MOMENTS of JOY and HEARTBREAK

66 SIGNIFICANT EPISODES IN THE HISTORY OF THE PITTSBURGH PIRATES

EDITED BY JORGE IBER AND BILL NOWLIN

ASSOCIATE EDITORS: RUSS LAKE AND LEN LEVIN

Society for American Baseball Research, Inc.
Phoenix, AZ

Moments of Joy and Heartbreak: 66 Significant Episodes in the History of the Pittsburgh Pirates
Edited by Jorge Iber and Bill Nowlin
Associate Editors: Russ Lake and Len Levin

All photographs in this book were generously provided through the courtesy of the Pittsburgh Pirates.
Thanks to Samantha Lynn.
Front cover photograph shows Pedro Alvarez homering at PNC Park in
Game Four of the 2013 National League Division Series.

Book design: Gilly Rosenthol

Society for American Baseball Research
Cronkite School at ASU
555 N. Central Ave. #416
Phoenix, AZ 85004
Phone: (602) 496-1460
Web: www.sabr.org
Facebook: Society for American Baseball Research
Twitter: @SABR

CONTENTS

1. **INTRODUCTION** 1
    by Jorge Iber, PhD

2. **MAY 10, 1882** 3
    The First Major-League
    Game in Pittsburgh
    by Tom Hawthorn

3. **APRIL 22, 1891** 6
    Opening Day 1891: The
    Storm After the Rain
    by John Bauer

4. **OCTOBER 4, 1892** 9
    Pirates Finish Exceptional Season
    By Setting Wins Record
    by Gordon J. Gattie

5. **OCTOBER 13, 1903** 12
    The Final Game of the First World Series
    by Bill Nowlin

6. **SEPTEMBER 20, 1907** 15
    Nick Maddox Tosses First
    No-Hitter in Pirates History
    by Gregory H. Wolf

7. **JUNE 29, 1909** 19
    Farewell to the Old Yard
    by Seth Moland-Kovash

8. **JUNE 30, 1909** 22
    Forbes Field, The House of Thrills,
    Celebrates Opening Day
    by Harry Schoger

9. **JULY 3, 1910** 25
    Chief Hits for the Cycle
    by Jeff Findley

10. **AUGUST 22, 1912** 28
    "Wagner Wields Willow," Hits for
    the Cycle, but Pirates Lose
    by Mike Huber

11. **OCTOBER 2, 1920** 31
    Three for a Half A Buck! The Only
    Major-League Tripleheader
    by Bill Nowlin

12. **JUNE 30, 1921** 35
    Moses "Chief" Yellow Horse
    Defeats Adolfo Luque
    by Jorge Iber, PhD

13. **JUNE 20, 1925** 38
    Cuyler, Carey, and Co. Steamroll Brooklyn
    by T.S. Flynn

14. **OCTOBER 15, 1925** 41
    Game Seven of the 1925 World Series
    by T.S. Flynn

15. **JUNE 24, 1933** 44
    Pirates Defeat Dodgers 15-3 as Arky
    Vaughan Hits for the Cycle and Goes 5-for-5
    by C. Paul Rogers III

16. **JUNE 19, 1934** 47
    Pie Traynor Replaces George
    Gibson as Pirates Manager
    by Jack Zerby

17. **APRIL 27, 1938** 51
    Arky Vaughan Slams Cubs, Edges Cubs
    by Joseph Wancho

18. **MAY 4, 1938** 53
    Lloyd Waner's Big Game
    by Blake W. Sherry

19. MAY 30, 1939 56
Johnny Rizzo's Nine RBIs:
A Pirates All-Time Record
by Bob LeMoine

20. AUGUST 27, 1949 59
Tiny Bonham's Last Game
by C. Paul Rogers III

21. JUNE 25, 1950 61
Kiner Scores 4, Drives in 8, in Hitting
for Cycle Against the Dodgers
by Mike Huber

22. SEPTEMBER 23, 1951.......................64
Murry Dickson's 20th Win
by Richard "Pete" Peterson

23. JUNE 6, 1952.................................67
Dickson and the Bucs Shave "The Barber"
by Paul Hofmann

24. APRIL 13, 1954 70
Vern Law Celebrates Return from Military
Service with Opening Day Win
by Gordon J. Gattie

25. MAY 16, 1954 73
Pioneering Rookie Curt Roberts Collects
Three Hits, Continues Steady Defense
by Jack Zerby

26. SEPTEMBER 24, 1955........................77
Bob Friend Clinches NL ERA Title
Despite Pitching for Last-Place Pirates
by Gordon J. Gattie

27. JULY 25, 1956 80
Clemente Grand Slams and
Runs to Pirates' Victory
by Steven C. Weiner

28. JULY 18, 1957 83
Luis Arroyo's Final Victory for Pittsburgh
by Robert E. Bionaz

29. MAY 1, 1958 87
Frank Has A Big Day
by Matt Keelean

30. MAY 26, 1959 90
Harvey Haddix Pitches 12 Perfect
Innings; Adcock's Double in 13th
Gives Braves 1-0 Victory
by Mark Miller

31. AUGUST 6, 1960 93
"We Had 'em All the Way"
by Alan Cohen

32. OCTOBER 13, 1960 96
Mazeroski's Heroic Homer Brings
Championship to Pittsburgh
by Mike Huber

33. APRIL 15, 1961................................100
Bob Friend Bests Don Drysdale
in a Record-Setting Game
by Robert E. Bionaz

34. SEPTEMBER 21, 1963.......................103
Gene Baker: The First African
American to Manage in the Majors
by Jorge Iber, PhD

35. JULY 22, 1964 106
Mazeroski, Lynch, and Stargell
Lead Rout of Cardinals
by Mike Huber

36. JUNE 1, 1965 108
Bob Veale's 16 Strikeouts
by Blake W. Sherry

37. OCTOBER 2, 1966.............................111
Matty Alou Claims the 1966 Batting Title
by Jorge Iber, PhD

38. MAY 15, 1967 114
Clemente Blasts Three Homers and
Knocks in All Seven Runs in Bucs' Loss
by Gregory H. Wolf

39. SEPTEMBER 20, 1969 117
A Trophy No-Hitter: Bob Moose Bites
the Amazin' Mets in the Big Apple
by Gregory H. Wolf

40. JUNE 12, 1970 120
Dock Ellis Throws A No-Hitter
by Richard Puerzer

41. JUNE 28, 1970 122
Human Locusts Have Their Day
by Jeff Barto

42. AUGUST 14, 1971 125
Gibby Fires a No-Hitter
by Gregory H. Wolf

43. AUGUST 23, 1971........................ 128
Best Game for Al Oliver
by Blake W. Sherry

44. SEPTEMBER 1, 1971........................ 131
The First All-Black Lineup
by Richard Puerzer

45. OCTOBER 17, 1971........................ 134
Blass, Clemente Lead Pirates to Victory
in World Series Game Seven
by Wayne Strumpfer

46. SEPTEMBER 30, 1972.....................137
Clemente Collects Number
3,000 in Last At-Bat
by Gregory H. Wolf

47. APRIL 6, 1973.....................140
Something's Missing: No
Clemente in Right Field
by Gregory H. Wolf

48. JUNE 13, 1973 143
Steve Blass Loses Control
by Richard Puerzer

49. SEPTEMBER 16, 1975.................... 146
Stennett Leads Pirate Rout With
Seven Hits in Nine Innings
by Doug Feldmann

50. SEPTEMBER 25, 1976.................... 149
The Tragic Death of Bob Moose: His
Last Appearance in the Majors
by Robert E. Bionaz

51. OCTOBER 3, 1976 152
Danny Murtaugh's Final Games
as Pirates Manager
by Robert E. Bionaz

52. OCTOBER 17, 1979 155
"Pops" Named MVP as Pirates Complete
Comeback to Win World Series
by Frederick C. Bush

53. MAY 19, 1981......................... 158
Jim Bibby's Near No-Hitter
by Eliza Richardson

54. SEPTEMBER 25, 1985.....................160
Rick Reuschel Inspires Struggling
Bucs with Strong Finish
by Gordon J. Gattie

55. OCTOBER 13, 1992......................... 163
Pirates Back Wakefield with Offensive
Explosion, Send 1992 NLCS to
Decisive Seventh Game
by Frank Ittner

56. JULY 12, 1997 166
Cordova, Rincon, and Smith
Provide Fireworks in 10-Inning
No-Hit Victory over Astros
by Frederick C. Bush

57. JULY 28, 2001.................................. 169
Pirates' Unforgettable Comeback
by Paul E. Doutrich

58. JULY 2, 2010 172
Ross Ohlendorf Wins His Only
Game of the Season
by Jorge Iber, PhD

59. JULY 26, 2011.................................. 175
Pirates Lose on a Really, Really Bad Call
by Jorge Iber, PhD

60. SEPTEMBER 9, 2013.................... 178
Pirates End the Streak
by Stephen Peterson

61. OCTOBER 1, 2013 181
Losers No More: The Pittsburgh Pirates
Win 2013 NL Wild Card Game
by Rock Hoffman

62. JUNE 20, 2015 184
Scherzer Loses Perfect Game in the Ninth,
Throws No-Hitter Against the Pirates
by Bob Webster

63. OCTOBER 7, 2015 186
Pirates Lose to Cubs in National
League Wild Card Game
by Thomas J. Brown Jr.

64. APRIL 26, 2016 189
Andrew McCutchen Hits Three
Home Runs in One Game
by Thomas J. Brown Jr.

65. CONTRIBUTORS 192

MOMENTS OF JOY AND HEARTBREAK: 66 SIGNIFICANT EPISODES IN THE HISTORY OF THE PITTSBURGH PIRATES

INTRODUCTION

BY JORGE IBER, PHD

MANY OF THE BOOKS GENERATED about a particular franchise, regardless of the sport, tend to focus on the "greatest games" in that team's history. This is certainly a worthwhile undertaking; who among us don't get a warm and wonderful feeling when we recall grand and glorious triumphs of our favorite squad? Certainly, in the minds of my generation of Pirates fans, the years 1971 and 1979 stand out. Pittsburgh's last two World Series titles featured fantastic performances and stirring comebacks from 3-to-1 deficits against the Baltimore Orioles. For example, recent works by Bruce Markusen (on the 1971 team) and a SABR collection edited by Bill Nowlin and Greg Wolf on "The Family" are among the most beloved books I have ever read. Given our team's decades-long "downturn" since "the slide" in 1992, these are memories near and dear to the hearts of Pirates fans.

While it is wonderful to recall intoxicating moments of victories, the histories of all such organizations are made up of more than just joyful occasions. Indeed, most fans certainly recall instances when their beloved team snatched defeat from the jaws of victory in crucial moments of a particular season. Given that I now live in western Texas, there are plenty of Rangers fans around who still haven't gotten over being one strike away from a title against the St. Louis Cardinals in 2011. Heartbreak does not only happen on the field, however. In September of 2016, for example, it was my sad duty to inform my father, a man who spoke no English, that his favorite Miami Marlins player, José Fernandez (affectionately referred to as "Joseito" by most Cuban Americans in the city) had met his demise in a (drug-induced) boating accident off Miami Beach. The pain on his face at the moment he understood what had happened reminded me of an instance that took place some 43 years previously, and which forever sealed my ties to the Pittsburgh Pirates.

As a young boy newly arrived in the United States from Cuba, I brought along much of the baggage that other immigrants of the Freedom Flights (which took place between 1965 and 1973) carried: a sense of confusion at having to leave behind one's homeland and a sense of apprehension as to how life would proceed in a foreign land. Another element that I carried, as did many other *Cubanos*, was a love for baseball. Once my family had settled into a small house in the Little Havana section of Miami, it was time to get down to the serious business of life in the United States, and among the first things I had to do was learn English. I quickly realized that by watching the *NBC Game of the Week* with Curt Gowdy it was possible to brush up on my new language, as well as enjoy my favorite sport. It was not too long before I noticed the stellar play of one Latino in particular: Puerto Rican Roberto Clemente. While I cannot recall specifically when I saw him and the Pirates play for the first time, the fascination with Clemente and the Pirates' pullover jerseys was instantaneous. Yes, there were Cubans on other teams: Tony Oliva, Tony Perez, Cookie Rojas, to name just a few. I cheered for my countrymen as well, but Clemente was different in my eyes. He carried himself with such poise and dignity that even a 9- or 10-year-old could sense there was something truly special in his persona. After seeing him star in the 1971 World Series, and most specifically asking for his parents' blessing, after Game Seven, I was hooked and proudly proclaimed to all my buddies in the barrio that I was a Pittsburgh Pirates fan for life!

On the morning of January 1, 1973, as my parents and I drove around Coral Gables, the horrible news came on the air via WQBA, then the one radio station for our community's *noticias* (news). The great Clemente was on a plane that had crashed into the ocean near San Juan. His body was lost at sea. I was absolutely devastated. At that time, I had not yet experienced the death of a "loved one." Suddenly and unexpectedly, here was that moment in my young life. After grieving the loss of this wonderful athlete and hero, I found my ties to the Pirates became stronger still. The team, the city, and I would carry on, my 11-year-old mind told me, urged on and encouraged by the benevolent spirit of a great man. When the 1979 club claimed the Series, it felt as if number 21 was in the dugout at Memorial Stadium.

Memories and emotions like these helped guide decisions about the games/events included in this work. Yes, there is coverage of important victories, such as Neil Maddox's no-hitter in 1907, and the wonderful game pitched by Jim Bibby in 1981. There are also essays that pay deference to the heartbreak that fans of the Pirates have endured over the decades. While Bream's slide in 1992 broke our collective hearts, there was almost as much pain in enduring the 19-inning "loss" to the Atlanta Braves in July of 2011. While the death of Clemente was a shock, so was that of Tiny Bonham in 1949 and, of course, Bob Moose's passing in 1976. Additionally, there are moments of joy in the midst of the gloom of the past two-plus decades, such as victory number 82 in 2013, the great comeback versus the Astros on July 28, 2001,

and Ross Ohlendorf's lone victory for the miserable 2010 squad against the hated, and division-winning, Philadelphia Phillies. While the Pirates are recognized for fielding the first all-minority lineup, in 1971, featured here also is one of the first matchups in the majors to involve two nonwhite starting pitchers (a Native American versus a Cuban) in June of 1921. All of these essays are designed to provide readers with a sense of the totality of the Pirates' experiences: the joy, the heartbreak, and other aspects of baseball (and life) in between. May sharing these memories, both good and unpleasant, remind us of why we love this team and its history.

A word about our project's organization is in order. Readers will note that there are 64 essays, but the title refers to 66 episodes. This difference is due to our having 62 essays that deal with individual games. We have two pieces, the one on the tripleheader and the last two games managed by Danny Murtaugh, that deal with multiple contests. The tripleheader, given the uniqueness of this event in Pirates and major-league baseball history, we considered three games (thus bringing us to 65 "episodes") while the last two outings managed by Murtaugh we chose to view as one "episode," thus leading to the figure used in the title of the work.

Putting this work together has been a great experience, and I would like to thank my co-editors, particularly Bill Nowlin, for their assistance in bringing this project to a successful conclusion. Additionally, I would like to thank all of the contributors for sharing their time, talents, and passion for the history of the Pittsburgh Pirates.

THE FIRST MAJOR-LEAGUE GAME IN PITTSBURGH

MAY 10, 1882: ALLEGHENYS (PITTSBURGH) 9, ST. LOUIS BROWN STOCKINGS 5, AT EXPOSITION PARK

BY TOM HAWTHORN

THE CHARTER ALLEGHENY CLUB OF the fledgling American Association played its first four games of the circuit's inaugural season of 1882 on the road against the Red Stockings in Cincinnati. The visitors from Pittsburgh won the opening match by 10-9, then lost two in a row to the home side by 7-3 and 19-10 before rebounding with a stellar 2-0 victory, greeted in the *Cincinnati Enquirer* with the headline, "The Smoky City Lads Shut Out the Porkopolitans."[1]

With a 2-2 record, the Allegheny team returned home for a debut in a city deprived of quality baseball for three seasons.[2] On May 9, the St. Louis Brown Stockings came to western Pennsylvania after splitting their first six games. The Alleghenys were leading 8-2 with one on and one out in the third inning when the game was called because of rain, part of a weather system that also canceled Cincinnati's game at Louisville. An anonymous *Enquirer* writer warned the Browns in print about the strong hitting of the Pittsburgh team: "One can safely wager before the latter delegation leaves the Smoky City their eyes will be protruding several feet from their heads."[3]

On the following afternoon, May 10, about 2,000 people gathered at Exposition Park, a diamond built on the north shore of the Allegheny River across from downtown Pittsburgh on a field susceptible to flooding. The previous day's rains were followed by heavy morning showers, leaving the field damp and soggy. Despite the poor conditions, the game went ahead.

Six months earlier, representatives of several prospective teams had met in Cincinnati to forge a new independent baseball association. The representatives who gathered at Gibson House, a fine hotel, sought to create a money-making rival to the stuffy National League. The ambition was to make money by selling beer in the stands and playing games on Sunday, both of which had been outlawed by the senior circuit. With teams based in rollicking river cities with large immigrant populations, such as Cincinnati and Pittsburgh, the American Association would be dubbed the Beer and Whiskey League.

Each club was expected to have at least $5,000 (and preferably more) in capital from which to launch the new league. Louisville was represented by J.H. Pank of the Kentucky Malting Company, while wholesale grocer Chris von der Ahe sought membership for St. Louis. The Pittsburgh owner was 33-year-old Harmar Denny McKnight, an iron merchant and the son of a lawyer elected to Congress. McKnight was elected the league's president at the Cincinnati meeting.[4]

The return of professional baseball after a three-year hiatus shared headlines with other news. Elsewhere in the state, Republicans gathered in convention at Harrisburg to nominate James Beaver, a Civil War general who lost his right leg in battle, for governor. He would lose, only to gain the office in an election four years later. Across the state line in Ohio, a forgotten stick of dynamite killed a worker in a tunnel in Steubenville. In Pittsburgh, the Kirkpatrick grocery on Liberty Street announced the arrival of a shipment of prunes, plums, and apricots from California.

At waterlogged Exposition Park, the visitors took to the field to start the game. (In earlier games, the order of batting was determined by a coin toss.) Pitching for St. Louis was George Washington McGinnis, a 196-pounder known as Jumbo. He kept the home Alleghenys off the scoreboard for three innings before being touched for two runs in the fourth.

The Pittsburgh hurler was Harry Arundel, a right-hander who had pitched in a game for the Brooklyn Atlantics of the National Association in 1875. He gave up two runs in the second, two more in the fifth and a final tally in the sixth.

"Arundel did not let up once in the entire game," the *Pittsburgh Commercial Gazette* reported. "He pitched effectively from beginning to end. He has coolness and nerve. Some of his best work was done when the bases were all covered and none out."[5]

The Alleghenys broke the 2-2 tie in the fifth inning. The tall first baseman Jake Goodman drove a McGinnis pitch deep into center field for a double. John Peters popped out to St. Louis third baseman Jack Gleason. (Peters and Arundel would be the only two Alleghenys to go hitless in the game.) Arundel walked. George Strief's base hit knocked in Goodman to give the Pittsburgh side a lead it would not relinquish. The catcher Jim Keenan, batting ninth, sent a towering fly to center under which Oscar Walker settled.

McGinnis failed to limit the damage in the inning, as Ed Swartwood and then Billy Taylor reached base on hits. Three more came home, as Arundel, Strief, and Swartwood all scored. When Swartwood again came to the plate in the eighth, McGinnis had had

Exposition Park (1891-1909)

enough. He "deliberately sent him to his base on balls, refusing to pitch even one of which he might strike with some show of success."[6]

Both starting pitchers finished the game, with Arundel and the Alleghenys prevailing by the score of 9-5. Arundel would go 4-10 for the season, the poorest result on a three-man rotation including Harry Salisbury (20-18) and Denny Driscoll (13-9).

Swartwood and Billy Taylor each had three hits in the game, half of the Allegheny dozen (four doubles and eight singles). The visiting Browns also had 12 hits (one double and 11 singles), but failed to bunch them.

McGinnis, the losing pitcher, would finish 43 of the 45 games he started in 1882, going 25-18. St. Louis third baseman Jack Gleason, the Brown Stockings' leadoff man, wielded a big bat for the visitors with a double and a trio of singles, though he was stranded each time, failing to score a run. His younger brother, shortstop Bill Gleason, also a St. Louis product, batting second, had a single in five plate appearances. Each Gleason brother committed an error, as did teammate Bill Smiley at second base. The Allegheny errors were charged to Taylor at third base and Goodman at first.

Gone unnoticed in game reports of the two-hour match was the tall, 22-year-old St. Louis first baseman, a right-hander born in Chicago by the name of Charlie Comiskey. Batting fourth, he hit a single and struck out once in five plate appearances, and made nine putouts at first without error. Of all the men on the field on May 10, 1882, he went on to have the greatest impact on baseball as an owner of the Chicago White Sox and builder of a ballpark in his hometown bearing his name.

The Browns were skippered by player-manager Ned Cuthbert in their inaugural season, but Comiskey would be a sometime playing manager in the following two seasons before taking over the reins full-time in 1885, leading the Browns to four consecutive American Association pennants and an 1886 world-championship victory over the Chicago White Stockings of the National League.

The Alleghenies were managed by Al Pratt, a Civil War veteran and a former pitcher for the Cleveland Forest Citys of the National Association.

The May 10 game got good reviews from sportswriters, who were even then given to ballyhoo and hyperbole. The *Gazette*'s writer liked the Alleghenys' 32-year-old shortstop, the oldest starter on either team. "Peters merits credit, not only for his good general work," he wrote, "but because he plays to win, and not to make an individual record."[7] In a brief report, the *Pittsburgh Daily Post* stated: "The attendance of spectators was quite large and the game was good enough to be thoroughly enjoyable."[8] The *Cincinnati Enquirer* promised: "Look out for some bold, bad, wicked work to-morrow."[9] As it turned out, the next day's game would be rained out.

The Alleghenys ended the American Association season in fourth place in the six-team league with a 39-39 record, a whopping 20½ games behind Cincinnati (55-25). The Pittsburgh team finished ahead of St. Louis (37-43) and the woeful Baltimore Orioles (19-54), while trailing the Eclipse of Louisville (42-38) and the Philadelphia Athletics (41-34). Pittsburgh was runner-up to Louisville for the most doubles with 110 (Swartwood led the league with 18; teammates Mike Mansell and Taylor tied for third with 16), while the Alleghenys' 18 home runs (four by Swartwood) led the circuit. Swartwood also led the league in runs (87) and total bases (161).

In the great card shuffling of late nineteenth-century baseball, the clubs would swap leagues and nicknames, the Brown Stockings becoming the Cardinals and the Alleghenys the Pirates, National League rivals to this day. The city of Allegheny was annexed by Pittsburgh in 1907, erasing a historic name from the geographic record books, though of the course the river from which it took its name was one of the Three Rivers for which the Pirates' ballpark was named when it opened in July 1970.

SOURCES

In addition to the sources cited in the Notes, the author also relied on baseball-almanac.com, baseball-reference.com, and retrosheet.org.

NOTES

1 "Chicagoed, The Smoky City Lads Shut Out the Porkopolitans," *Cincinnati Enquirer*, May 9, 1882: 2.

2 An earlier team, also known as Allegheny, is credited with playing the city's first professional game, defeating the Xanthas of the International Association by 7-3 at Union Park on April 15, 1876. The team disbanded midway through the 1878 season, according to William E. Benswanger's article "Professional Baseball in Pittsburgh," originally published in 1947. upress.pitt.edu/htmlSourceFiles/pdfs/9780822959700exr.pdf.

3 "Base-Ball Notes," *Cincinnati Enquirer*, May 10, 1882: 5.

4 "Well Done," *Cincinnati Enquirer*, November 2, 1881: 5.

5 "A fine game, the St. Louis beaten by the Alleghenys," *Pittsburgh Commercial Gazette*, May 11, 1882: 4.

6 Ibid.

7 Ibid.

8 "Alleghenies win again, by a score of 9 to 5," *Daily Post* (Pittsburgh), May 11, 1882: 4.

9 "The Alleghenys win from St. Louis," *Cincinnati Enquirer*, May 11, 1882: 5.

OPENING DAY 1891: THE STORM AFTER THE RAIN

APRIL 22, 1891: CHICAGO COLTS 7, PITTSBURGH PIRATES 6 (10 INNINGS), AT EXPOSITION PARK

BY JOHN BAUER

SURELY, PREPARATION WOULD NOT be an issue for Pittsburgh's 1891 National League campaign. The club spent two months training in the South, getting in shape for the new season. The new manager was also familiar to the squad. Still an active player, Ned Hanlon was in the nascent stages of a managerial career that would generate five NL pennants with the Baltimore Orioles and Brooklyn Superbas over the next decade. Hanlon had skippered the Pittsburgh Alleghenys for the final third of the 1889 season before joining the city's Players League entry, the Burghers, the following year. With the Players League defunct after one season, he now returned to pilot the NL team and, as a player, remained "admired by all and stands among the leading centerfielders of the country."[1]

Depleted by the Brotherhood war,[2] Pittsburgh finished the 1890 NL campaign dead last at 23-113. Expectations were high for the much-changed team heading into the April 22, 1891, season opener against Chicago. Among the changes, Pittsburgh was commonly referred as the Pirates. Hanlon predicted a first- or second-place finish based on the quality of players assembled in the offseason.[3] Pete Browning joined Pittsburgh after eight years with Louisville in the American Association and a stint with Cleveland's PL club. Browning was deemed "a terror to all pitchers, good, bad and indifferent and their hearts quiver whenever they see his lengthy form towering over the plate."[4] Charley Reilly moved over from the AA Columbus Solons and was viewed as "a young man full of ambition, [who] will play every point to win."[5] Connie Mack, formerly with Washington's NL club and a member of the PL Buffalo Bisons, gave Pittsburgh a top backstop who "did great work and

was admired by everybody."[6] Lou Bierbauer signed with Pittsburgh after playing with John Montgomery Ward's PL club in Brooklyn. Hanlon was thought to have "made a ten-strike"[7] in landing Bierbauer. A player who "hits like a Trojan and fields with consummate skill,"[8] Bierbauer would man second base for Pittsburgh. Chicago player-manager Cap Anson shared the optimism about Pittsburgh, remarking, "Captain Hanlon has spent a barrel of money and has what you might call an all-star aggregation. ... Pittsburg has corralled some of the champion hitters of the country."[9]

There was a festive atmosphere around Exposition Park ahead of the 3:30 P.M. first pitch. The grounds were in good shape after a large group of workers spent the prior day on preparations.[10] Fans crowded into the vicinity for the Opening Day parade as "[t]he band played and the base-ball season was inaugurated with a grand street pageant."[11] The joyous mood dampened briefly when storms rolled through, but "[w]hen the clouds broke and the sun showed a winning hand there was a yell of satisfaction."[12] The rain was thought to have limited the eventual 5,263 attendance, but fans purchased tickets despite the weather.

Chicago arrived by train the morning of the game. Anson's club also entered the season with high expectations. The *Chicago Tribune* called the team "as evenly balanced a ball club as ever stepped on the field, and its discipline is almost perfect."[13] For the opener, the Colts were weakened by the absence of Tom Burns, who was laid up with an injured arm;[14] Bill Dahlen, at 21, would make his major-league debut filling in for Burns at third base. Anson trusted the pitching to another freshman, 22-year-old Pat Luby. Because

Luby "pitches in a way that proves very painful to most batsmen,"[15] the move may have been viewed as a good one.

Though playing at home, Pittsburgh batted first. Fans greeted Doggie Miller[16] with enthusiastic cheers as he approached the plate, an act that would be repeated for the rest of the home team's lineup. Luby allowed a leadoff walk to Miller, but his teammates could not bring him home. Chicago scored in the bottom of the first, when Anson's double brought Dahlen across the plate in his first major-league inning. Chicago added gradually to its lead. The Colts scored another run in the second inning when Fred Pfeffer worked his way around the bases after a leadoff walk. The visitors got two more in the fourth inning to take a 4-0 lead. In fielding a groundball off Cliff Carroll's bat, Reilly belied his strong reputation playing third base by throwing wildly to first. Carroll landed at third base by the end of the play. Pfeffer brought him home with a single to center field. Three batters later, Elmer Foster singled to score Pfeffer.

By the seventh inning, Pittsburgh still trailed 4-0 and the Pirates partisans despaired. "Everybody had given up hope of scoring a run, to say nothing of winning the game," wrote one of the local papers.[17] After holding Pittsburgh scoreless through six innings, Luby unraveled. He hit leadoff batter Mack in the shoulder and followed that with four bad throws to put Reilly on base. Pitcher Pud Galvin "rapped out a clear single"[18] to load the bases. At this point, "Luby evidently feared the consequences of pitching over the plate"[19] and walked Miller on four pitches, which scored Mack. Luby surrendered another walk to Jake Beckley, which scored Reilly. With his pitcher "wild as a March hare,"[20] Anson tried to calm Luby. His words did not have the desired effect as Luby walked Fred Carroll, thereby scoring Galvin. With Pittsburgh now within one run, Anson called upon Bill Hutchinson to stem the tide.

Swapping pitchers did not stop the momentum, however. Browning's sharply hit single to center field scored Miller to tie the game, 4-4. The bases remained loaded and there were still no outs. Bierbauer's hit to Dahlen was collected by the Colts

third baseman, who threw home to force Beckley. Hanlon's drive into the outfield grass brought home Carroll and Browning, putting Pittsburgh ahead 6-4. "Pandemonium reigned in grand stand and bleachers. Two runs ahead was a cyclonic surprise," a Pittsburgh sportswriter rhapsodized.[21] Though dejected after the disastrous seventh, Chicago halved the deficit in the bottom of the inning. Hutchinson flied out to Browning in left-field foul territory and Malachi Kittridge grounded out to Miller at shortstop, but Foster started a two-out rally by reaching first after Miller bobbled a groundball. Jimmy Ryan uncorked a long double into center field that scored Foster. Jimmy Cooney struck out to end the frame but Chicago had pulled within one run.

Neither club scored in the eighth, but Chicago came close. With one out and Dahlen on third base, Cliff Carroll sent a high fly toward Fred Carroll (no relation) in right field. Dahlen neglected to take a chance on scoring, and would not make it home that inning. Pittsburgh did not add to its lead in the top of the ninth. Nonetheless, sensing victory, "the Pittsburgers put on their coats, and with a smile of satisfaction prepared to leave the grounds."[22] Chicago would provide reason for them to stay. Hutchinson sent a high fly to Fred Carroll, but the right fielder misjudged the ball and muffed the catch. With Hutchinson on second, Kittridge brought home his batterymate by singling to left field. The game now tied, 6-6, the Exposition Park crowd "resumed their seats with a thud that shook the stand."[23] Chicago would not find the winning run in the bottom of the ninth, and the season opener headed into extra innings.

Only the 10th inning would be required to settle the matter. The Pirates' Mack and Reilly began the top of the inning by striking out, adding to the anxiety in the grandstand. Galvin singled to keep the inning going, and Miller followed by drawing a walk from Hutchinson. The rally ended with Fred Carroll's fly out to Cliff Carroll in right field. In Chicago's half of the inning, Dahlen smacked the ball down the left-field line, almost reaching the outfield fence, and Dahlen was safe at third as a "sickening chill spread through the stands."[24] Anson popped up to shortstop Miller, and Dahlen held third. He would not need to do so when Cliff Carroll drove the ball to left-center, allowing Dahlen to score the winning run. Chicago 7, Pittsburgh 6. Despite the loss, the local newspaper observed some reason for optimism: "While they show a lack of team work, still there is evidence that this will be remedied in a game or two. ..."[25] In truth, the optimism proved unjustified. Although Pittsburgh's record was above .500 at the beginning of June, the team finished 55-80, placing it in the same spot as the season before: last place in the National League.

NOTES

1   "About the Boys," *Pittsburgh Commercial Gazette*, April 22, 1891: 6.

2   For information about the "Brotherhood War" related to the formation of the Players League, see, e.g., baseball-reference.com/bullpen/Players_League.

3   "News, Gossip and Comment," *Sporting Life*, April 25, 1891: 3.

4   "About the Boys."

5   Ibid.

6   Ibid.

7   Ibid.

8   Ibid.

9   "Anson's Review," *Sporting Life*, April 25, 1891: 3.

10   "Sporting Notes," *Pittsburgh Commercial Gazette*, April 22, 1891: 6.

11   "Lost the First," *Pittsburgh Commercial Gazette*, April 23, 1891: 6.

12   Ibid.

13   "Opening of the Campaign," *Chicago Tribune*, April 23, 1891: 5.

14   Ibid.

15   "Lost the First."

16   Miller was referred as "Kid Miller" in a season preview article in the *Pittsburgh Commercial Gazette*. "About the Boys."

17   "Lost the First."

18   Ibid.

19   Ibid.

20   "Opening of the Campaign."

21   "Lost the First."

22   "Opening of the Campaign."

23   Ibid.

24   "Lost the First."

25   Ibid.

PIRATES FINISH EXCEPTIONAL SEASON BY SETTING WINS RECORD

OCTOBER 4, 1902: PITTSBURG PIRATES 11, CINCINNATI REDS 2, AT EXPOSITION PARK III

BY GORDON J. GATTIE

THE 1902 PITTSBURG PIRATES WERE one of the greatest teams in baseball history; during the season's last weekend, they were on the verge of completing the season with an exclamation point. In the midst of a three-year reign atop the National League, the Pirates handily won the 1901 NL pennant with a 90-49 record, the first time Pittsburg won a league title and attained 90 wins.[1] Led by Hall of Fame outfielder-manager Fred Clarke, Hall of Fame shortstop Honus Wagner, and 20-game winners Jack Chesbro and Deacon Phillippe, the Bucs finished 7½ games in front of the second-place Philadelphia Phillies. The 1902 Pirates started the season with mostly the same key personnel from the previous season: first baseman Kitty Bransfield, second baseman Claude Ritchey, third baseman Tommy Leach, and outfielders Ginger Beaumont and Lefty Davis. The most significant changes included returning catcher Harry Smith, who jumped from Pittsburg to the American League's Philadelphia Athletics the previous year, and Wid Conroy, who was originally slated to be Wagner's backup at shortstop but started the season there, with Wagner moving to the outfield.[2]

The early 1900s were especially tumultuous for professional baseball, as Ban Johnson's American League played its inaugural season during 1901 and numerous players were jumping leagues for better opportunities and higher salaries.[3] During the first three years of the AL's existence, over 100 players joined the AL[4] with Johnson constantly fighting for new talent;[5] by 1903, many believed the American League was the superior league.[6] However, Pittsburg owner Barney Dreyfuss successfully retained his top stars through 1902, while most NL teams lost significant players.[7]

During 1901-1902, the Pirates lost only four players: third baseman Jimmy Williams (to Baltimore), shortstop Fred "Bones" Ely (to Philadelphia), Smith (who returned), and catcher Jack O'Connor (left following 1902 season). Other teams faced greater losses, ranging from Philadelphia and St. Louis (highest with 16 players jumping) to Cincinnati (second fewest with eight players jumping).[8] In addition, Dreyfuss helped stabilize NL ownership before the 1902 season, and thereby prevented Pittsburg itself jumping from the National League to the American League.[9] He also helped eliminate the possibility of an AL entry based in Pittsburg for 1902, although efforts undermining the NL Pirates continued after the season ended.[10] The Pirates entered the 1902 season in good shape, with manager Clarke "highly pleased with the outlook, and if the weather is good from now on for another week, he says his boys would be in condition second to none in the league."[11] The Pirates started fast, winning their first five games and ending April with an 8-2 record, up 1½ games on the Chicago Cubs. After compiling a 22-4 record during May and 11-6 record during June, the Pirates never looked back.

Conversely, the 1902 Reds were looking to improve upon the previous season's last-place finish, as their 52-87 record was 38 games behind Pittsburg. Although seven Reds switched leagues before the 1901 season, only outfielder Dick Harley left before the 1902 season started. In addition, four star players, pitcher Noodles Hahn, outfielder Sam Crawford, first baseman Jake Beckley, and pitcher Bill Phillips, remained with the club.[12] The Reds dropped their first three games and struggled through May and June before improving during the second half. During

September, Cincinnati assembled a 15-12 record and climbed to a more respectable fourth place, flirting with a .500 finish.

Four-year veteran Phillippe started Pittsburg's final 1902 game. He attained 20 wins and amassed at least 270 innings during each of his first three seasons, and was pitching for his 20th win facing Cincinnati. Phillippe was one of the many players traded from the Louisville Colonels to Pittsburg after the 1899 season. He spent the rest of his 13-year career in Pittsburg, and was voted the greatest right-handed pitcher in Pirates history in 1969.[13] A 6-foot right-hander possessing a fastball and curveball, Phillippe had legendary control; his career record 1.25 walks per nine innings is the lowest ratio once the modern 60-foot 6-inch pitching distance was established in 1893.[14]

His mound opponent that afternoon was Beckley, better known as a Hall of Fame first baseman than a starting pitcher. Beckley's career spanned 20 seasons with five different teams, including seven-plus years with the Pirates and a single year (1890) with the Players League Pittsburgh Burghers during their only year of existence. After nearly 2,000 games played at first base, Beckley was making his lone career pitching appearance as part of Cincinnati manager Joe Kelley's protest over sloppy weather conditions. Rookie reliever Rube Vickers served as Beckley's catcher; newspaper reports describing the game didn't sugarcoat the Reds' behavior, noting, "Beckley's weak throwing arm is notorious in baseball circles, but Jake proved a better pitcher than Vickers did a catcher."[15]

Although Pittsburg already clinched the NL pennant, they were tied with the 1892 and 1898 Boston Beaneaters with 102 wins in a single season. The Pirates' winning percentage was higher because they played in fewer games, but Dreyfuss and his players wanted to break the single-season wins record. A heavy storm rained upon Pittsburg that morning, but the Reds were informed that the game would be played if the storm passed and the field drained. During the early afternoon, the Reds learned the game was going forward, but they arrived late and Kelley generated a laughable lineup.

During the opening frame, Kelley, who was also hitting third and playing third base, emphasized his unhappiness by walking to the plate while smoking a cigarette. Umpire Hank O'Day threatened Kelley with expulsion before he complied with the umpire's request to extinguish the cigarette.[16] With the Reds barely trying, the Pirates scored three runs in the first inning. In the second inning, the Reds' Harry Steinfeldt reached on an error and scored on a Vickers single. The Pirates responded with four more runs in the bottom half and now built a 7-1 lead. At that point, a furious Dreyfuss announced that the 1,200 patrons attending the game would receive ticket refunds, and the Reds would be paid nothing for the game.[17]

The Pirates added a run in the fourth inning, which the Reds countered an inning later when Beckley doubled home outfielder Mike Donlin. In the fifth inning, Kelley acquiesced slightly when he inserted outfielder Cy Seymour, who was playing third base that afternoon, as a relief pitcher. Seymour, who pitched years earlier for the New York Giants and won 25 games in 1898, was effective for two innings before allowing three runs on two walks and two hits in the eighth inning.[18] The game ended on a double play; with one out and Donlin on second base, Kelley lined out to Jimmy Sebring, who doubled off Donlin. Phillippe pitched a complete game, allowing two runs on nine hits and two walks while striking out five. Six different Bucs had at least two base hits, with Bransfield going 3-for-5 with a double and triple. Pittsburg trounced Cincinnati 11-2 to win its 103rd game.

Pittsburg won its second consecutive NL pennant, 27½ games ahead of the Brooklyn Superbas. The Pirates had a dominant 56-15 home record, a .789 winning percentage. Their superior team offense led the NL with 5.45 runs per game, a full run ahead of second-best Cincinnati; 1,410 hits; 189 doubles; 95 triples; .286 batting average; and .374 slugging percentage. Individually, Beaumont paced the NL with a .357 batting average; Wagner led the NL with 105 runs, 30 doubles, 91 RBIs, and a .463 slugging percentage; and Tommy Leach hit six home runs for the league lead. The top four run scorers were all from Pittsburg: Wagner, Clarke (103), Beaumont (100), and Leach (97). The pitching staff had the second-lowest team ERA (2.30), but allowed the fewest runs per game (3.10). In addition, the Pirates pitchers compiled the highest team strikeout total (564), issued the fewest walks (250), and allowed the fewest home runs (4). The staff included three 20-game winners: Jack Chesbro (28-6, 2.17 ERA over 286⅓ innings), Jesse Tannehill (20-6, 1.95 ERA over 231 innings), and Phillippe (20-9, 2.05 ERA over 272 innings). Their success carried over into the following year, when they won their third consecutive NL pennant and appeared in the first modern World Series.

SOURCES

Besides the sources cited in the Notes, the author consulted Baseball-Almanac.com, Baseball-Reference.com, Retrosheet.org, and the following:

Thorn, John, and Pete Palmer, et al. *Total Baseball: The Official Encyclopedia of Major League Baseball* (New York: Viking Press, 2004).

NOTES

1   Jim Trdinich and Dan Hart, *2016 Pittsburgh Pirates Media Guide* (Pittsburgh: Pittsburgh Pirates, 2016), 264.

2   Sam Bernstein, "Wid Conroy," SABR Biography Project, sabr.org/bioproj/person/9202a5e3.

3   "War That Crippled National League," *New York Times*, December 7, 1913: 36.

4   Geoffrey C. Ward and Ken Burns, *Baseball: An Illustrated History* (New York: Alfred A. Knopf, 1994), 65.

5   "American to Fight," *Washington Times*, May 2, 1902: 4.

6   Tom Simon, ed., *Deadball Stars of the National League* (Washington: Brassey's, Inc., 2004), 15. See also John S. Bowman and Joel Zoss, *The National League* (Rocky Hill, Connecticut: Great Pond Publishing, 1992), 26.

7   *Deadball Stars of the National League*, 141.

8   "War That Crippled National League."

9   Ronald T. Waldo, *The 1902 Pittsburgh Pirates: Treachery and Triumph* (Jefferson, North Carolina: McFarland, 2015), 62-67.

10 "Dreyfuss Has a Talk with Spalding in Chicago — No American League for the Pittsburg Pirates," *Pittsburg Daily Post*, January 19, 1902: 12; "Another Park for Johnson," *Pittsburg Press*, October 19, 1902: 18.

11 "Champions Begin Their Spring Training," *Pittsburg Daily Post*, April 2, 1902: 6.

12 Cincinnati had three managers during the 1902 season: Bid McPhee (27-37), Frank Bancroft (9-7), and Joe Kelley (34-26).

13 Mark Armour, "Charles Phillippe, Pittsburgh," *Deadball Stars of the National League*, 159.

14 Ibid.

15 "Reds Made Farce Out of Finish," *Pittsburg Press*, October 5, 1902: 18.

16 Ibid.

17 "The Champion Pirates Finish the Season of 1902 by Breaking the World's Record of Games Won," *Pittsburg Daily Post*, October 5, 1902: 2.

18 "Reds Made Farce Out of Finish."

THE FINAL GAME OF THE FIRST WORLD SERIES

OCTOBER 13, 1903: BOSTON AMERICANS 3, PITTSBURG PIRATES 0, AT HUNTINGTON AVENUE GROUNDS, BOSTON

GAME EIGHT OF THE 1903 WORLD SERIES

BY BILL NOWLIN

THE FIRST WORLD SERIES EVER played was a best-of-nine competition, and after seven games, it was Boston with four wins and Pittsburgh with three. All three of the Pirates' victories went to Deacon Phillippe—Game One, Game Three, and Game Four. He had pitched Game Seven, too, but lost. With limited options available to him, manager Fred Clarke went with Philippe again in Game Eight. Boston manager Jimmy Collins countered with the 2-1 (and well-rested) Bill Dinneen. When Collins had put together the American League team in 1901, Big Bill Dinneen—who had been a 20-game winner for the National League's Boston Beaneaters in 1900—was a hurler the manager brought with him.

Dinneen won 21 games in 1902 and the same number again in 1903. He'd been 21-13, with a 2.26 ERA. Teammate Cy Young had been 28-9, with an ERA of 2.08, including seven shutouts; Dinneen had six.

Phillippe had been 25-9 (2.43) for the Pirates and his teammate Sam Leever had been slightly better (25-7, 2.06.)Leever hurled seven shutouts, and Phillippe had done so four times. Sixteen-game winner Ed Doheny had suffered a mental breakdown and was in an insane asylum. To make matters worse, Leever hurt his right shoulder late in the season, while trapshooting, and it was undeniably Phillippe who was the only top Pirates pitcher in condition at the end of the grueling regular season. Given the dire circumstances, Clarke was compelled to rely on Phillippe.

This game could determine the championship of the world. "The game meant something more than victory. It was a question of supremacy between two great leagues, a question which for the past two years has agitated the entire baseball world."[1] Should Pittsburgh win, the Series would be even at four wins apiece. Should Boston triumph, the honor would be theirs.

Despite the importance of the game, attendance was only 7,455, way below the 18,801 of Game Three (the fourth through seventh games were played at Pittsburgh's Exposition Park), because so many large blocks of tickets had been snapped up by speculators who hoped to cash in—but, wrote the *Chicago Tribune*, "the public would not submit to the extortion."[2]

Dinneen retired the Pirates on seven pitches in the first inning. He was perfect through the first three innings. Jimmy Sebring's slashing drive back to the mound (which he fielded and threw to first) in the top of the third split Dinneen's finger, but "despite the bleeding that continued to stain the balls he threw throughout the game, the gritty right-hander continued to pitch well."[3]

Phillippe was effective, too, allowing just two singles over the three frames. A walk and a single marred Dinneen's start in the top of the fourth. The Pirates might have scored. They had runners on first and third with two outs, when Wagner stole second base on the front end of a double steal, but the Bostons were wise to the play and catcher Lou Criger threw to Collins at third base and got Tommy Leach out, 2-5-2.

In the bottom of the inning, slugger Buck Freeman—Boston's right fielder, who had led the American League with 104 RBIs, hit a leadoff triple deep to center field. Freddie Parent reached first on a fielding error by catcher Ed Phelps on a ball hit in front of home plate. Freeman didn't dare attempt to score, nor did he on Candy LaChance's sacrifice bunt—though Parent took second. Hobe Ferris singled to center field and drove in both Freeman and Parent. Ferris advanced to second when Criger grounded back to Philippe. With two outs, Dinneen singled, but Ferris was thrown out at home trying to go for a third run. Right fielder Jimmy Sebring's throw cut him down. There was every anticipation that the game would be a low-scoring affair, and that staking Dinneen to a two-run lead would likely be sufficient. The *Boston Post*'s inning-by-inning game account said, "Nobody cared that Criger followed with an out, that Dineen *(sic)* singled and Ferris was thrown out trying to reach home. Boston had scored two runs off the great Phillippe and everyone believed that those two runs meant victory."[4]

Sebring himself tripled in the top of the fifth, but there were two outs and Dinneen struck out catcher Phelps to end the threat.

Another triple set up another run for Boston in the sixth. There were two outs when LaChance tripled to right field. Ferris then singled to center—his third RBI of the game. As it transpired, there were no other runs scored in the game. Ferris alone drove in all the runs.

Phillippe hadn't pitched poorly at all. He didn't walk a single Boston batter, and one of the three runs scored off him was unearned. The problem was that Bill Dinneen simply pitched a better game. Just as he had in Game Two, he shut out the Pirates—and by the same 3-0 score. The Pirates committed three errors; Boston, none. Indeed, Boston's fielding was superlative. The *Post* in particular praised third baseman Jimmy Collins, who "covered acres of ground and threw as only he can throw." The team's infield work made the Pirates "look amateurish by comparison."[5]

Dinneen allowed just four hits, and the denouement was especially apt—he retired Fred Clarke and Tommy Leach on fly balls in the top of the ninth inning, and then struck out the great Honus Wagner. The *Boston Herald* rhapsodized about the final pitch: "No more artistic conclusion to the great series was possible. Slowly the big pitcher gathered himself up for the effort, slowly he swung his arms about his head. Then the ball shot away like a flash toward the plate where the great Wagner stood, muscles drawn tense, waiting for it. The big batsman's shoulders heaved, the stands will swear that his very frame creaked, as he swung his bat with every ounce of power in his body, but the dull thud of the ball, as it nestled in Criger's waiting mitt, told the story."[6]

Dinneen struck out seven and walked only two. He improved his Series mark to 3-1 with the win, finishing with a 2.06 ERA, and he remains one of the few pitchers to win three games in a given World Series.

Phillippe wound up with five decisions in one World Series, every one being a complete game. This is something we will almost certainly never see again. Phillippe posted a 3.07 ERA for the Series, but had two defeats to go with his three victories. Sam Leever was 0-2 for the Pirates and Brickyard Kennedy bore the loss in Game Five. Pittsburgh manager Fred Clarke conceded to the *Boston Journal*, "Boston won on its merits. We were weak in pitchers."[7]

For Boston, Cy Young was 2-1, with a 1.85 earned-run average. Tom Hughes was 0-1; he had pitched just two-plus innings of Game Three before being relieved by Cy Young. In fact, Dinneen and Young had combined to pitch all but two innings of the eight games.

The first world championship in modern baseball history belonged to the Boston Americans. The *Boston Journal*'s headline the following day indeed said it all: "Boston Americans Are Now the Champions of the World."

The fans who were present reveled in the championship. For his part, Jimmy Collins credited the support shown the team by the Boston fans. "The support given the team by the 'Royal Rooters' will never be forgotten. ... [N]o little portion of our success is due to this selfsame band of enthusiasts. Noise—why they astonished Pittsburgh by their enthusiasm."[8]

As for the Pirates, they knew they had suffered such losses among their own pitching staff that it was impossible to put their best nine on the field at all times. The *Pittsburg Post* still called them "the best baseball team in the world, take it from all points," and said that as they left the field of play, they "moved proudly out of the park and to the bus. Not a man among Captain Clarke's force but felt the defeat keenly, yet every head was high in the air as with firm strides the National League champions skirted the howling mob and bid farewell. ... The Pittsburgs, although not at all used to playing second fiddle, took their Waterloo philosophically and had nothing but good words for their conquerors, the umpires and the spectators."[9]

Despite Tom Hughes being a 20-game winner in 1903, Collins was uncertain about the pitcher and he was sent to New York after the season, traded in December for pitcher-outfielder Jesse Tannehill. Dinneen had an even better year in 1904, going 23-14. Cy Young won fewer games in 1904, but he still won 26, with a 1.97 ERA. The Boston Americans won the AL pennant again, though it was a battle down to the final day with the New York Highlanders. John

McGraw and his New York Giants simply refused to play them in the World Series.

SOURCES

In addition to the sources cited in the Notes, the author also consulted numerous other newspapers, Retrosheet.org, and Baseball-Reference.com. Thanks to Thomas Mueller for providing the *Pittsburg Post*.

NOTES

1   "World's Champion Bostons Win 3 to 0," *Boston Post*, October 14, 1903: 5.

2   "World's Series Goes to Boston," *Chicago Tribune*, October 14, 1903: 6. "Considering the weather, the crowd of 7500 was considered extremely large," wrote the *Post*. "The speculators did little or no business and lost big money." See "Speculators Lost On Yesterday's Ball Game," *Boston Post*, October 14, 1903: 5.

3   Bill Nowlin and Jim Prime, *From The Babe to the Beards: The Red Sox in the World Series* (New York: Skyhorse Publishing, 2014), 18.

4   "World's Champion Bostons Win 3 to 0."

5   Ibid.

6   "Boston Americans Champions of World," *Boston Herald*, October 14, 1903: 5.

7   W.S. Barnes Jr., "Boston Americans Are Now the Champions of the World," *Boston Journal*, October 14, 1903: 1.

8   Bob Ryan, *When Boston Won the World Series* (Philadelphia: Running Press, 2003), 157.

9   John H. Gruber, "Dineen Shuts Out the Pirates," *Pittsburg Post*, October 14, 1003: 8.

NICK MADDOX TOSSES FIRST NO-HITTER IN PIRATES HISTORY

SEPTEMBER 20, 1907: PITTSBURGH PIRATES 2, BROOKLYN SUPERBAS 1, AT EXPOSITION PARK

BY GREGORY H. WOLF

FROM PITTSBURGH'S INAUGURAL season in the National League, 1887, when the club was known as the Alleghenys, to 1971, only one pitcher tossed a no-hitter in the Smoky City. Rookie right-hander Nick Maddox, a stout 6-foot 20-year-old, just about three months shy of his 21st birthday, turned the trick on September 20, 1907, in what the *Pittsburgh Press* hailed as "one of the most remarkable games ever played" in the city.[1] Not only did Maddox became the first Pirate in franchise history to throw no-hitter, he remains, as of 2017, the second youngest big-league hurler to author a no-no, trailing only Amos "The Hoosier Thunderbolt" Rusie (about a month younger), who accomplished the feat on July 31, 1891.

Few, if any, pitchers in Pirates history have begun their career with such a dominant stretch as Maddox. Widely considered one of the hardest-throwing pitchers in baseball, Maddox tossed an overpowering five-hit shutout, striking out 11, to beat the St. Louis Cardinals, 4-0, in his major-league debut on Friday, September 13, 1907, at Exposition Park in Pittsburgh.[2] As SABR member Bill Lamb discussed in his biography of the player on the BioProject, the Pirates had owned the rights to Maddox since September 1 of the previous year, and had farmed him to the Wheeling (West Virginia) Stogies of the Class-B Central League, where he had pitched for most of the season and fired two no-hitters.[3] Three days later, Maddox notched his second straight complete-game victory over the Cardinals, 4-2, in St. Louis.[4] After just two starts, local papers touted him as a star. "His coolness at all times is capital and his generalship is the sort that conquers the most dangerous diamond foes," gushed Edward F. Balinger in the *Pittsburgh Post*.[5] In an era when baseball players were often seen as uncouth or unsavory, hard-drinking characters, Balinger praised Maddox's temperament (indeed temperance): "He is said to be steady in his habits, which virtue is lacking among many slabmen."[6] In Maddox's third start in eight days, he made history.

With just 18 games left to play, the Pirates, led by player-manager Fred Clarke since 1900, had no chance of capturing their first pennant since the last of three consecutive in 1903. Despite a stellar 82-54 record, they were in second place, a whopping 15½ games behind the streaking Chicago Cubs. The previous afternoon, on September 19, they kicked off their last homestand (14 games) of the campaign by defeating the fifth-place Brooklyn Superbas on Tommy Leach's dramatic ninth-inning walk-off single for a 4-3 victory.[7] Maddox was expected to contribute to the momentum, both his own and the team's, against Brooklyn's Elmer Stricklett, regarded by many historians as one of the originators of the spitball. The 5-foot-6, 30-year-old right-hander was in the last of his four big-league seasons during which he went 35-51 before jumping to an "outlaw" league in California, and was subsequently blacklisted from the majors by the National Commission.[8]

A ferocious early afternoon rainstorm threatened a Friday afternoon of baseball, but by 3:30 the skies had cleared and the sun was bright. A crowd of about 2,380, according to the *Pittsburgh Post*, packed Exposition Park, located on the north side of the Allegheny River, several blocks south of where PNC Park would be inaugurated in 2001.[9] This geographical area had been an independent municipality called Allegheny City until it was annexed by Pittsburgh

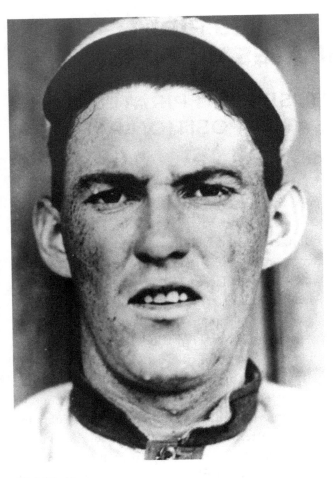

Nick Maddox

earlier that year, and became known as Pittsburgh's North Side.

The fast-paced contest quickly revealed itself as a pitchers' duel. Both hurlers held their opponents hitless through three frames, while Maddox walked two and Stricklett one. With two outs in the fourth, Pittsburgh flinched first. Maddox fielded Emil Batch's chopper back to the mound and threw high to first baseman Harry Swacina, who could not hold onto the ball, enabling Batch to scamper to second. Maddox remained "perfectly cool," opined the *Pittsburgh Post*, "and behaved himself like a veteran."[10] Al Burch followed with a routine grounder to shortstop Honus Wagner, whose high throw caromed off Swacina's glove and rolled into right field, allowing Batch to score easily. "I didn't hold that against Honus," said Maddox decades later. "He saved my no-hitter in the ninth."[11]

The Pirates' Clarke collected the game's first hit in the fourth by ripping a one-out double over Batch's head in left-center, but was left stranded at the keystone sack. His teammates finally got on the board the next inning owing to Swacina's "daring baserunning."[12] On first via walk, Swacina took off when Alan Storke executed a sacrifice bunt to third base. By the time first baseman Tim Jordan caught Doc Casey's throw, Swacina had rounded second. According to the *Brooklyn Daily Eagle*, catcher Bill Bergen darted to third base to take Jordan's throw, which sailed high, permitting Swacina to race home and tie the score.[13]

"[T]he game was speedy in every way," opined the *Pittsburgh Press*.[14] While Maddox overpowered the Superbas with his fastball, with an occasional slowball tossed in, Stricklett's "moist slants" and their corresponding dances to the plate deceived the Pirates.[15]

Skipper Patsy Donovan's Superbas threatened in the seventh when Burch led off with a walk, and moved up two stations on a sacrifice and a groundout. With poor-hitting Stricklett at the plate, the speedy Burch attempted an audacious steal of home, but was tagged out by catcher George "Moon" Gibson.

With mounting tension, Honus Wagner led off the Pirates seventh with a walk. Ed Abbaticchio followed with a tailor-made double-play grounder which Jordan fielded cleanly, but threw wildly to second base to force Wagner, who easily reached third when the ball rolled into left field. After Storke drew a one-out walk to load the bases, Gibson drove in Wagner on a grounder forcing Storke at second. Stricklett retired Maddox to keep the pressure on his mound mate.

While Stricklett yielded his second hit of the game, a two-out single by Clark in the eighth, Maddox mowed down all six batters he faced in the eighth and ninth innings. Honus Wagner recorded the final out when he fielded Billy Maloney's chopper over Maddox's head and rifled a bullet to Swacina to end the game in 1 hour and 30 minutes. "The ball seemed to hang in the air," recalled the Hall of Famer. "When it finally came down, I let fly to first base without even looking for the bag. The throw just beat the runner."[16]

In fashioning the Pirates' maiden no-hitter, Maddox fanned five, walked three, and hit a batter. The *Pittsburgh Post* reported that the Superbas did not manage a "semblance" of a hit.[17] The "boy behaves as though he had been working in major league company for ten years instead of ten days," wrote Balinger enthusiastically of Maddox.[18] A tough-luck loser, Stricklett walked four; however, newspaper accounts considered it noteworthy that he did not register a strikeout considering the effectiveness of his spitter, which the Pirates chopped into the grass all afternoon.

Prior to Maddox's gem, there had been three no-hitters in Pittsburgh, each of which occurred when the Alleghenys were members of the American Association. Guy Hecker of the Louisville Colonels tossed the first on September 19, 1882. Ed Morris of the Columbus Buckeyes fashioned the second, on May 29, 1884. Both of those took place at the first incarnation of Exposition Park. On October 7, 1886, Matt Kilroy of the Baltimore Orioles held the Alleghenys hitless in front of 600 spectators at Recreation Park, situated several blocks north of where Exposition Park had been built around 1880. At that time, pitchers threw from a box 50 feet from home plate; the pitcher's box was removed in 1893 and was replaced by a pitcher's plate, located 60 feet 6 inches from home plate.

Two days after Maddox's historic performance, team owner Barney Dreyfuss and the Pirates traveled by Pullman coach to Wheeling to play an exhibition game with the Stogies on what the *Pittsburgh Press* called "Nick Maddox Day."[19] While Stogies fans clamored for the Pirates' new favorite son to start the game, manager Clarke kept his wits, but sent Maddox to the mound for only the first three innings in the Pirates eventual 5-3 victory in 11 innings.[20]

Maddox continued his hot pitching in his fourth start with a distance-going six-hit victory, 14-1, against the New York Giants in Pittsburgh on September 25. Impressively, he extended his hitless streak to 13 innings.[21] The next Pirates hurler to win his first four big-league starts was Gerrit Cole in 2013. Maddox completed all six of his starts in 1907, winning five

of them, and permitting just five earned runs in 54 innings (0.83 ERA). After winning 23 games in 1908, and helping the Pirates to their first World Series championship in 1909, Maddox developed arm problems in 1910 and was sold to the Kansas City Blues in the American Association, never to return to the big stage. In four years with the Pirates he posted a 43-20 record.

SOURCES

In addition to the sources cited in the Notes, the author also accessed Retrosheet.org, Baseball-Reference.com, the SABR Minor Leagues Database, accessed online at Baseball-Reference.com, SABR.org, and *The Sporting News* archive via Paper of Record.

NOTES

1   "Pirates Win a Great Game," *Pittsburgh Press*, September 21, 1907: 8.

2   "Won Fine Game From St. Louis," *Pittsburgh Press*, September 14, 1907: 5.

3   Bill Lamb, "Nick Maddox, SABR BioProject, sabr.org/bioproj/person/1ee85e7c.

4   "Pirates Got an Even Break," *Pittsburgh Press*, September 17, 1907: 10.

5   Edward F. Balinger, "Review of Sports During the Week," *Pittsburgh Post*, September 22, 1907: 16.

6   Ibid.

7   "Fine Finish by Pirates, "*Pittsburgh Press*, September 20, 1907: 22.

8   Stephen V. Rice, "Elmer Stricklett," SABR BioProject, sabr.org/bioproj/person/e350a2d2.

9   "Maddox Proves Bright Star in Sensational Slab Battle," *Pittsburgh Post*, September 21, 1907: 7.

10 Ibid.

11 Paul Meyers, "September 20, 1907: Nick Maddox pitched the first no-hitter in Pirates franchise history," *Pittsburgh-Post-Gazette*, September 20, 2007, post-gazette.com/sports/2007/09/20/September-20-1907-Nick-Maddox-pitched-the-first-no-hitter-in-Pirates-franchise-history/stories/200709200425/.

12 "Superbas Fail to Make a Hit, Yet Nearly Win the Game," *Brooklyn Daily Eagle*, September 21, 1907: 12.

13 Ibid.

14 "Pirates Win a Great Game," *Pittsburgh Press*.

15 "Maddox Proves Bright Star in Sensational Slab Battle," *Pittsburgh Post*.

16 Meyers.

17 "Maddox Proves Bright Star in Sensational Slab Battle,"
    Pittsburgh Post.

18 Balinger.

19 "New Man to Help Locals," *Pittsburgh Press*, September
    22, 1907: 18.

20 "Wheeling Is Beaten in Bitter Struggle," *Pittsburgh Post*,
    September 23, 1907: 7.

21 "Nick Maddox Invincible," *Pittsburgh Press*, September
    26, 1907: 14.

FAREWELL TO THE OLD YARD

JUNE 29, 1909: PITTSBURGH PIRATES 8, CHICAGO CUBS 1, AT EXPOSITION PARK

BY SETH MOLAND-KOVASH

THE PITTSBURGH PIRATES CAME home from a six-game road trip to St. Louis and Cincinnati with excitement in the air on Tuesday, June 29, 1909. A new ballpark was about to be opened to much fanfare and the guests for the occasion were the 37-21 Chicago Cubs, led by manager Frank Chance. Over the past month, the Pirates had opened a 6½-game lead over these same Cubs in the race for the National League pennant and were excited to extend that lead even further. The Pirates and Cubs had last played May 29-30. At the start of that series, the Pirates led the Cubs by just a half-game. Over the past month, Fred Clarke's Pirates had gone an impressive 21-3 to enter the day with a record of 43-14 and that 6½-game lead they were hoping to extend.

Hope was high for Pirates fans. That morning's *Pittsburgh Press* included a feature item on the sports page entitled "Pirates and Tigers Likely to Clash for The World's Pennant."[1] Pirates fans knew that in order to make that prediction a reality, their team would have to go through the defending world champion Chicago Cubs. The Cubs and Pirates were to play the first game of this important five-game set at Exposition Park on Tuesday before moving across town to inaugurate the brand-new Forbes Field on Wednesday. The local papers were full of notes that morning both about the importance of the game to the season standings, but also the closing of Exposition Park and the anticipation of opening Forbes Field the next day. A few highlights:

- Last game at Exposition Park.
- Dedication ceremonies at Forbes Field tomorrow start at 2:30, and the Cubs-Pirates contest at 3:30.

- The Pittsburgh baseball club now has two big canvas coverings for its infield. Both will be spread over Forbes Field tonight.
- President Dreyfuss [president of the Pittsburgh Pirates] yesterday received a letter from [United States] President W.H. Taft, expressing regret over his inability to attend the opening of Forbes Field.
- The Cubs won the only game they have played in Pittsburg this season. It was that memorable 11-inning battle of May 29, played in the presence of President William H. Taft.
- It is fitting that Chicago should be the attraction in the last game at Exposition Park. A Chicago team was the first to play the locals in that historic game, the game occurring on April 22, 1891. The Pirates were defeated in 10 innings, 7-6.[2]

The Sporting News previewed the series by talking about the important race between the front-runners but also the historic closing of an old home and opening of a new home for the Pirates. "Five games are to be played, starting on Tuesday, which marks the final appearance of any ball team at Exposition Park, which has been the home of the bold Buccaneers for many years. Base ball history has been made there, but the field has grown too small to accommodate the large crowds that want to attend the games."[3]

Exposition Park (actually the third incarnation of a park with that name, so sometimes referred to as Expo III) was built in 1890 by the Pittsburgh Burghers of the Players League on the north side of the Allegheny River near where PNC Park stands today. It had a capacity of 10,000 in two-tiered covered wooden grandstands and giant deadball dimensions: 400 feet to each line and 450 feet to center. When the Players League folded after just one season, the Pittsburgh Alleghenies of the National League (just renamed the Pirates) moved in for the 1891 season. The high point of Exposition Park history came in 1903 when the Pirates, led by Honus Wagner, faced off against Cy Young's Boston Americans in the first modern World Series. The first Series game to be played in a National League Park was at Exposition Park on October 6, 1903, which the Pirates won, 5-4, in front of 7,600 fans before eventually losing the best-of-nine Series, five games to three. Continual problems with flooding and sewage backup in the field due to its location near the river, as well as a small capacity, led the Pirates ownership to build Forbes Field, which held 25,000, in Bellefield, in Pittsburgh's East End, far from any rivers.[4]

Perhaps saving their excitement for the new park, only 5,545 fans paid for a ticket that Tuesday to say goodbye to Exposition Park.[5] At the same time, hundreds of baseball fans watched the game for free from their picnic seats on the bluffs surrounding Exposition Park.[6] They were all treated to an offensive showing by the home team as the Pirates, behind Albert "Lefty" Leifield, beat Mordecai "Three-Finger" Brown and the Cubs, 8-1. The scoring started in the first inning as the Pirates scored four runs on three hits off the right-handed Brown, including a two-run triple by rookie second baseman Jack "Dots" Miller, earning him two of his 87 RBIs for the year; he trailed only his famous teammate, shortstop Honus Wagner, for the team lead. (Wagner led the team as season's end with 100 RBIS.) Pittsburgh added another run in the bottom of the third, also driven in by Miller.

After six innings, Heinie Zimmerman pinch-hit for Brown in the top of the seventh. Left-hander Jack Pfiester took over mound duties for Chicago; he finished the 1909 season with a 17-6 mark and a 2.43 ERA, the final one of four very good seasons pitching for the Cubs. Brown had given up five runs on nine hits and a base on balls; Pfiester gave up three runs on five hits, without walking a batter. All three runs off Pfiester scored in the seventh, with Dots Miller collecting his fourth RBI of the afternoon.

Meanwhile Leifield held the Cubs to seven hits, struck out four, and finished the game on his own. The Cubs scored their lone run in the eighth inning.

Leifield struck out Cubs catcher Jimmy Archer for the final out, and baseball at Exposition Park was no more. The time of game had been 1 hour and 40 minutes, with future Hall of Fame umpire Hank O'Day working the plate and veteran Bob Emslie, in the midst of his 35 years as a National League umpire, working at first base. The *Pittsburgh Press* commented, "The Pirates proved stronger than their opponents in every department, in spite of the fact that Chicago had the services of Frank Chance for the first time in six weeks. The Cubs saw plainly that they were up against it, and tried to cover up some of their shortcomings by arguing with the umpires, but this ruse failed to work."[7] Two errors were committed during the game, both by Chicago.

Even before the end of the game, while the Cubs were still at bat in the ninth inning, the farewell ceremonies began. The *Pittsburgh Daily Post* described the scene in serious tones:

> When the champions went to bat in the ninth, the notes of a bugle broke the silence. Commodore Charles Zieg, the well-known local musician, had quietly taken a position on the circus seats back of middlefield, and as soon as it was certain that Chicago had been hopelessly crushed, he sounded "taps" through his cornet. At the same time Groundskeeper Jim O'Malley commenced lowering the big flag, and just as Old Glory touched the ground and the last note of the farewell bugle call ceased, [Cubs' catcher Jimmy] Archer struck out and the historic old baseball lot had passed into history.[8]

Perhaps not surprisingly, the *Chicago Tribune*'s reporter did not share the sentimentality in reporting the same events:. "In the Cubs' half of the ninth inning a pathetic scene was enacted," wrote Ring Lardner, "the bugler playing taps with more or less accuracy while the American flag was let down from the top of the pennant pole, which hasn't held a pennant for some time and never will again."[9]

Whatever anyone thought of the closing of Exposition Park, the season was a great success for the Pirates. That Tuesday's 8-1 victory was one of 110 games won during the 1909 season as the Pirates held off the Cubs to win the pennant by 6½ games. In October, they did indeed face off with Hughie Jennings' Detroit Tigers, winning the World Series in seven games. Meanwhile, the Pirates played the next 61 years at Forbes Field before moving near the river to Three Rivers Stadium in July 1970.

SOURCES

In addition to the sources cited in notes, the author also used Baseball-Reference.com and Retrosheet.org.

NOTES

1   D.L. Reeves, "Pirates and Tigers Likely to Clash for The World's Pennant," *Pittsburgh Press*, June 29, 1909: 8.

2   Excerpted from "Baseball Notes," *Pittsburgh Press*, June 29, 1909: 8. Taft had attended the May 29 game.

3   Ralph S. Davis "Test for Pirates," *The Sporting News*, July 1, 1909: 4.

4   "Exposition Park: Birthplace of Pittsburgh Baseball & Site of First World Series," *Pittsburgh Post-Gazette*, July 11, 2006: 8.

5   "Curtain at Exposition Park Falls After Pirate Victory," *Pittsburgh Daily Post*, June 30, 1909: 8.

6   Ibid.

7   "Pirates Win Last Game at Expo Park," *Pittsburgh Press*, June 30, 1909: 18.

8   Ibid.

9   R.W. Lardner, "Pirates Take First Game of Series From Cubs, 8-1," *Chicago Tribune*, June 30, 1909: 12.

FORBES FIELD, THE HOUSE OF THRILLS, CELEBRATES OPENING DAY

JUNE 30, 1909: CHICAGO CUBS 3, PITTSBURGH PIRATES 2, AT FORBES FIELD

BY HARRY SCHOGER

IT WAS A BRILLIANT DAY FOR A BALL-
game. The skies were clear and azure blue, the temperature in the low 80s. Wednesday, June 30, 1909, was the culmination of a glorious week of parties and galas in Pittsburgh celebrating the opening of owner Barney Dreyfuss's million-dollar brainchild, Forbes Field, the new home of the Pittsburgh Pirates.[1] The first-ever game in this magnificent new steel and concrete stadium was scheduled for 3:30 P.M. It pitted the Pirates against their nemesis for the two previous seasons, the vaunted Chicago Cubs, the reigning World Series champs. The Pirates had come in second both times to the Cubs. In 1908 just one game separated them for the pennant. On this day, league-leading Pittsburgh enjoyed a 7½-game lead over its visiting rivals.

The new baseball palace was located in the elite Oakland/Schenley area of Pittsburgh on property on the southern boundary of the newly named University of Pittsburgh, which moved there in 1907 from downtown, nearly three miles west. Visionary Andrew Carnegie himself had spearheaded an extended development program to make it an area to rival downtown. He succeeded beyond expectations. Schenley Park, the most pristine in the city, abutted the ballpark along the outfield wall. From their seats, fans could see Carnegie Institute, Carnegie Tech, the University of Pittsburgh, and a host of affluent homes and mansions.

It was a day for the fans and the city of Pittsburgh to relish. Many firms had closed for the day to allow employees to attend the game. Patrons began to arrive at the park at 9:00 A.M. to buy 25-cent bleacher seats, since all reserved seats and most grandstand admittance seats were gone. The gates were scheduled to open to the general public at 1:00 P.M. By that hour thousands of baseball patrons of every class milled about in front of the red, white, and blue bunting that patriotically festooned the elegantly adorned façade and gates. The B&O Railroad had put on extra cars to bring in excursion groups from outlying communities. In spite of a strike settled just the day before, the trolley system proved up to the task of handling its largest day's traffic in history. The throng was abuzz with revelry, laughter, excitement, and awe over the spectacular new ballpark they were about to enter.

Fans came attired in their Sunday best. The ladies wore garments in delicate tints and bonnets of every description. The men wore suits, ties (noticeably bows), coats, and hats. Hats of every kind. By far the most popular were straws: sailors, Milans, and Panamas.[2]

The stands, when filled, looked like a massive sea of waving straw hats. Dreyfuss had lined up an army of attendants to take care of the grandstand spectators. Red, white, and blue megaphones were passed out, largely to the ladies, accentuating the colorful flow of revelers.

Because of the overflow crowd, men and boys without seats "were perched on girders or clung to pillars."[3] From the end of the grandstand to the end of the bleachers in left field and along the outfield wall was a necklace of humanity seated on the ground. Failing to get a seat on the grass, males climbed to the top of the walls to sit, legs dangling.

While the massive crowd was locating seats, it was entertained by two lively bands, the Nirella and the Fourteenth Regiment, stationed at either end of the huge grandstand. Once the crowd was settled in the dedication ceremonies began. "Come the trumpeters from the Nirella Band, clad in gaudy red coats, hats of the helmet brand with white plumes, sound the glad greeting that all is well and it is time for the real fun to begin."[4] The blare of the instruments brought a mighty roar from the crowd of 30,000.

The two bands converged at home plate to lead the dedication procession. From clubhouses beneath the grandstand contingents began to emerge: the current Pirates team, led by player-manager Fred Clarke, the men in suits (city fathers, baseball-team owners and magnates, prominent businessmen), and the Chicago Cubs team. The crowd roared when one final contingent emerged, the old warriors of Pirates teams past. They were the honorees this day and led by "Uncle" Al Pratt, the founder and manager of Pittsburgh's first professional baseball team, the Alleghenys.[5]

The current ballplayers removed their caps and opened ranks with great respect to allow the "old warriors" to pass through and take their place of honor behind the bands. Harry Pulliam, president of the National League, and Ban Johnson, president of the American League, led the "suits" and current players. The entire line marched slowly to the center-field flagpole, where the bands began to play *America*. "A monster flag was raised to the top of the flagstaff."[6] The crowd rose in unison when it reached its pinnacle. There followed "a touching silence, which became profound when the flag was dropped to half mast out of respect to Israel W. Durham of the Philadelphia club, who died this week."[7] The curtain came down on the dedication ceremonies when Pittsburgh Mayor William Magee threw out the first pitch.

Certainly, the Pirates faithful wanted to cap off this spectacular and historic week with a victory. The game turned out to be a well-fought pitchers' duel between a pair of veteran right-handers, Vic Willis for the Pirates and Ed Reulbach for the Cubs. The latter had led the NL in winning percentage for the previous three seasons. Willis, as it turned out, was playing his last season with the Bucs.[8]

Willis had a bit of a shaky start. He hit the lead-off batter, Johnny Evers. Jimmy Sheckard walked. Solly Hofman laid down a sacrifice, advancing both runners. Cubs player-manager Frank Chance got his only hit of the day, a single, scoring Evers. Sheckard tried to take home on the hit but was thrown out at the plate.

Both pitchers settled in and allowed no further scoring until the sixth, when the Pirates tied the game. The "Flying Dutchman," Honus Wagner, singled. Rookie Bill Abstein sacrificed and Wagner scored when another rookie, Dots Miller, singled.

The deadlock was broken in the eighth. Evers singled and Sheckard sacrificed, gaining second on an errant throw into the crowd by third baseman Jap Barbeau. After Hofman flied out, Chance hit a grounder to second baseman Dots Miller, who threw home to get Evers. But Evers got his second run of the day when catcher George Gibson dropped the throw. Harry Steinfeldt laid down a bunt that Gibson could have played to get Sheckard coming home. Instead he went for a seemingly easy out at first to get Steinfeldt. Sheckard scored before Abstein made the putout. The Cubs were up by two runs, 3–1.

The Pirates rallied in the bottom of the eighth. Or did they? With one out, Clarke walked. Wagner flied out. Uncharacteristically, Evers muffed an easy fly ball, allowing Abstein to reach first. Dots Miller hit a ball to deep center field. Although enthusiasm ran high throughout the game, "pandemonium broke loose when Miller made his hit in the eighth inning, which looked like the game winning wallop."[9] Or was it?

While fielding the hit, Solly Hofman touched the ball, which spurted into the crowd. All three runners—Clarke, Abstein, and Miller—came home. However, the umpires held a conference and decided the play was subject to a ground-rule double due to the involvement of the spectators. Clarke scored but Abstein was sent back to third and Miller to second. Left-handed-swinging rookie Ham Hyatt pinch-hit for Chief Wilson and struck out, ending the inning. Neither team could mount an offense in the ninth as the Pirates left the tying run on third base during the game-ending force play at second base. The score held up: Cubs 3, Pirates 2. The time of game was 1 hour and 50 minutes.

The Pirates had five hits to the Cubs' four, and Reulbach had walked six Pirates to Willis's three, but the Cubs put across three runs to Pittsburgh's two.

Owner Dreyfuss, who sorely wanted to cap off one of the most memorable weeks in Pittsburgh history with a win, lamented: "What a shame we had to lose that one. I'd have given my share of the gate to have won on this day."[10]

At the end of the day 30,338 baseball patrons had passed through the turnstiles of the new baseball palace, which seated only 25,000. It was the largest crowd that ever witnessed a baseball game up to that time.[11] In spite of the loss, the Pirates went on to win the National League pennant by 6½ games over the Cubs and defeated Ty Cobb and the Detroit Tigers in seven games to win its first World Series.

Forbes Field arguably spawned the most spectacular kickoff of any stadium in baseball history on June 30, 1909. After the din died down, the new stadium took on the daily task of serving the Pirates and their faithful followers and the Pittsburgh community. It served both spheres admirably and honorably. Over the next six-plus decades it became an iconic symbol of the spirit of the region it served.

SOURCES

In addition to the sources cited in the Notes, the author also consulted Baseball-Reference.com and the following:

Bernstein, Sam. "Barney Dreyfuss," sabr.org/bioproj/person/29ceb9e0.

Constans, L.H. "Forbes Field: The Great Stadium of the Pittsburgh Pirates," library.la84.org/SportsLibrary/BBM/1913/bb1m07u.pdf.

Ritter, Lawrence S. *Lost Ballparks* (New York: Penguin Group, 1992), 63-71.

Smith, Curt. "Forbes Field (Pittsburgh)," sabr.org/bioproj/park/forbes-field-pittsburgh.

"Beautiful Forbes Field," *Pittsburgh Press*, July 1, 1909.

"Opening Day Crowd Greatest on Record," *Pittsburgh Press*, July 1, 1909.

"Pirates Lose First Game on Forbes Field," *Pittsburgh Daily Post*, July 1, 1909.

"Showed He Was Game," *Pittsburgh Press*, July 1, 1909.

"Straw Hat Sale Enters Last Lap," *Pittsburgh Press*, June 28, 1909.

"World's Greatest Baseball Park to Open Wednesday," *Pittsburgh Press*, June 29, 1909.

NOTES

1   Forbes Field was named for a British officer, John Forbes, who was a hero in the French and Indian Wars. In 1758 Colonel Forbes (later promoted to general) led the campaign to capture Fort Duquesne from the French. As the enemy fled, it burned the fort. Forbes immediately rebuilt it, naming it Fort Pitt after British Secretary of State William Pitt the Elder. Forbes also named the settlement at the junction of the Allegheny and Monongahela Rivers Pittsburgh.

2   Haberdashers in downtown Pittsburgh conducted sales campaigns to dress every male fan in a straw hat for this game.

3   "New Home of Pirates Taxed," *Pittsburgh Post-Gazette*, July 1, 1909.

4   Ibid.

5   Al ("Uncle Al") Pratt was a pitcher-outfielder for the Cleveland Forest Citys in 1869-1870. The team was in the Professional League of Baseball Players, the first professional league in America. In 1880 he founded the first major-league club in Pittsburgh, the Alleghenys, which joined the American Association. The team began play in 1882 with Pratt as its manager through 1883. He dropped out of major-league baseball at the end of the 1883 season.

6   "New Home of Pirates Taxed."

7   Ibid. Israel Wilson Durham was a state senator from Philadelphia and briefly the president and principal owner of the Philadelphia Phillies in 1909.

8   Vic Willis pitched in the NL for 13 years, four of which were with the Pirates. He was a mainstay of the Pittsburgh starting rotation. He went 22-11 in 1909 and led the league with 35 starts. Before the start of the 1910 campaign, he was a Cardinal. In 1911 he was out of baseball. He was elected to the Hall of Fame in 1995.

9   "Immense Throng at Forbes Field," *Pittsburgh Press*, July 1, 1909.

10 Daniel Levitt, "Vic Willis," SABR BioProject. sabr.org/bioproj/person/3c061442.

11 The Forbes Field opener exceeded the previous attendance high for a baseball game, 30,247, on October 4, 1908, in Chicago. That game was also a Pittsburgh-Chicago game.

CHIEF HITS FOR THE CYCLE

JULY 3, 1910: PITTSBURGH PIRATES 10, CINCINNATI REDS 2, AT PALACE OF THE FANS

BY JEFF FINDLEY

ON JULY 3, 1910, THE REIGNING world champion Pittsburgh Pirates were visiting Cincinnati, completing the final contest of a five-game series with the Reds, the first games of which had been played in Pittsburgh. The third-place Pirates were just a half-game ahead of Cincinnati in the standings but, of more significance, trailed the Chicago Cubs by 7½ games in the National League race. An individual game in the middle of a long major-league season held minimal prominence in that day's news cycle, because most newspapers were focused on the heavyweight boxing match between Jack Johnson and James Jeffries, the anointed "Battle of the Century," which was scheduled to take place the following day.

But an uncharacteristic performance by the Pirates' Owen "Chief" Wilson made the day a memorable one for baseball fans.

The location was Cincinnati's Palace of the Fans, a ballpark that hosted the city's major-league baseball team from 1902 through 1911. Unique in that it sported what Reds historians Greg Rhodes and John Erardi called "the most distinctive grandstand ever built at a major league baseball park,"[1] the structure was inspired by the neoclassical White City structures at the 1893 World's Columbia Exposition in Chicago. This location in Cincinnati would later make way for Redland Field in 1912, and ultimately Crosley Field in 1934, the Reds' home until Riverfront Stadium hosted its first major-league game in June 1970.

The visiting Pirates sent Howie Camnitz to the mound, a 28-year-old right-hander who won 25 games the previous season. At 4-5, he had yet to match his 1909 brilliance, and in fact had given up four runs in a start that lasted just four innings two days earlier, a 4-1 loss at the Pirates' own Forbes Field.

The Reds countered with Harry Gaspar, who sported a modest 7-6 record after posting wins in his previous two outings. And for three innings, the right-handed Gaspar continued his effectiveness, suffering little damage at the hands of the Pirates except for a bunt single by Wilson.

But when the Chief stepped to the plate with two outs in the fourth, a crooked number quickly adorned the scoreboard.

From the *Pittsburgh Post*: "Wilson's four-ply hit vanished the Reds defense into thin air. For four rounds after Billy Klem, the master of ceremonies, had introduced the principals, Camnitz and (George) Gibson for Pittsburgh, and Gaspar and (Larry) McLean for Cincinnati, the game progressed in such a scientific manner that spectators were in doubt about the outcome. Then Wilson got busy. With two down in the fourth and (Honus) Wagner on second the Texan successfully robbed Gaspar of his good name as a pitcher, wheeled Wagner home and made the entire circuit while (Mike) Mitchell was returning the ball to the infield."[2]

Gaspar managed to hang around until the sixth inning, but Wilson's third hit of the day, a double, drove in Ham Hyatt with the final run of the frame after Fred Clarke and Wagner had previously scored. Gaspar managed to retire Gibson and Camnitz to end the inning, but his day was terminated after he allowed five runs and nine hits.

For Camnitz's part, the Pirates pitcher hadn't allowed a run through six frames, a vast improvement over his performance against the Reds two days earlier. He wasn't dominant, scattering 12 hits in the contest, but the Kentucky-born hurler was able to keep Cincinnati from mounting a serious rally, allowing single runs in the seventh and ninth innings, after the outcome had presumably been decided. It was the most safeties allowed in a game by Camnitz in his mediocre 1910 campaign (he also allowed 12 hits in a win over Boston on May 18), but he still tallied a win for his efforts

With three innings remaining, Cincinnati manager Clark Griffith sent Rube Benton to the hill. An interesting character, Benton has been described as "a hard-throwing, fast-living left-hander" who "had a reputation for drinking, gambling, and driving too fast."[3] The Reds had purchased his contract a few days earlier (he was a Class-D player at the time), and this represented only his second appearance in the big leagues.

It didn't go well, as intimated in the *Pittsburgh Post*: "Like all bush leaguers Benton relies on his alleged ability to strike out opposing batsmen. The minor leaguers fish at balls which do not come over the plate, but the ball players on the Pittsburgh and Chicago clubs just fold their arms and let the Rube hang himself with his own rope. In language more easily understood they wait and wait and Rube walks and walks."[4]

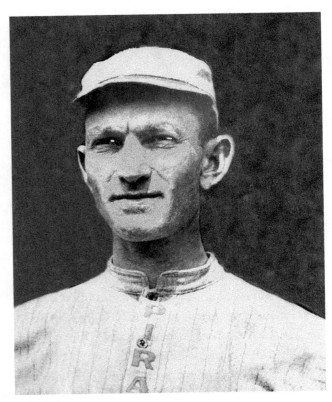

Owen "Chief" Wilson

Benton did walk four in three innings, and he also surrendered five hits, including a single by Tommy Leach and an RBI double by Clarke, the second and third batters he faced. Three Pirates scored in the seventh before Benton struck out Gibson to end the attack, and the Pirates had jetted to an 8-0 lead.

In the bottom of the seventh, Cincinnati finally tallied a run, on consecutive singles by Mike Mitchell, Dode Paskert, and McLean, three of the 12 hits allowed by Camnitz in the contest. Despite the offensive prowess shown throughout the contest, the Reds had only themselves to rely on, as Camnitz didn't issue a single free pass, nor did his fielders commit an error.

Unsympathetic, Pittsburgh answered with two more runs in the eighth on two walks and two hits, including Clarke's third counter of the game. The runs pushed the Pirates' lead to 10-1, and although the top of the ninth was scoreless, with one out, Wilson delivered a triple to complete the cycle. He was left stranded at third when the inning concluded.

Wilson reached base in all five plate appearances, including an eighth-inning error by Cincinnati second baseman Sam Woodruff, a stand-in for Dick Egan, who was ailing with a lame arm.

An insignificant run in the final frame for the Reds came from hits by Dick Hoblitzell, Mitchell, and McLean, and the Pirates left town with a 10-2 victory, heading directly to Chicago for a four-game series with the league-leading Cubs.

Cincinnati's hurlers were anything but stellar, with Gaspar and Benton each allowing five runs, while the Pirates' Camnitz avenged his subpar outing of two days earlier.

Offensively, the Reds' McLean had three safeties, as did Clarke for the Pittsburgh side. Wagner scored three times while being credited with two hits, but it was the Chief who stole the headlines with 10 total bases and a hit of each variety.

Cincinnati Enquirer sportswriter Jack Ryder summed up the contest this way:

"It was one of those games which reminded one of the champs of last season, with everyone hitting the ball hard and getting a lot of runs from their hard poling. Chief Wilson had a great picnic at the bat, a regular Fourth of July celebration all by himself. He cut in with every variety of bingle, from a single to a home run. Five times up, he got on every time, making a single, a double, a triple and a home run, and reaching first the other time on a fumble by Woodruff."[5]

The win kept the Pirates in third place in the National League standings, but they never got within reasonable distance of the Cubs, who won the pennant in 1910 by 12 games over the second-place New York Giants. Pittsburgh was a distant third, 17½ games back.

Notably, Chief Wilson's outstanding performance was the only time a major-league player hit for the cycle in Palace of the Fans ballpark.

SOURCES

In addition to the sources cited in the Notes, the author also consulted Baseball-Reference.com, Retrosheet.org, and SABR.org.

NOTES

1   Jeff Suess, "Reds' Legendary Palace of the Fans Symbol of Baseball's Growth," *Cincinnati.com*, April 7, 2017, cincinnati.com/story/news/2017/04/05/reds-legendary-palace-fans-symbol-baseballs-growth/100063096/, September 4, 2017.

2   "World's Champions Have Easy Time Beating Reds," *Pittsburgh Daily Post*, July 4, 1910.

3   Bill Bishop, "Rube Benton," posted online at sabr.org/bioproj/person/36b8167d.

4   "World's Champions Have Easy Time."

5   Jack Ryder, "After Six Rounds Against the Pirates, Mr. Gaspar Failed to Hold the Champs Safely," *Cincinnati Enquirer*, July 4, 1910.

"WAGNER WIELDS WILLOW,"[1] HITS FOR THE CYCLE, BUT PIRATES LOSE

AUGUST 22, 1912: NEW YORK GIANTS 8, PITTSBURGH PIRATES 6 (SECOND GAME), AT FORBES FIELD

BY MIKE HUBER

BEFORE A SOLD-OUT AND BOISTER-ous Forbes Field crowd, future Hall of Famer Honus Wagner "had his bat working overtime,"[2] producing seven hits (in two games) as his Pittsburgh Pirates split a doubleheader with the visiting New York Giants. About 25,000 were on hand to witness the pair of contests.[3] In the opener, Wagner had two singles, a double, and a stolen base, and he scored two of his team's runs, ensuring that Pittsburgh edged past the Giants, 3-2. Howard Camnitz out-dueled New York ace Christy Mathewson, holding "the Gotham gang to half a dozen hits."[4] In the second game, Wagner accomplished the rare feat of hitting for the cycle, unfortunately in a losing cause.

Despite banging out 16 hits in the second contest, the Pirates could not beat New York's Rube Marquard, who tossed a complete game to secure his 25th win of the season. The left-handed-throwing Marquard had won his first 19 starts of the season before losing to the Chicago Cubs on July 8. His confidence was high each time he took the ball. His opponent on the mound was Pittsburgh right-hander Claude Hendrix, who "suffered a bombardment in the first four innings."[5] From July 4 through August 14, Hendrix had 11 straight starts of at least eight innings, but in his last starting effort before this game, he had been knocked out after three innings and was used out of the bullpen once; for four innings two days earlier.

Pittsburgh started the action in the bottom of the first inning, as leadoff batter Solly Hofman doubled down the right-field line and scored on a single by Wagner. The Flying Dutchman promptly stole second base, his second steal of the day, but Dots Miller grounded out to pitcher Marquard to end the threat.

In the top of the second, New York's Red Murray led off with a triple, and scored on a double down the right-field line by Fred Merkle. After Buck Herzog sacrificed Merkle to third, Chief Meyers followed with a single, but Merkle did not score. So with Art Fletcher batting, Giants manager John McGraw put on the double steal. Pirates catcher George Gibson threw the ball into center field trying to get Meyers at second, and the error allowed Merkle to motor home. Merkle was credited with a stolen base as well. The Giants now led, 2-1.

In the fourth inning, Herzog tripled, Meyers singled, and Fletcher tripled, and New York had two more tallies to make the score 4-1. In the fifth inning, Pirates skipper Fred Clarke replaced Hendrix with Ed Warner, a rookie left-hander. Hendrix had yielded seven hits to the 19 batters he faced. Warner would also face 19 batters and give up four runs.

In the sixth inning, each team scored once. New York manufactured its run when Herzog was hit by a pitch, motored to third on a single by Meyers, and scored on a fielder's choice when Fletcher grounded to Wagner, who forced Meyers at second. "The Corsairs got this run back"[6] when Wagner led off with a triple to the fence in left-center. He trotted home when Miller singled up the middle to cut the Giants' advantage to 5-2. Then, in the bottom of the seventh, Pittsburgh struck again as Hofman singled to right, followed by Max Carey, who lifted a fly ball down the left-field line that dropped in for a double as New York's Fred Snodgrass, who had raced over to make a shoestring catch, instead saw the ball slip through his fingers. Hofman halted at third. Snodgrass insisted that the ball had landed foul, but umpire Bill Klem, from home plate, "declared it safe."[7] Wagner drove a ball to center, and this time it was Beals Becker who couldn't make the play, and the ball dropped in. This double enabled Wagner to trade places with Carey, who scored behind Hofman. Miller then singled again, and "Wagner carried the tying run across the pan."[8] The score was now tied at 5-5.

Four New York hits resulted in three more runs in the Giants' half of the eighth. With one out, Herzog singled. Meyers doubled him home, and then scored on Marquard's single into center field. Snodgrass drove a triple to deep left, and "Marquard waltzed home."[9] Pittsburgh manager Clarke called on right-hander King Cole to pitch the ninth, and Cole retired the Giants in order.

The Pirates tried to mount a two-out rally in the ninth. According to the *Pittsburgh Daily Post*, "Wagner sailed the sphere over the left field fence above the twelfth panel, but nobody was on when it happened and the jig was up."[10] Miller, who was 3-for-5 in the game, came up next and doubled to center, but he was stranded as Alex McCarthy, pinch-hitting for Chief Wilson, flied out to Larry Doyle past second base for the final out of the game. The Giants had won, 8-6.

The *New York Times* described Wagner's performance with great praise. His "quartet of hits figured in every Pittsburgh run, three being scored by the Teuton and the other three chased home by his timely smashes. On the paths he showed that Father Time is still a stranger by stealing two bases, and in the field he galloped nimbly on all sides of his position, accepting fourteen chances out of a possible fifteen."[11] In the last four innings of the tight second game, the 38-year-old Wagner had come to bat three times, and produced a triple, double, and home run.

Of the 29 hits between the two squads, 13 went for extra bases. Wagner hit the only home run, but there were five triples and seven doubles. The distances to the fences in left, center, and right field were 360 feet, 462 feet, and 376 feet, respectively,[12] so the spacious stadium allowed for extra-base hits. In the cycle, Wagner was 4-for-5 and added a stolen base. His

Honus Wagner

fifth home run of the season instantly became "the longest over-the-fence home run ever poled at Forbes Field."[13] The game was "an old-fashioned slugging bee, with doubles and triples coming so fast that the outfielders were legweary from chasing the ball."[14] In addition to Wagner's four safeties, Pittsburgh's Hofman, Carey, and Miller each had three hits in the losing effort. Gibson and Warner were the only other Pittsburgh players to get hits.

For Pittsburgh, Hendrix and Warner combined to allow eight earned runs to the Giants; Cole pitched one scoreless inning. Warner picked up the loss, the only loss of his major-league career.[15] Every New York batter except Becker got at least one hit. Meyers had the most productive day for New York, going 4-for-4 with two runs scored and two batted in. Five different New Yorkers pushed runs across home plate.

At the end of the day, the Giants stood at 78-33, atop the National League, while the third-place Pirates had a record of 67-45. In the first two weeks of September, the Pirates won 12 games in a row, but remained mired in third. After September 2, they went 21-5, finally climbing to second by the season's last week. They ended the campaign with a sterling record of 93-58-2, but 10 games behind New York.

New York fans might have been disappointed, as McGraw used his two aces, Mathewson and Marquard, and his Giants lost a half-game in the standings to the second-place Cubs, who were now four games behind. The Giants had been alone in first place since May 21, due to three nine-game winning streaks and another of 16 games, which carried through to July 3. McGraw's team finished at 103-48-3, taking the second of three consecutive National League pennants.

Wagner's cycle was the fifth in Pittsburgh franchise history. Fred Carroll had the first, on May 2, 1887. Player-manager Clarke cycled on July 23, 1901, and again on May 7, 1903. Chief Wilson accomplished the rare feat on July 3, 1910. After Wagner's accomplishment, Pirates fans would have to wait nine years before Dave Robertson hit for the cycle on August 30, 1921. From Fred Carroll (May 2, 1887) to John Jaso (September 28, 2016), 24 Pirates have hit for the cycle, the most of any major-league team, as of the beginning of the 2017 season.

NOTES

1   Ed F. Balinger, "Buccaneers and Giants Break Even in Bargain on Forbes Field," *Pittsburgh Daily Post*, August 23, 1912: 13.

2   Ibid.

3   Retrosheet lists the attendance at 25,000. The *Pittsburgh Daily Post* proclaimed 20,000 fans, the *New York Times* listed 27,000 spectators, but the *Pittsburgh Post-Gazette* recorded 25,000. According to *Forbes Field: Essays and Memories of the Pirates' Historic Ballpark, 1909-1971*, the stadium capacity was 25,000. See David Cicotello and Angelo J. Louisa, *Forbes Field: Essays and Memories of the Pirates' Historic Ballpark, 1909-1971* (Jefferson, North Carolina: McFarland & Company, Inc., 2007).

4   Balinger.

5   James Jerpe, "Wagner and Camnitz Star While Pirates and Giants Draw Even," *Pittsburgh Post-Gazette*, August 23, 1912: 8.

6   Balinger: 14.

7   Ibid. In 1912, only two umpires worked the game. Klem was behind home plate and Jim Johnstone worked first base.

8   Ibid.

9   Ibid. Marquard was a decent hitter, sporting a .215 average at this point in the season. In 1912, he had 10 runs batted in, helping his cause on the mound.

10   Balinger: 13.

11   "Giants Divide With Pirates," *New York Times*, August 23, 1912: 7.

12   Michael Gershman. *Diamonds: The Evolution of the Ballpark* (Boston: Houghton Mifflin, 2003), 90.

13   Jerpe. Forbes Field opened in 1909, so it had been home to the Pirates for just three seasons.

14   *New York Times*.

15   Warner's major-league career lasted for two months. He appeared in 11 games in 1912, starting three. He got one victory, a shutout of the Boston Braves.

THREE FOR A HALF A BUCK!
THE ONLY MAJOR-LEAGUE TRIPLEHEADER

OCTOBER 2, 1920: CINCINNATI REDS 13, PITTSBURGH PIRATES 4 (FIRST GAME);

CINCINNATI REDS 7, PITTSBURGH PIRATES 3 (SECOND GAME);

PITTSBURGH PIRATES 6, CINCINNATI REDS 0 (SIX INNINGS) (THIRD GAME), AT FORBES FIELD

BY BILL NOWLIN

"It's a great day for a ball game; let's play two!" — Ernie Banks

IT'S BEEN A CENTURY SINCE THERE was a tripleheader played in major-league baseball. Research has turned up only three instances of tripleheaders. The most recent one was played at Pittsburgh's Forbes Field on October 2, 1920, and it definitively determined which team would finish in third place in the National League that year.

After the close of play on September 30, the Brooklyn Robins were in first place and the New York Giants in second place. Bad weather prevented games between the reigning world champion but now third-place Cincinnati Reds (80-69) and the fourth-place Pittsburgh Pirates (77-73) on either September 30 or October 1. The two teams each had four games left on their schedule, three against each other and one against other teams on October 3 (the Pirates in Chicago against the Cubs, with the Reds hosting the Cardinals.) Mathematics shows that should the Pirates and Reds get in their three games and the Pirates sweep, both teams would have 80 wins. Third place would be resolved on October 3; at the time, finishing third earned the team a share of the World Series proceeds. Fourth place earned nothing.[1]

Pirates owner Barney Dreyfuss suggested three games in one day, beginning at noon. Sunset on October 2 was at 6:01 P.M. National League President John Heydler agreed to Dreyfuss's suggestion.[2] Everyone in Pittsburgh knew that "one defeat this afternoon will kill the Buccos' chances."[3]

"Talk about your bargain days," wrote *Pittsburgh Post-Gazette* sportswriter Charles J. Doyle. "Come early and bring your lunch. The big show begins at 12 o'clock and will continue for five or six hours. All for one price of admission, folks, and the sideshow thrown in."[4] Doyle said the gates would open "some time after breakfast" and "last, but not by any means least, the baseball writers will be served a lunch. It will not be in liquid form. Tough luck."[5]

Pirates manager George Gibson, wrapping up his first season as skipper, assigned the starting role for the first game to Pittsburgh's ace, left-hander Wilbur Cooper, who entered the game with a record of 24-14 and an ERA of 2.25. He got shelled. He gave up one run in the first thanks to an Edd Roush double, and another run in the second after shortstop Larry Kopf tripled to the scoreboard and Greasy Neale singled over second base. Cooper saw his team take a 3-2 lead in the bottom of the second on two walks and two Reds errors (both by Kopf), and Charlie Grimm's single.

But then he collapsed, surrendering six runs to the Reds in the top of the third. Jake Daubert led off with a triple over Max Carey's head in center field. Heinie Groh doubled to right field. After one out, Pat Duncan reached on rookie Pie Traynor's error, then stole second, and Kopf drove in both Groh and Duncan.[6] Neale was hit by a pitch. Catcher Bill Rariden singled and drove in Kopf, and then Reds pitcher Ray Fisher helped his own cause with a two-run single over first base.

Cooper was pulled with only one out in the third. He hadn't walked a batter, but he had allowed 10 hits. Whitey Glazner and Jack Wisner relieved.

Manager Pat Moran's choice of pitcher for Cincinnati was righty Ray Fisher. He was 9-11 (2.79). Of the four runs he gave up in his complete-game win, only one was earned. He scattered eight hits and walked three.

The big bats of the first game were Groh and Kopf (who tripled twice), each with three RBIs. Every Reds player had at least one base hit. The Reds ran free on the bases, stealing seven bases (left fielder Duncan stealing three); the Pirates stole none at all.

The Reds scored four more runs in the top of the ninth, an inning featuring two double steals, the second of them seeing Groh take second base while Daubert scored from third. By game's end the Reds had won, 13-4, and any hope the Pirates had had to finish third in the standings was gone. The game had taken 2:03 to play.

Cincinnati Reds 7, Pittsburgh Pirates 3 (second game)

The two games that followed were anticlimactic in terms of the standings, but played nonetheless. However, the *Pittsburgh Press* said they "were farces as far as the use of the regular lineups were concerned. Manager Moran used pitchers and catchers in infield and outfield positions and in the third spasm, Manager Gibson followed his lead and used a pitcher and catcher in the outfield."[7] In the second game, pitcher Dutch Ruether played first base for the Reds and Fritz Coumbe played center field. Hod Eller, yet another Reds pitcher, played second base and then

first base. Rube Bressler, a pitcher who was transitioning to become an outfielder, played right field.

Both starting pitchers went the distance. Righty Lynn Brenton pitched for the Reds. He'd pitched in one game for Cleveland in 1913 and 11 in 1915. In 1920, he made the majors again, working in four September games for Cincinnati with a 1-1 record prior to this October 2 start. Opposing Brenton was Jimmy Zinn. Also a right-hander, Zinn had been 1-3 for the Phillies in 1919, and entered this game with a 1-0 record, winning a 12-inning complete game, 2-1, against the Cardinals on September 25.

The Pirates scored first, in the bottom of the first, but only once, on rookie Cotton Tierney's sacrifice fly. They added another run in the bottom of the fourth when third baseman Clyde Barnhart hit a ball to the cinder path in left field, scoring right fielder Fred Nicholson, and things were looking better. Zinn was giving up a lot of hits, but the baserunners weren't scoring. Only two of the 14 hits off him went for extra bases, both doubles. He walked two, but struck out seven and had managed to keep the Reds scoreless until the seventh inning. Six of the 14 Cincinnati hits, however, all came in the top of the seventh.

The Reds scored seven times. A hit on a bad hop, an infield hit, and a walk loaded the bases, an error and a wild throw saw the first two runs come in, the second on one of second baseman George Cutshaw's two errors. Morrie Rath singled in another run on another poor fielding play. Shortstop Ed Sicking, purchased from the Giants in early July, drove in two with a single to center. Third baseman Sam Crane singled to center and drove in another. Sicking got caught in a rundown between third base and home, but made it back safely to third while Crane alertly moved up to second. Sicking got thrown out at the plate when the next batter was up, but then Eller, the pitcher who played infield (and had a 3-for-4 day), drove in two more Reds runs, the final two runs of the seven-run seventh, with a double to left field.

Cincinnati won the game, 7-3, the Pirates scoring one final run in the bottom of the ninth on a single by Nicholson and a triple over first base and down the right-field line by Possum Whitted.

Brenton allowed only six hits — three singles, two doubles, and a triple. He walked two and struck out five. All three of the runs off him were earned. The Reds committed only one error, but the Pirates made three. The game took 1:56 to play.

Pittsburgh Pirates 6, Cincinnati Reds 0 (six innings) (third game)

Umpires Pete Harrison (a native of England) and Hank O'Day worked all three games, Harrison working home plate for the full tripleheader.

The opposing pitchers were two right-handers, Johnny Morrison for the Pirates and Buddy Napier for the Reds. It was only Morrison's second big-league game. He'd pitched one scoreless inning on September 28. Napier had some scattered major-league experience, in seven games for the 1912 St. Louis Browns and one game for the 1918 Cubs. He was 4-1 with a 1.05 ERA for the Reds in 1920, though.

The Pirates struck first, in the first, scoring three runs off Napier. Leading off was Cotton Tierney. He singled to right field. Traynor was hit by a pitch. Nicholson doubled to left field. Cliff Lee's sacrifice fly enabled Traynor to score from third base. Grimm singled to score Nicholson. That was all it took.

Morrison kept the Reds scoreless through six, scattering four hits and walking only one. One of the hits was by Eller, who played first base once more.

Pittsburgh's Zinn, who had pitched game two, played right field in game three. He was 1-for-3 at the plate.

Napier allowed three more runs by the Pirates in the sixth inning. With one out, Grimm singled to center field. Bressler dropped Zinn's fly ball; Grimm took third and Zinn took second. Catcher Bill Haeffner singled over second and Grimm crossed the plate. Morrison reached on a force out that retired Haeffner. Tierney doubled to left field, scoring both Zinn and Morrison.

Darkness encroached and the game was called at 6 o'clock on account of said darkness. It had taken one hour and one minute to play. The Pirates won, 6-0. Only two of the runs were earned.

The Pirates were eliminated from third-place contention after the first game; the Reds ultimately shared $10.744.14 for finishing third.[8]

Each team had players who appeared in all three games. For the Pirates, they were Cotton Tierney, Fred Nicholson, and Clyde Barnhart, and for the Reds, they were Morrie Rath and Pat Duncan.

Five Baseball Hall of Famers took part in one or more of these three games — Max Carey, Pie Traynor, and Billy Southworth of the Pirates, and Edd Roush of the Reds. Officiating was Hall of Fame umpire Hank O'Day. In 1920, Roush batted .339, with a career-high 90 RBIs. Carey batted .289 in 1920, with a league-leading total of 52 stolen bases. Traynor, as noted, was just beginning his long career. Southworth played right field in the first game. He appeared in 146 games in 1920, batting .284. Though he finished with a career .297 mark, it was his 13 years as a manager, leading the Cardinals to three World Series and the Boston Braves to one that punched his ticket to the Hall. A fifth Hall of Famer played this day, too. Earle "Greasy" Neale played for the 1919 World Series champion Cincinnati Reds and was enshrined in the Pro Football Hall of Fame in 1969 primarily for his work as head coach of the Philadelphia Eagles from 1941 to 1950.

Total playing time for the three games came to precisely five hours — 2:03, 1:56, and 1:01. There was a scheduled 10-minute break between each of the games.[9] The length of an average game in 2016 was 3 hours and 26 seconds.[10]

The first of the two prior "tripleheaders" was on Labor Day, 1890 — September 1. The two teams were the Brooklyn Bridegrooms, who finished first in the National League that year, and the Pittsburgh Alleghenys, who finished last with a record of 23-113 (with two ties). Brooklyn swept all three games — 10-9, 3-2, and 8-4. The first game was quite a thriller. Brooklyn had led 10-0 heading into the ninth inning, but Pittsburgh scored nine runs and had the tying run thrown out at home plate for the final out on what would have been an inside-the-park home run. In 1891, the Pittsburgh team became the Pirates.

The first game had started at 10:30 A.M. There was a separate admission for that game from the two games played in the afternoon—hence, it was not a true tripleheader.

The same was true for the Labor Day "triple-header" on September 7, 1896, between Baltimore and Louisville. That year Baltimore finished first and Louisville finished last. Again, one game was played in the morning and the other two as a doubleheader in the afternoon. Baltimore swept, winning the games by scores of 4-3, 9-8, and 12-1 (the third game lasting eight innings.)

Thus the games at Pittsburgh's Forbes Field on October 2, 1920, constitute the only true tripleheader played in major-league baseball.[11] How many fans took in the games? The *Pittsburgh Post-Gazette* said "about 8,000 fans sparked themselves in the cool stands during the afternoon, but less than half of this number were present when the flitting shadows played."[12]

The 24 innings played were three fewer than the 27 innings the Pirates and Cubs played against each other on June 28, 1916—when the Pirates won a nine-inning game, 3-2, and then an 18-inning game by the same score.

After the game, Charles J. Doyle declared, "All in all, it was a very exciting afternoon—but the day proved that too much is too much."[13]

SOURCES

Thanks to Steve Krevisky who suggested the topic and did some initial research. Thanks to Mike Huber for assistance. The author relied upon Retrosheet.org for many details. Other articles consulted include:

Jackson, Frank. "The Longest Day," *Hardball Times*, January 20, 2014.

Willard, Jim. "Baseball's Last Triple-Header Was Certainly One for the Record Books," *Loveland* (Colorado) *Reporter-Herald*, November 20, 2011.

NOTES

1   Dan Hughes, "The Last Tripleheader," *Baseball*, October 6, 2015. Hughes led his article with the very apt Ernie Banks quotation. baseballmagazine.wordpress.com/2015/10/08/the-last-tripleheader/.

2   "Play Three Games Today," *Philadelphia Inquirer*, October 2, 1920: 16. See also A.D. Suehsdorf, "The Last Tripleheader,"

Baseball Research Journal, 1980. Suehsdorf wrote, "Barney Dreyfuss, the Pirates' energetic owner, proposed this to Pat Moran, the Reds' manager, who sensibly if not sportingly, refused. Undaunted, Dreyfuss got in touch with John A. Heydler, the National League's president, in New York. As has happened once or twice before in baseball, the owner got his way. Heydler telegraphed Moran to play the three games."

3   L.H. Wollen, "Triple-header Carded Today," *Pittsburgh Press*, October 2, 1920: 1. The first game to be played was the game originally scheduled for Saturday, October 2. The second game was to be the game which had originally been scheduled for Thursday, September 30, and the third game would make up the October 1 game.

4   Charles J. Doyle, "Pirates and Reds Play Tripleheader Today," *Pittsburgh Post-Gazette*, October 2, 1920: 9. Ticket prices had been increased from 1919, with the cheapest bleacher seats jumping from 25 cents to 50 cents. Ralph S. Davis, "All Ticket Prices To Be Higher," *Pittsburgh Press*, February 22, 1920: 20. Thanks to Dennis VanLangen for tracking down this article on Forbes Field ticker pricing.

5   Ibid.

6   For Traynor, it was the 16th game of his career. He played shortstop. Traynor played in only seven games in 1921, but settled in as Pittsburgh's regular third baseman from 1922 to 1934, ultimately voted into the National Baseball Hall of Fame.

7   L.H. Wollen, "Reds Cinch Third Place," *Pittsburgh Press*, October 3, 1920: Sporting Section 1.

8   A.D. Suehsdorf.

9   "Play Three Games Today."

10 foxsports.com/mlb/story/mlb-game-average-length-increase-how-to-fix-051716.

11 Due to rainout the preceding day, there was a minor-league tripleheader scheduled for May 4, 2016, between the Potomac Nationals and the Lynchburg Hillcats, affiliates of the Washington Nationals and the Cleveland Indians, for May 5, but one of the games was not played and it became a doubleheader instead. Tim Hagerty of *The Sporting News* wrote about the time in 1899 the New England League's Manchester Manchesters and the Portland Phenoms played six games all in one day, starting at 9:00 A.M. He says, "the Manchesters won all six games to clinch the division title, but baseball officials were furious about the sneaky scheduling change and later decided only two of the six wins counted, returning the second-half championship to Newport." Tim Hagerty, "Sextupleheader: Two Minor League Teams Played Six Games in One Day," The Sporting News, August 17, 2014. sportingnews.com/mlb/news/sextupleheader-six-games-in-one-day-portland-manchester/16y3fiygv405r1bwf9rjrnahxm.

12 Charles J. Doyle, "Bucs Suffer Two Defeats by Reds in Tripleheader," *Pittsburgh Post-Gazette*, October 3, 1920: 20.

13 Ibid.

MOSES "CHIEF" YELLOW HORSE DEFEATS ADOLFO LUQUE

JUNE 30, 1921: PITTSBURGH PIRATES 5, CINCINNATI REDS 3, AT FORBES FIELD

BY JORGE IBER, PHD

ALL MAJOR-LEAGUE FRANCHISES have had their share of noteworthy moments concerning the racial aspects of the sport's chronicle. The Pirates, for example, have participated in one of the most renowned events in this narrative, with the game on September 1, 1971, a prime example. On that evening at Three Rivers Stadium, manager Danny Murtaugh wrote out a lineup card that featured the first all-minority starting nine in major-league history. Pittsburgh was also enmeshed in a lesser known racial episode—the first time an African-American managed in the majors. That mostly ignored happening occurred on September 21, 1963, when Murtaugh and coach Frank Oceak were both tossed for arguing a call late in a contest against the Los Angeles Dodgers. The man who skippered the Bucs over the last two innings of that game, Gene Baker, not only broke down the managerial barrier (albeit but briefly) at the highest level, he was also the first man of his background to manage a minor-league squad for a major-league organization (when the Pirates signed him to manage Class-D Batavia in 1961). The story described here falls into this second, less well-recognized, category; though it is no less significant. On June 30, 1921, for only the third time in major-league history, both starting pitchers were nonwhite: one Latino (Adolfo Luque) and the other Native American (Moses Yellow Horse, a Pawnee).

A review of the careers of both men demonstrates the stereotypes so prevalent for Latinos and Native Americans at play during these years. The Cuban-born Luque was a "hothead," and the Native American competitor was someone who could have triumphed if only he had not been (genetically, it would have been argued then) susceptible to liquor. The two previous occasions for such a matchup took place that same season, when the Luque faced off against Cubs hurler Virgil Cheeves (Cherokee) on May 5 and June 25. The right-handed Luque also pitched in another historic start, on September 2, 1918, when he and fellow Cuban Oscar Tuero became the first Latino tandem to oppose each other on a major-league mound.

Moses Yellow Horse had a brief but significant, career with the Pirates, playing in only 38 games, starting eight and finishing with eight victories, four defeats, and one save. Overall, he toiled for 126 innings and finished his time in the majors with a 3.93 ERA. Yellow Horse's story has been covered in various works, but the most important rendering comes from Jeffrey Powers-Beck in his 2004 book, *The American Indian Integration of Baseball*.[1] Not surprisingly, Yellow Horse and other Native Americans endured "verbal and physical abuse both on and off the diamond" as he made his way up to the majors.

He started in the sport "late," given the paucity of equipment and facilities at the Pawnee Agency. In Oklahoma, Yellow Horse started by playing for the Chilocco Indian School team in 1916, and also played for Ponca City in the "Horseback League." He subsequently came to the attention of Des Moines of the Class-A Western League, which signed him in 1918. After success in that circuit, a former teammate with Chilocco recommended him to the Arkansas Travelers, where Moses helped the squad win the Class-A Southern Association pennant in 1920 by going 21-7. This was where Yellow Horse came to the attention of the Pirates, who bought his contract for $8,000. Powers-Beck argues that "although he lasted only two big league seasons, the sale was a bargain for Pirate fans."[2]

The young hurler made an immediate impact with the Pirates. On Decoration Day of 1921, for the first time, the fans at Forbes Field shouted out what would become a rallying cry for the team's aficionados: "Put in Yellow Horse!" On that holiday, May 30, the Pawnee pitcher cemented his status with fans by going 7⅔ scoreless innings and helping the Pirates to a 6-3 game-two victory over the Chicago Cubs to sweep a doubleheader. His response to the adulation was "restrained and gentlemanly," and he soon befriended other players, such as Drew Rader and Rabbit Maranville. Unfortunately, as many players of this era did, Yellow Horse (and particularly, Maranville too) imbibed quite a bit, and the rabble-rousing eventually led team owner Barney Dreyfuss to rid his team of the presence of what many in the majors considered to be nothing more than a "drunken Indian." The Pirates sold Yellow Horse to Sacramento of the Pacific Coast League for 1923. There, he continued to shine, sporting a 22-13 mark for the Senators.[3] Local papers did not note any behavior problems (alcohol-related or otherwise) that would have kept Yellow Horse from returning to the majors. But a shoulder injury in 1924 in a game against the Salt Lake City Bees created control problems and decreased the speed of his fastball, making a return to the big leagues impossible. Subsequently, "depressed and with a badly aching arm, Moses resorted to liquor as his painkiller of choice." As Powers-Beck noted in his work, on cue, *The Sporting News* played up the "drunken Indian" stereotype, stating that "Chief Moses Yellow Horse has gone the way of all bad Injuns. The Chief would not keep in condition, and was no longer of use to the team."[4]

All the negative events noted above lay in the future, however, as one month beyond his Decoration Day heroics, Moses Yellow Horse had the fans in Pittsburgh once again voicing their acclaim of his pitching prowess after he took the mound and went the distance in a contest against the Cincinnati Reds.

The Pirates hurler was sharp from the opening frame, with a quick first, striking out Sam Bohne,

Moses Yellow Horse

inducing a fly out from Jake Daubert, and walking Heinie Groh, who was then caught stealing. The Pirates broke through in their half of the frame, with singles by Carson Bigbee, a fly out by Max Carey, a single by Maranville, a fielder's choice by Clyde Barnhart, and a triple by Ray Rohwer plating two tallies. Cotton Tierney popped out to third to end the rally.

The score remained 2-0 until the top of the fifth. In that inning, the Reds broke through after two outs on walks to Larry Kopf and Rube Bressler and a two-run double by Luque that tied the score. The Pirates put the game away, and knocked out the Latino hurler, scoring three in the bottom of the seventh with a double by Charlie Grimm, a single by Walter Schmidt, a single by Bigbee, a double by Carey, and a single by Maranville. This flurry chased Luque, who was replaced by Lynn Brenton on the hill for the Reds. Cincinnati scored a final run in the top of the eighth on a walk to Ivey Wingo, a wild pitch by Yellow Horse, and a single by Pat Duncan. In the ninth, the visitors went down in order with Bressler grounding out, Bubbles Hargrave (who batted for

Brenton) doing likewise, and finally Bohne flying out to end the game.

While his record with the Pirates was excellent, it appears that team management, swayed in part by the stereotypical perception of Native Americans extant at that time (and also some inappropriate behavior by Moses as well), gave up on Yellow Horse too quickly. Here was a pitcher who had a decent 2.98 ERA in 1921 and won twice as many games as he lost (8-4) over a truncated two-season major-league career. Perhaps if the Pirates had not been so quick to pull the trigger on getting rid of him, Yellow Horse might have contributed to other squads during the 1920s and even beyond. Yellow Horse returned to Oklahoma and lived out the remainder of his life on the agency, passing away in 1964.

For Yellow Horse's opponent on the mound this day, there were also examples of how the broader American society stereotyped Latinos; for example, an incident that took place in Cincinnati in 1923 in which Luque charged outfielder Bill Cunningham of the Giants after enduring numerous "remarks" about his Cuban heritage. Even though he was a member of two World Series winners (the 1919 Reds and the 1933 Giants), Luque's nearly 200 major-league victories are often overlooked in lieu of characterizing him as a "hot-headed" Latin. Thus, on this day at Forbes Field, two pitchers who overcame great odds to make their way to the majors squared off and pitched well. Their mere presence on the mound that day was a challenge to the racial/ethnic status quo. This is yet another historically significant moment in Pirates history that deserves to be remembered.

SOURCES

In addition to the sources cited below, this essay also utilized information from Retrosheet.org and Baseball-Reference.com.

NOTES

1   Jeffrey Powers-Beck, *The American Indian Integration of Baseball* (Lincoln: University of Nebraska Press, 2004).

2   Powers-Beck, 143-144, 148-149.

3   Powers-Beck, 156-158.

4   Powers-Beck, 159.

CUYLER, CAREY, AND CO. STEAMROLL BROOKLYN

JUNE 20, 1925: PITTSBURGH PIRATES 21, BROOKLYN ROBINS 5, AT FORBES FIELD

BY T.S. FLYNN

PROMOTED AS A FATHER'S DAY GAME because Sunday ball still ran afoul of Pittsburgh's blue laws, the Saturday Robins-Pirates matinee drew an impressive crowd of 18,000 (about 8,000 more than the Forbes Field average in 1925).[1] The holiday throng would be treated to an orgy of offense that commenced shortly after the conclusion of a staid pregame ceremony that included a congregation of Missouri Synod Lutherans presenting a gold watch and other gifts to Bucs captain Max Carey.[2] The Pittsburgh center fielder had attended Concordia Lutheran Seminary in St. Louis prior to pursuing a career in baseball,[3] and he responded to the benevolent shower with a historic performance that afternoon, becoming the first switch-hitter to hit for the cycle. In most cases, such a deed would dominate the headlines. On this day, however, Carey's exploits paled in comparison to those of teammate Hazen "Kiki" Cuyler, who collected four hits (three of the extra-base variety), 5 runs, 6 RBIs, and 12 total bases.

Cuyler had emerged as a formidable offensive threat during his 1924 rookie season. His average peaked at .380 on September 6. Handicapped by a shoulder injury down the stretch, he finished with a .354 batting average in 117 games.[4] Now, a few months into the 1925 campaign, the 26-year-old Cuyler was healthy and proving he belonged in the bigs. He had hit for the cycle against the Phillies on June 4 and was batting .343 with 57 runs in 53 games entering the Father's Day tilt.

A pair of two-out first-inning Brooklyn singles initiated the scoring against Pittsburgh starter Babe Adams. After his base knock, Zack Wheat went from first to third on Jack Fournier's safety and scored when Pirates second baseman Eddie Moore muffed Cuyler's throw from right field. Moore and Cuyler retaliated in the home half of the first with a single and home run, respectively, giving the Bucs a 2-1 lead. They never looked back. Three more first-inning hits, including a run-scoring triple by Glenn Wright and a single by Stuffy McInnis, ended Brooklyn starter Jesse Petty's day. Predictably, Pittsburgh's right-handed lineup had shredded the southpaw. Petty had been pressed into the start because Brooklyn manager Wilbert Robinson had exhausted his right-handed starting options (Burleigh Grimes, Dazzy Vance, Tiny Osborne, and Rube Ehrhardt) in the first three games of the series.

Robins righty Bill Hubbell provided some offense in the second when he doubled in Dick Loftus. But the prodigious Pirates offense was just getting started. Moore singled and Cuyler was hit by a pitch. A flurry of hits followed: Wright doubled, McInnis and Adams singled, and Carey doubled. Meanwhile, Brooklyn inserted its third pitcher of the afternoon, lefty Nelson Greene. When the dust finally settled, Pittsburgh's lead had swollen to 9-2 on six second-inning hits and five more runs.

The Robins continued to battle and plated a run in the third via Eddie Brown's triple. They still faced a formidable six-run deficit to the Pirates, an offensive juggernaut that entered the weekend batting .323 as a team, 12 points better than the second-best Phillies.[5] In the bottom of the frame, Brooklyn kept Cuyler off the bases. It was a small victory negated three batters later when Clyde Barnhart and Pie Traynor both scored on Greene's two-out wild pitch. Just like that, the Bucs led 11-3.

The scoreboard operators enjoyed a break in the fourth; both teams failed to score. But the Bucs provided some excitement. Carey tripled on a shot into the right-field corner, and Moore followed with a base on balls. Then, with two outs and an eight-run lead, the Pirates attempted a double steal. Carey was tagged out at the plate.

The Pirates began the day 2½ games behind the National League-leading New York Giants, who were in Cincinnati, battling the third-place Reds. Just nine days earlier the Robins owned second place and 6½ games separated the Giants and third-place Bucs. Then Pittsburgh went on a tear. "In the week which closed yesterday," the *Daily Post* summarized, "the Pirates dealt with the two teams generally agreed upon as the clubs which make the most trouble for pennant contenders."[6] They swept the Giants in four games and, so far, had taken two of three from Brooklyn, leapfrogging the Robins in the standings. The Father's Day game was the concluding date of a homestand that seemed likely to change the tone of the Pirates' season. They had won 11 of 15 during that stretch and the *Daily Post* declared, "Leaving home soil the Pirates are in much better shape than when they left their neighbor's territory. The pitchers have reached shape and the team is hitting like none other."[7] By the end of June the Pirates and Giants would share the league lead. On October 4, the season's last day, the Corsairs would celebrate winning the pennant by 8½ games.

The Brooklyn club, on the other hand, entered this late-June Pittsburgh series in dire need of pitching. Bill Doak, a steady presence in their 1924 rotation, retired over the offseason to become a Florida real-estate salesman.[8] By early June, the club had failed to find a suitable replacement and manager Robinson urged Doak, a right-hander, to reconsider his decision. He declined. The *Daily Post* joked, "'Only a stone's throw from the nearest car line,' Doak is telling prospective customers these days, while Robbie sighs and informs mourners, 'Only a good pitcher removed from the flag.'"[9]

Pitching woes aside, the Robins needed more offense this day, but in their half of the fifth they laid another egg. The Pirates added another crooked number to their nest, thanks to Cuyler's leadoff single and Wright's ninth home run of 1925. The blast struck the facing in front of the right-field grandstand and bounded the seats. It sailed out of the ballpark and a dozen children chased the bouncing ball down into Panther Hollow (an Italian immigrant neighborhood bordering Forbes Field).[10] Pittsburgh's pair of runs made it 13-3.

In the sixth, the Robins surrendered in order again. Then the Pirates offense resumed the onslaught. Adams singled and Carey hit a long fly into the left-field corner. Adams held at second, limiting Carey to a single. Greene balked and then walked Moore. Cuyler smoked a drive past Eddie Brown in center, and the super sophomore sprinted around the bases for an inside-the-park grand slam, his second round-tripper and third hit of the game. The Pirates' lead expanded to 17-3.

Kiki Cuyler

The visitors gamely added a pair of runs in the top of the seventh on a Hod Ford single, Charlie Hargreaves's triple, and a single by Greene, but it was a death rattle. Brooklyn's fifth run would be its last of the day. The Bucs, however, had more in store. Following a walk to McInnis and Johnny Gooch's single, Adams bunted the runners to second and third. Carey stepped to the plate needing a home run for the cycle. He delivered a drive into the left-field corner and didn't stop running until he crossed the plate. After Johnny Rawlings popped out, Cuyler tripled to center for his fourth hit. He trotted home on Barnhart's single with his fifth run, the team's 21st of the day (all earned).

Two eighth-inning Brooklyn singles brought their hit total to 12 for the game (they'd add another in the ninth). In the home half, McInnis lobbed a Texas Leaguer behind third for a double, the Bucs' 25th safety of the day. The offensive excess had noticeably sapped the fans. According to the *Post Gazette*, "the holiday audience weakened under the strain of shouting and handclapping. An extra base hit by the Pirates after the seventh inning could not stir the fed up throng. There were so many homers of varied hue to cheer in the first half of the so-called contest that when the ninth arrived thousands were missing from the seats they cherished before the alleged battle started."[11] It ended Pittsburgh 21, Brooklyn 5.

The Bucs traveled to St. Louis next, where they thumped the Cardinals 24-6, for a two-game total of 45 runs scored in 17 innings. Paced by their captain Carey and the ascendant Cuyler, the Pirates hit .307/.818/.449 as a team in 1925. The 35-year-old Carey stole 46 bases in 133 games and hit to the tune of .343/.909/.491. Cuyler amassed an astounding 144 runs, 220 hits, and 41 stolen bases while hitting.357/1.021/.598 in 153 games. He lost the Most Valuable Player Award to Rogers Hornsby

(403/1.245/.756), who authored his second Triple Crown season for the Cardinals in 1925. But Carey and the Pirates crowned their season with the World Series championship. After falling behind Washington three games to one in the Series, the Bucs won the next two, and the season culminated in a thrilling Game Seven against Walter Johnson in the rain at Forbes Field. Pittsburgh trailed until the bottom of the eighth, when Cuyler stroked a two-out, two-run double off the Big Train to seize the lead. They finished off the Senators to complete their sensational comeback.

SOURCES

In addition to the sources identified in the endnotes, the author consulted Baseball-Reference.com and Retrosheet.

NOTES

1   The crowd size was noted by Edward F. Balinger, "Pirate Sluggers Have Field Day in Robin Finale, 21-5," *Pittsburgh Daily Post*, June 21, 1925: 22.

2   "Bucs Smother Robins Under 21-5 Count," *Pittsburgh Post-Gazette*, June 21, 1925: 22.

3   John Bennett, "Max Carey," Society for American Baseball Research, sabr.org/bioproj/person/e3347ea3.

4   Gregory H. Wolf, "Kiki Cuyler," Society for American Baseball Research, sabr.org/bioproj/person/7107706b.

5   "Pirates Lead National Loop in Club Batting," *Pittsburgh Press*, June 21, 1925: 17.

6   "What the Post Clock Saw: Post Clock Ticks," *Pittsburgh Daily Post*, June 21, 1925: 23.

7   Ibid.

8   Steve Steinberg, "Bill Doak," Society for American Baseball Research, sabr.org/bioproj/person/1359e4e2.

9   "What the Post Clock Saw: Post Clock Ticks."

10   Ibid.

11   "Bucs Smother Robins."

OCTOBER 15, 1925: PITTSBURGH PIRATES 9, WASHINGTON SENATORS 7, AT FORBES FIELD

GAME SEVEN OF THE 1925 WORLD SERIES

BY T.S. FLYNN

MORE THAN 40,000 FANS FILLED Forbes Field on a cloudy, wet Wednesday afternoon for Game Seven of the 1925 World Series, the Pirates faithful hoping the home team would complete an unlikely comeback against the Senators. Walter Johnson stood in the way. The Washington fireballer had already won Games One and Four, allowing just one run on 11 hits in 18 innings, and he would take the ball for Game Seven. But the Corsairs had regained Series momentum, having won Game Five in Washington and Game Six in Pittsburgh to tie the Series at three games each. Rain had dogged the Series all week and it returned shortly after Game Six ended, falling until midmorning Wednesday. A mist lingered through the early afternoon, but 10 minutes before Game Seven's scheduled 2:00 p.m. first pitch, strong rain again pelted Pittsburgh and puddles formed across the infield. At precisely 2:35 p.m., Commissioner Kenesaw Landis postponed the tilt.[1]

The damp conditions continued into Thursday, but the grounds crew worked through the morning, burning gasoline and spreading sawdust to dry the infield. Peering through a veil of fog, 42,856 hardy fans huddled in their seats for Game Seven.[2] They were rewarded with one of the most thrilling games in World Series history.

Washington's Sam Rice poked Pittsburgh starter Vic Aldridge's third pitch of the game into center field for a single. After retiring Bucky Harris on a fly out, Aldridge threw a wild pitch on a 2-and-0 count, allowing Rice to take second. Two pitches later, Goose Goslin walked. Again behind on a 2-and-0 count, this time to Joe Harris, Aldridge bounced another wild pitch, which moved Rice to third and Goslin to second. Harris walked on the next pitch

to load the bases with just one out. Aldridge then issued a walk to Joe Judge and Rice trotted home for the game's first run. Next, Ossie Bluege nearly homered to left, the ball striking the top of the screen so hard he was held to a run-scoring single. Pirates skipper Bill McKechnie had seen enough, and Aldridge's day ended after just one-third of an inning with the sacks packed, his team trailing by two runs. Johnny Morrison took the ball for the Bucs and Washington's Roger Peckinpaugh welcomed him with a hard grounder to shortstop Glenn Wright, who fired the ball to catcher Earl Smith for the force at home. But Harris was ruled safe due to catcher's interference by Smith against Peckinpaugh. All runners advanced one base, Peckinpaugh was awarded first. The Senators' lead increased to 3-0, the bases still loaded, still just one out. Morrison then induced a groundball to second from Muddy Ruel, but Eddie Moore bobbled the ball and Judge scored Washington's fourth run.

Pittsburgh had battled back from three games to one to reset the Series; now, to win it, they'd have to climb out of a four-run hole against Walter Johnson. The mist became a sprinkling rain. Eddie Moore led off with a bunt. Johnson, 37 years old and nursing a sore leg, fielded the ball cleanly and retired Moore with a crisp throw. Working very slowly, the Big Train then went after Bucs captain Max Carey, who doubled to deep right field on the seventh pitch of the at-bat.[3] With Carey on second and the Pittsburgh crowd energized, Johnson dispatched Kiki Cuyler with three fastballs. Clyde Barnhart fell behind 0-and-2 on a pair of heaters before waving at a wide curve to end the inning.

Morrison got the quick inning he needed in the second, retiring the Senators in order. With one down in the Pittsburgh second, Wright singled to center. Stuffy McInnis followed with a bingle up the middle. But Smith grounded to Harris, who tagged McInnis and fired to Judge for an inning-ending 4-3 double play. The Bucs had collected another two hits but still had no runs on the board. The rain persisted. According to the *New York Times*, "It was so dark the serried rows of fans in the far right field grand stand were just one inky blur."[4]

Judge led off the third with a single. After a Bluege popout, Peckinpaugh knocked a low fly into shallow right-center. Moore and center fielder Carey raced toward it, but it was Cuyler who dived between his teammates and snared the ball as he hit the ground with a splash. In his haste to double off Judge, Cuyler threw wide of first and the Senators first baseman advanced to second. That was as far as he'd get.

Finally, the Pirates drew blood in the bottom of the third. Moore followed Morrison's leadoff single with a double to left, scoring the Bucs pitcher. Carey singled on the next pitch and the fans erupted. At 4-2, the Pirates were back in the game. McKechnie ordered a hit-and-run[5] and Carey advanced to second on Cuyler's groundout. Carey stole third without a throw, and he scored easily when Barnhart blooped a single to right. The inning concluded with the Senators' lead shaved to 4-3.

The visitors responded in the fourth, scoring two runs on singles from Rice and Goslin and a Joe Harris double. 6-3 Senators. Sprinkling rain fell from the dark, low sky, muddying the basepaths and mound, and slicking the outfield grass.[6] Pittsburgh left a man on first, and did not score in its half of the fourth frame.

Pirates reliever Ray Kremer kept the Senators in check in the fifth, too. Carey smacked the first pitch of the home half of the inning into right-center for a double, and Cuyler followed with a double to deep left. Carey crossed the plate for the fourth Pittsburgh run. Johnson recovered and the score remained 6-4 in favor of the Senators through six.

The rain intensified as the seventh inning began,[7] and the Senators were retired in order. The home seventh opened with a Peckinpaugh error on a fly

so high off the bat of Moore that he reached second base. Carey then lashed his third double of the game and Moore scampered home to again cut the Washington lead to one. Cuyler sacrificed Carey to third. After Barnhart was retired on an unproductive groundout, Pie Traynor laced a shot to right. Carey plated the tying tally and watched as Traynor raced around the bases with an inside-the-park home run in mind. The on-target relay from Joe Harris to Bucky Harris to Ruel prevented Carey's completion of the circuit, but the Pirates had leveled the score to 6-6 through seven.

The Senators retook the lead in the eighth on Peckinpaugh's redemptive solo home run into the temporary left-field seats in front of the scoreboard, but that's all Washington could muster in its half. Johnson retired Wright on a foul pop in steady rain. After missing with his first pitch to McInnis, the Big Train asked home-plate umpire Barry McCormick to allow more sawdust for the muddy mound. When the arbiter assented, Johnson filled his cap with the stuff and personally groomed his station.[8] Two pitches later, McInnis flied out. Earl Smith doubled to right and gave way to pinch-runner Emil Yde. Pinch-hitter Carson Bigbee doubled to left, tying the score. The rain-soaked Pittsburgh faithful erupted with raucous cheering. Moore walked on seven pitches, bringing the red-hot Carey to the dish. The Pirates rally appeared to die when he grounded to Peckinpaugh, but the Washington shortstop's toss to second was wide — his eighth error of the Series — and the bases were loaded with two outs. Cuyler took Johnson's first pitch for a ball. The umpires paused the game again while more sawdust was applied to the mound. Kiki fouled off four pitches and then sliced the next one just inside the first-base bag, down the right-field line. Pirates reliever Tom Sheehan, who was warming up next to the line, insisted that none of the Pirates in foul territory touched the ball. "Joe [Harris] came over and fielded the ball," he said, "but the sphere was all over mud and it was hard to handle."[9] Cuyler circled the bases, beating the muddy ball home. Forbes Field rang with an ecstatic din while the umpires huddled. Determining the ball had struck a Pirates reliever, they sent Carey back to third and Cuyler to second. The eighth ended on Barnhart's subsequent fly ball, but the Pirates had scored three and enjoyed their first lead of the day, 9-7.

It proved sufficient. With rainwater "coursing over the brims of felt hats"[10] in the stands, Red Oldham took the mound for the top of the ninth and retired the Senators in order. Damon Runyon described the scene: "As the game ended, at least 20,000 of these well soaked spectators poured out into the muddy field, and surrounded the red-coated bandsmen, who shook the water out of their instruments, and blared 'There'll Be a Hot Time in the Old Town Tonight.'…"[11] Indeed there was. Across the city, Pittsburgh fans took to the streets to celebrate their team's second world championship, partying into the wee hours Friday.[12] It had been a Game Seven and a World Series for the ages, and the Pirates had come from behind to capture both.

SOURCES

In addition to the sources identified in the Notes, the author consulted Baseball-Reference.com and Retrosheet.org.

NOTES

1   James C. Isaminger, "Unbeaten Hurlers to Battle Today in Game to Settle Baseball Championship," *Philadelphia Inquirer*, October 15, 1925: 18.

2   "Facts and Figures About World Series," *Philadelphia Inquirer*, October 16, 1925: 18.

3   "Step-by-Step Account of Pirates' Victory March," *Pittsburgh Post-Gazette*, October 16, 1925: 12.

4   "Crush at the Gates Too Much for Police," *New York Times*, October 16, 1925: 15.

5   "Step-by-Step Account."

6   Ibid.

7   Ibid.

8   Ibid.

9   Charlie Doyle, "World's Series Chillysauce," *Pittsburgh Post-Gazette*, October 16, 1925: 13.

10   "Crush at the Gates."

11   Damon Runyon, "Pirates Should Take Rank with Greatest of Clubs, Runyon Says," *Pittsburgh Post-Gazette*, October 16, 1925: 13.

12   "Roar of Victory, Din of Celebration Encompass City as Tribute Is Paid to Greatest Ball Club in World," *Pittsburgh Press*, October 16, 1925: 1.

PIRATES DEFEAT DODGERS 15-3 AS ARKY VAUGHAN HITS FOR THE CYCLE AND GOES 5-FOR-5

JUNE 24, 1933: PITTSBURGH PIRATES 15, BROOKLYN DODGERS 3, AT EBBETS FIELD

BY C. PAUL ROGERS III

THE PITTSBURGH PIRATES WERE nursing a four-game losing streak heading into a Saturday-afternoon contest against the Brooklyn Dodgers on June 24, 1933. Pittsburgh had finished in second place in 1932, just four games behind the pennant-winning Chicago Cubs, and had high hopes for a pennant in 1933. The team had shot out of the gate by winning seven out of eight and was in first place almost continually through the end of May before faltering and losing 14 of 23 thus far in June. With their current losing streak, the Pirates had slipped to third place with a 33-29 record and had fallen to a season-high five games off the pace. The Dodgers, coming off a third-place finish in 1932, were in fifth place, six percentage points ahead of the sixth-place Cincinnati Reds, and were four games below .500 for the year.

Prospects for a Pirates win looked pretty good considering right-hander Bill Swift was toeing the rubber for Pittsburgh. Swift, who had just turned 25 and was in his second year in the big leagues, already had eight wins for the season and sported an outstanding 2.91 earned-run average. He was opposed by 34-year-old Sloppy Thurston, who was on the downside of a nine-year big-league career. As a spot starter and reliever, the right-handed Thurston was 4-2.[1]

Both hurlers retired the side in order in the first inning, giving promise of a pitchers' duel. In the top of the second, Pirates shortstop Arky Vaughan hit his sixth home run of the year when he "pasted a drive into the right field chicken wire" with one out and no one on to break the brief scoring drought.[2] After Swift retired the Dodgers in their half of the second on three fly balls, the Pirates extended their lead to 2-0 on a one-out double to left field by Adam Comorosky that drove in Freddy Lindstrom, who had reached on a bunt single.[3] Paul Waner hit a comebacker to Thurston, who caught Comorosky in a rundown for the second out as Waner reached on the fielder's choice. Pie Traynor singled to left to put runners on first and second and Vaughn loaded the bases with an infield single to first. But Thurston induced Gus Suhr to ground out to second baseman Tony Cuccinello on a 3-and-0 pitch to avert further damage.[4]

The Dodgers closed the gap to 2-1 in the bottom of the third on singles to left field by Al Lopez and Danny Taylor followed by a two-out single to center by Johnny Frederick to score Lopez and send Taylor to third. Swift regrouped to retire Joe Stripp on a fly ball to Waner in right to end the threat. After a scoreless, hitless fourth, the Pirates extended their lead to 4-1 in the top of the fifth, all with two outs and no one on. Paul Waner worked what seemed like a harmless walk, but Traynor made Thurston pay with a ringing double to left that plated Waner from first. The lefty-swinging Vaughan followed with his third hit of the game, a single to right to drive in Waner with the Pirates' fourth run of the day.

Neither team threatened for the next inning and a half, heading into the top of the seventh. Through six innings Swift had allowed only three singles, all in the third inning, and showed no signs of weakening. After the Pirates batted in the seventh, however, it was largely academic, as they scored four runs to extend their lead to 8-1. Comorosky tagged Thurston for a one-out solo home run, his first of the season, and after Waner grounded out to Jimmy Jordan at shortstop for out number two, Traynor kept the inning alive with a bloop single behind second base. That brought up the firecracker-hot Vaughan, who promptly laced his fourth hit of the day, a double to right to score Traynor from first.

With that, Dodgers manager Max Carey came out to get Thurston and waved in veteran southpaw Fred Heimach. As things turned out, Carey should have reconsidered. Heimach immediately gave up run-scoring singles to Suhr and Tommy Thevenow before retiring the side on a comebacker from Hal Finney. Cuccinello reached Swift for a solo home run, his team-leading eighth round-tripper of the season, in the bottom of the seventh to bring the score to 8-2 heading into the eighth.

Heimach's shaky performance in the seventh pre-saged a complete pounding by Pirates bats in the eighth as they scored seven more runs from a total of three triples and five singles. Seven of the hits were consecutive with two outs and included Vaughan's cycle-completing two-run triple, his fifth hit of the game in five at-bats. Manager Carey left Heimach in to finish the inning and take one for the team. His ugly totals were 10 hits and eight runs allowed, all earned, in 1⅓ innings.[5] Heimach's earned-run average from the outing jumped more than three runs, to 8.69.[6]

In the bottom of the eighth, Swift, after retiring pinch-hitter Chink Outen on a popup to second baseman Thevenow, was touched for another solo home run, this time by Taylor, to bring the score to 15-3. In the top of the ninth Vaughan batted with two out against reliever Rosy Ryan with a chance for his sixth hit of the day, but settled for a walk. In the bottom half, Swift retired Hack Wilson on a foul pop to Finney behind the plate and got Sam Leslie on a fly ball to Lindstrom in center field before allowing a double to Cuccinello. But Lopez flied harmlessly to center to seal Swift's complete-game victory in a brisk hour and 55 minutes.

Swift, in running his record to 9-5, allowed six hits and did not walk a batter. For the afternoon, the Pirates manufactured 21 hits and 36 total bases, which included eight extra-base hits. The 21-year-old

Vaughan was in just his second big-league season. In addition to going 5-for-5 and hitting for the cycle, he reached base all six times, drove in five runs, and scored three. After batting .318 as a 20-year-old rookie in 1932, he finished the 1933 season with a .314 batting average and was well on his way to a Hall of Fame career. He again hit for the cycle on July 19, 1939, again going 5-for-5, this time against the New York Giants in the Polo Grounds.

Vaughan's best season was with the Pirates in 1935 when he was batting .401 in mid-September before tailing off slightly to .385 to lead the league. He also led in walks (97), on-base percentage (.491), and slugging percentage (.607) while reaching career highs in home runs (19) and runs batted in (99). In 14 major-league seasons, Vaughan compiled a .318 batting average, making the National League All-Star team nine times. Tragically, he was killed in a boating accident in Northern California in 1952 when he was just 40 years old.[7]

The 1933 Pirates, despite having five future Hall of Famers in their lineup including Vaughan,[8] again finished in second place, this time five games behind the Giants. The excitement of a second consecutive pennant race must have been a nice diversion for the people of Pittsburgh from the depths of the Great Depression, but the team drew only 288,747 fans, fifth best in the National League.[9]

NOTES

1   Thurston had won 20 games with the Chicago White Sox as a 25-year-old in 1924 but had not come close to replicating that success. His career record was a respectable 89-86.

2   Harold Parrott, "Pirates Beat Dodgers 15-3," *Brooklyn Daily Eagle*, June 25, 1933: D1.

3   According to the *Brooklyn Eagle*, Comorosky was playing left field because Lloyd Waner had come down "with a spell of the grippe." Parrott: 36.

4   Not surprisingly, Suhr's swinging on a 3-and-0 pitch with the bases loaded resulted in "a call down" from Pirates manager George Gibson. Parrott: 36.

5   One news report called Heimach "a good, game chap by standing up under 10 hits in pitching only one and one-third innings." "Pirates Stop Losing Streak, Win 15-3," *Pittsburgh Press*, June 25, 1933: Sports Section 1. The *Brooklyn Eagle* was not so charitable. Its subheading for the game read, "Heimach,

Massacred in Relief Role, Gives Up Eight Hits in One Inning." A subheading in the middle of the game story read, "Heimach Luckily Escapes With Life," *Brooklyn Daily Eagle,* June 25, 1933: D1.

6   Heimach's next outing, on July 17 also against the Pirates, was even worse. Relieving in the eighth inning of a game the Dodgers were losing 5-2, he gave up nine earned runs in one-third of an inning. At 32 he was at the end of the line of a journeyman career that spanned 13 seasons. Pitching for four teams, he finished with a lifetime record of 62-69 and an earned-run average of 4.46.

7   Ralph Moses, "Arky Vaughan," SABR Bioproject: sabr.org/bioproj/person/4e00be9b.

8   The others were Pie Traynor, Freddie Lindstrom, Paul Waner, and Lloyd Waner.

9   That figure means that the Pirates averaged about 3,750 fans a game without taking into account doubleheaders for which the Pirates charged only one admission. The Pirates had drawn almost the exact same number of fans (287,262) to their second-place finish in 1932.

PIE TRAYNOR REPLACES GEORGE GIBSON AS PIRATES MANAGER

JUNE 19, 1934: NEW YORK GIANTS 5, PITTSBURGH PIRATES 3, AT FORBES FIELD

BY JACK ZERBY

WHEN PIE TRAYNOR[1] REACHED THE major leagues as a 21-year-old rookie with the Pittsburgh Pirates in 1920, his manager was George Gibson, a rookie skipper and a local fan favorite throughout his Deadball Era tenure as the team's catcher. Although Gibson delivered a positive overall 201-171 record in two-plus seasons at the Bucs' helm, by June 30, 1922, Pittsburgh stood a game under .500 and Gibson resigned in favor of a popular local native, Bill McKechnie.[2]

By 1932 McKechnie's Pirates had won the 1925 World Series but "Wilkinsburg Bill" had packed off to the St. Louis Cardinals as a coach (1927),[3] Donie Bush (1927-29) and Jewel Ens (1929-31) had come and gone, and the Pirates brought Gibson back for an encore as manager. Traynor was still there and solidly entrenched as arguably the best third baseman in baseball. As Pittsburgh began the 1934 season Gibson was still the skipper. Traynor, now 35, although off to a solid start at the plate, had played sparingly in the early season due to a sore throwing arm.[4] By Tuesday, June 19, the Pirates, atop the National League at 20-11 in late May, had stumbled to fourth place, losing seven of eight games from June 8 to stand a pedestrian 27-24; they trailed the New York Giants by 7½ games. Those first-place Giants had strutted into town on June 16 and defeated the Bucs twice. The Sunday, June 17, loss was particularly ugly, as "for the first time in his latest term as pilot, a stretch of three seasons, Gibson was roundly booed by 15,000 customers" every time he trudged from the dugout to the third-base coaching box.[5]

The Pirates got a much-needed rainout on Monday, but Tuesday morning there was big news — Gibson was once again stepping down during the season, this time to be replaced by Traynor as player-manager. Announced just prior to the game with the Giants at Forbes Field, the move was "by mutual agreement."[6] That Gibson had already resigned once in Pittsburgh and had a reputation as a leader "intolerant of mental mistakes and his temperament left him ill-suited to the task of managing locker-room politics"[7] may have been factors in the move.

Fans got their beloved Pie's "promise to give the opposition plenty of headaches" by "stealing every time [we] get a break; we've all got to hustle." Of the Giants' lead, he said: "A couple of winning weeks and that lead will be washed up. That old flag isn't lost yet — we've got lots of time."[8] He named respected four-year veteran first baseman Gus Suhr to replace him as team captain[9] and was ready to go, all in the span of a few hours.

Traynor, who had missed 17 of Pittsburgh's 51 games to this point in the season but was hitting .320, penciled himself in at the number-3 slot of the batting order, at third base and between two other future Hall of Famers, right fielder Paul Waner and shortstop Arky Vaughan. He tabbed lefty Larry French, as close to an ace as the Pirates had, to start the contest. French, 26, was in his sixth Pittsburgh season since having broken into the majors in 1929. He'd had 11 starts for the season and sported an uninspiring 3-5 record and a 4.17 ERA.

New York's own player-manager, Bill Terry, countered with 23-year-old "Prince Hal" Schumacher. He was a 19-game winner for the Giants in 1933 and was 8-4 so far in 1934, coming off a shutout in Cincinnati five days before. The consistent young righty was at this point in his career giving the Giants' older lefty

Pie Traynor

"King Carl" Hubbell a run for his money as ace of the staff.

The rapid succession of events culminating in a managerial change, which wasn't even reported in the papers until the next day, plus the reality of a midseason Tuesday game before the advent of night baseball[10] combined to hold the Forbes Field attendance to "around 2,500" as the Pirates took the field under Traynor for the first time.[11]

The new manager nicked Schumacher for the first safety of the game in the Pittsburgh first but, trying to practice the hustle he preached, was out attempting to stretch the hit into a double. Mel Ott opened the scoring in the Giants' second with a two-bagger of his own, coming home on Blondy Ryan's double after French had managed two outs.

Vaughan continued the game's doubles carousel leading off the Pittsburgh second and moved to third on Suhr's infield grounder. Vaughan had to remain at third as Cookie Lavagetto rolled out to second, but the Pirates then evened the score at 1–1 when Woody Jensen singled to score Vaughan.

With Tom Padden batting next, Schumacher wild-pitched Jensen to second base. Padden then hit a shot that Giant shortstop Travis Jackson booted. With two outs, Jensen churned around third and headed home, but a "heroic heave"[12] by Jackson from short left field, atoning for his error, nipped Jensen at the plate to preserve the tie.

French got two outs in the New York third before a single by Hughie Critz and a walk to Terry put two on. They didn't stay there long, as the always dangerous Ott lashed a bases-clearing triple to right field. The Giants, 2½ innings in, led 3–1.

The Pirates tried a comeback in their half of the third. After French struck out, Lloyd Waner singled. Then brother Paul singled and advanced to second as the Giants' attempt to get Lloyd at third base failed. The Pirates were set up nicely with the Waners in scoring position and Traynor batting. Even Schumacher seemed unnerved as he unleashed his second wild pitch of the game in that crucial situation. He reacted quickly, though, to cover home plate successfully on catcher Gus Mancuso's throw to nab Lloyd Waner. The "out" call by home-plate umpire Beans Reardon was "hotly contested"[13] by the Pirates — conveniently, manager Traynor was already on the scene. Still up, but with two outs, Pie could have used a duplicate of his first-inning hit here to score Paul Waner from third; instead, he grounded to short and the Pirates got nothing out of the once-rosy situation.

In the fourth inning, both teams got runners to third but failed to score. Pittsburgh started its sixth with promise, but Suhr was cut down at third on a botched sacrifice attempt for the first out and pitcher Red Lucas,[14] pinch-hitting for Padden, grounded into a double play; New York's 3–1 lead stood.

The Giants bumped that to 5–1 in their seventh on Terry's clutch two-run single with two outs. Pittsburgh countered in the bottom of the eighth as Jensen's single scored Suhr with the second run of the inning and chased Schumacher. With the score now 5–3, two outs, and lefty-hitting Earl Grace, who had replaced Padden, coming to the plate as the potential tying run, Terry played some book baseball and brought in his ace, the portsider Hubbell.[15] It worked, as Grace lined out to Homer Peel in center field for the third out.

The game ended 5-3, Giants. The Pirates advanced Lloyd Waner as far as second base with two outs in the ninth with Traynor up. There were no storybook heroics, though—as the rookie skipper flied out to center.

A little more than a week later, Pittsburgh had won seven of 11 games under Traynor and had closed to within 5½ games of the Giants.[16] Over the new manager's 1934 tenure, however, the Pirates were a lackluster 47-52, and finished fifth, 19½ games behind the pennant-winning Cardinals. Pitching was the problem. It had been spotty under Gibson and with Traynor at the helm the hurlers didn't get better. Although the Pirates hit .287, their 4.20 ERA against a league average of 4.06 essentially assured the middle-of-the-pack finish. An undaunted Traynor, however, looked at the bigger picture. The October 2, 1934, *Pittsburgh Press* sports section carried a page-wide banner headline look ahead to the 1935 season hinting at why the club had installed him back in June.

"Pie Traynor peeled off his coat in the Pirates' winter baseball headquarters today and announced to the world that he is going to make every effort to give Pittsburgh a stronger baseball team next season. ... Traynor isn't trying to kid himself and he knows there is plenty of work to be done before the Pirates go to spring training next March."[17]

Acknowledgments

James Forr's SABR biography of Pie Traynor provided a good overview for my research, as did *Pie Traynor, A Baseball Biography* (Jefferson, North Carolina: McFarland & Co., Inc., 2010), which Forr co-authored with David Proctor.

SOURCES

In addition to the sources listed in the Notes, I used the Baseball-Reference.com and Retrosheet.org websites for box scores, play-by-play, player, team, and season pages, pitching and batting games logs, and other material pertinent to this account. The Newspapers.com website provided access to all of the cited newspaper articles except the item from *The Sporting News*, accessed through PaperofRecord.com.

NOTES

1   Born Harold Joseph Traynor on November 11, 1898, in Framingham, Massachusetts, Traynor acquired the nickname "Pie" in boyhood. The name stuck throughout his baseball and later business careers and appears with Traynor's given name on his Hall of Fame plaque.

2   McKechnie was born in Wilkinsburg, Allegheny County, Pennsylvania. The Pirates brought him to the majors in 1907, and after a two-season sojourn in the minors he played in Pittsburgh from 1910 through 1912. The Pittsburgh managerial post was his first in the majors, although the ultimate Hall of Fame inductee gained experience as a player-manager with the Newark (New Jersey) Federal League team in 1915.

3   McKechnie coached for the Cardinals in 1927, then managed them in 1928 and 1929. His 1928 team won the National League pennant. Mitchell Conrad Stinson, *Deacon Bill McKechnie: A Baseball Biography* (Jefferson, North Carolina: McFarland & Co., Inc., 2012), 123-128.

4   Chester L. Smith, "The Village Smithy," *Pittsburgh Press*, April 23, 1934: 27.

5   Volney Walsh, "Gibson on 'Spot,' But He Laughs at Fans' Boos," *Pittsburgh Press*, June 18, 1934: 27.

6   Edward F. Ballinger, "Pie Traynor Given Gibson's Manager Post," *Pittsburgh Post-Gazette*, June 20, 1934: 16-17.

7   Trey Strecker, "George Gibson," SABR Baseball Biography Project, sabr.org. See also: "Pie Traynor," SABR Baseball Biography Project, sabr.org, where Traynor historian James Forr notes: "Officially, the Pirates said Gibson had resigned, but he admitted to friends that he had been fired."

8   Jack Berger, "A Pencil Interview With Our New Manager," Sports cartoon, *Pittsburgh Press*, June 20, 1934: 26.

9   Ralph Davis, "Traynor, as Pilot, Insists Bucs Make Better Use of Their Speed," *The Sporting News*, June 28, 1934: 1.

10 The first night game at Forbes Field was played on June 4, 1940. Lester Biederman, "Bees Open Night-Light Season Tuesday," *Pittsburgh Press*, June 2, 1940: 27.

11 "Pirate Notes," *Pittsburgh Post-Gazette*, June 20, 1934: 17. The Pirates had drawn 15,000 for the Tuesday home opener back in April and 40,000 for a Memorial Day doubleheader.

12 Chester L. Smith, "Traynor Gives Bucs Command—'Hustle,'" *Pittsburgh Press*, June 20, 1934: 26, 28.

13 Ibid. Smith opines that Reardon badly blew the call and laments, "Something always turns up to thwart [the Pirates'] efforts," in reporting this play.

14 Lucas, who had 157 pitching wins in his major-league career, was often used as a pinch-hitter. Over 16 seasons (1923-1938)

and 1,606 plate appearances, all in the National League, he hit .281 and drove in 190 runs.

15   In addition to 35 starts in 1934, Carl Hubbell made 14 relief appearances for the Giants. His eight saves (retroactively calculated) would have led the 1934 National League had that statistic then existed.

16   "Pirate Notes," *Pittsburgh Post-Gazette*, June 28, 1934: 14.

17   Volney Walsh, "Pie Plans to Rebuild Pirates for Next Season: This Year's Outfit, Without Changes, Will Wind Up in Third or Fourth Place Again Next Year, Pirate Manager Announces," *Pittsburgh Press*, October 2, 1934: 29.

ARKY VAUGHAN SLAMS CUBS, EDGES CUBS

APRIL 27, 1938: PITTSBURGH PIRATES 6, CHICAGO CUBS 5, AT FORBES FIELD

BY JOSEPH WANCHO

THE PITTSBURGH PIRATES BEGAN THE 1938 season on a hot streak. They swept a three-game series over both the St. Louis Cardinals and the Cincinnati Reds. The Bucs were finding some "late-inning magic" to pull out a few of those games. In the season opener on April 19 at Sportsman's Park, Pittsburgh scored two runs on the strength of a clutch two-run, ninth-inning homer by Arky Vaughan to win, 4-3. Two days later the Pirates broke a 4-4 tie and again scored two runs in the top of the ninth inning to win, 6-5.

The Pirates opened the home portion of their schedule against Cincinnati. In the third game of the series, on April 24, Paul Waner singled home Ray Berres with two out in the bottom of the eighth inning to provide a 2-1 lead. That ended up being the final score as the Pirates won their sixth straight game.

The Chicago Cubs invaded Forbes Field next, and the Pirates edged the Cubs 8-6 when they scored four runs in the bottom of the eighth inning. Vaughan again came through, with a bases- loaded single that plated two runs. Gus Suhr and Bill Brubaker also knocked in a run in the inning. Pittsburgh finally lost in the second game of the series with the Cubs, as Chicago scored two runs in the top of the 10th inning and won, 5-3.

The Cubs entered the game on April 27 game against the Pirates with a 5-3 mark. Like the Pirates, the Cubs also opened their schedule against Cincinnati and St. Louis, winning two out of three games in each series. The starting pitchers were southpaw Larry French for Chicago (1-0, 0.00 ERA) and righty Cy Blanton for the Pirates (1-0, 1.32 ERA). French, a former Pirates hurler, had shut out the Cardinals in his first start of the season, on April 23. He scattered four hits and struck out four in the 4-0 Cubs win. Blanton had a victory on that same day as the Pirates beat the Reds, 6-2. Blanton went the distance, striking out three and giving up two runs, one earned.

Through the first three innings, both pitchers found little resistance from the opponent's batting order. But in the top of the fourth inning, the Cubs struck first. With two down, Joe Marty walloped the first pitch from Blanton so hard that it cleared the scoreboard in left field. Chicago was not finished, as Augie Galan singled and stole second base. Tony Lazzeri followed with a free pass. Pirates backstop Al Todd rifled a quick throw in an attempt to erase Galan, who had loitered far off the second-base bag. But with no middle infielder to retrieve the baseball, it sailed into center field and Galan took third base. Galan crossed home plate with the Cubs' second tally after Ken O'Dea singled to right field.

The Cubs added a run in the top of the fifth inning when Stan Hack tripled to left-center field. Billy Herman flied out to right field, but it was not deep enough for Hack to attempt to score. Ripper Collins took care of that with a single to right field to make the score 3-0 in favor of the North Siders. In five innings of work, Blanton gave up three earned runs and he struck out two.

That was the end of the day for Blanton. He was removed for a pinch-hitter and right-hander Mace Brown entered the game in the sixth inning. But the change of hurlers did not seem to matter to the Cubs. With two outs, Lazzeri walked and O'Dea singled to right field. French ambled to the plate and sent a pop fly just beyond second baseman Pep Young. Neither Young nor right fielder Paul Waner could nab it, and Lazzeri raced home with the Cubs' fourth run.

Arky Vaughan

The score remained 4-0 until the bottom of the seventh inning. Brubaker led off with a walk and went to third base on Young's single to left field. Johnny Dickshot pinch-hit for Brown, and lifted a fly ball to center field that scored Brubaker. Woody Jensen singled to right and Young moved to second. Both runners moved up a base when Paul Waner grounded out to first baseman Collins. Johnny Rizzo walked to load the bases.

Vaughan stepped to the plate and smashed the baseball on a line to right field. It kept rising until it cleared the screen and landed in the right-field extension in the upper deck. The Pirates grabbed the lead, 5-4 on Vaughan's tremendous clout. "French just gave me a good pitch and I hit it right," said Vaughan.[1]

The Pirates added an insurance run in the bottom of the eighth. Cubs right-handed reliever Charlie

Root made his way to the mound. With one out, Root walked Brubaker. He stole second base when Young struck out. Bob Klinger, who had relieved Mace Brown in the top of the frame, singled. The detail of Klinger's hit was described in the *Chicago Tribune*: "Klinger bounced one straight at (shortstop) Lazzeri who let the ball roll up one arm, around his neck and down the other wing. It was a good act, but the ex-Yankee really didn't know where the ball was at. By the time he located it, Brubaker had scored from second. Klinger was credited with an undeserved hit."[2] As it turned out, they would need the extra cushion.

Hack led off the ninth and hit a smash that went right through Vaughan's glove at short. As Jensen in center and Rizzo in left field gave chase, Hack motored around the bags. Jensen then booted the ball and Hack checked into third base with no outs. Billy Herman doubled him home. Collins followed with a bunt attempt, but Todd jumped on the ball and fired it to third. Brubaker applied the tag on Herman for the first out. Frank Demaree ended any further drama as he bounced into a 6-4-3 double play.

The win put the New York Giants and the Pirates into a first-place tie. But in the end, it was the Cubs who got the last laugh. On September 25, the Pirates had a two-game lead over the second-place Cubs. But they faltered down the stretch, losing six of seven games. Included in the Pirates downturn was a three-game series at Wrigley Field. The Cubs won all three games to pull ahead and eventually win the NL pennant.

NOTES

1   Lester Biederman, "Pirate Patter: All in a Day's Work," *Pittsburgh Press*, April 28, 1938: 28.

2   Irving Vaughan, "Vaughan Knocks Home Run With Three On Base," *Chicago Tribune*, April 28, 1938: 20.

LLOYD WANER'S BIG GAME

MAY 4, 1938: PITTSBURGH PIRATES 9, BROOKLYN DODGERS 5, AT FORBES FIELD

BY BLAKE W. SHERRY

THE 1938 SEASON WAS A GOOD ONE for the Pittsburgh Pirates: a second-place finish, just two games out. But it was the heartbreaking September collapse that made it a season Pirates fans don't enjoy talking about.[1] The team featured four future Hall of Famers: manager Pie Traynor, shortstop Arky Vaughn, and outfielders Paul and Lloyd Waner. The Waner brothers were known as Big Poison and Little Poison, with the popular theory being they got their nicknames because they were "poison" to pitchers of their era. Another theory is someone misheard "person" as "poison" and the names stuck with the press.[2]

The Pirates started the season reeling off seven consecutive wins. A series-opening 7-2 loss to the Brooklyn Dodgers the previous day was their fifth straight loss. Just before the game on May 4, Lloyd Waner reportedly said to his brother Paul, "I think I'll do the hitting today for the Waner family."[3] And with that Lloyd Waner had one of the most explosive days of his Hall of Fame career. He finished the day 4-for-4 with a home run, two triples, and a single. He scored three runs and drove in five.

Right-hander Russ Bauers was on the mound for the Bucs, facing righty Luke Hamlin for the Dodgers. Bauers was in his second full year in the majors, coming off an excellent 13-6 record with a 2.88 ERA.

The Dodgers took a 1-0 lead in the first inning, scoring on a bases-loaded fly by Gibby Brack. The lead didn't last long. Lloyd Waner, hitting second in the lineup, began his big day by smacking a triple over Brack's head in right-center field. The next hitter was his brother Paul, who drove him home with a fly ball to left, knotting the score.

After an uneventful second inning, the Dodgers went back up 3-1 in the third inning. Johnny Hudson and Ernie Koy led off with walks. Hudson scored on an error by third baseman Lee Handley and Koy came home on Leo Durocher's fly ball. But in the bottom half of the inning, Lloyd collected an RBI infield single.[4] Now within one run, the Bucs tied it again at 3-3 in the fourth on Johnny Rizzo's triple and Vaughn's fly ball.

After an RBI triple by Dolph Camilli, Traynor pulled Bauers and called on reliever Joe Bowman with no outs. A spot starter in 1937, Bowman entered the game and got the next three outs, which included Durocher's fly ball to score Camilli from third. From then on Bowman pitched nearly flawless baseball.

With the Bucs down 5-3, Lloyd Waner was ready to do damage again. Following a bunt single by Bowman and two balls to Handley, an irritated Dodgers manager Burleigh Grimes brought inBill Posedel to replace Hamlin. The walk to Handley was completed, and then Lloyd Waner laced his second triple of the day, down the right-field line, tying the game. Again his brother drove him in with a fly ball, and the Pirates had a lead they would not relinquish. It was reported that the sudden removal of Hamlin caused a bit of a stir in the Dodgers locker room. An angry Hamlin said a few unkind things about Grimes's managerial style.[5] General manager Larry MacPhail came to Pittsburgh the next day to support Grimes and calm the team down.[6]

In the seventh, Lloyd followed Handley's double with a homer to deep right field for an 8-5 lead. It was Waner's first of the year, and only the second time he reached that deep right-field section in his career. It was such an anomaly for the slight player of only 145 pounds[7] that he took some friendly ribbing from the Brooklyn bench as he rounded the bases. He responded with a smile and pointed to his arm muscle.[8]

Ray Berres capped the Pirates' scoring in the eighth with a single to score Gus Suhr, who had tripled. It was the fifth triple of the game. Forbes Field, with its spacious outfield, was known for triples.[9]

Joe Bowman shut Brooklyn out in the ninth, giving the Bucs a 9-5 win. Bowman got the win after yielding just one baserunner in five shutout innings. He retired his first 13 batters before Goody Rosen's pinch-single in the ninth. If Waner had to share a headline with any teammate that day, and he did, it was with Bowman.[10]

After a mediocre start of 20-20 as of June 6, the Pirates went on an impressive second-half run, winning 42 of 57 games (.737) through August 9. They held a seven-game lead on September 1. But on September 21 a hurricane raged up the East Coast, resulting in several postponed games, and Pittsburgh lost its momentum and swagger.

A collapse in the final week did them in. The Bucs won just one of their last seven games, which included a crucial three-game series in Chicago with the second-place Cubs. The Cubs won all three games. The backbreaker in many fans' eyes was of the second game of that series, in which Gabby Hartnett hit a clutch two-out ninth-inning home run as dusk fell at Wrigley Field. In Pirates and Cubs lore, it unaffectionately (for the Pirates, at least) became known as the "homer in the gloamin'."[11]

The second-place Pirates finish was a tremendous disappointment. So sure of a pennant was the club that in the late summer a special press stand was added to the roof of Forbes Field, and 1,000 press buttons were printed for the World Series.[12] While team owner Bill Benswanger agreed that Hartnett's home run was a damaging blow, he felt the pennant was lost by the effect of the hurricane, observing, "As we sat around hotel lobbies during the storm, a hot team cooled off and never regained its winning momentum. The Hartnett homer was an anticlimax, but not the cause of our defeat."[13]

Lloyd Waner's monster day was part of the only season in which he was selected as an All-Star, though

he didn't get into the game. He hit .313 and struck out only 11 times in 659 plate appearances. His career strikeout ratio of one every 44.9 at-bats ranks him third to Willie Keeler (63.2) and Joe Sewell (62.6) for batters with 3,000 plate appearances or more. Lloyd would finish in the Top 10 toughest batters to strike out 12 times, and led the National League five times, including 1938.

The 1938 was the last in which the Waner brothers played over 145 games. Their playing time began to diminish in the 1939 season, and by 1940 the brothers were spare parts. After 14 years of sharing the Pirate outfield, Paul was released by the Pirates after the 1940 season. Lloyd was traded to the Boston Braves in May 1941, and then sent to the Cincinnati Reds a month later. Both extended their careers as a result of the shortage of major-league players during World War II.[14] Their combined hit total of 5,611 is first among major-league brother combinations.

Beyond his 2,459 hits, Lloyd was regarded as a fine outfielder. Bill James in his *Historical Baseball Abstract* would have awarded Waner eight gold gloves from 1927 through 1937.[15] James's *Win Shares* analysis rated Lloyd an A+, the highest defensive rating, for his career.[16] A gentleman on the field, he was never ejected from any of his 1,993 games.[17]

Paul was elected by the Baseball Writers Association of America to the Hall of Fame in 1952. Lloyd joined him in the Hall in 1967 after being selected by the Veterans Committee. Having retired in 1945, and after such a long wait Lloyd was surprised when he got the call. He did not know that he was still being considered.[18] His selection made the Waner brothers the only playing brothers in the Hall of Fame. (Brothers George and Harry Wright are also in the Hall, but were selected as Executive/Pioneers.)

NOTES

1   Frederick G. Lieb, *The Pittsburgh Pirates* (New York: G.P. Putnam's Sons, 1948), 260.

2   Lieb, 229.

3   Lester Biederman, "Pirate Patter: Waner Act Revived!" *Pittsburgh Press*, May 5, 1938: 28.

4   Edward Balinger, "L. Waner Hits Two Triples, Homer, Single," *Pittsburgh Post-Gazette*, May 5, 1938, 20.

5   Roscoe McGowen, "Lucas, Pirates, Beats Dodgers 4-2; MacPhail Backs Action on Hamlin," *New York Times*, May 6, 1938: 28.

6   Chester L Smith, "Dodgers' Rebellion Quelled by MacPhail," *Pittsburgh Press*, May 6, 1938: 45.

7   Clifton Blue Parker, *Big and Little Poison* (Jefferson, North Carolina: McFarland & Company, Inc., 2003), 303.

8   Ronald T. Waldo, *Pennant Hopes Dashed by the Homer in the Gloamin'* (Jefferson, North Carolina: McFarland & Company, Inc., 2013), 92.

9   Parker, 112.

10   Biederman, "Bucs' Powerhouse Flashes Old Form to Shake Slump," *Pittsburgh Press*, May 6, 1938: 28.

11   Waldo, 202.

12   Parker, 198.

13   Lieb, 263.

14   Parker, 261.

15   Bill James, *The New Bill James Historical Baseball Abstract* (New York: Simon & Schuster, 2001), 755.

16   Bill James and Jim Henzler, *Win Shares* (Morton Grove, Illinois: STATS Publishing, 2002), 153.

17   Parker, 310.

18   Parker, 303.

JOHNNY RIZZO'S NINE RBIs: A PIRATES ALL-TIME RECORD

MAY 30, 1939: PITTSBURGH PIRATES 14, ST. LOUIS CARDINALS 8 (SECOND GAME OF DOUBLEHEADER), AT SPORTSMAN'S PARK

BY BOB LEMOINE

JASON BAY OF THE PITTSBURGH Pirates had eight RBIs in a game twice in his career and both within a year of each other: September 19, 2003, and July 2, 2004. Bay may not have realized it, but he just missed the all-time Pirates single-game record of nine in a game set by Johnny Rizzo on May 30, 1939. The right-handed-swinging Rizzo spent seven seasons in the minors with the St. Louis Cardinals' organization before an October 13, 1937, trade to Pittsburgh, followed by his breakout rookie season of 1938 in which he pounded 23 home runs. Ironically, this record was also broken by Bay, who had 26 home runs in 2004, batting .301 with 111 runs driven in. Left fielder Rizzo, a 26-year-old Texan in his second year in the majors, struggled in the early going, batting only .219 in April and .210 (17-for-81) with no home runs and a woeful .289 on-base percentage since May 8. On May 29, at Sportsman's Park in St. Louis, Rizzo managed a run-scoring double in five at-bats during a Pittsburgh victory, but he also grounded into a first-inning 5-4-3 triple play. He went hitless in four trips to the plate in game one of a holiday doubleheader on May 30 against the Cardinals. Game two would be a totally different story.

St. Louis won the first game, 7-2. With the victory, St. Louis was in second place, 22-13, 4½ games ahead of fourth-place Pittsburgh (18-18). Both clubs, along with the Chicago Cubs, were chasing the front-runner Cincinnati Reds in the National League. A crowd of 14,178 was on hand to celebrate Decoration Day (later known as Memorial Day) in St. Louis.

The second-game pitchers for both clubs were making their first starts of the season. The Cardinals sent left-hander Clyde Shoun to the mound. Shoun had pitched 15⅔ innings out of the bullpen over seven games with a 2.30 ERA. Pittsburgh countered with Russ Bauers, a righty who had pitched 6⅓ scoreless relief innings this season but started 34 games the previous year. The Pirates struck for a run in the first when Arky Vaughan walked and Rizzo doubled to the wall in left field. This lead evaporated quickly, however, when Bauers walked Johnny Mize and Don Gutteridge in the Cardinals second inning. Enos Slaughter doubled to the wall in left, scoring both, and then made it to third on a wild pitch. Herman Franks' sacrifice fly to center scored Slaughter to give St. Louis a 3-1 lead.

The hits kept on coming for the Cardinals in the third. With Stu Martin on first, Pepper Martin hit a sure double-play ball, but Lee Handley's throw from third was dropped by second baseman Bill Brubaker. Joe Medwick doubled in both Martins to make the score 5-1 and end the day for Bauers. Right-hander Bill Swift came in from the bullpen to try to stop further damage, but allowed a triple to Mize, scoring Medwick, and Slaughter's bloop double to right, scoring Mize. The Cardinals enjoyed a 7-1 lead, and were primed for a doubleheader sweep.

The score remained 7-1 into the fifth. Shoun walked both pitcher Swift and Paul Waner. With two out, Rizzo blasted his second home run of the season, into the left-field seats, and all of a sudden the Pittsburgh deficit was 7-4, with Rizzo accounting for all four runs. After a walk, right-hander Mort Cooper replaced Shoun on the mound, and retired the Pirates. Swift retired the side in order in the fifth and sixth innings, but St. Louis still held a three-run lead.

In the seventh, Vaughan walked and Rizzo singled him to second. A walk to rookie Fern Bell loaded the bases with one out, and right-hander Curt Davis relieved Cooper. Brubaker lined out to left field and Medwick's quick throw forced the runners to hold. Gus Suhr singled to right, scoring Vaughan and Rizzo, cutting the deficit to 7-6. Handley's single to left tied the score, but pinch hitter Lloyd Waner lined out to retire the Pirates. The game was now even in the bottom of the seventh. Lloyd Waner stayed into the game to play center field and Ray Berres went in to catch for the Pirates. Swift hurled another scoreless inning, and the game remained tied into the eighth.

Swift reached first on a bunt down the third-base line that St. Louis hoped would roll foul. He moved to third on Paul Waner's double to right center. Though Rizzo was 3-for-4 with four RBIs, St. Louis opted to pitch to him with the bases loaded, intentionally walking Vaughan. Rizzo cleared the bases with a double to left center, giving the Pirates a 10-7 lead. "The ball was hit with such force that it bounded off the wall, away from Medwick and Pepper Martin," wrote Lester Biederman of the *Pittsburgh Press*.[1] The hit drove Curt Davis from the game in favor of right-hander Bob Bowman. He surrendered a fly ball to Handley that scored Rizzo and extended the Pirates' lead to 11-7. In the bottom of the eighth, Swift gave up a leadoff single to Medwick and a double to Slaughter to cut the Pittsburgh lead to 11-8, but pinch-hitter Don Padgett popped out to third to end the inning.

Mickey Owen, who had caught all of game one for St. Louis, now went in to catch the ninth inning. Bowman allowed a one-out single to Paul Waner. Vaughan bunted to third and Gutteridge threw to an uncovered second base the ball ending up in right center for an error. Waner scored from first and Vaughan took third. Interestingly, with first base open, Rizzo was pitched to again … and he drilled his second home run of the contest. He finished the game 5-for-6 with two doubles and a single and nine RBIs. He scored four runs. The polite St. Louis crowd

Johnny Rizzo

by this point was cheering Rizzo "despite their rude awakening to the realization that the big Italian boy was wrecking their favorites with his blasts in and out of the park," wrote Edward F. Balinger in the *Pittsburgh Post-Gazette*.[2]

Swift pitched a scoreless ninth, locking up the 14-8 victory. He completed 6⅔ innings of relief, allowing only five hits and one earned run, and striking out five in his first win of the season. Davis, who allowed four earned runs in two-thirds of an inning of relief, took the loss and fell to 7-3. The game took 2:26 to play. Pittsburgh's 14 runs came on 14 hits and one Cardinals error. St. Louis had eight runs on seven hits and one Pittsburgh error. The Pirates left nine on base and the Cardinals stranded three. While the Pirates would fight to stay above .500 into early August, they were far out of the pennant race. An 8-22 month of August sank them to a sixth-place finish at 68-85. The disappointing season ended the managerial career of Pittsburgh legend Pie Traynor.

Rizzo had two of his six home runs for the season that day in St. Louis, and his nine RBIs represented 16 percent of his 1939 total of 55. Despite having a strong rookie season, Rizzo fizzled to a mediocre five-year career, batting .270 with 61 home runs and 289 RBIs, ending his major-league career with the Cincinnati Reds, Philadelphia Phillies, and Brooklyn Dodgers.

But Rizzo's feat of nine RBIs in a game was still a Pirates record as of 2017.

SOURCES

In addition to the sources listed in the Notes, the author also consulted Baseball-reference.com, Retrosheet.org, and "Detail on Pirates' Games," *Pittsburgh Post-Gazette*, May 31, 1939: 17.

NOTES

1   Lester Biederman, "First Night Game With Phillies Is Slated Tomorrow," *Pittsburgh Press*, May 31, 1939: 25.

2   Edward F. Balinger, "Rizzo's Five Blows Help Pirates Capture Nightcap," *Pittsburgh Post-Gazette*, May 31, 1939: 14, 16.

TINY BONHAM'S LAST GAME

AUGUST 27, 1949: PITTSBURGH PIRATES 8, PHILADELPHIA PHILLIES 2, AT SHIBE PARK, PHILADELPHIA

BY C. PAUL ROGERS III

THE PITTSBURGH PIRATES WERE firmly entrenched in sixth place heading into their August 27, 1949, game in Philadelphia against the fourth-place Phillies. The Pirates, near the middle of a long road trip, had taken two of the first three of the four-game series heading into the Saturday afternoon tilt. Thirty-six-year-old Ernie Bonham, known throughout baseball as Tiny,[1] was to take the mound for the Pirates against another veteran, 39-year-old Schoolboy Rowe, who was playing out the string with the Phillies after starring for the Detroit Tigers in the 1930s.

After posting a 6-10 record for the Pirates in 1948, Tiny Bonham experienced a resurgence during the first half of the 1949 season. The right-handed Bonham had been a star twirler for the New York Yankees during the war years, winning 21 games in 1942, but had been plagued by back and arm injuries through much of his career. Although beset by those issues early in 1949, he won six decisions in a row in June and July before hitting a rough patch in August. As a result, he entered the August 27 game having not won a game in a month and with a 6-4 record and a 4.50 earned-run average. But none of the 6,070 in attendance in Shibe Park that day could have imagined that this would be Bonham's last game and that 19 days later he would be dead.

Rowe managed to escape the first inning unscathed despite two Phillies errors, one by Schoolboy himself when he mishandled Johnny Hopp's bunt attempt. After a scoreless inning and a half, the Phillies struck first when with two outs in the bottom of the second Willie "Puddinhead" Jones launched a drive into the left-center-field seats for a solo home run. Mike Goliat followed with a double to left and Andy Seminick walked before Bonham escaped further trouble by getting Rowe to ground to third baseman Pete Castiglione, who threw to second to force Seminick.

In the top of the third, Rowe gave up a two-out triple to right field to Hopp before retiring Tom Saffell on a fly to right to end the frame. In the bottom of the inning Bonham allowed only a one-out single to Granny Hamner and the teams headed into the fourth with the game shaping up like a bona-fide pitchers' duel.

Rowe, however, had been inconsistent both in and out of the bullpen and entered the game with a 3-6 record. He was making only his sixth start of the year and in the fourth the roof caved in. By the time the dust settled, the Pirates had scored four runs on a double by Wally Westlake mixed in with three singles and three Phillies errors, all before an out was recorded. Two of the errors were on bunts, meaning that the fumble-fingered Phillies defense botched three Pittsburgh bunts on the day.[2] When Bonham broke a 0-19 streak with a liner to left for his first hit of the season to drive in two runs, Rowe's day was done.[3] Blix Donnelly relieved and retired Stan Rojek on a sacrifice bunt for the first out of the inning. Hopp then smacked a fly to deep center field to drive in Clyde McCullough, who had reached base on one of the Phillies' errors, with the fifth run of the frame.

Bonham pitched a shutdown inning in the bottom of the fourth following his teammates' rally by retiring Bill Nicholson, Jones, and Goliat in order. Ralph Kiner then led off the Pittsburgh fifth with a line drive deep into the upper deck in left field to extend the lead to 6-1. It was his eighth home run in his last 15 games and his league-leading 37th of the year.[4]

Bonham mowed down the Phillies in their fifth, allowing only a one-out walk to Stan Hollmig, who was pinch-hitting for Donnelly.

Ken Trinkle in relief set the Pirates down in order in the sixth. In the bottom of the frame, Bonham got off to a shaky start, allowing leadoff singles to Dick Sisler and Del Ennis. But Nicholson lined out to Westlake in right and Jones grounded into an around-the-horn double play to keep the five-run lead intact. The Pirates, however, were not through with their sticks and touched Trinkle for two runs in the seventh to expand the lead to 8-1. Castiglione had the big blow, a two-run, two-out single that drove in Kiner, who had walked, and Westlake, who had doubled for the second time.

Bonham allowed only a leadoff single to Goliat in the Phillies' seventh but in the eighth was touched for a run on a Richie Ashburn single and a two-out double to center by Ennis. Meanwhile 21-year-old bonus baby Charlie Bicknell retired the Pirates in order in the eighth and ninth innings.[5]

In the bottom of the ninth Bonham kept the Phillies at bay despite allowing one-out walks to Goliat and Seminick. With runners on, he struck out pinch-hitter Stan Lopata for the second out. Ashburn tried to bunt his way on but catcher McCullough pounced on it and threw to first to end the game and secure Bonham's seventh win of the season by the score of 8-2. Pitching to contact, Bonham scattered eight hits, striking out only one and walking four[6] in a game that took 2 hours and 14 minutes.

The Pirates played errorless ball in the rout while the Phillies uncharacteristically made five errors. But the Phillies would rebound from their shoddy performance to win 12 of their next 16 games and would finish in third place, a precursor to their 1950 pennant-winning season as the Whiz Kids. The Pirates, on the other hand, were headed nowhere fast and remained in sixth place, finishing a dozen games below .500.[7]

For much of the summer, Bonham had been telling teammates that he intended to retire to his California farm after the season.[8] However, he began experiencing abdominal pain during the long road trip and told manager Billy Meyer that he felt tired all of the time.[9] He was admitted to Presbyterian Hospital in Pittsburgh for an appendectomy on September 8. The doctors, however, found intestinal cancer and performed additional abdominal surgery. After rallying, Bonham took a turn for the worse and died on September 15.[10] He was survived by his wife, Ruth, 6-year-old daughter, Donna Marie, and 4-year-old son, Ernie Jr.

Bonham's untimely death at the age of 36 shocked the baseball world, including his former teammates on the Yankees, for whom Tiny had pitched for seven years. Longtime New York shortstop and coach Frankie Crosetti called him "a great Yankee."[11] The Pirates, also stunned by the sad news, had to play on and on September 16, after a moment of silence for Bonham, defeated the Brooklyn Dodgers 9-2 behind southpaw Bill Werle.

NOTES

1   Bonham was listed as 6'2" tall and 215 pounds "with a torso like blacksmith." Warren Corbett, Tiny Bonham, SABR BioProject: sabr.org/bioproj/person/d7503bf4.

2   Two of the bunts were botched by Rowe.

3   Although that was Bonham's only hit for the year and his batting average for 1949 was .045, for his career he hit .161.

4   Les Biederman, "Kiner Hits 37th, Pirates Win, 8-2," *Pittsburgh Press*, August 28, 1949: 35.

5   It was arguably the best outing of Bicknell's brief major-league career. Because of the bonus rule then in effect, the Phillies were forced to carry Bicknell on their major-league roster in 1948 and 1949. Manager Eddie Sawyer relegated Bicknell to mopup duty, typically bringing him in in lost causes like this game. For his career Bicknell appeared in 30 games and, remarkably, the Phillies were 0-30 in those games. He started only one game, the only time he appeared when the Phillies were not already losing. His lifetime record was 0-1, reflecting that one short-lived start.

6   Bonham was uncharacteristically wild that day. For his career he walked just 1.67 batters per nine innings.

7   In 1950 the Pirates recorded only 57 wins and fell to the National League cellar.

8   Chester L. Smith, "The Village Smithy," *Pittsburgh Press*, September 16, 1949: 41.

9   Warren Corbett, Tiny Bonham, SABR BioProject: sabr.org/bioproj/person/d7503bf4.

10 "Ernie Bonham, Buc Pitcher, Dies," *Pittsburgh Press*, September 15, 1949: 1.

11 Oscar Fraley, "Yanks Stunned by Death of Ernie Bonham," *Pittsburgh Press*, September 16, 1949: 41.

KINER SCORES 4, DRIVES IN 8, IN HITTING FOR CYCLE AGAINST THE DODGERS

JUNE 25, 1950: PITTSBURGH PIRATES 16, BROOKLYN DODGERS 11, AT EBBETS FIELD

BY MIKE HUBER

"PITCHING IS CALLED 70 PER CENT OF baseball."[1] The Pittsburgh Pirates knocked 20 hits off 70 percent of the Brooklyn pitching staff, beating the Dodgers in an old-fashioned slugfest, 16-11, before 20,196 fans during a Sunday afternoon tilt at Ebbets Field. Ralph Kiner carried his team to victory, hitting for the and driving in eight runs. This was the final game of a three-game series. The Dodgers entered the game with a record of 34-22, while the Pirates started 14½ games behind Brooklyn, in seventh place at 21-38. In the loss, the "Brooks did some heavy hitting, too, but their efforts were dwarfed and their lead over the second-place Phils was cut to half a game."[2]

Pirates' rookie righty Vern Law started and faced Dodgers' 1949 National League Rookie of the Year Don Newcombe on the mound. From the outset, Newcombe, a 6-foot-4-inch right-hander, was not sharp, allowing a double to Stan Rojek to start the game. Ted Beard then walked, and Kiner followed with a home run, a line drive into the bleachers. Quickly, Newcombe and the Dodgers were down 3-0 before recording an out. The Brooklyn squad responded quickly. With two outs in the bottom of the first, Duke Snider walked, Jackie Robinson singled, and Carl Furillo doubled both home.

In the Pirates' third, Kiner singled with two outs. Gus Bell also singled, and Danny Murtaugh plated two runs with a double to center. Given the circumstances, Dodgers manager Burt Shotton did not hesitate to use his bullpen, since he had used just one pitcher on Friday, though he followed that with four hurlers on Saturday against the Bucs. He made the call for Joe Hatten to relieve Newcombe, and

the southpaw Hatten stemmed the tide, keeping the score at 5-2.

Brooklyn tied the game in the fifth as it appeared that Law had "tired in the terrific heat."[3] Pee Wee Reese bunted safely down the first-base line. George Shuba pinch-hit for Hatten and scorched a double to right, sending Reese to third. Billy Cox walked to load the bases, and Pittsburgh manager Billy Meyer called upon Cliff Chambers to end the threat. Lefty Chambers uncorked a wild pitch, bringing Reese home. Fly balls by Jim Russell and Snider created two outs, but also brought in two runs, to tie the game, 5-5.

Ralph Branca became the third Dodgers pitcher at the start of the sixth inning. After retiring the Pirates in order, the right-handed veteran ran into trouble in the seventh, walking Rojek and Beard to start the inning. Kiner, who had struck out in the fifth, again came to bat with two runners aboard. He hit a double to center, earning two more RBIs, and Branca was done. Shotton replaced him with right-hander Al Epperly, who had last pitched in the major leagues in 1938.[4] Epperly didn't fare much better than his predecessors, yielding a run-producing double to Bell, walking Murtaugh, and serving up another RBI double to Dale Coogan. Bell scored, but Furillo fielded Coogan's safety and fired the ball to Robinson, whose relay cut down Murtaugh at the plate. Just like that, the Pirates had scored four more times and had a 9-5 advantage. The Dodgers did get back one run, when Snider tripled in the bottom of the seventh and scored on Furillo's fly, but Pittsburgh struck again in the eighth. Beard hit his third home run of the season, a two-run shot, after Rojek's leadoff single, to bump Pittsburgh to an 11-6 lead. Epperly had "an undistinguished Flatbush debut, yielding three runs, four hits, and two walks in one inning."[5] That brought Erv Palica into the game, and the right-hander had to face the hot-hitting Kiner. Pittsburgh's left fielder laced a triple to right, completing the cycle, but the inning ended with Kiner still standing on third.

Brooklyn did not give up. Reese doubled with one out in the bottom of the eighth. Tommy Brown pinch-hit for Palica and tripled to right, bringing in Reese. Cox's fly ball brought home Brown, and after eight innings, the Pirates' lead had been pared to 11-8.

Billy Loes entered the game in the top of the ninth as the sixth Dodgers hurler; however, Loes never recorded an out. Pete Castiglione singled to left and Ray Mueller bunted toward the mound and legged it out. Chambers loaded the bases with a single to left. Shotton had seen enough and motioned once again to his bullpen. After Rex Barney (another right-hander) entered, Rojek greeted him with a two-run single to center field, but Chambers was thrown out at third. Barney then walked Beard. Kiner entered the batter's box and sent a Barney offering into the lower left-field stands for a three-run home run, his second round-tripper of the game. As a result, the Pirates had added five more runs, making the tally 16-8.

Even with an eight-run lead in the ninth inning, Pittsburgh skipper Meyer made a pitching change. Chambers was touched for singles by Snider and Robinson, so Bill Macdonald came on in relief. He managed to get one out before Gil Hodges blasted a three-run home run, his eighth of the season, to make it 16-11. Roy Campanella flied out and Reese struck out to end the game.

For the game, Kiner was 5-for-6, with four runs scored and eight runs batted in. This was the only time in the 1950 season that Kiner had more than three hits in a game. His 14 total bases in a single game rank second on the Pirates' all-time list, behind only Willie Stargell, who had 15 against the Chicago Cubs on May 22, 1968. Kiner's average jumped 15 points to .287 with this feat. Earlier in the season, on May 9, Kiner had also hit two home runs in a contest against the Dodgers, and he had driven in seven runs

Ralph Kiner

in that game. Rojek was 4-for-5 with four runs scored, and he had led off in four innings, reaching base three times. Bell also was productive with a 3-for-5 day. The first four batters in Pittsburgh's lineup scored 14 of the Pirates' 16 runs.

In the offensive outburst, the Pirates "walloped three homers, five doubles, and a triple, while the Brooks made one round-tripper, four doubles, and two triples."[6] The three-game series between the Dodgers and the Pirates was, simply put, a display of power. Together, the Pirates and Dodgers scored 76 runs. Brooklyn scored 45 runs and had to settle for one victory, one suspended game, and one defeat. Tommy Holmes of the *Brooklyn Daily Eagle* wrote, "It's plain that right now all batters are stepping in swinging from the handle and batting with all kinds of confidence, while the pitchers, poor wretches, work like terrorized fatalists."[7] Brooklyn had defeated the Dodgers on Friday, June 23, 15-3. Saturday night's game was suspended, because of the 11:59 curfew, with Brooklyn leading 19-12 with one out in the bottom of the eighth inning, just after Jackie Robinson had hit a grand slam and Furillo had singled. It was completed on August 1 with new umpires; during the interval from game suspension to resumption, Coogan and Earl Turner had left the Pirates, so defensive substitutions had to be inserted (the Dodgers eventually won, 21-12).[8] Sunday's game was 16-11, in favor of the Pirates.

The two home runs gave Kiner 18 "official" round-trippers for the season. He had hit one the night before (also off Barney), but the home run did not count until the game was completed in August. Even so, with 18 homers and 54 RBIs, he was leading the National League in both categories.[9]

Kiner's cycle was the 16th to date in Pittsburgh franchise history. He also added a second home run to his cycle. It came a little over a year after Wally Westlake accomplished the feat for the second time and almost one year before Gus Bell. For four consecutive seasons, a member of the Pirates had hit for the cycle: Westlake (July 30, 1948, and June 14, 1949), Kiner (June 25, 1950), and Bell (June 4, 1951).

NOTES

1 Tommy Holmes, "Dodger Pitchers Battered as Slugfest Engagement With Pirates Comes to End," *Brooklyn Daily Eagle*, June 26, 1950: 11.

2 Louis Effrat, "Pirates Overpower Dodgers With 20 Blows; Reds Top Giants Twice," *New York Times*, June 26, 1950: 32.

3 Jack Hernon, "Kiner's Big Bat Subdues Bums, 16-11," *Pittsburgh Post-Gazette*, June 26, 1950: 16.

4 Al Epperly pitched nine games for the Chicago Cubs in 1938, with a record of 2-0, and he did not return to the big leagues until 1950, making his debut in this game. For the season, he pitched in five games (all in relief) and did not record a decision. His final major-league game was on July 7, 1950.

5 Effrat.

6 Ibid.

7 Holmes.

8 retrosheet.org/boxesetc/1950/B06240BRO1950.htm.

9 Kiner finished the 1950 season with 47 home runs, leading the National League for the fifth consecutive year. He continued to be the NL's home-run king through 1952, a string of seven straight seasons. His 118 RBIs in 1950 were 8 behind Philadelphia's Del Ennis.

MURRY DICKSON'S 20TH WIN

SEPTEMBER 23, 1951: PITTSBURGH PIRATES 3, CINCINNATI REDS 0, AT CROSLEY FIELD

BY RICHARD "PETE" PETERSON

AFTER COMPETING FOR THE 1948 National League pennant before finishing in fourth place, the Pittsburgh Pirates, on January 29, 1949, purchased right-hander Murry Dickson from the St. Louis Cardinals for $125,000 in an effort to improve their pitching staff for the 1949 season.

Regarded as one of the craftiest pitchers in baseball, Dickson had made his major-league debut with the Cardinals in 1939 at the age of 22, but didn't become a permanent member of their staff until 1942. His best year with the Cardinals was in 1946, when he had a 15-6 record and started the seventh game of the 1946 World Series against the Boston Red Sox.

While the Cardinals won the deciding game, 4-3, on Enos Slaughter's celebrated "mad dash" around the bases, Dickson was so angry about being taken out in the eighth inning with the Cardinals leading 3-1 that he dressed and left the ballpark. He drove around St Louis and listened to the rest of the game on his car radio.

Overcoming his unhappiness, Dickson became the workhorse of the Cardinals pitching staff for the next two seasons until he was sold to the Pirates. With the Pirates, Dickson continued in that role. In 1949, he pitched in 44 games, 24 of them in relief. In 1950, he pitched in 51 games, including 29 relief appearances.

Despite his reliability, Dickson hadn't compiled a winning record since 1946, but all that changed in 1951. Used primarily as a starter, he won his first three games, including a 4-3 complete game against Don Newcombe and the Dodgers. By midseason, even with the Pirates floundering in the second division, he managed to stay at .500 or above. From July 15 through August 12, he won six games in a row to bring his record to 16-10 and on September 19 won his 19th game of the season, against the Boston Braves.

On September 23, Dickson, looking for his 20th win, started the first game of a doubleheader in Cincinnati. The Reds had struggled to score runs in 1951, but Dickson would still be facing a formidable lineup, led by sluggers Ted Kluszewski and Wally Post. He'd also have to beat Reds ace Ewell Blackwell in a matchup of pitching opposites.

Dickson, who stood 5-feet-10 and weighed 159 pounds, used a variety of pitches, including a knuckleball, and deceptive deliveries to get batters out. His former teammate Joe Garagiola claimed that players called him Thomas Edison because invented so many pitches.[1] The Cubs' Frankie Baumholtz hated facing Dickson: "His ball moved all the time and occasionally he'd sneak in a fastball. He was no fun to bat against."[2]

Blackwell, who stood 6-feet-6 and weighed 195 pounds, was known as the Whip. The right-hander intimidated hitters with a side-arm fastball, once clocked at 99.8 mph. He knew his side-arm delivery "was intimidating and I took advantage of it. .... I was a mean pitcher."[3] He could tell Pirates slugger Ralph Kiner "was scared. ... he'd bail out because my fast ball would break toward the batter."[4]

After Blackwell retired the side in order in the top of the first, Dickson struck out leadoff hitter Bobby Adams on his way to a one-two-three inning. Blackwell had to pitch his way around an error and a single by Jack Merson in the second, while Dickson, after giving up two singles, struck out Roy McMillan and got Hobie Landrith on a ground ball to work his way out of trouble. Blackwell and Dickson gave up harmless singles in the third inning and retired the side in order in the fourth.

The Pirates finally broke through against Blackwell in the top of the fifth, but it was thanks to a costly throwing error by second baseman Adams. George Strickland doubled, then scored with two outs on Adams's wild throw on a Pete Castiglione ground ball. With Castiglione on first, Blackwell walked George Metkovich, then gave up a run-scoring single to Gus Bell before striking out Kiner.

With a 2-0 lead, Dickson retired the Reds in order in the bottom of the fifth. After the Pirates failed to score in the top of the sixth, Adams led off the bottom of the inning with a single, then moved to third base on two groundouts. Kluszewski, however, flied out to right field to end the threat.

In the top of the seventh, Dickson, who would hit .273 for the season, singled and was sacrificed to second by Castiglione. After Metkovich lined out to third, Bell brought Dickson home with a single to right field to give the Pirates a 3-0 lead. When Dickson took the mound in the bottom of the seventh, he was nine outs away from a 20-win season

Murry Dickson

with a Pirates team that was struggling to stay out of last place.

With one out, Dickson walked Grady Hatton, then gave up a two-out single to Landrith. With Blackwell due up, Reds manager Luke Sewell went with pinch-hitter Joe Adcock. Facing the tying run at the plate, Dickson bore down and struck out Adcock to end the inning.

After the Pirates wasted a Clyde McCullough single in the eighth off Reds righty reliever Frank Smith, Dickson had his finest inning in the bottom of the frame. Facing the top of the Reds lineup, he struck out Adams, Johnny Wyrostek, and Post. When he walked off the mound, he still possessed a 3-0 lead and was one inning away from his 20th win.

Dickson led off the top of the ninth with his second hit, but after Castiglione sacrificed, Jack Phillips and Bell failed to bring him home. In the bottom of the ninth, Kluszewski led off by lining out to short and Hank Edwards grounded out to second. When Hatton lofted a fly ball to center fielder Frank Thomas, Dickson became a 20-game winner for a team that would win only 64 games for the season and finish in seventh place, only two games ahead of the Chicago Cubs.

The irony of Dickson's accomplishment in the 1951 season was that it was eclipsed by St. Louis Browns right-hander Ned Garver, who made history by becoming the first pitcher to win 20 games for a last-place team. His Browns finished the season with 102 losses and only 52 wins. Like Dickson, Garver was a craftsman on the mound. Satchel Paige once said that Garver knew more about pitching than anyone, except, of course, Paige himself.[5]

Unfortunately for Dickson, he would go on to pitch for a 1952 Pirates team, dubbed Branch Rickey's "Rickey Dinks," that set a modern Pirates record for ineptness with a record of 42-112. Dickson would make his own history by losing 21 games and becoming the first pitcher to have a 20-game-losing season after a 20-game-winning season.

After losing 19 games in 1953, Dickson was traded to the Philadelphia Phillies, where he lost 20 games in 1954. He bounced back in 1955 with a 12-11 record, and, after being sent to the Cardinals after a poor start in 1956, went on, at the age of 40, to win 13 games. After going 5-3 with the Cardinals in 1957, he ended his career as a part of the Kansas City-New York shuttle. With the Yankees, after spending most of the 1958 season with the A's, he appeared in two games in the 1958 World Series. He ended his career with the A's in 1959, just one year short of pitching in four decades.

Joe Garagiola was one of many teammates who admired Murry Dickson because of his intelligence and determination. He said that Dickson was "one of those guys who always wanted the ball and it was more than having a rubber arm. He was the kind of guy you wanted out there when things were tight."[6]

Dick Schofield, who was Dickson's teammate with the Cardinals in 1956 and 1957, remembered him as "a good guy ... and a real battler, who threw every day on the sideline and wanted to pitch in every game." Dickson's roommate, Ken Boyer, told Schofield that Dickson's regimen was to eat once a week and drink coffee all day long.[7]

While Dickson ended his career with a losing record at 172-181, his 172 wins were remarkable considering that he spent several seasons with awful baseball teams. Had he pitched for better teams, there is no doubt that he would have won over 200 games and earned a place in the Hall of Fame. But he had his moment of greatness in 1951 when he became a 20-game winner and, no doubt, inspired young pitchers Bob Friend and Vernon Law, who would go on to win 20 games for the Pirates and, in Law's case, become a Cy Young Award winner.

SOURCES

In addition to the sources cited in the Notes, the author also consulted Baseball-Reference.com, and Finoli, David, and Bill Ranier, eds. *The Pittsburgh Pirates Encyclopedia* (New York: Sports Publishing, 2015).

NOTES

1   Michael Gershman, David Pietrusza, and Matthew Silverman, eds., *Baseball: The Biographical Encyclopedia* (Kingston, New York: Total/Sports Illustrated, 2000), 287.

2   Daniel Peary, ed., *We Played the Game* (New York: Hyperion, 1994), 156.

3   Peary, 35.

4   Ibid.

5   Richard Peterson, ed., *The St. Louis Baseball Reader* (Columbia: University of Missouri Press, 2006), 313.

6   Gershman et. al., 288.

7   Peary, 355.

DICKSON AND THE BUCS SHAVE "THE BARBER"

JUNE 6, 1952: PITTSBURGH PIRATES 8, NEW YORK GIANTS 1, AT FORBES FIELD

BY PAUL HOFMANN

ON PAPER THE GAME APPEARED TO be a mismatch between teams on different ends of the continuum of competiveness. The defending National League champion New York Giants, losers of seven of their last nine games, entered the game in second place with a record of 28-15, three games behind the first-place Brooklyn Dodgers and with every hope of returning to the World Series. The Giants were in need of a victory to right a floundering ship and stay within striking distance of their crosstown rivals. The last-place Pittsburgh Pirates were riding a three-game losing streak and entered the game with an 11-37 record, a distant 22½ games off the pace. For the Pirates, the game was an opportunity to dismiss the long hoodoo of their great nemesis, Sal "The Barber" Maglie, who was riding a personal 13-game winning streak against the Bucs that dated to September 16, 1945.[1]

The pitching matchup pitted a pair of 1951 20-game winners against each other. The Giants started Maglie, a right-hander who entered the game with a 9-1 record and 1.46 ERA, while the Bucs turned to veteran right-hander Murry Dickson, who was 2-8 with a 4.77 ERA. Maglie, who was 50-11 since his 1950 return from a four-year stint in the Mexican League, finished 23-6 for the Giants in 1951.[2] Although he was off to a slow start to the 1952 season, Dickson was considered the ace of the Pirates rotation. Coming off a 20-win season himself, Dickson posted a 20-16 record in 1951 for a Pirates club that won only 64 games and finished in seventh place.[3] In addition to his being the Pirates most reliable hurler, Dickson entered the game with a team-leading .370 batting average.

The Friday night game drew a crowd of 20,163, well above the 8,917 fans the Pirates averaged at Forbes Field that season.[4] The game was played under partly cloudy skies with a game-time temperature of 83 degrees, slightly above average for an early June evening in Pittsburgh.

Dickson had an uneventful first inning, yielding a harmless two-out single to Giants third baseman Bobby Thomson. Maglie, coming off his first defeat of the season, four days earlier, also got out of the first unscathed. He gave up back-to-back one-out singles to rookie Bobby Del Greco and George Metkovich before striking out Ralph Kiner and retiring Joe Garagiola on a groundball to end the inning.

Don Mueller singled to lead off the top of the second and advanced to second when Al Dark grounded out to third. One out later, Chuck Diering drew a walk, giving Maglie an opportunity to help his own cause. However, the Giants hurler grounded out to shortstop to end the threat.

The Pirates opened the scoring in the bottom of the second. Rookie Jack Merson drew a leadoff walk. Following a strikeout by George Strickland, left-handed-swinging rookie first baseman Tony Bartirome sliced a short double down the left-field line, advancing Merson to third.[5] Just as Maglie had done in the top of the inning, Dickson also failed to help himself when he popped out to first. Pete Castiglione then followed with a single to center that plated both Merson and Bartirome. Castiglione hustled around first to second when he saw Diering attempt to throw Bartirome out at the plate. Giants first baseman Whitey Lockman alertly cut off the throw and tried to catch Castiglione advancing to second. However, Lockman's relay throw to second sailed into right-center and Castiglione came around to score.[6] A three-run Little League home run!

The Giants answered in the top of third when Thomson sent a two-out home run into the gardens, formerly known as Greenberg Gardens, in left-center.[7] Thomson's seventh home run of the season was the only offense the Giants produced off Dickson that night.

Maglie responded with a shutdown inning in the bottom of the third to keep the score at 3-1. Dickson was equally as effective in the top of the fourth when he struck out the side after giving up a leadoff infield single to Mueller.

The Pirates reached Maglie again in the bottom of the fourth. Strickland walked and came around to score when Bartirome singled to right and the throw to third from Mueller ended up in the box seats.[8] Bartirome was awarded third on the error and came around to score when Dickson singled to left to put the Giants up 5-1.

Maglie, who was scheduled to lead off the top of the fifth, was lifted in favor of pinch-hitter Bill Rigney. It was the shortest outing of the season to date for "The Barber." In four innings of work, Maglie gave up six hits, five runs (three earned), and three walks, while striking out three. Meanwhile, Dickson retired the Giants in order for his first 1-2-3 inning of the game.

George Spencer replaced Maglie on the mound for the Giants in the bottom of the fifth. After yielding a leadoff single to Metkovich, the right-handed Spencer retired the next three Pirates to end the inning.

Dickson successfully navigated his way through the heart of the Giants order in the top of the sixth. Following a leadoff walk to Thomson and a one-out single by Mueller, the crafty right-hander retired the next two Giants to keep the score at 5-1.

Spencer was less fortunate in the bottom of the sixth. Strickland started the inning with a walk and advanced to second when Giants catcher Wes Westrum failed to pick up Bartirome's attempted sacrifice bunt for an error. Two batters later, Castiglione bounced a one-out single off Spencer's shin that

rolled into short right field and plated Strickland with the Pirates' sixth run of the game.[9]

Dickson escaped potential trouble in the seventh inning after giving up a two-out triple to Davey Williams and a walk to Lockman. With runners on first and third, Dickson retired Thomson on a foul popup that Garagiola easily handled.

Right-hander Hoyt Wilhelm was summoned to pitch for the Giants in the bottom of the seventh. The future Hall of Famer and his Giants teammates were caught off guard when Kiner, the reigning six-time National League home-run leader, laid down a bunt on the third-base line that brought a roar from the crowd. Kiner said it was the only bunt he could remember resulting in a base hit.[10] The Pirates left fielder advanced to second on a passed ball and moved up to third when Merson singled to left. The light-hitting Bartirome, who was batting .191 coming in and had been inserted at first base because Gus Bell was too ill to play (Metkovich was switched from first base to right field),[11] collected his second double (and third hit) of the game, plating Kiner and Merson for the final margin of victory, 8-1.

Dickson retired the Giants in order in the top of the eighth and Wilhelm followed suit with a 1-2-3 inning of his own in bottom of the frame. Dickson started the top of the ninth by striking out Westrum and pinch-hitter and former Pirate Bill Howerton before giving up a two-out single to Bob Elliot. Dickson finished the complete-game victory by getting Williams to ground out to short, forcing Elliot at second. In all, Dickson scattered seven hits, walked three, and struck out six while yielding a single run to the Giants.

Dickson's ability to pitch out of trouble, Bartirome's and Castiglione's contributions at the plate and sloppy defense on the part of the Giants were the stories of the day for Dickson and the Pirates, who finally beat Sal Maglie after seven long years.[12]

After starting the season 9-0 with a 1.12 ERA, Maglie was 9-8 with a 3.98 ERA from the beginning of June on. He finished the season with a record of 18-8 and a 2.92 ERA as the Giants failed to replicate their magic of a year earlier. The team finished the season at 92-62, 4½ games behind the National League champion Dodgers.

Dickson, on the other hand, bounced back from his slow start to re-establish himself as the Pirates ace. From June 6 on he went 12-13 with a 3.15 ERA and finished the season with a record of 14-21 and ERA of 3.57. His 14 victories were double the number of victories of any other Pirates starter and his ERA was more than one run less than the team's collective ERA. Amazingly, Dickson accounted for 33 percent of the total number of victories for a Pirates team that finished a dismal 42-112, 54½ games behind Brooklyn. The turnaround for Dickson was the night he and the Bucs shaved "The Barber."

NOTES

1   Preacher Roe pitched a complete game as the Pirates beat Sal Maglie and the Giants, 3-2.

2   Ken Burns in his book, *Baseball: An Illustrated History*, stated Maglie earned five times more playing in Mexico than he would have with the Giants. See Geoffrey C. Ward and Ken Burns, *Baseball: An Illustrated History* (New York: Knopf, 2010), 353.

3   Warren Corbett, "Murry Dickson," SABR BioProject, Retrieved from sabr.org/bioproj/person/1bb26f23.

4   Forbes Field had a seating capacity of 33,730 in 1952.

5   Jack Hernon, "Bucs Chase Sal Maglie, Beat Giants, 8-1: Long Hoodoo Ends as Dickson Stars," *Pittsburgh Post-Gazette*, June 7, 1952: 12.

6   Jack Hernon.

7   The fences in left field were shortened by the Pirates for Hank Greenberg when he joined the Pirates in 1947 and the space beyond the left-field wall became known as Greenberg Gardens.

8   Lester Biederman, "At Last! Pirates Beat Sal Maglie: 'Barber' Loses First to Bucs Since 1945 as Giants Bow, 8-1," *Pittsburgh Press*, June 7, 1952: 6.

9   Jack Hernon.

10   Ibid.

11   Ibid.

12   Maglie continued his mastery of the Pirates throughout his career. In 38 games against the Pirates, "The Barber" was 25-6 with a 2.29 ERA. His 25 victories against the Pirates were the most wins he had against any opponent.

VERN LAW CELEBRATES RETURN FROM MILITARY SERVICE WITH OPENING DAY WIN

APRIL 13, 1954: PITTSBURGH PIRATES 4, PHILADELPHIA PHILLIES 2, AT FORBES FIELD

BY GORDON J. GATTIE

THE PITTSBURGH PIRATES WERE eager to open the 1954 season following a disastrous 1953. That year the Pirates went 50-104, finishing 55 games behind the league-leading Brooklyn Dodgers. On the "brighter" side, their record was an improvement over the 42-112 record of 1952. Throughout the mid-1950s, the Pirates frequently joined the Chicago Cubs in the National League's second division, well behind the pennant winners. The 1953 Pirates struggled offensively, finishing last in the NL in team runs, home runs, and OPS, and in pitching, finishing last in team ERA and next to last in strikeouts and walks issued. The '53 Pirates' pitching staff included only one pitcher whose ERA fell below 4.00 — Johnny Hetki, a reliever with a 3.95 ERA in 118⅓ innings.

Branch Rickey, now in his fifth year as general manager, was optimistic while acknowledging shortcomings. "Right now we're strong in catching and at first base. We're not so strong in pitching, infield and outfield but we will be."[1] Thirty-two rookies and two returning servicemen, pitcher Vernon "Deacon" Law and first baseman Dale Coogan, reported to spring-training camp in late February 1954.[2] Law was returning from US Army service, having enlisted after the 1951 season.[3] Pittsburgh scout Rex Bowen was pleased with Law's work as he commented, "I don't believe the boy has any traces of the sore arm which cut down his effectiveness,"[4] referring to an injury Law sustained while pitching in the Army. Law was rated a sure bet to stay with the staff;[5] he pitched with Pittsburgh for two years before his military service, compiling a 13-18 record and 4.72 ERA over 242 innings as a swingman, including 31 starts.

The Opening Day opponent on April 13 was the cross-state rival Phillies, who went 83-71 in 1953, tied with the St. Louis Cardinals for third place, 22 games behind Brooklyn. Philadelphia was led by pitching ace Robin Roberts, outfielders Richie Ashburn and Del Ennis, and second baseman Granny Hamner. All four reached the top 25 in MVP voting, with Roberts finishing sixth and earning a first-place vote. The Phillies experienced a resurgence during the early 1950s, finishing above .500 four times between 1949 and 1953 and making a World Series appearance in 1950. Philadelphia was harmed less than Pittsburgh by losing players to the military; only Paul Penson, a 22-year-old pitcher without Organized Baseball experience, had spent 1953 in the service, while the Pirates were still without Dick Groat, Tony Bartirome, and Johnny and Eddie O'Brien, all regular position players.[6]

Pittsburgh enjoyed Opening Day 1954 at home for the first time in 61 years. Prior to 1954, the last time the Pirates opened on home turf was in 1893, when they dropped a 7-2 decision to the Cleveland Spiders. Although Wagner couldn't attend because of health concerns, Mayor David L. Lawrence presented Wagner's daughter, Mrs. Harry Blair, with a plaque honoring his loyalty, high character, and playing skill.[7]Right-hander Bob Friend received the Opening Day nod from manager Fred Haney. During the spring, Haney was pleased with his top six pitchers: Friend, Law, Max Surkont, Bob Hall, Cal Hogue, and Hetki.[8] Friend was still learning his craft, going 8-11 with a 4.90 ERA in 170⅔ innings during 1953. He was dependable during his first three years, averaging 168 innings per season while steadily improving his control. Friend started his career with a sinking fastball and hard curve, and had completely reworked his unorthodox delivery with Haney's arrival.[9] Future Hall of Famer Robin Roberts was among the best pitchers in the NL during the 1950s, earning an All-Star selection while winning at least 20 games and pitching over 300 innings during each of the previous four seasons. In 1953, the right-handed Roberts went 23-16 with a 2.75 ERA, striking out a career-high 198 hitters and issuing 61 walks, amassing major-league highs in games started (41), complete games (33), and innings pitched (346⅔), and strikeouts. Coincidentally, Roberts opposed Law during Law's major-league debut on June 11, 1950.[10]

The Phillies' Ted Kazanski started the game by grounding out to the shortstop. Ashburn also grounded out and Earl Torgeson flied out. The Pirates' Cal Abrams lined out to center field to lead off the bottom of the first, and Curt Roberts, making his major-league debut as the Pirates' first African-American player, followed with the game's first hit, a triple to right field. Both Hal Rice and Sid Gordon popped out, stranding Roberts on third base. During the second inning, the Phillies loaded the bases on a walk, single, bunt groundout, and intentional walk, but Friend then struck out Stan Lopata and Roberts. Robin Roberts set down the Pirates in order in the bottom of the second, and Friend echoed his opponent's inning by inducing three consecutive groundouts in the Philadelphia third. Toby Atwell started the Pittsburgh half with a single to center field, but a pair of groundouts and a flyout kept the Pirates at bay. Neither team threatened to score during the fourth.

Willie Jones started the top of the fifth inning with a single to left, and Lopata followed with an infield single. Friend walked Roberts to load the bases. Kazanski grounded into a fielder's choice, with third baseman Gordon forcing Jones out at home. With the bases still loaded, Ashburn grounded into a fielder's choice, but with the force out occurring at second base, as Lopata scored the game's first run. Roberts advanced to third, and scored when Friend balked. Torgeson flied out to center, ending

the inning. Philadelphia led 2-0. Roberts continued pitching effectively, allowing a leadoff single but striking out Gair Allie and making Atwell hit into an inning-ending 4-6-3 double play.

Friend continued struggling into the sixth. Ennis flied out to left field, and then Hamner singled to left. After Johnny Wyrostek grounded out to first, Jones walked and Lopata reached first on an infield single, the third time Philadelphia loaded the bases. However, Roberts grounded out to second base for the third out. Pittsburgh's leadoff hitter in the sixth was pinch-hitter Gail Henley; Friend's day was complete with two runs allowed on six hits and four walks in six innings. Roberts continued blanking the Pirates, allowing a lone walk during the sixth.

Vern Law took over in the top of the seventh, hitting ninth. After not pitching in the major leagues for two years, Law set down the Phillies in order: Kazanski grounded out to third, Ashburn flied out to center, and Torgeson grounded out to first. Roberts continued frustrating the Pirates, equaling Law's effectiveness. Through seven innings, Roberts looked unstoppable, allowing only three hits and one walk.

Vernon Law

Law delivered another hitless inning with a fly out and two infield groundouts in the eighth.

Roberts walked Allie to start the Pittsburgh eighth inning, and Atwell followed with a single to right. Down two runs with runners on first and second, manager Haney pulled Law for pinch-hitter Eddie Pellagrini, who sacrificed to advance the runners. Abrams finally broke though the Philadelphia defense when Phillies left fielder Ennis lost Abrams' fly ball in the sun, resulting in a single that scored Allie.[11] Making his major-league debut, pinch-hitter Bob Skinner singled Atwell home to tie the score. Philadelphia manager Steve O'Neill summoned right-hander Jim Konstanty to relieve Roberts. Konstanty promptly surrendered a double to Hal Rice, an intentional walk to Gordon, and a sacrifice fly to Frank Thomas, giving Pittsburgh a 4-2 lead. Right-handed reliever Johnny Hetki pitched a scoreless ninth as the Pirates triumphed in Law's return and turned seemingly dismal defeat into victory.[12] Although Roberts delivered seven scoreless innings, the Pirates' four-run eighth-inning outburst saddled him with his third consecutive Opening Day loss.[13]

Pittsburgh finished the 1954 season with a 53-101 record, 44 games behind the first-place New York Giants. The team would continue struggling until the late 1950s. Law was 9-13 in 1954 with a 5.51 ERA in 161⅔ innings. He played a pivotal role in the Bucs' 1960 World Series victory, and would remain with the team until he retired in 1967.[14]

SOURCES

Besides the sources cited in the Notes, the author consulted Baseball-Almanac.com, Baseball-Reference.com, Retrosheet.org, and the following:

James, Bill. *The New Bill James Historical Abstract* (New York: The Free Press, 2001).

Thorn, John, and Pete Palmer, et al. *Total Baseball: The Official Encyclopedia of Major League Baseball* (New York: Viking Press, 2004).

NOTES

1   Lester J. Biederman, "Rickey Calls '54 Pirates Strongest He's Had," *Pittsburgh Press*, February 16, 1954: 24.

2   International News Service, "Size of Rookies Is Impressive in Buccaneer Camp," *Corsicana* (Texas) *Daily Sun*, February 24, 1954: 6.

3   C. Paul Rogers III, "Vern Law," SABR Biography Project, sabr. org/bioproj/person/9266780c#sdendnote20sym.

4   Jack Hernon, "Scout Bowen Pleased With Law's Mound Work," *Pittsburgh Post-Gazette*, February 25, 1954: 17.

5   Jack Hand (Associated Press), "Former GI's Rate Plenty of Attention," *Ogden* (Utah) *Standard Examiner*, March 21, 1954: 9.

6   Carl Lundquist, "Ex GIs Could Scramble Major Races," *The Sporting News*, April 7, 1954: 1.

7   Jack Hernon, "First Opener in Pitt in 61 Years Dedicated to Wagner," *The Sporting News*, April 21, 1954: 21.

8   Jack Hernon, "Hurlers Help Hitters Widen Haney's Grin," *The Sporting News*, March 31, 1954: 9.

9   Bill James and Rob Neyer, *The Neyer/James Guide to Pitchers* (New York: Fireside Books, 2004), 212.

10   C. Paul Rogers III, "Vern Law," SABR Biography Project.

11   "Games of Tuesday, April 13," *The Sporting News*, April 21, 1954: 21.

12   Al Abrams, "32,294 See 'New Look' Pirates Win," *Pittsburgh Post-Gazette*, April 14, 1954: 1-2.

13   "Games of Tuesday, April 13."

14   Les Biederman, "A Sad Moment for the Buccos — Vern Law Hangs Up His Spikes," *The Sporting News*, September 16, 1967: 30.

PIONEERING ROOKIE CURT ROBERTS COLLECTS THREE HITS, CONTINUES STEADY DEFENSE

MAY 16, 1954: CHICAGO CUBS 12, PITTSBURGH PIRATES 3 (FIRST GAME), AT FORBES FIELD

BY JACK ZERBY

BRANCH RICKEY, WHO HAD SHAKEN the foundations of Organized Baseball in 1947 when he orchestrated Jackie Robinson's integration of the sport with the Brooklyn Dodgers, was still innovating seven years later. He had left as Brooklyn's general manager to take over the same spot with the Pittsburgh Pirates in 1950. Before the 1952 season he purchased the contract of a promising 22-year-old African-American infielder, Curt Roberts, for the Pirates' Denver Bears affiliate in the Class-A Western League, allowed Roberts two more years of seasoning at Denver, then promoted him to the Pittsburgh spring-training roster for 1954. Rickey saw to it that manager Fred Haney gave Roberts ample work at second base that spring—Johnny O'Brien, the Bucs' primary second baseman in 1953, had been drafted into military service the prior September.[1]

Coming off a 50-104 season that had left them solidly in the National League cellar,[2] the 1954 Pirates had plenty of open spots.[3] Roberts brushed off competition from fellow rookie George Freese[4] and was Pittsburgh's Opening Day second baseman against the Philadelphia Phillies on April 13 at Forbes Field.[5]

Roberts, who had debuted in professional baseball as a 17-year-old with the Kansas City Monarchs in the Negro American League, "became the Pirates' first African American player. In the bottom of the first he batted second. Just as had Jackie Robinson, this retracing the historic steps more faithfully than anyone else who had come in-between."[6] This, because Rickey had "singled out Roberts for the identical set of qualities: tolerant attitude, competitive demeanor, admirable baseball skills" that he had used to select Robinson seven years earlier.[7]

As to Roberts' arrival, "It was a big deal," according to Bill Nunn, sports editor of the African-American *Pittsburgh Courier* in 1954, and Roberts's neighbor in the Schenley Heights section of the city. "But quite a few [black] guys had come into the major leagues, and Curt was an average ballplayer. Under the circumstances, he really didn't get the [attention] some of the other guys did." Still, according to the 1997 profile of Roberts in which Nunn is quoted, "like most of the others, Roberts was a target for racists, some of them at Forbes Field. He and his wife were briefed on what to expect by Rickey, who talked to the couple before spring training in 1954 much the way he had with Robinson seven years earlier."[8]

The slightly-built (5-feet-8, 165 pounds), right-handed, sometimes bespectacled Roberts got his career off to a fine start, touching perennial National League All-Star Robin Roberts for a triple in his first at-bat in the April 13 opener. Through May 15, Curt Roberts had played all but one inning of Pittsburgh's 28 games at second base, was hitting a decent .230, and had been charged with only three errors.

By then, though, the Pirates were predictably back in last place in the National League at 9-19. They stood 3½ games behind the seventh-place Cubs as new Chicago manager Stan Hack brought his club to Forbes Field for a three-game series starting with a Sunday doubleheader on May 16.

The Pirates had beaten Milwaukee behind Vern Law the day before and manager Haney hoped to keep things going with right-hander Bob Friend on the mound in the first game. At 23, Friend had yet to blossom into the ace he would ultimately become, but he had had a good spring and had gotten the call as Pittsburgh's Opening Day starter. In four starts, though, he had struggled to a 1-2 record and 6.75 ERA. This Sunday afternoon, in front of a crowd of 14,369,[9] he cruised through the first two innings. Cubs starter Paul Minner, a 6-foot-5 lefty from New Wilmington, Pennsylvania, 60 miles northwest of Pittsburgh, did the same. Roberts, again hitting number 2 in the order after also having been used in the leadoff and seventh slots, quickly took away Minner's no-hitter chances in the first inning with a single; Minner summarily erased him on Dick Cole'sdouble-play groundball.

Friend slipped in the Cubs' third inning. With one out, former Pirate Joe Garagiola, who had gone to Chicago with Ralph Kiner in the 1953 trade that included George Freese,[10] singled, moved to second as Minner made an infield out, then scored on Frank Baumholtz's single. The next batter, Dee Fondy, homered. Chicago led, 3-0.

Curt Roberts

Pittsburgh got one of those runs back in its half of the fourth. Roberts tripled, his third of the season, then scored on Frank Thomas's single. Maintaining their three-run lead, the Cubs answered with another run in the fifth on Garagiola's double, a single by Minner that moved the broadcaster-to-be to third, and another RBI single by Baumholtz to make it 4-1 Chicago.

The Pirates kept it competitive at 4-2 with a run in their fifth. Bob Skinner laced a leadoff triple and came home on Dick Hall's sacrifice fly to left field. Friend tried to keep things going with a single, but Minner retired Cal Abrams and Roberts to end the mild threat.

But Friend yielded a double to Ransom Jackson and singles to Kiner and Ernie Banks that produced a run to open the Chicago sixth inning and make it 5-2 before Haney replaced him withLen Yochim. Yochim allowed a bunt single to Garagiola that loaded the bases; Minner then drove home two runs with a double. After Yochim finally managed the first two outs of the inning, Gene Baker compounded the damage with another two-run single. Batting around, the Cubs plated five on six hits to take a 9-2 lead. They increased it to 10-2 in the seventh when Kiner walked, Garagiola singled, and Minner, who had to be immensely enjoying this day back in western Pennsylvania, nailed another double off Yochim to score Kiner.[11]

Roberts's third hit of the day, "a blooper back of second,"[12] drove in the Pirates' third run in their half of the seventh. That was it for the Pittsburgh offense.

Thirty-six-year-old Joe Page, signed by the Pirates in 1954 after a distinguished relief career with the New York Yankees that ended with a sore arm after the 1950 season, took over on the mound in the eighth. The lefty navigated that inning without damage, but the Cubs nicked him for two more runs in the ninth on a home run by Banks after Kiner's double. Garagiola, who was 5-for-5 in the game,[13] picked up another single, but Page retired the pesky Minner; the lefty then returned to the mound and retired the Pirates in order in the bottom of the inning to close out a tidy 12-3, complete-game win.

Roberts had done his part despite the shaky Pirate pitching. He chipped in three of Pittsburgh's 10 hits, scored a run, and drove in another. The three-hit game marked the first of three times Roberts managed the feat in the majors and lifted his season batting average from .230 to .246. He handled four defensive chances successfully.

And although 1954 was Roberts's only full season in the majors—Johnny O'Brien was back from the military in 1955 and Roberts played in only 37 more games as a Pirate before being bumped by 19-year-old Bill Mazeroski and traded to the Kansas City Athletics in June of 1956[14] -- Roberts' brief but pioneering time with Pittsburgh had "humanized the ongoing integration of baseball by thrashing the perception that African-Americans had to be superstars to find a place in a big-league world of white bench players."[15]

Acknowledgments

The deduced games initiative Dave Smith is leading at Retrosheet.org provided a helpful play-by-play of this game, done by Richard Weston.

SOURCES

In addition to the Sources cited in the Notes, I used the Baseball-Reference.com website for player and team pages and game logs. I used the box score for this game, Curt Roberts's and other player pages, and, as noted, the deduced play-by-play of this game at the Retrosheet.org website. I accessed articles from *The Sporting News* through PaperOfRecord.com. Other cited newspaper articles are from the digital archives of Newspapers.com.

NOTES

1 Johnny O'Brien's twin brother, Eddie, who had been Pittsburgh's primary shortstop in 1953, was drafted at the same time. *The Sporting News*, January 13, 1954: 17.

2 The 1953 Pirates finished 55 games behind pennant-winning Brooklyn and 15 games behind the seventh-place Chicago Cubs.

3 See: Jack Hernon, "Only Two Bucs Jobs Filled," *The Sporting News*, March 3, 1954: 16.

4 The Pirates had acquired George Freese, who had one at-bat of major-league experience with the Detroit Tigers, in a multiplayer June 1953 trade with the Chicago Cubs which sent Ralph Kiner to Chicago. Freese was assigned to Pittsburgh's

Double-A farm club in New Orleans out of 1954 spring training and didn't play for the Pirates at the major-league level until 1955.

5 Tom Alston debuted the same day (April 13, 1954) as the St. Louis Cardinals' first African-American player.

6 Tom Singer, "Curt Roberts Broke Pittsburgh Pirates' Color Line Admirably," MLB.com, February 2, 2012, Black History Month feature, accessed September 13, 2017.

7 Ibid. Curt Roberts is generally recognized as breaking the color line for the Pittsburgh franchise. It should be noted, however, that in 1953, Carlos Bernier, a Puerto Rican, was arguably the team's first black player. Bernier had 366 plate appearances in 105 games as a Pittsburgh outfielder in 1953, his only year in the majors. But Bernier "was competitive and aggressive on the ballfield, and some have speculated that this led to his having a long minor league career with only the one opportunity at the major-league level." "Carlos Bernier," Baseball-Reference.com Bullpen, accessed September 13, 2017. Presumably Bernier was not the player Branch Rickey, who added Roberts to the Pittsburgh roster after the 1953 season, wanted as a standard-bearer. See also: SABR member Joe Guzzardi's "Carlos Bernier, More Than a Footnote: Major League Baseball Doesn't Agree, but Carlos Bernier Was the Pirates' First Black Player, Argues Baseball Historian," *Pittsburgh Post-Gazette*, April 14, 2013: F-1, and Charles F. Faber, "Carlos Bernier," *Puerto Rico and Baseball: 60 Biographies* (Phoenix: Society for American Baseball Research, 2017), 46-51, where Faber states on page 48: "Pittsburgh promoted Bernier to the majors in 1953. He became the first black player to join the Pirates," and recognizes Curt Roberts only parenthetically.

8 Ed Bouchette, "'Little Man' Took Big Step," *Pittsburgh Post-Gazette*, May 15, 1997: 10.

9 This attendance figure is reported in the Retrosheet.org box score. The box score for this game in the *Pittsburgh Post-Gazette* (May 17, 1954: 22) reports attendance of 13,369.

10 See also: Note 4 relative to the trade; Both Kiner and Garagiola, former Pirates, "received a nice welcome by the fans," according to Pirates beat writer Jack Hernon. Jack Hernon, "Bunts and Base Hits," *Pittsburgh Post-Gazette*, May 17, 1954: 22.

11 After this game Minner was hitting a heady .313 for the 1954 season. He cooled off to .171 by the end of the year, but hit .219 over his 10-year career, with 6 home runs and 43 runs batted in.

12 *Pittsburgh Post-Gazette*, May 17, 1954: 22.

13 Over his major-league career, which began in 1946 and ended with this 1954 season, Garagiola had twice before collected four hits in a game. This was his only five-hit game.

14 The A's assigned Roberts to Triple-A Columbus in the International League. Before the 1957 season they transferred his contract to the New York Yankees as a "player to be named later." He stayed at the Triple-A level with the Yankees and Dodgers organizations through 1962, then retired at age 33 after

spending the 1963 season with the White Sox' Lynchburg club in the South Atlantic League (then Double-A).

15   Singer, mlb.com, February 2, 2012.

BOB FRIEND CLINCHES NL ERA TITLE DESPITE PITCHING FOR LAST-PLACE PIRATES

SEPTEMBER 24, 1955: PITTSBURGH PIRATES 6, BROOKLYN DODGERS 1 (SECOND GAME OF DOUBLEHEADER), AT FORBES FIELD

BY GORDON J. GATTIE

THE PITTSBURGH PIRATES SUFFERED through a miserable 1955 season, and entered the final weekend hosting the NL-leading Brooklyn Dodgers. Back in April, Pittsburgh GM Branch Rickey was optimistic heading into the season opener, citing outfield and pitching improvements, with third base as his major concern: "This 1955 club will be the best Pittsburgh has had in many years. The Pirates will be a happy surprise to our people sooner or later."[1] Fred Haney, Pittsburgh's manager, cautiously noted, "I won't hazard a guess as to where this year's Pirates will finish in the National League for the simple reason that I don't know how much the other seven clubs have improved." He also optimistically commented on his pitching staff, "Pitching wise we have a championship staff in the making."[2] Pittsburgh's season opened with a 6-1 loss to Brooklyn at Ebbets Field. Although Pirates starter Max Surkont started with five scoreless innings, he allowed a sixth-inning run before the Dodgers erupted for five runs in the seventh inning. The Dodgers' Carl Erskine pitched a complete game, allowing one run on seven hits in front of 6,999 fans on a cold and rainy afternoon.[3]

The season opener established the season's tone; Pittsburgh finished April with a 3-11 record. The Pirates pieced together a six-game winning streak from the second game of a May 1 doubleheader through May 6, but an 11-game losing streak from May 11 through 22 erased those gains. After the second game on May 22, the Pirates were only one game away from tying their modern-day record of 12 consecutive losses, established in 1939.[4] During their losing streak, they fell to last place and remained

there all season. The team struggled with losing records in June and July, but played above .500 baseball in August, managing a 14-12 record for the month. However, the Pirates' offensive production and defensive efficiency lagged throughout the season.

Conversely, the Brooklyn Dodgers were a strong and balanced team, led by future Hall of Famers Duke Snider and Roy Campanella with All-Stars Don Newcombe and Gil Hodges. The Dodgers won at least 90 games for the fourth straight season in 1954; during those years, they lost two World Series to the New York Yankees and narrowly lost the NL pennant to the New York Giants in the other two seasons. The Dodgers were eager to begin the 1955 season by atoning for two late-September losses against Pittsburgh the previous year which helped the Giants take the pennant.[5] Expectations were high among baseball insiders that the NL pennant would be a Dodgers-Giants battle once again in 1955. The Dodgers gained sole possession of first place on April 16 and never looked back; the Giants made an early-season push but ultimately finished third.

The Pirates won the September 24 twi-night doubleheader opener from Brooklyn, 4-3, when Gene Freese homered off reliever Don Bessent in the eighth inning. Pittsburgh led early after Dale Long delivered a three-run blast in the first inning, but the Dodgers rallied with two runs in the fifth and the tying run an inning later. Dick Hall pitched the complete game for his sixth win of the season.

Bob Friend took the mound for his 20th start, and 44th overall appearance, for the nightcap. The 24-year-old Friend was enjoying his breakout year, reaching double digits in wins, and had already established career highs in innings pitched and strikeouts. During the previous offseason, Friend altered his windup to deliver a more effective curveball, and his results improved.[6] Frequently used as a swingman, he started four times in his six September appearances and was riding a four-game winning streak. Friend's batterymate that evening was Jerry Lynch, who was catching for the second time as a major leaguer since Rickey started converting him from an outfielder into a catcher; his first appearance came in the opener of the doubleheader.[7]

Dodgers manager Walter Alston named right-hander Billy Loes as his starter. Loes was starting his 19th game of the season, on eight days' rest. A five-year veteran, the 25-year-old Loes had pitched at least 120 innings with 10 wins for the fourth straight season in 1955. He defeated the Pirates twice that season, giving up one run over seven innings on July 3 and going the distance on July 7. During the latter win, Loes struck out rookie Roberto Clemente with the tying run on third base to end the game.[8] However, Loes and Dodgers pitchers Karl Spooner,

Bob Friend

Johnny Podres, and Erskine were dealing with various arm injuries during the season's second half.[9]

Brooklyn's Jim Gilliam led off the game by grounding out to short. Sandy Amoros singled, and Snider followed with another single, advancing Amoros to third. Cleanup hitter George Shuba grounded out to first, and Amoros crossed the plate for the game's first run while Snider moved to second base. Hodges then grounded out to shortstop, ending the threat. In the bottom of the first, the ball didn't leave the infield as Pittsburgh batters grounded out twice and struck out looking. In the second inning, Brooklyn's Rube Walker singled to right field, but was removed on a subsequent double play. Don Zimmer singled, but Loes struck out to end the inning. In Pittsburgh's half, Long, who returned to the majors following a three-year absence, looked at strike three for the first out. After John Powers walked, both Frank Thomas and Johnny O'Brien flied out. In the third inning, Brooklyn managed a lone walk among three infield groundouts, while Pittsburgh was sent down in order.

Hodges singled to start the fourth, but Walker hit into a 1-6-3 double play. Don Hoak struck out, and Friend managed to quell any potential threats. Before the Pittsburgh half started, rookie Sandy Koufax replaced Loes, who had allowed only one hit through three innings. Koufax walked Freese and Lynch, the first two batters he faced. Long grounded out to Koufax, with both runners advancing a base. Clemente pinch-hit for Powers, and reached on a Hodges error as Freese scored and Lynch moved to third. With Thomas hitting next, Lynch scored on a wild pitvh by Koufax. After Koufax's third walk, Alston summoned reliever Ed Roebuck from the bullpen. Roebuck induced two groundouts and prevented further damage. Over the next two innings, the Dodgers threatened with runners on first and second, but couldn't push a run across. In the Pittsburgh fifth, Roebuck allowed a lone baserunner via walk who was stranded at second base.

With the Pirates maintaining a 2-1 advantage, Long began the sixth by tripling to center field. After Clemente popflied out to second, Thomas singled Long home and O'Brien followed suit by tripling

Thomas home for a pair of insurance runs, increasing Pittsburgh's lead to 4-1. Friend induced three infield groundouts in the Brooklyn seventh, including one by Pee Wee Reese, who pinch hit for Roebuck. In the bottom of the frame, new reliever Clem Labine allowed an O'Brien leadoff infield single and walked Freese. Lynch hit into a fielder's choice, advancing O'Brien to third. The right-handed Labine issued Brooklyn's sixth walk, which loaded the bases. Clemente also hit into a fielder's choice, and O'Brien scored; a throwing error by shortstop Zimmer resulted in Lynch scoring. Thomas grounded out to third, ending the frame with Pittsburgh leading 6-1.

Friend continued his strong performance, striking out two hitters and prompting a fly out in the eighth. Labine matched Friend by setting down the side on two groundouts and a line out. In the ninth, Walker reached first on a throwing error by O'Brien to start the inning. Hoak flied out to right, Zimmer flied out to center, then Friend caught Campanella looking to end the game and earn the complete-game victory.

Friend completed the season with a 14-9 record and 2.83 ERA over 200⅓ innings, winning the NL ERA title. He topped 200 innings for the first time, a milestone he reached for the next 10 seasons. The Cy Young Award was instituted the following year; however, Friend did finish with 6.0 Wins Above Replacement, also first in the NL that season. Friend's ERA achievement was especially noteworthy; he was the first pitcher since official ERA statistics were reported in 1912 to have the league's lowest ERA while pitching for a last-place team.[10] He also led Pittsburgh in wins, appearances (44), and strikeouts (98). Pittsburgh finished with a 60-94 record, 38½ games behind the Dodgers. The Pirates struggled all season with their offense, and their bench players didn't provide much support, as evidenced by their collective .217 batting average covering 20 players.[11] An early offseason report noted that Pittsburgh's only trade bait was in its pitching, some of whom should be traded for outfielders with power and additional catching.[12] Manager Fred Haney was fired after the season, and Branch Rickey retired in October.[13] Meanwhile, the Dodgers captivated the baseball world when they won their only World Series while based in Brooklyn by defeating the Yankees in seven games.

SOURCES

Besides the sources cited in the Notes, the author consulted Baseball-Almanac.com, Baseball-Reference.com, Retrosheet.org, and the following:

Bob Friend on SABR Bioproject: sabr.org/bioproj/person/c9od66d9.

O'Brien, Jim. *We Had 'Em All The Way: Bob Prince and His Pittsburgh Pirates* (Pittsburgh: Jim O'Brien Publishing, 1998).

Golenbock, Peter. *Bums: An Oral History of the Brooklyn Dodgers* (New York: Putnam Books, 1984).

NOTES

1   Branch Rickey, "Bucs Best in Years — Rickey," *Pittsburgh Post-Gazette*, April 14, 1955: 14.

2   Fred Haney, "Bucs Improved; How About Rivals? — Haney," *Pittsburgh Post-Gazette*, April 14, 1955: 16.

3   Jack Hernon, "Pirates Off and Losing as Dodgers Win, 6-1," *Pittsburgh Post-Gazette*, April 14, 1955: 20.

4   Jack Hernon, "Buc Streak Soars to 11 as They Lose 5-2, 5-3," *Pittsburgh Post-Gazette*, April 23, 1955: 18.

5   Owen Fitzgerald and Sid Frigant, "Giants Crush Flock in Flag-Clincher, 7-1," *Brooklyn Daily Eagle*, September 21, 1954: 1.

6   Rick Cushing, *1960 Pittsburgh Pirates: Day by Day: A Special Season, An Extraordinary World Series* (Pittsburgh: Dorrance Publishing, 2010), 363.

7   Jack Hernon, "Lynch Slated to Catch Against Bums Tonight," *Pittsburgh Post-Gazette*, September 24, 1955: 12.

8   Jack Hernon, "Buc Rally in 9th Fails as Dodgers Win, 4-3," *Pittsburgh Post-Gazette*, July 8, 1955: 18.

9   Roscoe McGowen, "Sore Arms Forced Use of Hurlers From Farms," *The Sporting News*, September 28, 1955: 9.

10   Jack Hernon, "Buccos' Friend First ERA King on Cellar Team," *The Sporting News*, October 5, 1955: 9.

11   Jack Hernon, "Bucs Pinched for Punching Sub Swingers," *The Sporting News*, October 12, 1955: 10.

12   "Major Needs for '56 in a Nutshell," *The Sporting News*, September 28, 1955: 6.

13   Jack Hernon, "Buc Pilot Haney Fired by Rickey," *Pittsburgh Post-Gazette*, September 26, 1955: 1; Jack Hernon, "New Pirate GM Talks About Plans," *Pittsburgh Post-Gazette*, October 26, 1955: 1; Jack Hernon, "Brown 'On Own' as Pirates New G.M.," *The Sporting News*, November 2, 1955: 5.

CLEMENTE GRAND SLAMS AND RUNS TO PIRATES' VICTORY

JULY 25, 1956: PITTSBURGH PIRATES 9, CHICAGO CUBS 8, AT FORBES FIELD

BY STEVEN C. WEINER

THE HEADLINE WRITER FOR THE front page of a daily newspaper is challenged to provide the reader with glimpses of tragedy and joy, victory and defeat, worry and elation, all appropriately befitting the day's news. When Pittsburgh awoke on the morning of July 26, 1956, the headline spread across the front page of the *Pittsburgh Post-Gazette* was "Luxury Liners Collide, 1,100 Abandoning Andrea Doria."[1]

Just before midnight, the Swedish ship *MS Stockholm* struck the Italian ocean liner *SS Andrea Doria* in dense fog off Nantucket Island. The *Andrea Doria* was severely damaged and badly listing before finally capsizing in the morning. The heroic efforts of rescuers saved 1,660 people but tragically, 51 others lost their lives.[2] No doubt the headline, the photo of the *Andrea Doria* and that first two-column story captured the tragedy and the actions taken in response during the early-morning hours.

For the sports fan, the smaller-print box in the middle of the front page, "Clemente Again, Pirates Win in Merriwell Finish, 9-8,"[3] provided that first glimpse of a unique baseball feat never seen before and never repeated as of the 2017 season. The 20-year-old Roberto Clemente brought his exciting style to Pittsburgh in his 1955 rookie season and earned a spot in the Pirates outfield. On this night, he clouted an inside-the-park grand slam off Cubs relief pitcher Jim Brosnan to end the game in a victory for the Pirates, right then and there.

Clemente was a free swinger, an impatient hitter who swung at almost any pitch including those outside the strike zone.[4] He became known as a primary example of a good "bad-ball hitter."[5] Playing for the Triple-A Montreal Royals in 1954, Jack Cassini was

Clemente's teammate. In Stew Thornley's interview for SABR's Clemente biography, Cassini said, "He could hit. He didn't need a strike. The best way to pitch him was right down the middle of the plate."[6] In fact, Clemente walked only 13 times in 572 plate appearances in 1956. In one stretch that season, covering 192 plate appearances, he went 50 games without walking.[7]

For a game pitting two teams that would finish the season last and next-to-last in the National League, respectively, the Pirates started their All-Star pitcher, Bob Friend (12-8, 3.24 ERA), and the Cubs countered with Warren Hacker (2-8, 5.37).

The Pirates started the scoring in the fourth inning when Clemente reached on an infield single and Dale Long hit his 20th home run of the season for a 2-0 lead. That home run set a record for Pittsburgh left-handed hitters, previously held by Hall of Fame shortstop Arky Vaughan, who hit 19 in 1935.[8] The Pirates scored their third run in the fifth inning. After Friend singled and Bill Virdon doubled, Bob Skinner was intentionally walked to load the bases for Clemente. No grand slam this time, just a sacrifice fly to center for a 3-0 lead. In the sixth inning, consecutive doubles by Frank Thomas and Jack Shepard added another run and Warren Hacker's pitching outing was over for the night when he was replaced by Vito Valentinetti.

Meanwhile, Bob Friend was sailing along into the eighth inning on a 4-0 four-hitter, but four singles that produced one run ended his evening. Roy Face, by now being used almost exclusively in relief, came in to pitch and was summarily hammered with doubles by Walt Moryn, Eddie Miksis, and Hobie Landrith each of whom knocked in two runs for a 7-4 Cubs lead. Each team scored once in its next at-bat for an 8-5 Cubs lead. In the case of the Cubs, they scored on three singles against Face after two were out. Nellie King replaced him and ended the top of the ninth inning by striking out Miksis on three pitches.[9] The stage was now set for the dramatic bottom of the ninth inning and the improbable feat about to unfold.

With Turk Lown pitching for the Cubs, a walk to Hank Foiles, a single by Bill Virdon, and another walk to Dick Cole loaded the bases for Clemente. Jim Brosnan relieved Lown and threw one pitch, described by Jack Hernon as "high and inside."[10] There was no doubt that Clemente would swing. He hit the ball over Jim King's head in left field and after the ball struck the fencing, it rolled along the cinder warning track toward center field. The three runners easily scored and Clemente ignored the outstretched arms and stop sign of Pirates manager and third-base coach Bobby Bragan as the relay throw came in from center fielder Solly Drake to Ernie Banks to catcher Hobie Landrith. The last moments of the improbable were captured in the *Pittsburgh Post-Gazette*: "He slid, missed the plate, then reached back to rest his hand on the rubber with the ninth Pirate run in a 9-8 victory as the crowd of 12,431 went goofy with excitement"[11]

Would Clemente be fined for roaring right past Bragan? The circumstances were ripe. After the game, Bragan's comments reflected conventional baseball strategy, "Clemente tied up the game, for sure and I threw up the stop sign. ... After all, we had some long-ball hitters coming up, no one out and getting Bobby home with the winning run looked easy."[12] Clemente readily admitted his deliberate action to ignore the stop sign.

Bragan was in his first year as Pirates manager, desperately trying to improve their lot after four consecutive years in the eight-team National League's cellar.[13] Bragan's penchant for fining players started early in the season. After a loss to the New York Giants in the second game of the season, he fined Clemente $25 for missing a squeeze-play sign and Dale Long the same amount for using bad judgment

in cutting off a relay from the outfield.[14] As Bragan put it, "A manager can get into serious trouble by letting the little things go unnoticed. They soon grow into big things, so let's put a stop to the little things now."[15]

A *Sports Illustrated* feature story by Robert Creamer also explained the rationale for those minor infractions—$5 for reporting late to the park, $10 for failing to throw a pitchout when it was called for, $20 for failing to slide into second base in a crucial moment. "The fines aren't much, but they sting a man's pride. And they help spread Bragan's basic idea that this club is too good to condone carelessness; carelessness is for eighth-place clubs."[16]

Clemente's heroics and the Pirates' victory maintained their position in fifth place. We can only speculate as to the mood of Bobby Bragan after the game. Clemente was not fined.

It would be 32 years before the term "walk-off" entered the baseball lexicon. As noted by Paul Dickson, "The term was coined by Oakland Athletics pitcher Dennis Eckersley for that lonely stroll from the mound after a pitcher gives up the winning run

Roberto Clemente

(Gannett News Service, July 30, 1988)."[17] Eckersley's use of the term had a rather negative connotation marking the losing pitcher as he leaves the field.[18] Common usage has evolved now to highlight the achievement of the batter and the celebratory mood of the winning team and its fans.

The drama created by the possibility of any walk-off home run and the elation felt when it occurs happens quite often. In fact, it occurred at another game on that very night. The author, attending the game with his father as a young teenager and avid Dodgers fan, saw Duke Snider hit a walk-off home run in Roosevelt Stadium, in Jersey City, New Jersey, as the Brooklyn Dodgers edged the Cincinnati Reds, 2-1.[19] But what happened in Jersey City pales in comparison to what happened in Pittsburgh!

"What Roberto Clemente accomplished in Pittsburgh on July 25, 1956, stupefied the tobacco-spitting baseball lifers all around him precisely because it transcended baseball, entering the realm of pure theater and then myth. Even his defiance of authority that day—running through hapless Bobby Bragan's sign—enhances the quality of the legend."[20]

Improbable as it may be, the uniqueness of Clemente's game-ending home run could be duplicated someday if the right set of circumstances align. Regardless, the inside-the-park walk-off grand slam is safe at home plate thanks to Roberto Clemente. We should celebrate what Clemente accomplished on this night and take the greatest of pleasures in what he brought to baseball in an exciting style we got to enjoy over his entire career.

SOURCES

In addition to the references cited in the Notes, the author also accessed Baseball-Reference.com and Retrosheet.org.

NOTES

1   "Hits Stockholm in Heavy Fog, Italian Ship Listing So Badly She Can't Lower Life Boats; Vessels Racing to Rescue," *Pittsburgh Post-Gazette*, July 26, 1956: 1.

2   Evan Andrews, "The Sinking of Andrea Doria," History.com, July 25, 2016, accessed September 12, 2017, history.com/news/the-sinking-of-andrea-doria.

3   "A Frank Merriwell finish: A dramatic and successful ending to a baseball game in the manner of Burt L. Standish's (pseudonym for Gilbert Patten) fictitious character Frank Merriwell, who triumphed each week in spectacular fashion by performing unmatchable feats of last-minute derring-do. Merriwell's exploits as a scholar sportsman captured the imagination of millions from 1896 to 1914 in *Tip Top Weekly*, a pulp-fiction magazine for boys." Paul Dickson, *The Dickson Baseball Dictionary, 3rd Edition* (New York: W.W. Norton & Company, 2009), 345.

4   Dickson, 347.

5   Dickson, 43.

6   Stew Thornley, "Roberto Clemente," SABR Baseball Biography Project (telephone interview with Jack Cassini, June 20, 2005).

7   Les Biederman, "Clemente in 50 Games Without Walk," *The Sporting News*, August 8, 1956: 18.

8   Jack Hernon, "Bucs Bounce Back After Losing Lead, Rally in 9th After Chicago's 7-Run 8th; Long Sets HR Mark," *Pittsburgh Post-Gazette*, July 26, 1956: 14.

9   After mention of such a performance, this author feels compelled to acknowledge Roy Face's outstanding 16-year career as captured in his SABR biography written by Gary Gillette. In this season alone, Face led the National League with 68 appearances and tied a major-league record by appearing in nine consecutive games September 3-13, 1956.

10   Hernon.

11   Hernon.

12   "Clemente Ignored Stop Sign on Slam, but Escaped Fine," *The Sporting News*, August 8, 1956: 18.

13   The Pittsburgh Pirates finished the 1956 season in seventh place in the National League with a record of 66-88 and only the Chicago Cubs trailed them; they remained a seventh-place team well into the 1957 season when Bragan was replaced by Danny Murtaugh in August.

14   "Bragan Cracks Down Early, Fines Clemente, Long $25," *The Sporting News*, April 25, 1956: 21.

15   Les Biederman, "Bear-Down Bragan Means Business, Buc Fans Learn," *The Sporting News*, May 2, 1956: 7.

16   Robert Creamer, "The Sad Song of Bobby," *Sports Illustrated*, May 6, 1957: 54-58.

17   Dickson, 919.

18   Although unconfirmed by the author, it is quite possible that Dennis Eckersley was referring to the Oakland-Seattle game at the Kingdome on July 29, 1988. Eckersley came into the game in the 10th inning seeking his 31st save of the season with the A's leading 3-2. Instead, Steve Balboni hit a three-run game-winning home run for the Mariners and the walk-off began.

19 Steven C. Weiner, "Dodgers Win on Snider Walk-Off Home Run in Jersey City," SABR Games Project.

20 Martin Espada, "The Greatest Forgotten Home Run of All Time," *The Massachusetts Review*, Volume 56, Number 2, Summer 2015: 249-255.

LUIS ARROYO'S FINAL VICTORY FOR PITTSBURGH

JULY 18, 1957: PITTSBURGH PIRATES 6, CINCINNATI REDS 5, AT FORBES FIELD

BY ROBERT E. BIONAZ

ANYONE OLD ENOUGH TO RECALL the spectacular 1961 major-league baseball season will likely remember Luis Arroyo. During that magical summer, the left-handed Arroyo became an indispensable performer on one of baseball's greatest teams; in 65 relief games he posted a 15-5 record, 2.19 earned-run average, and 29 saves (19 according to the rules in place in 1961). Additionally, he became inextricably linked with New York Yankees great Whitey Ford by saving more than half of Ford's 25 victories that season. To cap off his dream season, Arroyo won Game Three of the 1961 World Series as the Yankees rolled to an easy 4-1 win over the Cincinnati Reds. In an era that did not emphasize relief pitching, Arroyo was ranked sixth in MVP balloting.[21]

Nothing in Arroyo's major-league career offered a preview of his 1961 dominance. After years of pitching in Puerto Rico and the minor leagues, he broke into the majors in 1955 with the St. Louis Cardinals, posting an 11-8 record that year, primarily as a starting pitcher.[22] That season Arroyo got off to a great start; at the All-Star break he was 10-4 with a 2.44 ERA. He made the 1955 National League All-Star Team but did not pitch in the game at Milwaukee's County Stadium, and his second half proved miserable, as he went 1-5 with an ERA of 8.19. In 1956, after an ineffective spring with the Cardinals, Arroyo found himself back in the minors. On May 7, 1956, the Cardinals sent Arroyo to the Pittsburgh Pirates for pitcher Max Surkont. Arroyo pitched well at first; after eight appearances he was 1-0 with a 1.08 ERA. After two starts a week apart in mid-June, Arroyo returned to the bullpen and pitched poorly; by July 1, his ERA had ballooned to 4.64. Although the team was desperate for pitching, the Pirates sent Arroyo to the Hollywood Stars of the Pacific Coast League, where he was 7-5 with a 2.81 ERA. He returned to the Pirates for three games in relief during September.

Sports Illustrated opined in its 1957 baseball preview issue: "Even more than most managers, [Bobby] Bragan is badly in need of another starting pitcher—or maybe two. ... there are only possibilities. Some of them: Luis Arroyo, who at the moment looks like the No. 4 man."[23] Despite that unenthusiastic appraisal, during spring training in 1957, Arroyo earned a job in the Pirates' starting rotation. He started the second game of the season on April 18 at Ebbets Field against the Brooklyn Dodgers and took a 6-1 loss although he allowed only two runs in four innings. Against the New York Giants at the Polo Grounds four days later, he pitched 4⅔ innings in a 3-1 loss. His next 24 appearances included only eight starts, and on June 20, 1957, he made his final major-league start at St. Louis. After pitching two scoreless innings, he hit Cardinals pitcher Murry Dickson with a pitch, gave up an infield single to Don Blasingame, a run-scoring double to Alvin Dark, and an intentional walk to Stan Musial before being relieved by Roy Face. When Blasingame and Dark eventually scored, Arroyo was charged with three earned runs in his two-plus innings of work. At that point, his 1957 record as a starter stood at 0-6 with a 4.61 ERA. His overall mark of 2-7 with a 4.03 ERA suggested he might be more effective in relief. Pirates managers Bobby Bragan and then Danny Murtaugh evidently thought so, too; after June 20, Arroyo made 28 more appearances in mainly long or middle relief.

Arroyo pitched well in his first four relief assignments: 8⅔ scoreless innings, dropping his season ERA on June 25 to 3.64. However, mirroring his 1955 second-half problems, from that point until the end of the season, his ERA was 6.70 and he allowed eight home runs in only 41⅔ innings of work. Nonetheless, in the midst of this ineffective pitching, Arroyo won his third and final game for the Pirates on July 18, 1957.

The Pirates had lost six of their previous seven games and were ensconced in seventh place. Arroyo had pitched only once since July 5, a two-inning mop-up role on July 11. One week later at Forbes Field, Arroyo entered the game in basically another mop-up situation, as the Pirates trailed the Chicago Cubs 4-2 in the eighth. In the top of the inning, Arroyo allowed an inside-the-park home run to Chuck Tanner to make the score 5-2. After pitching a scoreless ninth, Arroyo had allowed nine earned runs and three home runs in his last 9⅓ innings of pitching. As the Pirates came to bat in the bottom of the ninth, the game looked like nothing more than another loss in an already long and unsatisfying season.

Turk Lown, who had entered in the seventh and snuffed out a Pirate rally, started the ninth on the mound for the Cubs. He ran into trouble immediately. Pinch-hitter Roman Mejias singled. Johnny O'Brien ran for Mejias and went to third on a single by pinch-hitter Gene Freese. Dee Fondy hit a sacrifice fly scoring O'Brien to make it a 5-3 game; Lown then walked Bob Skinner. When Dick Groat tripled, the game was tied at 5-5. At that point, with the winning run at third base and only one out, Cubs manager Bob Scheffing brought left-hander Dick Littlefield into the game to face Bill Virdon. Bragan countered by sending Jim Pendleton up to hit for Virdon. Littlefield walked Pendleton intentionally. Scheffing then summoned right-hander Jim Brosnan from the Cubs bullpen to face Frank Thomas, the Pirates' most dangerous hitter. Brosnan walked Thomas intentionally, loading the bases. Bill Mazeroski then singled to win the game, 6-5, improving Arroyo's season mark to 3-8.

Arroyo made 16 more relief appearances after July 18, posting a 0-3 mark. Rory Costello aptly described his final 1957 ledger, 3-11 with a 4.61 ERA in 54 games as "forgettable."[24] His two years with Pittsburgh fell into the same category, a 6-14 won-lost record with an ERA of 4.69. Obviously unimpressed, the Pirates kept Arroyo at Triple-A Columbus in 1958, where he posted a 10-3 record and a 4.01 ERA almost exclusively in relief. In December of 1958, the Pirates sent Arroyo to Cincinnati for a career minor-league outfielder, Nino Escalera, whose only major-league experience had come in 1954 with the Reds. After starting the 1959 season at the Cincinnati's Triple-A Havana farm team, Arroyo returned to the majors in June. He pitched only 10 games that season. When Fred Hutchinson took over as manager on July 9, he sent Arroyo back to Havana; as Arroyo told Costello, "Hutchinson let me go without even a look." At age 32, having been sent down again by a team in desperate need of pitching, Arroyo's career seemed over.

Arroyo spent the first several months of the 1960 season at Havana, then in Jersey City after the

Luis Arroyo

team relocated due to Cuba's revolutionary turmoil. On July 20, the Reds sold him to the Yankees. The Yankees began using Arroyo as a late-inning stopper. Between his Yankees debut on July 26 and the end of the season, Arroyo won five games and saved seven (three according to 1960 rules), with a 2.88 ERA. Despite some good late-season work, *Sports Illustrated* remained unimpressed, writing in its 1961 baseball preview, "Luis Arroyo was sharp in spots last year, but cannot be regarded as day-in, day-out stopper." Similarly dismissive, *The Sporting News's* analysis of each major-league team's best player in a number of categories listed "none" for the Yankees "best relief pitcher."[25] However, Arroyo's 1961 pitching confounded the experts. He led the American League in appearances (tied with Philadelphia's Jack Baldschun for the major-league lead) with 65; his 119 relief innings led the American League, and were second in the majors only to San Francisco's Stu Miller, who pitched 122 innings. After 1961, Arroyo pitched two more seasons in the majors, both marred by injuries. When he retired, he owned a 40-32 won-lost record with a 3.93 ERA. After going 18-22 as a spot starter/reliever in the National League, Arroyo posted a 22-10 record as a Yankee.

Although Arroyo's 1956-57 service with the Pirates proved unsuccessful, during the mid-1950s he developed and refined the pitch that defined him in 1961: the screwball.[26] Using the pitch to lethal effect that season, Arroyo held American League hitters to a .199 average and in a year of impressive home-run production, allowed only five in his 119 innings of work. While Arroyo enjoyed only "middling" success during his career, "in 1961 he was the best reliever in the game, a prototype of the late-inning specialist now known as a closer."[27] On July 18, 1957, Arroyo won a basically meaningless game for a bad Pirates club, his last victory for Pittsburgh. At the end of that season, his major-league career seemed over. Who could have imagined where he would be four years later?

NOTES

1   All the statistical information and game accounts in this article come from the following sources: Retrosheet, retrosheet.org/boxesetc/index.html; Baseball Reference, baseball-reference.com/; J.G. Taylor Spink, Paul A. Rickart, and Clifford Kachline, *Baseball Guide and Record Book 1961*, *Baseball Guide and Record Book 1962* (St. Louis: Charles C. Spink & Son, 1962, 1963).

2   For a description of Arroyo's Puerto Rican accomplishments, see Rory Costello, "Luis Arroyo," SABR Biography Project, sabr.org/bioproj/person/6a29b50a, accessed April 3, 2017.

3   *Sports Illustrated*, April 15, 1957: 81.

4   Rory Costello, "Luis Arroyo."

5   *Sports Illustrated*, April 10, 1961: 72; *The Sporting News*, April 19, 1961: 2.

6   For a discussion of the development of Arroyo's screwball see Costello, "Luis Arroyo"; William J. Ryczek, *The Yankees in the Early 1960s* (Jefferson, North Carolina: McFarland, 2008), 69-70; Rich Marazzi and Len Fiorito, *Baseball Players of the 1950s: A Biographical Dictionary of all 1560 Major Leaguers* (Jefferson, North Carolina: McFarland, 2004), 17.

7   Bruce Weber and Daniel L. Slotnick, "Luis Arroyo, Baseball's Best Reliever in '61, Dies at 88," *New York Times*, January 14, 2016: nytimes.com/2016/01/15/sports/baseball/luis-arroyo-baseballs-best-reliever-in-61-dies-at-88.html?_r=0, accessed March 29, 2017.

FRANK HAS A BIG DAY

MAY 1, 1958: PITTSBURGH PIRATES 8, LOS ANGELES DODGERS 3, AT THE LOS ANGELES COLISEUM

BY MATT KEELEAN

THE GAME ON THURSDAY, MAY 1, 1958, pitting the Pirates against the née Brooklynites, came in the midst of the Bucs' first visit to Los Angeles after the Dodgers' relocation. In the first two games of the five-game series, the Pirates prevailed, and would do so again in the third contest. Indeed, the game itself was a matchup of two teams heading in distinctly opposite directions. The Pirates would remain relevant in the 1958 National League pennant race, finishing second to the defending World Series champions, the Milwaukee Braves. The Dodgers would struggle in their first season in their new home, finishing in seventh place, a mere two games ahead of the perpetual basement-dwelling Philadelphia Phillies.

The Pirates won this contest 8-3, despite an ordinary pitching effort from right-handed starter Vern Law, on the strength of Frank Thomas's big game, one of many such games he would enjoy for as long as the Dodgers called the Los Angeles Coliseum home. But on May 1, he had arguably his most impressive outing in the unintentional ballyard, going 4-for-5 with two runs scored, three RBIs, two home runs and 10 total bases. Although Law gave up two earned runs in the 5⅓ innings he worked, he did help his own cause with a three-run homer in the midst of a fine 2-for-3 day, taking advantage of the short porch (250 feet) and tall fence (40 feet) in left field in much the same manner as his third sacker did.

The opposing starter, the venerable Dodger hurler Don Newcombe, was just coming back from a rest to heal a sore right arm, having thrown only a single inning since April 17 (in relief on April 29). His return to the rotation came at a critical moment for the Dodgers, who were struggling in the early part of the season and desperately needed a return to

form from their big veteran right-hander. However, Newcombe's rest period did not last long enough; he was shelled for five runs (all earned) over five-plus innings, giving up eight hits, including the two homers to Thomas (the second of which chased the starter from the game in the top of the sixth), while recording only two strikeouts.

In Thomas's first at-bat, in the top of the second with one out, the game was still in its early stages. Newcombe had thrown only 11 pitches to that point, and had retired the Pirates in order. Up stepped Thomas, ready to take his cuts and pepper the oversized yard fence in left. He fouled off three straight pitches, then let ball one pass by without response. Facing the 1-and-2 pitcher's count, Thomas proceeded to stroke a solid base knock to the opposite field. But he was eliminated from the basepaths by a fielder's choice off the bat of Bill Mazeroski for the final out of the inning.

Thomas's next trip to the plate, as the leadoff batter in the top of the fifth, found the Bucs trailing 2-0. Staying true to his hack-first approach, Thomas drove the first pitch served over the 40-foot barrier in left field for what was variously categorized the following day as both "a cheapie" (by the *Pittsburgh Post-Gazette*)[1] and "strictly legit" (by the *Los Angeles Times*).[2] At this point, Newcombe began to struggle. He had been cruising comfortably through the first four frames, giving up only the single to Thomas in the second, and had thrown a modest total of 43 pitches, but had barely escaped the fifth inning after giving up four more singles (including three in a row) and two more runs for a 3-2 Pittsburgh lead.

With the score tied, 3-3, Thomas's next at-bat proved to be Newk's undoing. Still unsteady after the debacle in the previous frame, Newcombe proceeded to serve up a 1-and-2 fastball to Pirates cleanup hitter Ted Kluszewski, who drove it back up the middle into center field for his first hit of the series. Thomas followed his fellow slugger by punching the second pitch thrown to him over that now-familiar chain-link wall in left field for a two-run shot, a fly ball "… that barely cleared the barrier" in left field, according to the *Times*,[3] or a shot that he "conked … pretty far over the screen …" per the *Post-Gazette*, depending on one's perspective (or perhaps bias).[4] At that point, Thomas had shown beyond any doubt his preference for not only hitting off Newcombe, but hitting in the so-called shallow concrete oval in downtown Los Angeles. And while Newk's day was done, Thomas and his teammates still had more firepower to offer. Right-handed reliever Ed Roebuck allowed a one-out double and a walk before Law cleared the fence for his fifth career circuit clout to produce an 8-3 cushion. Manager Walter Alston pulled Roebuck in favor of southpaw Jackie Collum, but the Bucs' offensive damage had been done.

In the top of the seventh inning, Thomas faced the third relief pitcher of the evening for the Dodgers, right-hander Don Bessent. Thomas continued his big day at the plate without regard as to the opposing hurler. Once again the leadoff batter for the inning, he worked the count even at 1-and-1, and then drove the third pitch deep into left field for another solid single, described in the *Pittsburgh Press* as having "… just missed" being "… a third circuit blow."[5] One can imagine that the shot ricocheted off the tall fence back toward Don Demeter, limiting Thomas to a safety. However, he no sooner reached first base than he was eliminated on the next pitch, as Roman Mejias hit into a 4-3 twin killing.

Finally, in the top of the ninth, one final plate appearance awaited Thomas. Facing the Dodgers' top reliever of the past two seasons, right-hander Clem Labine, Thomas worked the count to his favor, 2-and-1, and then slapped a shot to his opposite number with the Dodgers, Jim Gilliam. Gilliam gobbled up the ball and threw it across the diamond to Gil Hodges at first base to record the final out of the Pirates' frame.

In the bottom of the ninth, righty Ron Blackburn, who had relieved Law in the bottom of the sixth after Law yielded three consecutive singles, continued his mastery of the Dodgers, retiring Duke Snider, Hodges, and Charlie Neal in order to preserve the victory. The heart of the Dodgers lineup went down ignominiously on a mere 10 pitches, only one of which was a ball.

The game vaulted the Bucs into second place in the National League, wrapping up an early-season six-game winning streak after a 2-5 start to the 1958 campaign. For Thomas, the 4-for-5 night carried him closer to the top 10 in batting average (.345) in the National League.

That Thomas would have a big game against Newcombe in the favorable confines of the Coliseum is, in hindsight, obvious. On top of his success in that venue, Thomas enjoyed even greater success against Newk: over 67 plate appearances, Thomas laced 25 hits, including eight home runs, for a slash line of .391/.418/.813, giving him an astonishing 1.231 OPS. Newk never conceded to Thomas individually nor to the in-game situation when facing Thomas, as he intentionally walked Thomas only once.

Thomas also greatly enjoyed hitting in the Coliseum. In 42 lifetime games played there, over 177 plate appearances from 1958 to 1961, Thomas was .294/.345/.620, for a total OPS of .964, or 144 OPS+. He hit 17 home runs, and had 31 RBIs and 101 total bases. For this particular five-game series, Thomas would collect 11 hits in 21 at-bats, five of which were home runs, and seven RBIs. This astonishing performance gave Thomas a slash line of .524/.545/1.238, and a total OPS of 1.783 for the five-game set. According to chroniclers, Thomas believed that if he had played in Los Angeles for an entire season, he could have challenged Babe Ruth's then-single season record of 60 home runs.[6] Performances such as his evening on May 1 also added to Thomas's overall success in 1958, as he not only started at third base for the National League in the All-Star Game at Memorial Stadium in Baltimore on July 8, but he also finished a strong fourth in the voting for the National League Most

Valuable Player Award. In contrast, Newcombe, the 1956 National League MVP and Cy Young Award winner, continued to struggle with the Dodgers, going winless against six defeats before being traded to Cincinnati on June 15.

Much in the same manner as the two teams playing that evening of May 1, Thomas and Newcombe's seasons became emblematic of their teams' seasons. In something of an ironic twist, the following season would find both players as teammates on a middling 1959 Cincinnati ballclub. While that season would be an utterly forgettable experience for Thomas, it proved to be Newcombe's last good season as a professional, as he managed a very respectable 13 wins against 8 defeats for the fifth-place Reds.

SOURCES

In addition to the sources cited in the Notes, the author also consulted BacktoBaseball.com, Baseball-Reference.com, Retrosheet.org, *The Sporting News*, SABR's BioProject, and

Lowry, Philip J. *Green Cathedrals: The Ultimate Celebration of All Major League Ballparks* (New York: Walker and Company, 2006).

NOTES

1   Jack Hernon, "Thomas Swats 2, Bucs Win 6th in Row, 8-3," *Pittsburgh Post-Gazette*, May 2, 1958.

2   Frank Finch, "Thomas Smacks Two as Pirates Win, 8-3", *Los Angeles Times*, May 2, 1958.

3   Ibid.

4   Hernon.

5   Lester J. Biederman, "Thomas Continues Home-Run Blasting in Dodger Coliseum," *Pittsburgh Press*, May 2, 1958.

6   Bob Hurte, "Frank Thomas," SABR Baseball Biography Project. sabr.org/bioproj/person/ff969dc6.

HARVEY HADDIX PITCHES 12 PERFECT INNINGS;

ADCOCK'S DOUBLE IN 13TH GIVES BRAVES 1-0 VICTORY

MAY 26, 1959: MILWAUKEE BRAVES 1, PITTSBURGH PIRATES 0, AT COUNTY STADIUM

BY MARK MILLER

MARCIA HADDIX WAS AT HOME—ON a Clark County, Ohio, farm—when her mother-in-law called to tell her to turn on the radio—her husband was pitching a pretty good game in Milwaukee. The reception of Pittsburgh's KDKA was poor so she got in her car and drove a few miles to park on a hill where she knew she could pick up the broadcast.[1]

In the sixth inning, the KDKA engineers decided to start recording the game on a vinyl album, which was not something they typically did.

In Milwaukee, Harvey Haddix was ill. "I had the flu, I felt terrible," Haddix said. "We took a morning flight over from Pittsburgh the day of the game, and we didn't have a lot of rest. I took throat lozenges the whole game to try to keep from coughing."[2]

The Pirates started the 1959 season slowly, but on May 26 they were riding a five-game winning streak. In their pregame scouting meeting, Harvey spoke up. "Going over the hitters, I figured I would have some fun so I got into the high and tight and low and away stuff. Don Hoak broke up the meeting with, 'If you do that you will throw a no-hitter.'"[3]

In the grandstand was a 24-year-old Allan "Bud" Selig. "I was a great Braves fan in those days," said the former baseball commissioner. "It was an amazing night, just a great baseball night. A game you never forget. It was unbelievable."[4]

The Pirates' lineup did not include injured right fielder Roberto Clemente, who was replaced by Roman Mejias. Manager Danny Murtaugh had Dick Schofield at short, rather than Dick Groat, and Rocky Nelson at first, rather than Dick Stuart or Ted Kluszewski.

Braves pitcher Bob Buhl recalled that the Braves' bullpen had pilfered the Pirates' signs. If catcher Smoky Burgess called for a fastball, they flashed a towel to the batter. On breaking pitches, the towel was out of sight. "Smoky couldn't bend over very far when he caught, so with binoculars, you could pick up every sign from the bullpen," Buhl said. "Harvey had such marvelous movement and changes of speed that night that it didn't matter if the hitter knew what was coming or not."[5]

The Braves lineup was very formidable. Selig remembered, "The Braves were a wonderful, wonderful team and had just won the pennant in '57, '58, and would tie in '59. They could really hit."[6] They began the game with a .290 team batting average. Pitching for the Braves was veteran right-handed All-Star Lew Burdette.

The weather at game time was 77 degrees. It was cloudy with a stiff wind blowing in from right field and thunderstorms were forecast.

In the first inning Schofield popped out to Eddie Mathews, Bill Virdon hit a ball in front of the plate that catcher Del Crandall fielded for out number two, and Burgess popped out to left. The Braves followed suit in their first. Johnny O'Brien grounded out to short on the first pitch. Mathews, batting second, worked the count to 3-and-2 before lining out to Nelson at first. It was Haddix's last three-ball count until the 13th inning. Five pitches later, Aaron flied out to center.

Nelson led off the second with a line-drive single to center. Bob Skinner hit a roller to first baseman Joe Adcock, who teamed with shortstop Johnny Logan on a 3-6-3 double play. Bill Mazeroski struck out to end the inning.

Many accused Burdette of throwing a spitball. Logan said, "I can't verify that but I will say he knew how to throw one. I called it a sinker. I got a feeling he was throwing one because we got a lot of double plays."[7]

Pirates shortstop Schofield said of Burdette, "He would load them up pretty good sometimes. The ball got a little wetter when men got on base."[8]

In the bottom of the second it took just 10 pitches for Haddix to dispose of Adcock on a strikeout and Wes Covington and Crandall on groundouts to second and third.

In the third Hoak led off with a single as he threw the bat at the ball and hit it back to Burdette, who dodged the bat and missed the ball.Mejias forced Hoak at second on a grounder to Mathews at third. That brought Haddix to the plate in what was the first of two key failed offensive opportunities. Haddix hit a shot off Burdette's leg and hustled down the line, beating the throw to first. But Mejias tried to advance from first to third and was thrown out. Schofield followed with a single to right that would have easily scored Mejias from second. Virdon then flied out to left field to end the inning.

In the third inning Harvey threw just seven pitches—he retired Andy Pafko on a fly to Mejias, got Logan to line sharply to Schofield, and struck out Burdette.

The Pirates fourth saw Burgess fly out to center and Nelson ground out to second before Skinner singled to center and Mazeroski flied out deep to center. In the Braves half, Haddix made quick work of O'Brien, Mathews, and Aaron with a strikeout and two flies to center.

In the fifth and sixth innings, Haddix needed just 11 pitches to complete a perfect second time through the order. Schofield commented, "Standing at short, I would turn around and look at the scoreboard and it seemed like they were all hitting with two strikes."[9]

The seventh through the ninth were more of the same for both teams. Haddix set them down in order and Burdette kept scattering hits, 12 in the game, and getting timely double plays. The Pirates' seventh inning brought their second near-miss. Skinner, Haddix's roommate, recounted, "I hit a ball to right field and I thought it was gone. But a windstorm had started. Aaron went back on it and kind of gave up on it when the wind blew it back and he caught it against the fence. I thought it was gone."[10]

Pirates pitcher Bob Friend recalled the mood on the Pittsburgh bench: "We were all squirming around in the dugout. Murtaugh kept asking Harvey, 'Can you go another?' Harvey said, 'I'm OK.'" Pirates closer Elroy Face typically stayed on the bench until the sixth inning before heading to the bullpen. Face said, "I never went to the bullpen, I stayed in the dugout so I could watch."[11]

After the eighth inning Pirates radio broadcaster Bob Prince shouted, "Don't go away. We are on the verge of … baseball history." When the ninth inning was over, Prince screamed, "Harvey Haddix has pitched a perfect no-hit, no-run game."[12]

The pattern continued through the top of the 13th as the Braves went out in order and the Pirates failed to score. In the 10th Milwaukee's Del Rice batted for second baseman O'Brien and Felix Mantilla went in at second.

Harvey Haddix went to the mound for what would be his unlucky 13th time. Through 12 innings he had thrown an unbelievably economical 104 pitches. He would throw only 11 more.

Mantilla led off the 13th by hitting the ball to Hoak at third. "About a five-hopper," Haddix said. "Don picked up the ball, looked at it in his glove … and threw it in the dirt. Rocky Nelson couldn't come up with it. Mathews bunted Mantilla to second base; I walked Aaron intentionally to set up a double play."Joe Adcock was next. "Hung a slider on the second pitch and he hit it out in right center."[13]

Mantilla scored. Aaron assumed the game was over, stopped, and cut across the infield, causing Adcock to pass him. Aaron eventually went to third and scored in front of Adcock but was ruled out. Adcock was credited with a double instead of a homer. Murtaugh argued that Aaron was called out before Mantilla, who went back to tag up, had crossed the plate. Umpires huddled and ruled Mantilla safe and allowed all three runs. National League President Warren Giles overturned that decision the next day. The final score: Braves 1, Pirates 0.

Mantilla explained, "When I crossed the plate I looked up and saw Hank walking across the pitcher's mound." Asked if he crossed the plate in time, he said, "It was close! We were lucky to win that game."[14]

After the game a despondent Haddix was surprised to hear he had done something (12 perfect innings) that had not been done before. That did little to console him. "It was just another loss, and that is no good."[15]

Burdette called the visitors' clubhouse and congratulated Haddix, and the next day asked for a raise since he was the winning pitcher in the "Greatest Game Ever Pitched."

Haddix became an instant celebrity. He was featured in *Life* and *Sports Illustrated* articles. He turned down an invitation to appear on *The Ed Sullivan Show*. At a ceremony in Pittsburgh, Giles presented him with an inscribed silver tea service with 13 silver cups.

SOURCES

In addition to those listed in the notes, the following sources were used.

Interviews:

Recorded at WHIO-FM radio studios, Dayton, Ohio (Darryl Bauer, engineer), April 9-16, 2009.

Interviewers were Mark Miller, president, Springfield/Clark County Baseball Hall of Fame, and Tim Bucey, retired sports editor, *Springfield* (Ohio) *News-Sun*.

Johnny Logan interviewed by Mark Miller, April 9, 2009; Felix Mantilla interviewed by Mark Miller, April 9, 2009; Dick Schofield interviewed by Tim Bucey, April 9, 2009; Commissioner Bud Selig interviewed by Mark Miller, April 16, 2009; Bob Skinner interviewed by Tim Bucey, April 16, 2009.

Recorded at PNC Park, Pittsburgh (Mark Miller, videographer), May 7, 2009.

Interviewers were David Jablonski, sports reporter, *Springfield News-Sun, and* Tim Bucey, retired sports editor, *Springfield News-Sun*.

Elroy Face and Bob Friend (joint video interview).

Wright State University major-league baseball panel discussion April 17, 1989, CD, produced by Professor Allen Hye, 2009.

baseball-reference.com

NOTES

1   Bob Sullivan, "'A Pitcher's Dream,' Says Wife Marcia of Haddix' Unprecedented Feat, "*Springfield* (Ohio) *Daily News*, May 27, 1959: 1-2.

2   Sid Bordman, "Haddix has perfected his tale of baseball epic," *Kansas City Star*, May 19, 1984.

3   Ibid

4   Interview with Bud Selig, April 16, 2009.

5   Bordman.

6   Selig interview.

7   Interview with Johnny Logan, April 9, 2009.

8   Interview with Dick Schofield, April 9, 2009.

9   Schofield interview.

10   Interview with Bob Skinner, April 16, 2009.

11   Interview with Elroy Face and Bob Friend, May 7, 2009.

12   "Sweet Smell of Failure." *Sports Illustrated*, June 8, 1959: 34-35.

13   Bordman.

14   Interview with Felix Mantilla, April 9, 2009.

15   "Sweet Smell of Failure."

"WE HAD 'EM ALL THE WAY"

AUGUST 6, 1960: PITTSBURGH PIRATES 8, SAN FRANCISCO GIANTS 7 (10 INNINGS), AT FORBES FIELD

BY ALAN COHEN

"When you win that kind, you've got to win the pennant. You appreciate that kind of game. The fellows really pulled me through today. It's been a long time since I've won that kind of game."—Vernon Law *after the Pirates had scored three 10th-inning runs to come behind and defeat the Giants 8-7.*[1]

"I never saw a club that won so many games that way. I was with the Dodgers when they won the pennant (1956), but they didn't win many games that way. They usually overpowered the other team." – Gino Cimoli.[2]

"I thought we were going to win. I'm like the fans—I always think we are going to win." —*Pirates manager* Danny Murtaugh.[3]

SAN FRANCISCO HAD A NEW BALL-park in 1960, but the Giants had experienced a June swoon. After contending in 1958 and collapsing at the end of 1959, ownership was frustrated when the team, after leading the league by one game on May 28, lost 12 of 20 games to fall four games behind the Pirates. They dispatched manager Bill Rigney 58 games into the season. When the Giants visited Forbes Field in August, they had sunk to fifth place, and as they took the field on the 6th, the Giants trailed the league-leading Pirates by eight games.

The Pirates had risen from the ashes. They were baseball's worst team in 1952 and had not been to the World Series since 1927. In 1958, they had escaped the second division. General manager Joe L. Brown

virtually completed the rebuilding job commenced by Branch Rickey by bringing on board Don Hoak, Smoky Burgess, and Harvey Haddix at the beginning of 1959. Role players like Gino Cimoli and Hal Smith were added in 1960. On May 30, 1960, after flirting with first place during the season's first 39 games, the Bucs gained undisputed possession of that slot, and by August 6 their league lead was four games.

A Saturday-afternoon crowd of 33,759 (28,246 paid) was at Forbes Field as Giants rookie pitcherJuan Marichal (3-0) took on Pirates ace Vernon Law (14-5). Marichal, who had been called up from Tacoma in July, had been nothing short of spectacular in his first three starts, winning each game and allowing only three runs in 28 innings. In his most recent start, at Philadelphia on August 2, he left the second game of a doubleheader in the seventh inning with a three-run lead, but the bullpen squandered the lead. Law, who had debuted with the Pirates in 1950, was having his best season.

The leadoff batter for the Giants was second baseman Don Blasingame, who was retired easily as were Jim Davenport and Willie Mays. In the bottom of the first inning with two outs, the Bucs broke on top as Bob Skinner homered on the first pitch he saw, his 13th of the season, slamming a ball into the upper deck of the right-field stands. It was the first homer Marichal had allowed as a Giant. Skinner had been slumping, and prior to the homer had gone 3-for-18.

The Giants moved in front in the third frame. Catcher Bob Schmidt led off with a single and when Blasingame tripled to right past Cimoli (playing for the injured Roberto Clemente), Schmidt scored the tying run. Clemente had injured himself in the series opener against the Giants. After making a spectacular catch on a ball hit by Mays, he went into the wall face first. For the next six games, he was replaced by Cimoli. The official scorer was generous in awarding the triple as the ball, which should have been only a single, had gone between Cimoli's legs. Jim Davenport's single plated Blasingame and the Giants led 2-1.

Marichal's control uncharacteristically eluded him in the bottom of the third, and he walked Bill Virdon and Rocky Nelson. Cimoli stroked a two-out triple past Willie Kirkland in right field and the Pirates regained the lead, 3-2. The Giants threatened in the fourth inning when Felipe Alou singled with one out and stole second base. He was left stranded as Law intentionally walked Andre Rodgers and retired Marichal on a fly ball that Pirates captain and shortstop Dick Groat corralled in short left field.

The Giants mounted a threat in inning five. A walk to Blasingame and a hit-and-run single by Davenport put runners at the corners with none out and Mays up. Willie grounded into a 4-6-3 double play, scoring Blasingame from third, but there was no further damage. The score was tied, but not for long.

Virdon led off the Pirates' fifth inning with a single, stole second base, and advanced to third on Groat's grounder to the right side. He scored on Skinner's single up the middle against the drawn-in infield. The Pirates took the 4-3 lead into the seventh inning and Giants manager Tom Sheehan lifted Marichal for pinch-hitter Jim Marshall. Marshall flied out and Law got through the inning unscathed. Sherman "Roadblock" Jones came in to pitch for the Giants and the Giants flirted with disaster in the Pirates' half of the seventh inning. With two outs, Bob Skinner hit a fly ball to short center field. Blasingame and Mays converged on the ball and collided. Blasingame made the catch for the third out. Pittsburgh then extended its lead in the eighth inning. Nelson singled and was moved to third by a Cimoli sacrifice and a groundout by Hoak. He scored on a single by second baseman Bill Mazeroski, and the score was 5-3.

Sheehan made several moves in the Giants' ninth inning. Veteran Dave Philley was sent up to hit for Schmidt and the lefty singled off Law, getting just enough of his bat handle on the ball. Sheehan inserted Billy O'Dell as a pinch-runner but the move proved unnecessary as former Pirate Dale Long, pinch-hitting for Jones, homered to tie the game. It was Long's third homer of the season, each in a pinch-hitting role. In the bottom of the inning, the Giants realigned their defense and Johnny Antonelli came on to pitch. One of the few remaining New York Giants, Antonelli dispatched the Pirates in the bottom of the ninth and the game went into extra innings.

The 10th inning provided end-to-end excitement. With one out in the Giants' at-bat, Mays singled and, after Kirkland flied to right, scored on Orlando Cepeda's 19th home run of the season. He took an outside pitch and lofted it to right field. The ball cleared the fence just inside the foul pole.

Defensive lapses, miscues, and omissions defined the Giants in the bottom of the 10th. Cimoli opened the inning with a single and advanced to third when Mays bobbled a single by Burgess. Dick Schofield ran for Burgess. Hoak's single scored Cimoli and advanced Schofield to second, closing the gap to 7-6. For Hoak, who had come into the game in an 0-for-11 slump, it was his first hit in 16 at-bats. Sheehan replaced Antonelli with the Giants' top reliever, Stu Miller. With runners on first and second, Mazeroski executed a perfect bunt to put the tying and winning runs in scoring position with one out. On the play, Giants third baseman Joey Amalfitano had a chance to force Hoak at second base, but elected to get the sure out at first. Dick Stuart was sent up to pinch-hit for Law and, when the count got to 2-and-1, was walked intentionally, loading the bases for Virdon.

Virdon's fly ball to short right field scored Schofield, and the game was knotted at 7-7. A close play at the plate was expected, but right fielder Kirkland threw to second base, preventing Hoak from advancing to third. Groat stepped to the plate. He had not missed a game all season and was playing in his 101st game. It had not been the best of days for Groat. He was in a 3-for-26 slump and had gone 0-for-5 in this game. He had seen his batting average drop from .317 on July 27 to .305. With one swing of the bat, he made his day, and that of the team, successful, singling past shortstop Davenport into center field. Hoak raced home ahead of the throw from Mays, giving the Pirates an 8-7 win.

The day's attendance pushed the Bucs' attendance for the season to over one million for the third consecutive season. They drew 1,705,828 for the season, a Forbes Field record. The Pirates would not draw that many again until 1988 at Three Rivers Stadium.

It was Law's 15th win of the season. For the season, he compiled a record of 20-9, tied Warren Spahn and Lew Burdette with a league-leading 18 complete games, and was named the National League Cy Young Award winner.

The Pirates, with the win, extended their league lead to 4½ games. They went on to win the National League pennant and defeat the New York Yankees in the World Series.

SOURCES

In addition to Baseball-Reference.com and the sources shown in the Notes, the author used:

Associated Press. "Bucs Get off Deck in 10th, Kayo Giants 8-7," *New Orleans Times Picayune,* August 7, 1960: 6-1.

Hernon, Jack. "Bucs Edge Giants in 10th, 8-7," *Pittsburgh Post-Gazette,* August 7, 1960: 3-1.

Judge, Walter. "Unbeatable Bucs Bop SF: 2 Giant Homers Wasted," *San Francisco Examiner,* August 7, 1960: III-1, III-5.

United Press International. "Pirates in Rally to Beat Giants, 8-7," *Springfield* (Massachusetts) *Republican,* August 7, 1960: B-1.

NOTES

1   Ray Kienze, "Bucs, Fans Temperatures High—It's Pennant Fever," *Pittsburgh Post-Gazette,* August 7, 1960: 3-1.

2   Ibid.

3   Ibid.

MAZEROSKI'S HEROIC HOMER BRINGS CHAMPIONSHIP TO PITTSBURGH

OCTOBER 13, 1960: PITTSBURGH PIRATES 10, NEW YORK YANKEES 9, AT FORBES FIELD

GAME SEVEN OF THE 1960 WORLD SERIES

BY MIKE HUBER

BOTTOM OF THE NINTH. GAME TIED. Series tied. Only one team can win. On the mound for the New York Yankees was 24-year-old Ralph Terry. Leading off the inning for the Pittsburgh Pirates was 24-year-old second baseman Bill Mazeroski. The crowd "sucked in their collective breaths"[1] as Terry delivered a shoulder-high fastball. Home-plate umpire Bill Jackowski called it a ball. No one was talking, except for those fans actually praying out loud. The tension was mounting. Terry took the sign from his catcher, John Blanchard, and delivered another fastball. It was "high but a touch lower than the last one."[2] Mazeroski, with "a baseball-sized chaw in his jaw,"[3] swung, sending it toward the left-center-field wall. Yankees center fielder Mickey Mantle raced over, as did left fielder Yogi Berra. Both hoped to make a play but could only look up as the ball cleared the wall, flying out of Forbes Field for a walkoff, 10-9 victory for the home team.

Coming into Game Seven, the Bronx Bombers had all the momentum. They had outscored the Bucs, 46-17, and their three victories came by a combined 38-3 score with two shutouts. Two of the blowouts had come in Pittsburgh.

After Pittsburgh starter Vern Law retired the Yankees in order in the first, the Pirates jumped on New York's Bob Turley. With two outs, Bob Skinner worked a full count and drew a walk. Rocky Nelson smashed Turley's 2-and-1 offering deep into the right-field seats, and Pittsburgh had a 2-0 lead. Law set down three more Yankees and Smoky Burgess started the Pittsburgh second with a single. Yankees

manager Casey Stengel strode to the mound, calling for Bill Stafford in relief of Turley. Stafford walked Don Hoak and then Mazeroski bunted down the third-base line for a single, loading the bases with no outs. Law came to bat and hit a comebacker to Stafford, who started the 1-2-3 double play, and it appeared as if the Yankees would escape unscathed. But Bill Virdon singled to right, plating both Hoak and Mazeroski for a 4-0 advantage. There was still a lot of ball left to play.

Law continued his effectiveness, allowing singles in the third (Hector Lopez) and fourth (Mantle). In the fifth, Bill Skowron got the Yankees on the board with a leadoff opposite-field home run to deep right. In the sixth, Bobby Richardson started a rally with a single. Tony Kubek walked, and Law was sent to the showers. Veteran reliever Roy Face entered for the fourth time in this Series and retired Roger Maris on a pop fly to third baseman Hoak in foul territory. Mantle drove a single up the middle, scoring Richardson. Berra then blasted an 0-and-1 pitch down the line and into the upper-deck grandstand in right, his 11th home run in World Series competition. Suddenly, New York had a 5-4 lead.

The Yankees struck again in the top of the eighth. Face retired Maris and Mantle, but Berra walked on a full count. Skowron hit a high bouncer to third; Hoak's throw to Mazeroski at second was too late to force Berra and New York had two baserunners. This was Skowron's 12th hit of the series, "tying the record held by many."[4] Blanchard followed with a single to right-center, and Berra crossed the plate with New York's sixth run. Clete Boyer jumped on

Face's next offering and lined a double down the line into short left field, driving in Skowron for a 7-4 Yankees cushion.

If the Pittsburgh faithful were deflated, they found their voices in the bottom of the eighth. Bobby Shantz had become the third New York hurler in the third inning and faced the minimum of 15 batters for five innings, thanks to two double plays. However, in the eighth he could not get an out. Gino Cimoli pinch-hit for Face and popped a single into short right-center. Virdon's sharp groundball to short took a bad hop and hit Kubek in the larynx, knocking him to the ground. Kubek left the game to an ovation by the crowd and Joe DeMaestri came in to replace him. Virdon was credited with a single. Dick Groat then deposited a clutch single into left field with Cimoli scoring, and Stengel had seen enough from Shantz.

He called for right-hander Jim Coates. Skinner's bunt advanced Virdon to third and Groat to second. Nelson lofted a fly ball to right. Virdon threatened to tag but "held third on [Maris's] perfect no-bounce throw to the plate."[5] Roberto Clemente beat out a slow chopper that was wide of first base. Skowron had to hold the ball as Coates was late to first base. Virdon scored, cutting the New York lead to 7-6. Hal Smith had come on as a defensive replacement behind the plate in the top half of the inning, and now he came to bat with two outs and two on. He revived the crowd with a home run to deep left, plating Groat and Clemente ahead of him. Terry came in to retire Hoak, but the Pirates had scored five runs on five hits and, with one inning to go, led 9-7.

It would not be that simple. Pittsburgh's Bob Friend came on to save the game. Friend had started

Pirate fans embrace their team, and each other, after Game Seven of the 1960 World Series.

Games Two and Six and was hit hard in each contest, allowing eight runs in six innings pitched. He faced two batters in the ninth, throwing only four pitches but giving up singles to both Richardson and pinch-hitter Dale Long. Pirates skipper Danny Murtaugh didn't waste any time. With the tying run on base, Murtaugh called on southpaw Harvey Haddix to face the heart on the Yankees' lineup. Maris popped out to the catcher in foul territory and then Mantle, batting right-handed, singled to right. Richardson scored and Long motored to third. Stengel inserted Gil McDougald to run for Long. Berra hit a sharp grounder to Nelson at first. Nelson "stepped on the bag to retire Berra but Mantle regained first base, evading Nelson's tag with a beautiful headlong slide."[6] While this was taking place, McDougald scampered home with the tying run. The official scorer credited Berra with an RBI. Skowron forced Mantle at second for the third out.

That set up the bottom-of-the-ninth heroics for Mazeroski. It was a titanic battle between baseball's David and Goliath. According to the *Pittsburgh Post-Gazette*, "Mazeroski, who must be the greatest .270 hitter in baseball—he is today, that's for certain—went sailing around the bases waving his hat in one hand and pandemonium broke loose among the 36,683 patrons."[7] As Maz rounded second, fans were climbing over the railings, and as the hero rounded third, "the crowd poured down on him like a mob attacking a public enemy."[8] They ran with him to home plate and swept over him and his ecstatic teammates. After 35 years, the Pittsburgh Pirates had once again won the World Series.[9]

After the game Mazeroski told reporters, "I thought it would go over. ... I was hoping it would. But I was too happy to think. All year we've been a fighting, come-from-behind ballclub. We always felt we could pull it out—even after the Yankees tied it in the ninth—but I didn't think I'd be the guy to do it."[10] Don Hoak said, "Maz is eighth in the batting order, a spot that doesn't exactly rank him as the greatest hitter of all time, yet he comes up after the Yanks have tied the score in the ninth, and bam!

I said, 'Get out of here, you rotten, stinking, beautiful baseball.'"[11]

Pittsburgh made all of its 11 hits count, leaving only one runner on base. Pirates batters hit four homers in the Series, and three came in Game Seven. (New York smashed 10 round-trippers with two in this contest.) Mazeroski, Virdon, and Burgess each collected two hits. Mantle was 3-for-5 in the losing effort. Richardson had two hits, broke the record for RBIs in a World Series game (six in Game Three) and in a Series (12), and his 11-for-30 performance in the Series earned him MVP honors.

Terry's line was one-third of an inning pitched, one hit, one run, and he took the loss.[12] Shantz pitched well enough to earn the victory, but it would not be. For the Pirates, Friend was charged with two more earned runs without getting an out. Harvey Haddix, even though he had blown the save opportunity in the top of the ninth inning, picked up his second World Series victory. The nine pitchers in the game combined for zero strikeouts while facing 77 batters.

After the game, the Yankees were still in shock. New York had come oh-so-close to a 19th Series championship, but the Steel City team had prevailed. In the clubhouse, Maris said, "What happened to us, for cryin' out loud, what happened?" Teammate Berra supplied the answer: "We just got beat, Roger, by the damnedest baseball team that me or you or anybody else ever played against."[13]

SOURCES

In addition to the sources mentioned in the Notes, the author consulted Baseball-Reference.com and Retrosheet.org.

NOTES

1   David Kelly, "Berra Tells Maris 'What Happened,'" *Pittsburgh Press*, October 14, 1960: 1.

2   Myron Cope, "This Was the Drama—Strategy, Tension of the Finish," *Pittsburgh Post-Gazette*, October 14, 1960: 30.

3   Ibid.

4   "How Pirates Won Final Game of World Series," *Pittsburgh Post-Gazette*, October 14, 1960: 32.

5   Ibid.

6   Ibid.

7   Jack Hernon, ""Pirates Come From Behind to Cop Series," *Pittsburgh Post-Gazette*, October 14, 1960: 1.

8   Cope.

9   The last Pittsburgh club to win the World Series was the 1925 Pirates (95-58). The 1960 Pirates finished the regular season with a record of 95-59. The 1971 Pirates won 97 games, and the 1979 champions won 98 games. Pittsburgh's first World Series victory came in 1909, when the team won 110 games.

10   Ray Kienzl, "Maz Hoped Hit Would Go for HR," *Pittsburgh Post-Gazette*, October 14, 1960: 28.

11   Don Hoak, "This Club Makes a Guy Proud Just to Be Part of It…," *Pittsburgh Post-Gazette*, October 14, 1960: 29.

12   Terry had also taken the loss in Game Four, after allowing three runs in the Pirates' fifth.

13   Kelly.

BOB FRIEND BESTS DON DRYSDALE IN A RECORD-SETTING GAME

APRIL 15, 1961: PITTSBURGH PIRATES 4, LOS ANGELES DODGERS 1, AT LOS ANGELES MEMORIAL COLISEUM

BY ROBERT E. BIONAZ

POSSIBLY THE MOST INTRIGUING thing about baseball is its unpredictability. Fans attending a game have no idea what they are about to see. On April 15, 1961, the 36,783 spectators at the Los Angeles Coliseum watched as the Pittsburgh Pirates and Los Angeles Dodgers tied a major-league record by hitting into nine double plays, seven on groundballs, and two on line drives. A couple of other noteworthy events occurred that evening: Pirates starter Bob Friend completed his first game in Los Angeles since his first Coliseum start on April 29, 1958, and for the third and final time in his major-league career, Pittsburgh center fielder Bill Virdon had a multiple-home-run game.

The early-season contest featured two highly-regarded teams. The Dodgers won the World Series in 1959 and Pirates were defending World Series champions as the 1961 season began. J.G. Taylor Spink picked the Dodgers first and the Pirates second in his 1961 predictions in *The Sporting News*. *Sports Illustrated* echoed Spink's enthusiasm, writing, "This could be the beginning of a Dodger dynasty to rival that of the Yankees or that of the old Brooklyn Dodgers (circa 1946-56). The talent is there; if it doesn't jell this year, it will next, or next after that." As for the Pirates, *Sports Illustrated* predicted: "Buoyed by a champion's *esprit de corps* and confidence, Pirates will be one-two."[1]

That Saturday evening, right-hander Friend made his second start of the 1961 season. He had come up to the majors in 1951 and pitched for some dreadful Pirates teams in the 1950s. Between 1951 and 1957, Pittsburgh finished last four times, seventh twice, and tied for seventh once. The club posted records of 42-112, 50-104, and 53-101 from 1952 through 1954. In Friend's first seven seasons in the majors, his team went 397-681. After four major-league seasons, Friend's record stood at 28-50. However, he blossomed in 1955 as he went 14-9 for a 60-94 last-place team and led the National League with a 2.83 ERA. In 1956, Friend became the workhorse of the Pittsburgh pitching staff. In the next 10 seasons, he made 368 starts and pitched 2,604⅓ innings, tops in the majors in both categories. In 1956 and 1957, the Pirates struggled to reach respectability, and in 1958, they broke their nine-year streak of losing seasons by finishing in second with an 84-70 record. Improving with his team, Friend led the majors (tied with Warren Spahn) with 22 wins that season. Both Friend and his team regressed in 1959; the Pirates finished fourth with a 78-76 mark and Friend had a disastrous 8-19 season. The 1960 season was a wonderland for Pittsburgh and Friend as the team won its first pennant since 1927, its first World Series since 1925, and the pitcher bounced back with an 18-12 record and a 3.00 ERA.

In contrast to the regular season, Friend had a nightmarish World Series. He started and lost Games Two and Six in Forbes Field, the first a 16-3 Yankees victory, the second a 12-0 drubbing. In Game Two, Friend turned in a fair performance; going four innings and allowing two earned runs before leaving for a pinch-hitter while trailing, 3-1. He then watched four of the five Pittsburgh relievers allow the Yankees 13 more runs. In Game Six, Friend started and went only two-plus innings, allowing five hits and five earned runs. Then, in Game Seven, he started the ninth inning with a 9-7 lead. With a chance to nail down the World Series crown and redeem himself in the balance, Friend gave up singles to Bobby

Richardson and pinch-hitter Dale Long. Having seen enough, Pirates manager Danny Murtaugh yanked him and brought in eventual winner Harvey Haddix. When the two runs for which Friend was responsible scored, his 1960 World Series pitching ledger stood at 0-2 with a 13.50 ERA in six innings. His poor 1959 performance along with his disastrous outings against the Yankees spurred some doubts about his 1961 prospects. The *Sporting News* wondered whether Friend and other Pirates who had comeback years in 1960 were "now due to suffer relapses ...?" Friend's teammate, third baseman Don Hoak, acknowledged that Friend "still carries a bit of a scar from the Series" and hopefully added, "and he'll be a better pitcher because of his experience with the Yankees."[2] Friend's Opening Day performance did nothing to ease the doubts. He lasted only 4⅔ innings against the San Francisco Giants, allowing six earned runs and two home runs, leaving with a 6-3 deficit. He managed to escape being tagged with the loss when the Pirates rallied for an 8-7 victory.

On April 15, both teams started the game with 2-2 records. The Dodgers sent Don Drysdale to the mound to oppose Friend. A durable, hard-throwing right-hander prone to temper tantrums, Drysdale was coming off a mediocre 15-14 mark in 1960, although he sported a stellar 2.84 ERA. Drysdale had come up at 19 with the Brooklyn Dodgers in 1956 and had won 17 games in two separate seasons, but had yet to harness his potential. He came into the game with a 1-0 record, having pitched seven innings against the Philadelphia Phillies in a 6-2 win on April 11. As with all games played in the Coliseum, pitchers always had to be cognizant of the short distance to left field, 250 feet with a 40-foot screen. With cavernous distances to right field, pop flies often settled into the left-field stands while tremendous drives to right died in outfielders' gloves. Drysdale hated pitching in the ballpark, telling Bob Verdi, "It's nothing but a sideshow. Who feels like playing baseball in this place?"[3]

The Pirates started with a bang, as leadoff man Virdon homered. The game remained 1-0 through the fifth inning. Although both teams managed to put runners on base, by the end of five frames, they had hit into eight double plays, four for each side. The Pirates extended their lead to 3-0 in the top of the sixth. Virdon singled and Dick Groat doubled, sending Virdon to third. After Drysdale walked Bob Skinner intentionally, he struck out Dick Stuart and got Roberto Clemente on a popout. However, Hoak doubled to left, scoring Virdon and Groat and giving Friend some breathing room.

In the top of the seventh inning, Virdon touched Dodgers right-handed reliever Larry Sherry for his second homer of the game, giving Friend a 4-0 lead. In the top of the eighth, Clemente grounded into the game's ninth double play. The 4-0 score held until the bottom of the eighth when the Dodgers struck for their only run of the game on a triple by pinch-hitter Jim Gilliam and a single by Willie Davis. Friend then struck out Tommy Davis and pitched a scoreless ninth inning for a 4-1 win, his first of 1961.[4]

For a short time, it looked as though the Pirates might be up to defending their National League title. On May 2, they went into first place with a 6-0 victory over the St. Louis Cardinals, running their record to 10-6. On May 24, the team stood in second place at 20-13, one game behind the San Francisco Giants. The club then bumped along at a .500 clip for the next seven weeks, finding itself in third at the first All-Star break on July 9, with a 42-35 mark, 8½ games behind the league-leading Cincinnati Reds. On that date, Friend's record stood at 9-9 with a 4.15 ERA. The season's second half proved disastrous for him and the Pirates. The team went 33-44 to finish sixth with a disappointing 75-79 record. Although he lowered his season ERA to a final 3.85, Friend won only five games the second half, losing 10 to make his final mark 14-19.

Friend pitched another four years for the Pirates, posting a 56-60 record and running his Pittsburgh win total to 191. In December 1965, the Pirates traded him to the New York Yankees and after a brief stay in the Bronx, Friend was sold to the Mets in June 1966. He retired after the 1966 season with a lifetime mark of 197-230 and an ERA of 3.58. Respectable totals for a pitcher who labored many years for a dreadful team. In an interview on November 17, 2012, Friend pointed to two career highlights: "[H]is 22 wins in 1958 and his durability—perhaps above all—stood out in his mind. 'I was able to pitch every third or fourth day for more than ten years and not miss starts,' he said." Friend's April 15 victory over the Dodgers provided a glimpse at a workmanlike and utterly dependable major-league pitcher turning in a professional effort. The hallmarks of a proud player nicknamed "The Warrior."[5]

NOTES

1 J.G. Taylor Spink, "Swami Spink Sees Dodger, Oriole Flags," *The Sporting News*, April 26, 1961: 7; *Sports Illustrated*, April 10, 1961: 55, 61.

2 *The Sporting News*, April 26, 1961: 7; Les Biederman, "Super-Heated Don Hoak Raps Experts Who 'Overlooked' Bucs," *The Sporting News*, April 19, 1961: 10.

3 Don Drysdale with Bob Verdi, *Once a Bum, Always a Dodger: My Life in Baseball from Brooklyn to Los Angeles* (New York: St. Martin's Press, 1990), 71; quoted in Don Zminda, "A Home Like No Other: The Dodgers in L.A. Memorial Coliseum," SABR. sabr.org/research/home-no-other-dodgers-la-memorial-coliseum. Accessed July 7, 2017.Between 1956 and 1965, Drysdale made 334 starts, pitching 2574⅔ innings, both marks second in the majors to Friend.

4 Game account from Retrosheet: retrosheet.org/boxesetc/1961/B04150LAN1961.htm, accessed August 14, 2017.

5 Clifton Parker, *Bob Friend*, sabr.org/bioproj/person/c90d66d9, accessed August 15, 2017.

GENE BAKER: THE FIRST AFRICAN AMERICAN TO MANAGE IN THE MAJORS

SEPTEMBER 21, 1963: LOS ANGELES DODGERS 5, PITTSBURGH PIRATES 3, AT DODGER STADIUM

BY JORGE IBER, PHD

THANKS IN NO SMALL PART TO BRUCE Markusen's 2009 work, *The Team That Changed Baseball: Roberto Clemente and the 1971 Pittsburgh Pirates*, even non-Pirates aficionados are now familiar with the story of how, at Three Rivers Stadium on September 1 of that year Danny Murtaugh filled out a lineup that featured, for the first time in major-league history, a starting nine made up exclusively of African-Americans and Latinos.[1] Certainly, as Markusen and others have noted, this was not done purposefully so as to break down racial and ethnic barriers in the sport; rather, the "Whistling Irishman" merely went with what he considered to be his best players for that specific contest against the Philadelphia Phillies: It resulted in a 10-7 victory for the home club. What many may not be aware of is that approximately 10 years before, the Pirates were involved in another racial milestone: the first time an African-American would manage a team at the major-league level. This momentous yet mostly overlooked event took place at Dodger Stadium on September 21, 1963, when both Murtaugh and coach Frank Oceak were tossed from the game by umpire Doug Harvey for arguing a close call at first base. Into the managerial breach now entered former Kansas City Monarchs, Chicago Cubs, and Pirates infielder (and at that time Pirates coach) Gene Baker. Although he guided the squad for but two innings, Baker made history and helped to pave the way for Frank Robinson to become the first African-American major-league manager in 1975 with the Cleveland Indians.

Gene Baker was involved in many "firsts" during his career on the diamond. He was the first African-American signed by the Chicago Cubs, in 1950. He played his first season in the minors in his home state of Iowa (in Des Moines), hit .321, and scored 50 runs in just 49 games. He was one of the first African-Americans to play in the Pacific Coast League, where he spent most of 1951 through 1953 with the Triple-A Los Angeles Angels. Over those years he hit .278, .260, and .284. His final campaign was punctuated by 20 home runs, his professional best. Given his success in the PCL, many in Chicago wondered why the club did not bring Baker up to replace the Cubs' regular shortstop during these years, Roy Smalley, who hit for considerably less average and power. Baker finally got his chance with the big club in the latter stages of the 1953 season. He was called up on August 31, but due to a back injury, he did not make his first appearance until September 20. By then Ernie Banks had already taken the field at shortstop for the North Siders. Club management decided to shift Baker to second and he and Banks formed a more-than-reliable double-play combination. Both players were named to the 1954 *Sporting News* rookie team. At the plate, Baker did not disappoint either, hitting .275, .268, and .258 over his time in the Windy City. He was a 1955 All-Star. Given that he was 32 after the 1957 campaign, the Cubs felt they could move him to another club; that turned out to be the Pirates, an organization that would employ Baker for the rest of his career.

As a Pirate starting in 1957, he backed up Bill Mazeroski and Dick Groat and played in 111 games. He was slotted as Pittsburgh's third baseman for 1958, but suffered a severe leg injury on July 13 and was lost for the rest of that season, as well as for 1959. Baker returned to the field in 1960, but in a utility role. He played sparingly during the regular season, and went hitless in three at-bats during the World Series against the New York Yankees. With the start of 1961, his role became even more restricted, and the Pirates waived him on June 15. Less than a week later, Baker was named manager of the Pirates' Class-D Batavia, New York, affiliate. With this announcement, the Pirates had broken a significant barrier: naming the first African-American to skipper a major-league-affiliated squad. Given the tenor and assumptions of many during these times, it was necessary for Pirates general manager Joe L. Brown to reassure fans that Baker was "capable" of handling the job. "He is a fine gentleman with outstanding baseball knowledge and experience. We're confident he will do a fine job in the managerial field," Brown said. His confidence was well placed, as Baker guided his team, which was in seventh place when he took over, to a third-place finish in the standings, as well as a victory in the first round of New York-Penn League playoffs. As a result, Baker earned a promotion in 1962 to the Pirates' Triple-A team in Columbus, and then to the big-league club for 1963. It was late in that season that certain events transpired and resulted in cementing Baker's status as a pioneer in the sport.[2]

After having played their final home game on September 18 against the Cubs, the Pirates took off to finish the season on a nine-game Western swing through Los Angeles, Houston, and San Francisco. The first game of the set against the Dodgers took place on September 20 and resulted in a 2-0 defeat for Pittsburgh, leaving the team at 72-82, 23 games behind LA. The next day's matchup featured a pitching duel between Bob Friend and Sandy Koufax. As usual, a large crowd of over 48,000 witnessed the proceedings at Chavez Ravine. Both hurlers were sharp from the outset and there was no scoring over the first three innings. In the Pirates' half of the fourth, Donn Clendenon homered off Koufax for the game's first tally. Friend continued his mastery over the first-place Dodgers through six frames. Pittsburgh scored again in the top of the seventh as, after a Clendenon flyout to deep center, Ted Savage singled and stole second as Mazeroski struck out, then scored on a single by Bill Virdon to make the score 2-0 for the

visitors. In the bottom of the frame the Dodgers scored twice to tie the game on singles by Jim Gilliam and Wally Moon, a groundout by Tommy Davis, a single by Ron Fairly (which scored Gilliam), then a single by Willie Davis off Harvey Haddix (who had replaced Friend). Johnny Roseboro grounded into a double play to end the rally.

In the top of the eighth, the Pirates regained the lead with singles by Clemente, Clendenon, and Savage. Mazeroski was then walked intentionally and Ron Perranoski replaced Koufax on the hill. The final out of the inning came when Bill Virdon grounded out, pitcher to first. Both Murtaugh and Oceak contested the call and were ejected. This left Gene Baker in charge of the Pirates for the final two frames. Of course, it would have been wonderful if there had been a victory to discuss after all of these significant events. It was not to be as Willie Davis hit a three-run home run in the bottom of the ninth off Tommie Sisk after singles by Tommy Davis and Ron Fairly, to win the game for Los Angeles.

While Gene Baker did not get "credit" in the won-lost column for his managerial effort in this

Gene Baker

contest, it was an important breakthrough. An African-American had managed in the majors and had demonstrated the ability to lead, if but temporarily, a team at this level. In 1964, Baker was once again assigned to lead the Batavia squad. This season did not turn out as well as did 1961, however. This team finished dead last in the circuit with a mark of 33-97. After that year, Baker and the Pirates parted ways in regard to managing, though he remained in the team's employ for the next 23 years. He returned to his hometown of Davenport, Iowa, and served as the Pirates' chief scout in the Midwest. Gene Baker died on December 1, 1999, from a heart attack. While he did not gain great notoriety from his exploits, he proved to the management of baseball that a man of his race was more than capable of leading men on the diamond. As his widow noted after Baker's passing: "He was very proud of some of the accomplishments that he made with the Pittsburgh Pirates. He was a black man in a white man's sport, and he did very well in that sport."[3]

SOURCES

In addition to the sources cited in the Notes, the author also used information from retrosheet.org and Baseball-Reference.com.

NOTES

1 Bruce Markusen, *The Team That Changed Baseball: Roberto Clemente and the 1971 Pittsburgh Pirates* (Yardley, Pennsylvania: Westholme Publishing, 2009).

2 Robert J. Puerzer, "Gene Baker: Unsung Hero in the Integration of Major League Baseball," *Black Ball*, Volume 4, Number 1, Spring 2011: 28-37.

3 Elizabeth Bloom, "Pittsburgh Pirates' Gene Baker Quietly Crossed Baseball's Color Lines," *Pittsburgh Post-Gazette*, February 7, 2016. See: post-gazette.com/sports/pirates/2016/02/07/As-a-Pirate-Gene-Baker-quietly-broke-baseball-s-color-barriers/stories/201602070090.

MAZEROSKI, LYNCH, AND STARGELL LEAD ROUT OF CARDINALS

JULY 22, 1964: PITTSBURGH PIRATES 13, ST. LOUIS CARDINALS 2, AT BUSCH STADIUM I

BY MIKE HUBER

THE PITTSBURGH PIRATES BOMBED the St. Louis Cardinals before a meager gathering of 11,089 spectators at Busch Stadium. Three Pirates batters connected for long home runs and on top of that, Willie Stargell hit for the cycle, en route to a 13-2 Pittsburgh victory.

At the 1964 All Star break, the fourth-place Pirates were 40-35, seven games behind the National League-leading Philadelphia Phillies. Thirteen games later, they came into this match at 46-42, still in fourth place. The sixth-place Cardinals were a game behind the Pirates with a 47-45 record. Bob Veale, with his 6-foot-6-inch frame, toed the rubber for Pittsburgh, seeking his fourth straight victory; he was opposed by right-handed veteran Roger Craig, pitching in his first season for the Redbirds.

Three Pittsburgh mainstays, Stargell, Jerry Lynch, and Bill Mazeroski, had not been contributing regularly on the offensive side, due to, respectively, injury, part-time playing, and a slump. Stargell's knees had been bothering him. Lynch was being platooned in left field with Stargell while routinely being subbed for defensively by Manny Mota. Gold Glove second baseman Mazeroski had been 4-for-26 (.154) during the seven games before this series.

Stargell got the party started in the very first inning. With one out, Bill Virdon, Roberto Clemente, and Lynch all reached on singles to the outfield. With one run in, Stargell sent a shot to deep center for a two-run triple. This extended his hitting streak to a modest four games.[1] Mazeroski followed with a sacrifice fly to left, driving in Stargell. Pittsburgh had staked Veale to a four-run lead. The Pittsburgh left-hander allowed three singles to St. Louis in the

first five innings, but the home team never threatened to score.

In the fifth inning, after a two-out walk to Clemente, Lynch hit his 10th homer of the season, a shot that cleared the nearly 37-foot-high pavilion roof in right-center. Cardinals manager Johnny Keane called to the bullpen and brought on Bob Humphreys to face Stargell. The Pirates slugger greeted the right-handed reliever with his 13th homer, making it a back-to-back barrage for a 7-0 Pittsburgh advantage. (His shot also cleared the roof in right.)

In the sixth, Lou Brock hit a two-out double for the Cardinals and scored on a single by former Buc Dick Groat, to break up Veale's shutout. Pittsburgh answered with three more runs in the top of the seventh. Righty Ray Washburn came on to pitch for St. Louis and was tagged by the middle of the Pirates lineup. Clemente singled with one out. After Lynch lined out, Stargell drove a single to left, and Mazeroski doubled to right for two more runs batted in. Jim Pagliaroni singled up the middle and Mazeroski came around to score. Veale and the Pirates now had a 10-1 lead.

Pittsburgh manufactured a run in the eighth on a single by Veale, an error by St. Louis right fielder Carl Warwick, and a sacrifice fly by Virdon. The Cardinals responded in their half with a meaningless tally to make it 11-2 on singles by Brock and pinch-hitter Charlie James. Ken Boyer lifted a sacrifice fly to right, and Brock scored the second and final run for the home team.

In the final frame, with 19-year-old rookie right-hander Dave Bakenhaster now doing the pitching duties for St. Louis, Stargell doubled to right, completing the cycle. Mazeroski slammed his seventh home run of the season, deep into the left-field seats, as Pittsburgh added two more tallies. Bakenhaster finished the inning without further damage, but this was his last outing in the major league. The young-ster was optioned the next day to Winnipeg of the Class-A Northern League, and never returned to the majors. The final score was 13-2.

Stargell joked with reporters after the game, saying, "The more hits I got the better my knee felt. I wanted to stay in the game even after we had a big lead because I felt good hitting."[2] The next day, he said, "If I can hit like I did last night, I'll run on one leg."[3] He had walked in the fourth inning, so he had reached base every time he came to the plate. He scored four runs and drove in three. Lynch also had three RBIs. Since July 13, Lynch was batting .480 (12-for-25) with three round-trippers and 17 RBIs. His batting average vaulted to .323. The *Pittsburgh Press* printed, "'I never felt better,' Lynch enthused. 'I want to play regularly because I feel I can help more.'"[4] Mazeroski drove in five runs in a 2-for-4 performance, adding a sacrifice fly. He delivered three hits in the first game of the series, driving in two runs. For the series, he had seven hits, eight RBIs, and six runs scored, and it seemed as if his slump was over.

As part of the 18-hit attack, Veale chipped in with three singles and a run batted in while picking up his 11th win of the season. Veale lost 15 pounds during the game, and he had to change his shirt three times![5] He struck out four and walked none in the com-plete-game outing, gaining his fourth straight win, improving his season's record to 11-6. Clemente added two hits and three runs scored to the attack, raising his major-league-leading batting average to .347.[6] Brock and Groat each had two hits for the Cardinals. Craig took the loss, evening his record at 5-5.

The win was the second in a Pittsburgh sweep over the Cardinals. In the three-game series, the Pirates pounded out 46 hits and scored 29 runs. But after beating St. Louis, the Pirates were 32-40 the rest of the season, falling to sixth place. St. Louis stood at 47-47, tied for seventh place, after this sweep. But then they played 46-22 ball to win the National League pennant on the last day of the regular season by a single game over Philadelphia and Cincinnati, and eventually beat the New York Yankees in the World Series.

Stargell's cycle was the 18th for the Pittsburgh franchise. It came 13 years after Gus Bell's cycle on June 4, 1951. Richie Zisk became the next Pirate after Stargell to cycle (on June 9, 1974). Stargell's cycle was the third of four in the 1964 season. The others who hit for the cycle were Jim King (Washington Senators, May 26), Ken Boyer (St. Louis Cardinals, June 16), and Jim Fregosi (Los Angeles Angels, July 28).

SOURCES

In addition to the sources mentioned in the notes, the author con-sulted baseball-reference.com and retrosheet.org.

NOTES

1 Over the next six games, Stargell continued hitting the ball well, elevating his batting average to .303 with a 10-game hitting streak, in which he hit three home runs and drove in 10 runs. In 1964, Stargell hit 21 home runs, beginning a string of 13 consecutive seasons with at least 20 round-trippers.

2 Lester J. Biederman, "Lynch's Big Bat Is Magic Wand for Pirates," *Pittsburgh Press*, July 23, 1964: 43.

3 Ed Wilks, "Ailing Bucs Enjoy Get-Well Cards," *St. Louis Post-Dispatch*, July 23, 1964: 47.

4 Biederman.

5 Les Biederman, "Veale Loses 15 Pounds in Game," *Pittsburgh Press*, July 23, 1964: 44.

6 Clemente finished the 1964 season at .339, which led the league. He also led the National League in batting average in 1961 (.351), 1965 (.329), and 1967 (.357).

BOB VEALE'S 16 STRIKEOUTS

JUNE 1, 1965: PITTSBURGH PIRATES 4, PHILADELPHIA PHILLIES 0, AT FORBES FIELD

BY BLAKE W. SHERRY

IN 1965, THE PIRATES MADE AN IM-pressive second-half run at the pennant. That year, as they would the following year, the Bucs finished third to the Giants and pennant-winning Dodgers. On a rainy June 1 evening, with the Pirates riding an 11-game winning streak, fireballer Bob Veale struck out 16 Philadelphia Phillies batters in front of 10,478 fans at Forbes Field. In so doing, the 29-year-old left-hander broke his own Pirates record for strikeouts in a nine-inning game, set the season before on September 22 against the Milwaukee Braves.[1] That 15-strikeout game had broken the Pirates record of 12, first established by Babe Adams in 1909 and tied by Veale himself twice. Veale struck out 16 batters in Cincinnati on September 30, 1964, but pitched 12⅓ innings to do so.

Veale was in the dawn of his prime years. His third full season and one year removed from a breakout 18-win season and a National League-leading 250 strikeouts, 1965 was the first of Veale's two All-Star years. His pitching opponent on June 1, 1965, was the Phillies' Art Mahaffey.

Veale was facing a Phillies lineup with three players hitting over .300: Cookie Rojas, Dick Allen, and Alex Johnson. Rojas and Allen finished the season over .300, while Johnson finished just under the mark at .294. The '65 Phillies also featured slugger Johnny Callison, who was in the midst of hitting a career-high 32 home runs. But Veale was also facing players still fighting demons stirred up from their epic collapse in 1964, when they lost a 6½-game lead with just 12 games to play.

After a slight rain delay before the game, two additional rain delays took place in the first two innings.[2] The first came with two outs in the first and lasted 85 minutes. Veale benefited from a first-inning lead

given to him on a sacrifice fly by Willie Stargell and a run-scoring single by Jerry Lynch. In the second inning, a rain delay of 40 minutes again halted the game. When the tarp was rolled back, Veale began his march toward the team strikeout record, getting Gus Triandos and Lew Burdette (who had relieved Mahaffey in the first) to strike out looking. In the third, Veale had back-to-back strikeouts of Dick Allen and Dick Stuart.

As the game progressed, Veale continued to shut down the Phillies, and with a strikeout and a double play in the fourth, he had his first three-up, three-down inning. Despite his 16 strikeouts, the sixth inning was the only one in which he struck out the side. He did it to the heart of the batting order: Allen, Stuart, and Johnson. After the game, Allen gave high praise to Veale, saying, "He's as tough as I've seen."[3] Dick Stuart echoed his comments: "He's as rough as I've batted against. Sandy Koufax has struck me out only once in his career. Veale got me three times the first time he faced me."[4]

The Pirates got two more runs in the sixth inning, and led 4-0. In the seventh Veale struck out pinch-hitter Wes Covington. After Rojas led off the eighth inning with a single, Veale struck out the next three batters—Callison, Allen, and Stuart—giving him 14 strikeouts through eight innings.

In the ninth inning, Veale struck out the first two batters before Triandos grounded out to third baseman Bob Bailey to end the game. Eleven of the last 15 outs were strikeouts. Veale finished with a five-hit shutout while walking only two batters and raising his season record to 5-2.

It was the Pirates' 12th consecutive win. After an 11-3 drubbing by the Reds on May 20, the Bucs had started their streak. And they needed the streak,

Bob Veale

as immediately before it they had lost the previous eight and were a lowly 9-24 after the loss to the Reds. Pittsburgh's 12-game streak ended the night after Veale's masterpiece, when the Bucs fell to the New York Mets, 8-6.

After his game, Veale said he felt he was tiring at the end. "I just felt tired, but (catcher) Jim Pagliaroni kept telling me I wasn't. I believe I had nine strikeouts on the fastball and seven on curves."[5] Veale even mustered some humor about the rain delays making for a long game. "This is the first time I've ever pitched two days running," he laughed, as he threw his first pitch at 8:20 P.M. Tuesday and his last at 12:40 A.M. Wednesday.[6] Phillies manager Gene Mauch marveled at Veale's stamina over the evening and said, "It was the longest fire I've ever seen."[7] Those few fans who stayed for the final outs in the eighth and ninth inning, cheering every strike, treated Veale with an appreciative standing ovation with the final out.[8] It was his third straight complete-game victory.

Heading into the 2018 season, Veale's record of 16 strikeouts remained the Pirates nine-inning record.

When he set it, it was two behind the record of 18 set by Bob Feller and later Koufax. Since then that record has been broken several times. As of 2018 the record for strikeouts in a game is 20 and is shared by three pitchers: Roger Clemens (twice), Kerry Wood, and Max Scherzer. For his part, Veale fanned a record 22 batters while pitching for the Triple-A Columbus Jets against Buffalo on August 10, 1962. He was lifted for a pinch-hitter in the 10th inning with the score tied and didn't get a win for the game.

The day after his 16-strikeout game, Veale said, "I can't recall when I've been faster. My fastball was moving and my curveball was going good. I was getting them out on both pitches."[9] The game reignited the debate over who was the fastest pitcher in the National League, Veale or Koufax. Most batters believed that Koufax had the better curveball, but that Veale had the better fastball.[10]

In his next start, on Sunday, June 6, Veale struck out six while shutting out the Mets and Warren Spahn 3-0 in the second game of a doubleheader sweep for the Bucs. His catcher Pagliaroni commented, "He didn't have the speed he had Tuesday but his ball was jumping more."[11]

Veale finished the season with 17 wins and struck out a career-high 276 batters. However, he finished second in the League to Koufax's incredible 382. He tied for third in shutouts, with seven. His fine season got him plenty of notice around the league, including that of pennant-winning Los Angeles Dodgers manager Walter Alston, who observed, "He throws hard and gets the job done."[12] But in the eyes of Giants star Willie Mays, Veale had gained better control by letting up on his fastball. Mays commented, "The reason he's so good is that he doesn't throw as hard as he once did. That may sound funny but when he threw hard, he didn't know where the ball was going. Since he let up on this fastball a little he throws strikes."[13]

Veale finished in the Top 10 in strikeouts four more times, and had six seasons in the top 10 for strikeouts per nine innings pitched. He also had two career highlights in 1971 with the Bucs. He won a championship ring, and had the distinction of pitching in relief in the historic game on September

1 when the Pirates started a lineup of all minority players for the first time in major-league history.

Thanks in part to the 12-game winning streak, the Bucs reached .500 at 26-26 on June 9, and finish strongly playing nearly .600 ball in the second half to finish in third place with a 90-72 record. They inched ahead of the Reds for third place on the next-to-last day of the season.

NOTES

1   Jack Hernon, "Veale Fans 16 as Bucs Make It 12 in a Row," *Pittsburgh Post-Gazette*, June 2, 1965: 22.

2   Ibid.

3   Lester Biederman, "Veale's 'Fanning Bee' Shortens Long Night," *Pittsburgh Press*, June 2, 1965: 59.

4   Ibid.

5   Ibid.

6   Ibid.

7   Lester Biederman, "Veale Faster at End Than Start of 16-Whiff Job Against Phils," *The Sporting News*, July 3, 1965: 13.

8   Al Abrams, "Sidelights on Sports: 'Superman Tag' Fits Veale," *Pittsburgh Post-Gazette*, June 3, 1965: 32.

9   Bill Nunn Jr., "Change of Pace," *Pittsburgh Courier*, June 12, 1965: 23.

10   United Press International, "Veale Gains Backing as Fast Southpaw," newspaper clipping from Baseball Hall of Fame files, June 3, 1965, source unknown.

11   Lester Biederman, "Veale Turns Heat on Mets," *Pittsburgh Press*, June 7, 1965: 32.

12   Lester Biederman, "Veale Shows He's on Way to Greatness," *Pittsburgh Press*, June 3, 1965: 51.

13   Ibid.

MATTY ALOU CLAIMS THE 1966 BATTING TITLE

OCTOBER 2, 1966: SAN FRANCISCO GIANTS 7, PITTSBURGH PIRATES 3 (11 INNINGS), AT FORBES FIELD

BY JORGE IBER, PHD

AFTER THE 1965 SEASON BILL VIRDON retired from the Pirates. Virdon was a solid contributor with a career batting average of .267 and nearly 1,600 safeties, as well as an excellent center fielder. In order to plug this chasm, manager Harry "The Hat" Walker and general manager Joe L. Brown traded pitcher Ozzie Virgil to the San Francisco Giants for outfielder and Dominican Republic native Matty Alou. The plan was to platoon the right-handed-hitting Manny Mota, who had split time in center during 1965 and hit .279, with his left-handed-hitting countryman. There was concern, however, since Alou hit a measly .231 in 1965 with San Francisco. Still, Walker saw potential, arguing, "[W]e feel we found a replacement who can run faster … (and) is capable of hitting .300. All he needs is a change of environment."[1] In 1966, Walker would prove quite a prophet: While "The Hat" has been criticized for his dealings with Latino ball players,[2] he connected with both Mota and Alou in terms of hitting. Three years later, Mota recalled that Walker convinced both players they should "hit the ball down and to all fields. He taught this old dog new tricks."[3] Alou noted in his first spring training under Walker that "I never hit to left field before in my life, but now I like it."[4] To the Pirates' benefit, Mota finished with a .332 batting average in 359 plate appearances while Alou claimed the National League crown with a .342 batting average.

One of the techniques Walker emphasized was to make better use of the bunt in order to take advantage of Alou's speed. By the middle of May, sportswriter Les Biederman put the National League on notice that the Buccos were making effective use of this weapon in their arsenal. "They're bringing the bunt back into the game and it's surprising what a

few good bunts do to a player's morale and his batting average."[5] By the end of the first six weeks of the campaign, Alou was hitting .329 and Mota was even more impressive at .370.[6] By early July, the top four spots in the National League batting race were occupied by Pirates; in addition to Alou and Mota, Roberto Clemente and Willie Stargell were among the league leaders.[7]

The results Alou generated were quite surprising to many who followed the game and team. How did this come about? It can be credited to both the player's talent as well as Walker's coaching. "You're trying to pull everything to right field to take advantage of the wind that blows in San Francisco. Well, you won't find any of that wind at Forbes Field and you won't find it in other parks in the National League."[8] The bunting and infield-hit trend continued to bolster Alou's average toward the end of the season as, by mid-September (through 135 games), he had amassed 20 safe bunts and 29 infield hits and had maintained an average around the .340 mark since the middle of July.[9]

One would think that this average would have allowed Alou to cruise toward a batting title, but he had some significant competition — from his brother Felipe, then playing with the Atlanta Braves. Since the All-Star break, Felipe Alou increased his average from .299 to as high as .331. While he did not catch his sibling, the eldest brother of the Alou trio finished second in the race with a .327 clip. Even more significantly, Felipe understood what this would mean to Latino ballplayers in general, as well as to fans of this background back in their native lands, as well as in the United States. "I love my country. That's the reason I would like for Matty or myself to win the batting championship. First, it would be good for the Alou family, and next it would be good for the Dominican Republic."[10] The final aspect of this familial, batting, and Latino drama culminated on October 2, 1966, at Forbes Field.

The Pirates finished with a respectable 92-70 mark, but wound up in third place, 3 games behind the pennant-winning Dodgers. Thus, when San Francisco, at the time occupying third place, came to town for the final three contests of the campaign, one of the few key questions still to be determined was whether Matty would manage to hold off Felipe. Things did not go well for the Pirates (they lost all three games), or for Matty to start. In a Saturday twin bill, Alou achieved but one hit in nine trips, appropriately enough, a bunt single in the fifth inning of the first game off Juan Marichal to spark a three-run rally.[11] As a result, his average dropped to .338. Although still ahead in the batting race by 11 points, there remained one contest for Matty to seal his status. That came on Sunday, October 2. The Pirates lost, 7-3 in extra innings, but Alou claimed his title with an impressive performance.

The contest featured a matchup between Gaylord Perry for San Francisco and Pittsburgh's Bob Veale and was witnessed by 33,827 fans. Both men had winning records that season, though the right-handed Perry was the more impressive, finishing with a 21-8 mark and an ERA of 2.99. Veale finished 16-12 with an ERA of 3.02. After Veale retired the visitors in order in the top of the first, Alou led off the Pirates' half of the frame with a single. He advanced to second on a groundout by Gene Alley, but was stranded at third after Mota grounded out and Clemente was called out on strikes. The Pirates scored first in the bottom of the second, as Donn Clendenon tripled to lead off and came home on a groundout by Bob Bailey after Bill Mazeroski struck out. In the top of the third, Jesus Alou singled with two outs and the Giants took the lead on Willie Mays's two-run home run over the scoreboard.

Alou took his second turn at bat in the bottom of the third and singled to left. He moved to third on Alley's infield single and an error by third baseman Jim Ray Hart. He then scored on an infield single by

Matty Alou

Mota and Alley advanced to third on another error by Hart. Alley scored as Clendenon hit into a double play. The inning ended on a fly out by Mazeroski After three innings, the score stood at 3-2 in the Pirates' favor. Alou singled again in the fifth. He faced Perry a final time in the seventh, and grounded out to first. There was no further scoring through the end of the eighth inning.

The Giants pushed across the tying tally in the ninth off Veale as Hart walked, was sacrificed to second by Jack Hiatt, and came home on a two-out pinch-hit single by Ozzie Virgil (after Ollie Brown had grounded out to short). Jim Davenport forced Virgil at second for the final out. In the bottom of the frame, the Pirates threatened when, with two outs, Alou bunted for a single and moved to third on a single by Alley. Mota walked to load the bases, but Clemente grounded out. There was no scoring in the 10th, although Alou came up for the final time and grounded out with the bases loaded, finishing the day 4-for-6. The Giants plated four runs in the top of the 11th to seal the victory.

Matty Alou went on to play parts of 10 more campaigns in the majors, including four more (1967-1970) with the Pirates, and then moved on to play in Japan for two-plus years. He finished his career with 1,777 hits and a .307 batting average. He came close to defending his title in 1967, averaging .338 and finishing behind Tony Gonzalez of the Philadelphia Phillies (.339) and teammate Clemente (.357).[12] Alou's '66 batting title marked the third consecutive year that a Pirate had won this award, Clemente having won in 1964 and 1965.

NOTES

1   Jack Hernon, "Roaming Around," *Pittsburgh Post-Gazette*, February 16, 1966: 23.

2   John H. Ingham, "Managing Integration: Clemente, Wills, 'Harry the Hat' and the Pittsburgh Pirates' 1967 Season of Discontent," *Nine: A Journal of Baseball History and Culture*, Fall 2012: 69-102.

3   James Collins, "Mota Was More Than a 'Throw-In.'" *Baseball Digest*, November 1959: 58.

4   Les Biederman, "A Tip by The Hat, Presto! Matty's a Terror at Dish," *The Sporting News*, March 26, 1966: 21.

5   Les Biederman, "Alert Buccos Reap Harvest Using Bunt as Deadly Weapon," *The Sporting News*, May 14, 1966: 7.

6   Les Biederman, "If You Could Buy Stock in Matty and Manny, Price Would Soar," *The Sporting News*, June 4, 1966: 15. See also retrosheet.org/boxesetc/1966/I1motam1010051966.htm, and retrosheet.org/boxesetc/1966/I1aloum1010071966.htm.

7   Les Biederman, "Blue Flame Trails Each Veale Pitch," *The Sporting News*, July 9, 1966: 11.

8   Les Biederman, "Swat Master Matty Learns Fast: Bunt, Speed Fatten Mark," *The Sporting News*, July 16, 1966: 8.

9   Les Biederman, "Bucs' Matty Lifts Mark 100 Points," *The Sporting News*, September 24, 1966: 3 and 6. See the dates noted at: retrosheet.org/boxesetc/1966/I1aloum1010071966.htm.

10   Wayne Minshew, "Brother vs. Brother in N.L. Bat Drama: Faith Helps Felipe Alou, Tepee Star," *The Sporting News*, September 24, 1966: 3, 6.

11   retrosheet.org/boxesetc/1966/B10011PIT1966.htm.

12   Mark Armour, "Matty Alou." sabr.org/bioproj/person/3d8b257b.

CLEMENTE BLASTS THREE HOMERS AND KNOCKS IN ALL SEVEN RUNS IN BUCS' LOSS

MAY 15, 1967: CINCINNATI REDS 8, PITTSBURGH 7 (10 INNINGS), AT CROSLEY FIELD

BY GREGORY H. WOLF

"IT WAS ALMOST LIKE ROBERTO Clemente playing the Reds all by himself," gushed sportswriter Les Biederman in the *Pittsburgh Press*, "and coming so close to wrecking them singlehandedly."[1] Affectionately nicknamed "Arriba" by Pirates radio broadcaster Bob Prince, Clemente belted three home runs and knocked in all seven Pirates runs, but his offensive heroics were not enough to overcome dreadful pitching and a relentless Reds hitting attack punctuated by Tony Perez's game-winning, walk-off double in the 10th. "[It was] one of those weird, sloppy but tingling battles that drive scorekeepers slap-happy and customers back to the park," wrote Lou Smith excitedly in the *Cincinnati Enquirer*.[2]

Skipper Dave Bristol's Reds were one of the early-season surprises in 1967. After a seventh-place finish the previous year, they had gotten off to a hot start and occupied first place (21-10), paced by one of the deepest pitching staffs in the league. Two games behind the Reds were manager Harry Walker's Pirates (16-9), the hottest team in baseball and winners of 13 of their last 17 contests. The Bucs' strength was hitting; they had led the majors in batting average in 1966 (.279) and duplicated the feat in 1967 (.277).

A cool, damp spring evening with temperatures hovering around 50 degrees suggested an advantage for the hurlers. Both clubs sent former All-Stars to the rubber in the first game of a three-game series: The Pirates' 31-year-old southpaw, Bob Veale, one of the hardest throwers in baseball, owned a 63-40 career record, including 5-0 with a stellar 2.49 ERA thus far in '67. The Reds' right-hander Milt Pappas, acquired from the Baltimore Orioles in the trade

for the immensely popular Frank Robinson, was a dependable workhorse with a 125-87 career record. Instead of a pitching duel, the paltry crowd of 5,222 spectators at Crosley Field was treated to a memorable offensive explosion.

After Matty Alou, the reigning NL batting champion (.342), led off the game with a single, Clemente belted what Charley Feeney of the *Pittsburgh Post-Gazette* considered a routine fly to right field, but it "got caught in the wind and sailed into the seats" for a two-run homer, his fourth of the season.[3] Clemente had gotten off to a slow start in 1967, but had been wielding what Feeney called a "booming bat" in the Pirates surge.[4] In that 17-game stretch, the seven-time All-Star and three-time NL batting king, had gone 29-for-71 (.408) to raise his batting average to a major-league-leading .368. Coincidentally, Clemente's home run also gave him a cycle in his last four at-bats; he had hit a double, triple, and single in his final three at-bats against the Atlanta Braves the day before.

Veale held the Reds hitless through the first four innings, but got a scare in the fourth when Pete Rose reached on Bill Mazeroski's error and moved to third on a wild pitch with no outs. After Perez fanned and Lee May walked, shortstop Gene Alley scoped up Don Pavletich's grounder and did what the Pirates did best: initiate a 6-4-3 twin killing; they led the big leagues with 186 double plays in 1967.

In the fifth the Pirates took advantage of Perez's error on Alou's routine one-out grounder. After Maury Wills forced Alou, and then stole second, Clemente whacked a two-out liner over the nine-foot fence in right field for a 4-0 Pirates lead. Long regarded as one of baseball's best pure hitters, Clemente tailored his game to fit cavernous Forbes Field in the Steel City, stretching doubles into triples. Never considered a power hitter, the reigning NL MVP had belted a career-most 29 round-trippers the previous campaign, well above his average of 17 over the last seven seasons (1960-66).

Veale survived a shaky fifth (single, balk, and walk), and then came unraveled in the sixth. He "lost rhythm on his fastball suddenly," opined Biederman, and threw more pitches in the inning than he had in the previous five combined.[5] Rose, Perez, and May led off with consecutive singles, the last of which resulted in the Reds' first tally. After Veale's wild pitch enabled the runners to each move up a base, Pavletich drove in Perez on a sacrifice fly, and Chico Ruiz's groundout plated May to pull the Reds to within one, 4-3. Leo Cardenas's single ended Veale's outing, before reliever Pete Mikkelsen ended the frame.

Dubbed a "one-man-show" by the *Cincinnati Enquirer*, Clemente greeted Darrell Osteen, the Reds' third hurler of the game, by spanking a double over Rose's head in left-center to drive in Mikkelsen and

Roberto Clemente

Wills (both of whom Osteen had walked) for a 6-3 Pirates lead in the seventh.[6]

Mikkelsen, a rubber-armed middle reliever who had appeared in 71 games the previous season, imploded just minutes later. Rose drew a two-out walk and scored on Perez's double to deep center field. May followed with a single to score Perez and the Reds were back within one run.

Both teams threatened in the eighth, but came up empty. In relief of Osteen, Gerry Arrigo uncorked a wild pitch to the first batter he faced, enabling Mazeroski (who had walked) to scamper to second with no outs. Making his first appearance since tossing a one-hit shutout against the New York Mets on April 29, Arrigo dusted off the cobwebs to escape the jam. In the Reds' half of the frame, pinch-hitter Art Shamsky, who had clouted three homers against the Pirates at Crosley Field on August 12 the previous season, led off with a double, but was stranded on third, setting the stage for two nailbiting innings.

In the ninth the Pirates tacked on an insurance run when Clemente blasted what Cincinnati sportswriter Lou Smith described as a "prodigious" home run that easily cleared the left-field fence.[7]

A two-run lead in the ninth inning on the road would normally have been an ideal situation for longtime Pirates reliever Elroy Face. However, the 39-year-old forkballer had pitched in each of the last three games, picking up two saves and a win versus the Braves, and remained seated. Walker counted on offseason acquisition Juan Pizarro to close the deal. Lee May, in his first campaign as a regular, greeted the former White Sox All-Star with a towering one-out, two-run round-tripper, driving in Perez (on first via a single) to tie the game, 7-7. Arrigo followed with what appeared to be another home run, over the right-field wall. "[T]he ball was over the fence for a home run," said Clemente, "when I jumped and kept it from falling in."[8] Crashing into the fence, Clemente prevented a game-winning clout, but could not hold onto the ball, which fell for a double. As the Bucs' bullpen remained silent, Pizarro ended the frame with runners on second and third.

After Arrigo set down the Pirates 1-2-3 in the 10th, Pizarro yielded a leadoff single to speedy Tommy Harper and punched out Vada Pinson. Third baseman Maury Wills made a "brilliant" backhanded and potentially game-saving stab of Rose's grounder and then fired to Maz at second to force Harper.[9] To the plate stepped Tony Perez, en route to his first of seven All-Star selections in his 23-year Hall of Fame career. With Steve Blass beginning to warm up in the Pirates 'pen, Perez walloped a double over center fielder Manny Mota's head and off the wall to drive in Rose for the winning run to end the game in 3 hours and 18 minutes. (Mota had replaced Alou to begin the ninth inning after the latter had been ejected by home-plate umpire Bill Jackowski for tossing his bat and helmet when he was called out on strikes.)[10]

"It was an unbelievable finish to an unforgettable game," opined Biederman with an air of disappointment.[11] The trio of Rose, Perez, and May victimized Bucs hurlers for eight of the team's 13 hits, scored all eight Reds runs, and drove in six off what Feeney bluntly called "bad" Pirate pitchers.[12] The "Reds had heroes all over the place," gushed Smith, and included Arrigo, who yielded only one hit—Clemente's homer—in three innings to earn the victory.[13]

"This could have been one of Clemente's great moments," wrote Feeney. "The defeat took away any joy he might have known."[14] Clemente became the fifth Pirate to hit three homers in a game, joining Ralph Kiner (who did it four times between 1947 and 1951), Frank Thomas, and Roman Mejias (both in 1958), Dick Stuart (1960), and Willie Stargell (1965). "[Y]es, my biggest game, but not my best," replied Clemente when asked to comment on his fifth multi-homer game in his 13-year career. "I don't count this one, we lost."[15]

Clemente hit 240 home runs in his 18-year career, which ended prematurely when he lost his life in a humanitarian mission to Nicaragua on December 31, 1972, just about three months after he notched his 3,000th and final hit. On August 13, 1969, he tied his career best by belting three home runs in a 10-5 victory against the San Francisco Giants in Candlestick Park. On 11 other occasions he hit two round-trippers in a game.

SOURCES

In addition to the sources cited in the Notes, the author also accessed Retrosheet.org, Baseball-Reference.com, the SABR Minor Leagues Database, accessed online at Baseball-Reference.com, SABR.org, and *The Sporting News* archive via Paper of Record.

NOTES

1   Les Biederman, "Clemente's 'Biggest' Game Wasted," *Pittsburgh Press*, May 16, 1967: 34.

2   Lou Smith, Perez's Double Scuttles Pirates in 10th, 8-7," *Cincinnati Enquirer*, May 16, 1967: 23.

3   Charley Feeney, "Cincinnati Overpowers Clemente by 8-7," *Pittsburgh Post-Gazette*, May 16, 1967: 26.

4   Ibid.

5   Biederman.

6   Smith.

7   Ibid.

8   Biederman.

9   Smith.

10   Feeney.

11   Biederman.

12   Feeney.

13   Smith.

14   Feeney.

15   Biederman.

A TROPHY NO-HITTER: BOB MOOSE BITES THE AMAZIN' METS IN THE BIG APPLE

SEPTEMBER 20, 1969: PITTSBURGH PIRATES 4, NEW YORK METS 0, AT SHEA STADIUM

BY GREGORY H. WOLF

A MOOD OF NERVOUS, ANXIOUS EX- citement permeated Shea Stadium on an abnormally cool 60-degree Saturday afternoon, September 20, 1969, as the New York Mets took on the Pittsburgh Pirates in the third tilt of a five-game series. The Mets were on the verge of a miracle, but a celebration in the Big Apple was far from certain. Beginning on August 16, skipper Gil Hodges' squad had won 29 of 36 games going into the Pittsburgh series, transforming a 10-game deficit in the newly formed National League East into an unlikely five-game lead for the division crown, overtaking the fading Chicago Cubs. The Mets had seemed invincible, but "showed they were partly mortal," opined *New York Times* writer Leonard Koppett when the third-place Pirates ambushed them in a double-header to kick off the series, defeating them 8-2 and 8-0 behind route-going outings by hard-throwing Bob Veale and Luke Walker.[1] Despite those defeats, the magic number for the Mets (91-60) to capture their first crown in just their eighth season of existence since losing a major-league record 120 games as an expansion club in 1962 dropped to seven (any combination of Mets victories and Cubs losses) with 11 more games to play as they faced the ever-dangerous Bucs (81-70).

The pitching match-up featured two promising youngsters. The Mets' 22-year-old rookie right-hander Gary Gentry (11-11, 3.65 ERA) formed the "Big Three" with aces Tom Seaver and Jerry Koosman. Toeing the rubber for the Pirates was right-hander Bob Moose, about three weeks shy of his 22nd birthday. As a rookie swingman in 1968, Moose compiled a misleading 8-12 record that was offset by a robust 2.74 ERA. On June 14, 1968, he came within four

outs of tossing the first no-hitter in the 60-year history Forbes Field when he held the Houston Astros hitless for 7⅔ innings before settling for a two-hit shutout. "He's the reason we traded Jim Bunning," said Pirates skipper Jim Shepard about Moose's potential. "We just had to be able to start him regularly. He's the sort of kid a manager would give a million dollars to have."[2] After tossing complete games to win his first two starts of 1969, Moose struggled and spent much of the season in the bullpen before moving back in the starting rotation in mid-August. With an impressive 11-3 record (3.18 ERA), Moose was coming off two excellent starts, including an overpowering 14-strikeout performance in a victory against Philadelphia and a tough-luck 1-0 loss to the Mets eight days earlier, when he yielded yielding just five hits and a run while fanning 10 in eight innings in the Steel City. "Any way I want to use him I know he's ready," gushed Shepard. "He has the ideal temperament for a pitcher."[3]

The Shea Stadium crowd of 38,784, plus an additional 16,000 Midget Mets youth baseball players and 2,500 Ladies Day ticket holders, seemed restless. According to Koppett, their "attention was on the Met situation in the pennant race more than on the game itself."[4] Their distraction was excusable. At almost the same time as home-plate umpire Augie Donatelli yelled "Play Ball!" in Queens, New York, the Cubs commenced their game against the St. Louis Cardinals in Wrigley Field.

The first three innings shaped up as a classic pitchers' duel with only two baserunners. Gentry yielded a leadoff single to Matty Alou and Moose issued a one-out walk in the third to Ed Kranepool, an original Met.

All of that changed in the fourth. "It was the only bad inning Gentry had," opined Koppett, "but it was plenty."[5] Rookie Dave Cash, subbing for the perennial Gold Glove Award winner Bill Mazeroski at the keystone sack, led off with a walk and moved to second on Willie Stargell's single to center. With Roberto Clemente at bat, Cash and Stargell darted off in a double steal and slid easily into their respective bases as catcher J.C. Martin dropped Gentry's offering and did not attempt a throw. After the "Great One" worked the count to 3-and-2, three successive pitches decided the game. Ball four to Clemente was a wild pitch, enabling Cash to score the game's first run and Stargell to reach third. The next pitch hit rookie Al Oliver on the wrist to load the bases. Stargell dashed home when Gentry unleashed another wild pitch while facing Manny Sanguillen. Emerging as one of the best-hitting catchers in just his first full season in the majors, Sanguillen grounded to third, driving in Clemente to increase the Pirates' lead to 3-0. Gentry retired the next two batters with Oliver on third.

While Moose mowed down the Mets, the partisan crowd was eerily silent. At Wrigley Field the Cubs maintained a 1-0 lead on the Redbirds as that game also entered the middle innings.

After the game Moose said that he began thinking about the no-hitter in the sixth inning. "That's when I started checking the lineup on the scoreboard," said the western Pennsylvania native, who grew up in Export, about 22 miles east of Pittsburgh.[6] After pinch-hitter Jim Gosger struck out and Tommie Agee grounded to second, Wayne Garrett connected for the Mets' first and only hard-hit ball. "When he hit the ball," admitted Moose, "I thought it was gone, but then I saw the wind hold it up. I knew that if anybody could catch it, Roberto would."[7] Clemente raced to the warning track and made what Koppett described as a "leaping catch" against the right-field wall to preserve the no-hitter.[8]

The eighth inning saw what the *Times* called "one of those bizarre climaxes that only the Mets can achieve."[9] As Ron Swoboda struck out for the first out, Shea Stadium burst into a raucous roar as the scoreboard announced that the Cardinals had just scored two runs in the top of the eighth and led the Cubs, 3-1. That news suddenly energized the crowd. The buzz continued even after Moose fanned Martin and Ron Hunt to end the frame.

After retiring the first seven batters he faced, reliever Tug McGraw gave up one-out singles to Sanguillen and Richie Hebner in the ninth. He then unfurled the Mets' third wild pitch of the game, with Moose at the plate, allowing Sanguillen to race home for the Pirates' fourth run.

As fate would have it, the Mets came to bat in the ninth at the same time the Cubs took their last swings against the Cardinals. Moose seemed impervious to the tension of the moment. "The big thing about Moose is that nothing bothers him," said Pittsburgh pitching coach Vern Law, who had fashioned a 162-147 record in 16 seasons with the Pirates, including a 20-9 record and a Cy Young Award for the world champions in 1960.[10] Moose issued his third walk of the game, to Rod Gaspar, to lead off the ninth, then quickly retired Agee on a pop foul to first and Garrett on a grounder to third. "[Moose] was in control at all times," gushed Koppett about the stocky 6-foot, 200-pounder who kept the Mets guessing all afternoon with a steady diet of fastballs, breaking balls, and an occasional kunckler.[11] Moose dispatched Art Shamsky on a slow roller to second to complete the no-hitter in 2 hours and 8 minutes.

As expected, Moose was mobbed by his teammates (and a "few civilians," reported the *Times*[12]) upon tossing the majors' sixth no-hitter of the season.[13] It was just the third no-hitter in Pirates history. The other two were by Cliff Chambers against the Boston Braves at Braves Field on May 6, 1951, and by Nick Maddox versus the Brooklyn Superbas at Exposition Field, in Pittsburgh, coincidentally also on September 20, albeit 62 years earlier (1907).

The Shea Stadium crown stood clapping calmly after Moose's masterpiece, then began cheering loudly three or four minutes later when the scoreboard flashed the Cardinals' 4-1 victory over the Cubs. Despite suffering what Koppett considered the "ultimate indignity" of a no-hitter, the Mets saw their magic number drop to six with the Cubs' loss.[14]

"I think they must be a little nervous," said Moose of the Mets. "They say they don't feel the pressure, but you can't help feel it some."[15] The Mets hadn't lost three straight since August 11-13 in Houston, immediately preceding the club's dramatic push for the crown. The Mets inched closer to the miracle the next day when they swept a doubleheader behind complete games by Koosman and Don Cardwell. Gentry, who picked up the loss against the Pirates, redeemed himself in his next start by tossing a stellar four-hit shutout against St. Louis at Shea to clinch the NL East crown on September 24.

Moose continued his torrid September, winning his final two starts and picking up his fourth save of the season to finish 14-3 with a 2.91 ERA (easily the lowest among starters on the staff) in 170 innings. Seven years later, Moose died tragically at the age of 29 in an automobile accident on his birthday, October 9. A valuable contributor to the Pirates, Moose fashioned a 76-71 record in parts of 10 seasons.

SOURCES

In addition to the sources cited in the Notes, the author accessed Retrosheet.org, Baseball-Reference.com, the SABR Minor Leagues Database, accessed online at Baseball-Reference.com, SABR.org, and *The Sporting News* archive via Paper of Record.

NOTES

1   Leonard Koppett, "Mets Lose to Pirates, 8-2 and 8-0," *New York Times*, September 20, 1969: 34.

2   "Moose Makes No Hit With Mets as He Keeps Pressure on Them," *New York Times*, September 21, 1969: 53.

3   Charley Feeney, "Moose Just Kid, Acts Like Vet," *The Sporting News*, September 20, 1969: 19.

4   Leonard Koppett, "Pirates Beat Mets, 4-0, on No-Hitter; Cubs Lose, Moose Is Victor," *New York Times*, September 21, 1969: S1.

5   Ibid.

6   "Moose Makes No Hit."

7   Ibid.

8   "Pirates Beat Mets."

9   Ibid.

10 "Moose Just Kid."

11 "Pirates Beat Mets."

12 Ibid.

13 The others were by Houston's Don Wilson, Cincinnati's Jim Maloney Montreal's Bill Stoneman, the Chicago Cubs' Ken Holtzman, and Baltimore's Jim Palmer. Wilson's and Maloney's came on consecutive days in a Houston-Cincinnati series.

14 "Pirates Beat Mets."

15 "Moose Makes No Hit."

DOCK ELLIS THROWS A NO-HITTER

JUNE 12, 1970: PITTSBURGH PIRATES 2, SAN DIEGO PADRES 0 (FIRST GAME OF DOUBLEHEADER), AT SAN DIEGO STADIUM

BY RICHARD PUERZER

ON JUNE 12, 1970, DOCK ELLIS pitched one of the greatest games in the history of the Pittsburgh Pirates, throwing a no-hitter in San Diego against the Padres. It was only the fourth official no-hitter in Pirates history.[1] Given what came to light years later, the claim that Ellis was under the influence of LSD when he threw the no-hitter, the game perhaps was one of the most unusual in the history of professional baseball.

The game was played on a Friday evening at San Diego Stadium, and was the first game of a twilight-night doubleheader. The Padres, managed by Preston Gomez, entered the game with a record of 26-35 and were in last place in the National League West Division, already 17½ games behind the first-place Cincinnati Reds. The Pirates, led by manager Danny Murtaugh, came into the game with a record of 28-29, holding onto second place in the National League East, 4½ games behind the Chicago Cubs. The right-handed Ellis was matched up against Padres lefty starter Dave Roberts. A light mist fell throughout the game. Dock Ellis was in his third season with the Pirates and the 25-year-old hurler was quickly becoming one of the best pitchers on the staff.

But throughout this game, Ellis was not terribly sharp. In the first inning, he walked two batters, but got out of the inning by striking out Padres right fielder Ollie Brown. In the fifth and sixth innings, he also walked two batters but was able to get the Padres out without allowing any baserunners to advance. He also had trouble holding runners on at first base, and allowed three steals of second for the Padres. In all, he walked eight batters, including three walks to Padres

third baseman Steve Huntz. He also hit one batter, center fielder Ivan Murrell.

Although the Padres had very few hard-hit balls, Ellis relied on his defense quite a bit; they pulled off at least three tough defensive plays. In the second inning, center fielder Matty Alou made a running one-handed grab in right-center of Padres Chris Cannizzaro's line drive. In the eighth inning, Alou made another running grab, this time of a line drive off of the bat of Padres cleanup hitter Nate Colbert. But the defensive gem of the game came in the bottom of the seventh inning when leadoff batter Ramon Webster, pinch-hitting for pitcher Dave Roberts, hit a ball sharply up the middle. Pirates second baseman Bill Mazeroski made a diving backhanded play on the ball, taking the base hit away.[2] The ninth inning was one of Ellis's smoothest: He got the Padres to go down 1-2-3, with the game ending on a strikeout looking of pinch-hitter Ed Spiezio. It was reported that Ellis threw about 150 pitches in the game, and the game was played in 2 hours and 13 minutes.[3]

Ellis and the Pirates eschewed the tradition of not speaking of the no-hitter on the bench as the game progressed. In the fourth inning, Ellis turned to Pirates rookie and reserve second baseman Dave Cash, who was sitting next to him on the bench, and said, "Hey, look, I've got a no-no going." Cash then reminded Ellis at the end of every inning, "Remember, now, you're still on the no-no."[4]

The Pirates offense was kept in check for much of the game, managing only five hits and no walks. However, left fielder Willie Stargell belted two solo home runs, his 11th and 12th round-trippers of the season, one in the second inning to left field and the

Dock Ellis

other in the seventh inning to right, to account for the only two runs scored in the game.[5] Offensively, Ellis went 0-for-3, with two strikeouts and a groundout.

After the game the Pirates mobbed Ellis on the mound. However, as this was the first game of a doubleheader, the team had to prepare for the second game, putting a damper on an extended celebration. It was mentioned however, that Ellis was "particularly cooperative" with the sportswriters after the game, something that was not always the case for the sometimes combative pitcher.[6] The Pirates lost the second game, 5-2. The split gave the Pirates had a record of 29-30, and they would go on to win 89 games and finish first in the National League East.

It was not until 1984 that Dock Ellis began to tell the public he had been under the influence of LSD when he threw the no-hitter. The explanation he gave was that he was at his home in Los Angeles on the day of the game, and mistakenly believed that the Pirates had an offday. At around noon, he ingested LSD. At 1 P.M., his girlfriend read in the newspaper that the Pirates in fact did have a game that day in

San Diego, and that Ellis was scheduled to pitch. Ellis got to the airport and flew from Los Angeles to San Diego, arriving at the park in time to pitch.[7]

In describing his experiences pitching in the game, Ellis said that as he pitched, it felt to him that the ball changed size throughout the game, that at times the batter looked like Richard Nixon or Jimi Hendrix wielding a guitar instead of a bat, and that he sometimes did not see the catcher as he pitched.[8]

After his baseball career ended in 1979, Ellis said he had always been under the influence of drugs, including amphetamines or "greenies," or alcohol when he pitched. But he insisted that this was the only time he pitched while on LSD. After retiring as a player, Ellis entered drug treatment. He later became a drug counselor and remained sober for the rest of life. Ellis died in 2008 of cirrhosis of the liver. He is buried in Inglewood Park Cemetery in Inglewood, California. *No No: A Dockumentary*, a 2014 documentary film, provides an excellent and often moving overview of Ellis's life, including, of course, his no-hit game.

SOURCES

In addition to the sources cited in the Notes, the author also consulted Baseball-Reference.com.

NOTES

1   David Finoli and Bill Ranier, *The Pittsburgh Pirates Encyclopedia* (New York: Sports Publishing, 2003), 623. This does not include Harvey Haddix's performance on May 26, 1959, in which he pitched 12 perfect innings, but ultimately lost the game by a score of 1-0 in 13 innings.

2   Charley Feeney, "Ellis Fires No-Hitter Against Padres, 2-0," *Pittsburgh Post-Gazette*, June 13, 1970: 10-11.

3   Bill Christine, "No Hit Ellis Knows About Pressure," *Pittsburgh Press*, June 13, 1970: 6.

4   Donald Hall with Dock Ellis, *Dock Ellis in the Country of Baseball* (New York: Coward, McCann, and Geoghegan, New York, 1976), 134.

5   Christine.

6   Feeney.

7   Paul Smizik, "Ellis: I Pitched No-Hitter on LSD," *Pittsburgh Press*, April 8. 1984: D1.

8   *No No: A Dockumentary*, directed by Jeff Radice, 2014.

HUMAN LOCUSTS HAVE THEIR DAY

FORBES FIELD FINALE: JUNE 28, 1970: PITTSBURGH PIRATES 4, CHICAGO CUBS 1 (SECOND GAME), AT FORBES FIELD

BY JEFF BARTO

AT 11:00 A.M., THE ROOKIE PITCHER relaxed in a booth on Forbes Avenue. Five hours later he would start the final baseball game at Pittsburgh's Forbes Field. James Lorin Nelson recalled that morning: "I remember sitting in McDonald's having a cup of coffee about a block from the park and watching people going to the park and how excited they were. I was pitching the second game so I was in no hurry to get there because I didn't want to get too excited so early."[1]

It was June 28, 1970, and the Pirates scheduled a doubleheader to close out their aging ballpark. That Sunday morning nearly 10,000 tickets were still available.[2] But by the time Nelson took the mound for the nightcap, 40,918 fans packed the park, its fourth largest regular-season crowd ever.[3] Back on June 30, 1909, Forbes Field opened as one of the first concrete and steel ballparks. The Pirates lost, 3-2, that day to the Chicago Cubs, who now looked to repeat that result in closing down Forbes Field almost 61 years later.

As an early-morning haze burned off, the temperature peaked at 76 degrees by noon. Across the street from the ballpark stood a couple of curbside hot-dog stands. Smells of boiled franks permeated the area along with the odor of stogie cigars, roasted peanuts, and stale popcorn.[4] Fans stopped by the open-air stands to munch on one last dog before heading in. Tom Evans owned Tom and Jerry's Hot Dogs for 33 years on Sennott Street near home plate. He lamented his future loss of revenue: "You might say this is involuntary retirement."[5]

The first game started at 1:05 P.M., and the Pirates won 3-2. Between games Pirates broadcaster Nellie King interviewed the Bucs' star right fielder, Roberto Clemente. Clemente earlier purchased several dozen baseballs that he signed, dated, and personalized for King and other Pirate officials.[6] Clemente then reflected on his fading workplace, "This will mean a great deal to me because I've been here 16 years, almost half my life. I've been here 16 years in this ballpark … and the fans have been great for me here. …"[7] Clemente left the interview to watch the rest of the afternoon from the bench, sitting out Forbes Field's final contest.

A cloudless sky greeted the Bucs as they took the field at 4:17 P.M. Full sunshine warmed the crowd with a balmy 73 degrees. Though the sun's glare affected several outfield plays, it was a critical infield error in the fifth inning that would cost the Cubs the game. Little else attracted interest during Forbes' finale. It would be the events afterward that left memories of panic, chaos, and damage.

Forbes Field never hosted a no-hitter and when Don Kessinger singled on the game's third pitch, game number 4,728 wouldn't be one either.[8] Nelson recalled how quickly the Cubs greeted him in the first inning: "When I came out to warm up, there was electricity in the air. The first three hitters got hits to start the game, and it was 1-0 with runners on first and third. Jim Hickman was the cleanup hitter, and the count went to 3-and-2 before he hit into a unique double play. He hit a ground ball to (Richie) Hebner at third, who threw to Maz at second, who threw to home to get the runner at the plate.[9] Then I got the next hitter to pop out, and the crowd went nuts."[10] The run completed the Cubs scoring for the afternoon as the right-handed Nelson settled down over the next seven innings.

Chicago's starter, right-hander Milt Pappas, recently acquired from the Atlanta Braves, opposed

Nelson in his Cubs debut. Pappas yielded four fly balls in the first inning, three of them for outs. The fourth fly produced the last home run at Forbes Field. Al Oliver replaced Clemente in right field and lifted a 3-and-2 pitch high and five rows deep over the 28-foot screen atop the right-field fence. It stood as the Bucs' only home run in an 11-game homestand; it tied the score at 1-1.[11]

The next three innings became a fly-ball fest, producing neither groundouts nor runs. Nelson forced eight fly outs and a strikeout while Pappas scattered three strikeouts among six fly-ball put-outs. In fact, over his six innings, Pappas induced only one groundball. It was in the fifth inning and it proved to be pivotal. Bob Robertson started the Bucs' fifth with a single to left and stole second. After Gene Alley popped out to first and Jerry May struck out, Pappas intentionally walked Bill Mazeroski to get to his mound mate, Nelson. Ron Santo fielded Nelson's weak grounder to third, but first baseman Hickman dropped the knee-high throw to load the bases. Leadoff hitter Matty Alou then chopped a ball through to right field for a two-run single to break the tie and put the Pirates ahead to stay, 3-1. The Bucs tacked on the final run at Forbes Field in the sixth inning. Oliver doubled, moved to third on Willie Stargell's long fly out, and scored on Robertson's sacrifice fly. The final three innings produced little action. Lefty Larry Gura relieved Pappas in the seventh inning and pitched two solid innings of relief, yielding a harmless double to Mazeroski. Nelson pitched a flawless seventh. In the eighth, Hickman grounded to shortstop Gene Alley, who flipped to second, as Maz fittingly turned the final double play at Forbes Field to erase a leadoff single.

After throwing 132 pitches in eight innings, Nelson was done.[12] Pirates manager Danny Murtaugh made a double switch to start the ninth. Right-hander Dave Giusti came in to pitch, replacing left fielder Stargell as the cleanup hitter. Outfielder Johnny Jeter took over for Stargell in left while batting in Nelson's ninth spot. Giusti got Cleo James to ground out to shortstop and J.C. Martin to fly out to Jeter. Pinch-hitter Willie Smith then stroked the last base hit at

Forbes Field, a single to center. Finally, Kessinger stepped to the plate and tapped a soft bouncer over the mound. Mazeroski charged the ball, took it on the second hop, and continued to the bag to force Smith. It was only proper that Maz made the final putout at old Lady Forbes.

The game itself was unremarkable. The Bucs claimed their seventh straight win, which tied them for first place in the NL East by the end of the day. When Maz touched second at 6:31 P.M., shadows covered the entire infield. Pirates players signed their caps to be given away, and then watched the proceedings from their first-base dugout. "Auld Lang Syne" blared throughout the PA system as security roped off both foul lines. The Pirates planned to raffle over 50 souvenirs and asked Pirates announcer Bob Prince to do the honors from the home-plate area.

At first, the fans flowed quietly onto the field, filling in behind the ropes. They listened to Prince announce winners of clubhouse chairs used by Clemente and Mazeroski. Other prizes raffled off included the players' autographed caps, home plate, bases, and bricks from the outfield wall.[13] The throng of fans still pouring onto the field eventually forced people around to the back of the infield. Feeling completely surrounded, Prince sensed their impatience and pleaded, "Please … please stand back," as panic crept into his voice.[14] Public-address announcer Art McKennan supported Prince with a firmly worded message that echoed throughout the park, "The Pirates are desirous of turning Forbes Field over to the University of Pittsburgh in satisfactory condition."[15] By 7:30 P.M., it was anything but satisfactory.

A headline in the *Pittsburgh Press* the next day captured the tone of the after-game chaos: "Human Locusts Have Their Day."[16] As Prince packed up to escape to the dugout, fans stormed the hand-operated scoreboard baked by the left-field sun. Tom Link, a fan that day, led the rush. "I was one of the first to reach the scoreboard but was crushed by much bigger kids and grown men who literally scrambled over me, some almost using me as a ladder to get up to that scoreboard."[17] Fans climbed and crawled about the hole-riddled scoreboard, forming a giant honeycomb of human bees. They hung from the scoreboard with one hand while flinging the wooden numerals through the air like Frisbees. As the numbers disappeared, fans began to tear the ivy from the outfield walls. Soon the clatter of seats being kicked, ripped, and uprooted from their concrete bases filled the grandstands. Hundreds of fans hauled away rows of seats along with tufts of grass, bathroom signs, bullpen phones, and turnstiles. Even Barney Dreyfuss's plaque, honoring the man who built the ballpark, was stripped from its right-center-field monument, but later returned.[18]

Despite the dismantling of the historic ballpark, there were no injuries, violence, or arrests. People were mourning the loss of their childhood and just wanted a piece of the place. Indeed, even after 13-year-old Jeff Barto claimed his two seats, he still had to phone home for a ride. "The driver of the 61C bus told us 'no way' were we carting them onto his bus," Barto said.[19] To this day those seats sit in his den and sparked the inspiration for this article.

NOTES

1   David Cicotello and Angelo J. Louisa, *Forbes Field, Essays and Memories of the Pirates' Historic Ballpark, 1909-1971* (Jefferson, North Carolina: McFarland Publishing, 2007), 179.

2   Bob Smizik, "Fergie Funny Stuff Fools Alou," *Pittsburgh Press*, June 28, 1970: 4.1.

3   Cicotello and Louisa, 103.

4   The author attended this doubleheader, bought hot dogs from Tom and Jerry's, and does recall the smells described here that followed him into the park.

5   John Place, "Somehow, Oakland Won't Be the Same," *Pittsburgh Press*, June 28, 1970: 2.

6   Charley Feeney, "Twin-Bill Sweep Closes Forbes Field," *The Sporting News*, July 11, 1970: 5; Cicotello and Louisa, 100.

7   The Miley Collection, Chicago Cubs vs. Pittsburgh Pirates, June 28, 1970, Game Two, Historic Radio Broadcasts (1926-1993) Complete Game Broadcast Recordings, Baseball Direct. baseballdirect.com/product/baseball-audio/audio-broadcasts/audio-1970s/audio-1970/1970-628-pittsburgh-4-chicago-nl-1/.

8   Curt Smith, SABR Bioproject: Forbes Field (Pittsburgh), sabr.org/bioproj/park/forbes-field-pittsburgh.

9   Note: Play-by-play scoring shows 5-4-2-5, with Hebner (5) tagging out runner (Popovich); Retrosheet.

10   Cicotello and Louisa, 179.

11   Charley Feeney.

12   Cicotello and Louisa, 94-119. Note: Nelson's 132 pitches were counted from the transcript of the game on the pages indicated. The Miley audio tape (Note 8) also supplemented the count.

13   Charley Feeney.

14   Phil Musick, "Human Locusts Have Their Day," *Pittsburgh Press*, June 29, 1970: 14.

15   Ibid.

16   Ibid.

17   Tom Link, "Portfolio/Baseball Lore: Nothing Topped Forbes Field, Especially on Last Day," *Pittsburgh Post-Gazette*, May 22, 2015: A2.

18   Charley Feeney.

19   Note: The author attended these games, watched, and participated in the aftermath of souvenir hunting that was mostly peaceful. He waited nearly two hours until his friend's mother could steer her station wagon through crowded Forbes Avenue to bring the seats home.

GIBBY FIRES A NO-HITTER

AUGUST 14, 1971: ST. LOUIS CARDINALS 11, PITTSBURGH PIRATES 0, AT THREE RIVERS STADIUM

BY GREGORY H. WOLF

BOB GIBSON THOUGHT HE WAS RUN-
ning out of time. At 35 years of age, the hard-throw-ing right-hander from Omaha had accomplished almost everything a pitcher could as the 1971 season commenced. The five-time 20-game winner twice tossed complete games to win Game Seven of the World Series (1964 and 1967), won the Cy Young and MVP awards in 1968 on the strength of his record-shattering 1.12 ERA and 13 shutouts, and picked up another Cy Young trophy in 1970. However, a no-hitter had thus far proved elusive. He had come close just a year earlier when he held the San Diego Padres hitless for 7⅔ innings on June 17, ultimately settling for his second one-hitter. All that changed on August 14, 1971, when Gibby held the eventual World Series champion Pittsburgh Pirates hitless in an overpowering performance. "This was the greatest game I've pitched anywhere," said Gibson, who fanned 10.[1] "I didn't think that I'd ever throw a no-hitter," admitted the hurler. "I'm a high-ball pitcher and not many high-ball pitchers throw no-hitters."[2]

The St. Louis Cardinals were trying to make a late-season push to capture their fourth pennant in eight years. After losing four straight at Busch Stadium, skipper Red Schoendienst's squad had taken the first two games of a four-game set at Three Rivers Stadium to inaugurate a season-long 13-game road trip. The Redbirds (66-54) trailed the reeling Pirates by only six games. Manager Danny Murtaugh's Bucs (71-48) had been in sole possession of first place since June 10, but had won only six of their last 20 games.

In his 13th big-league season, Gibson was having a very un-Gibson-like campaign (10-10, 3.39 ERA), especially after posting otherworldly numbers in his previous three seasons (a 65-29 record, 2.13 ERA, and

an average of 304 innings pitched and 270 strike-outs per season). Bothered by a sore leg for most of May, Gibson landed on the DL at the end of the month and missed three weeks. The talk of baseball was that the seven-time All-Star with a 4-5 record and 4.27 ERA was washed up. But the competitive hurler had regained his status as one of the game's fiercest since his return, winning six of his previous nine starts, posting a stellar 2.25 ERA and holding opponents to a .212 batting average. His previous vic-tory, a route-going affair in the Gateway City against San Francisco on August 4, was his 200th (against just 126 losses), easily within striking distance of Jesse Haines's franchise record 210. Gibson looked to carry his momentum against the major leagues' highest-scoring offense, affectionately known as the Lumber Company.

Just as the crowd of 30,678 in Three Rivers Stadium was getting comfortable on a Saturday evening, the Cardinals wasted no time attacking the Pirates starter, 28-year-old right-hander Bob Johnson (7-7, 3.21). Johnson was coming off a shutout six days earlier, but this day was forgettable. After former Pirate Matty Alou led off with a walk and moved to second on rookie Jose Cruz's one-out single, Joe Torre and Ted Simmons belted RBI singles to right field. Joe Hague followed with his 11th round-tripper of the season to make it 5-0 and send Johnson to the show-ers. Swingman Bob Moose (7-7, 4.19 ERA) yielded a single to the first batter he faced, Ted Kubiak, but immediately picked him off first before settling into a groove for the next few innings.

Gibson took advantage of a lineup that was miss-ing two of its integral pieces, the venerable Roberto Clemente, batting .323, and Manny Sanguillen, whose .328 average placed him fourth in the NL.

Both had scheduled days off. Supported by what probably seemed an insurmountable five-run cushion, Gibson breezed through the first four innings, allowing three baserunners. Milt May, catching in place of Sanguillen, reached first on a wild pitch after striking out in the second. Jackie Hernandez and Willie Stargell drew walks in the third and fourth, respectively.

The Cardinals, who would lead the majors in hitting with a .275 average and score more runs than any NL team other than the Pirates in 1971, went on another barrage in the fifth. Following Torre's one-out single and Simmons's double, Moose intentionally passed Hague to set up an inning-ending double play. That strategy failed when light-hitting Kubiak stroked a two-run double to right field. Playing the percentages despite a 7-0 score, Moose issued another free pass, to Dal Maxvill to load the bases again. Gibson whacked a sacrifice fly to deep right field to drive in Hague, as the other runners advanced a station. But the third time was a charm for Moose, who retired Ted Sizemore on a fly ball to end the inning after his third intentional walk of the frame.

"You keep looking up at that big scoreboard and see they don't have any hits," remarked Gibson about the growing tension of his no-hitter. "Starting in the seventh, I was really concentrating."[3] Gibson began the seventh by punching out Stargell for his eighth strikeout. May followed with the first hard-hit ball of the game, sending Jose Cruz deep into center field where he made, according to the Associated Press, a "running catch" at the warning track.[4] After Bob Robertson drew Gibson's third and final walk, Bill Mazeroski lined sharply to shortstop Maxvill to end the frame.

The Redbirds scored their final three runs in the eighth inning off reliever Bob Veale, the former major-league strikeout king (250 in 1964 but now on the tail end of a 13-year career). He loaded the bases on one-out singles by Simmons and Hague and a walk by Kubiak. After Maxvill drew a walk to plate the Cardinals' ninth run, Gibson, one of the league's best hitting pitchers, lined a two-run single.

"In the last two innings, I was bearing down extra hard," Gibson said. "I was trying not to make bad pitches. Even when I was getting behind in the count, I was careful not to groove the ball."[5] Gibson set down the side in order in the eighth, benefiting from a stellar play by third baseman Torre, who made a "leaping stab" of Dave Cash's grounder and rifled a throw to first.[6] After Nellie Briles, the Pirates' fourth reliever of the game, tossed a scoreless frame, Gibson began the ninth with a no-hitter intact for the first time in his career.

Gibson was "mixing his fastballs and sliders well and even throwing in a few changeups," reported Neal Russo of the *St. Louis Post-Dispatch*.[7] A noted fly-ball pitcher, Gibson had the Pirates reaching for pitches well out of the strike zone. Vic Davalillo and Al Oliver grounded to short and second, respectively, to begin the ninth. Up stepped Stargell, leading the majors with 39 homers, 101 RBIs, and a .660 slugging percentage, and whom Pirates radio broadcaster Bob Prince often introduced with the phrase, "Spread some chicken on the hill, Will." On a 3-and-2 count, Stargell kept his bat on his shoulder as home-plate umpire Harry Wendelstedt emphatically called strike three ending the game in 2 hours and 22 minutes. Cardinals catcher Ted Simmons rushed to the mound to embrace Gibson as other teammates quickly joined the celebration.

"It thrilled me," said Gibson, who threw 124 pitches to record his 48th career shutout and also reached double digits in strikeouts for the first time that season. "I felt as if we'd won the seventh game of the World Series."[8] The 22-year-old Simmons seemed awestruck by Gibson's dominance: "Man, he was throwing hard."[9]

The Cardinals banged out 16 hits, led by eventual NL MVP Joe Torre, who tallied four singles to improve his major-league-leading batting average to .360. Simmons also had four hits, including a double; he and Hague scored three times each.

"I was looking for a fastball and then that slider cut over the plate at the last second," said Stargell of the strikeout that concluded Gibson's masterpiece, Willie's third whiff. "All those people who said that

Gibson was washed up should have had to bat against him tonight."[10] Stargell was right. Gibson continued his second-half surge, tossing a three- and a four-hit shutout and winning five of his last eight starts to finish with a misleading 16-13 record, tying for the NL lead in shutouts (5) and ranking third in complete games (20).

Gibson's gem was the sixth no-hitter in Cardinals history and the first since Ray Washburn defeated San Francisco, 2-0, on September 18, 1968, at Candlestick Park. It was just the second no-hitter in the Steel City and the first since 1907 when the Pirates Nick Maddox defeated the Brooklyn Superbas, 2-1, on September 20 at Exposition Park. From 1909 through June 28, 1970, the Pirates played in cavernous Forbes Field, which was never the site of a no-hitter.

SOURCES

In addition to the sources cited in the Notes, the author accessed Retrosheet.org, Baseball-Reference.com, the SABR Minor Leagues Database, accessed online at Baseball-Reference.com, SABR.org, and *The Sporting News* archive via Paper of Record.

NOTES

1   Neal Russo, "Gibson Fires First No-Hitter," *St. Louis Post-Dispatch*, August 15, 1971: 1B.

2   Ibid.

3   Ibid.

4   Associated Press, "Bullet Bob Gibson's no-hitter buries Pirates, 11-0," *Sunday News and Tribune* (Jefferson City, Missouri), August 15, 1971: 13.

5   "Gibson Fires First No-Hitter."

6   Associated Press, "Bullet Bob Gibson's No-Hitter Buries Pirates, 11-0."

7   "Gibson Fires First No-Hitter."

8   "Bob Gibson Pitches His First No-Hitter," *St. Louis Post-Dispatch*, August 15, 1971: 1. The pitch count is from Neal Russo, "Gibson's Reward: A Party," *St. Louis Post-Dispatch*, August 16, 1971: 3C.

9   "Gibson Fires First No-Hitter."

10   Ibid.

BEST GAME FOR AL OLIVER

AUGUST 23, 1971: PITTSBURGH PIRATES 15, ATLANTA BRAVES 4, AT ATLANTA STADIUM

BY BLAKE W. SHERRY

ON AUGUST 23, 1971, 24-YEAR-OLD AL Oliver had one of the greatest games in his 18-year major-league career. The game got little media attention locally, partly due to a newspaper strike against the *Pittsburgh Press* and *Pittsburgh Post-Gazette* that ran from mid-May until September.[1] In the second game of a twilight-night doubleheader at Atlanta Stadium, Oliver went 5-for-6 with two home runs, five RBIs, and four runs scored.

In the dog days of August in Atlanta, the Pirates entered the day in first place, 4½ games ahead of the Chicago Cubs, and had just lost three straight to the Cincinnati Reds. They had seen an 11-game lead cut by more than half over the past month. The Lumber Company, as the Pirates were called, needed to stop the bleeding and a twin bill in Georgia heat hardly seemed a tonic for turning things around.

Oliver's big game was also sandwiched between two games of great significance in Pirates and major-league history. The first occurred two weeks previously, when the Pirates were no-hit by the St. Louis Cardinals' Bob Gibson. Since Forbes Field opened in 1909, there had never been a no-hitter there in 60 years. Yet it took just 102 games for one to be pitched at Three Rivers Stadium. Gibson dominated the Bucs with 10 strikeouts in an 11-0 rout, for the only no-hitter of his career.[2]

In the second notable game, a week after Oliver's slugging outburst, Danny Murtaugh submitted a historic lineup populated entirely of African-American and Latino players. Oliver started at first base, hitting seventh. The game is covered in detail in a book published in 2006, *The Team That Changed Baseball*, by Bruce Markusen, and in a 2017 MLB Network documentary, *The Forever Brothers*.

Nothing in game one of the August 23 doubleheader forecast the offensive explosion Oliver would have in game two. In the first game, playing center field, he had only a single in five trips to the plate as the Pirates' combination of Steve Blass and Dave Giusti defeated Phil Niekro, 4-3. For the Bucs, the play of the game was a two-run, two-out triple in the sixth inning by catcher Manny Sanguillen that broke a 1-1 tie. It had followed a two-out walk to Willie Stargell and Bob Robertson's reaching base on an error. Only one of the Pirates' runs was earned in the game.[3]

In the second game, Murtaugh penciled in the same lineup. It included Rennie Stennett at second, Oliver in center, Roberto Clemente in right, Stargell in left, Robertson at first, Sanguillen behind the plate, Dave Cash at third, and Jackie Hernandez at shortstop. He sent right-hander Bob Moose (7-7) to the mound against Braves right-hander Tom Kelley.

Game two started out quickly enough for Oliver. After a leadoff strikeout by Stennett, Oliver got his hitting barrage started with a single, but he was then erased on the basepaths by a double play. In the third inning, with the Bucs down 2-1, Oliver continued hitting his stride. He tripled to score Stennett, who had walked, and then scored himself as Clemente homered, giving the Pirates a lead they would not surrender.

In the top of the fourth, Oliver followed Stennett's double with the first of his two home runs. It was a blast off reliever Jim Nash that put the Bucs up 8-2. They added to their lead with another run on an error by second baseman Felix Millan on a Sanguillen grounder. The rout was on.

Oliver's fourth consecutive hit of the game came leading off the sixth inning with a single off reliever Steve Barber. He scored three batters later on Robertson's 25th homer of the season. (The blast gave Robertson 25 homers for the second straight season, but he would hit only one more during the regular season, then clubbed three in Game Two of the National League Championship Series against the San Francisco Giants.)

In the seventh inning, Oliver flied out to center field to end the inning with a runner on second. It was the only time in the game the Braves retired him.

In the ninth inning, with the Bucs now up 13-4, Oliver strode to the plate needing a double to complete the cycle. But with reliever Nellie Briles on third base after a double of his own and a fielder's choice, he did two bases better. Oliver belted his second homer of the game, capping his 5-for-6 day. The final score was 15-4. Clemente also hit well in the game, finishing 3-for-5, with a home run, before Murtaugh replaced him with Vic Davalillo in the bottom of the eighth.

In relief, Nellie Briles was arguably the second star of the game. He gave up only one single in four

Al Oliver

innings. The game proved important to Briles, as it gave Murtaugh the confidence to insert him in the starting rotation for the remainder of the season.[4]

In Oliver's start the next day, he cooled off a bit but still ripped a two-run triple in four at-bats and scored on Clemente's groundout. But it would not be nearly enough as the Braves turned the tables on the Pirates with a 15-run game themselves, winning 15-5. The back-to-back days also presented fans an opportunity to see Hank Aaron hit a home run and move past Ty Cobb for career total bases (August 23)[5] and then pass Tris Speaker for career runs scored (August 24).[6]

Commenting about Oliver, one of the Lumber Company's leading long-ball hitters, Willie Stargell said, "It was a treat to see a dedicated individual and a great pure hitter come along. We knew right off the bat that we had a diamond. He came in with a tremendous amount of self-confidence as well."[7] Dock Ellis had similar comments several years later after Oliver was traded to the Giants: "He was one of our team leaders. If a team listens to him, it can feed off his confidence, and that was the case with the Pirates. We were roommates coming up through the system, and he always used to say, 'If you can hit, you can hit. I don't need batting practice.' He was extremely confident, in a positive way."[8]

Years later, Oliver would recall this game as one of his best days, but not the most memorable. In a doubleheader on August 17, 1980, when he was with the Texas Rangers, he tied Jimmie Foxx of the Philadelphia A's for the American League record for most total bases in a doubleheader: 21.[9] Oliver went 3-for-5 in game one with a double, triple, and a home run. He followed that with a three-homer game in the nightcap, going 3-for-4, with four RBIs. Foxx had solely owned the record since 1933, and it remains the AL record today. Nate Colbert has the National League record with 22 total bases.

The doubleheader sweep in 1971 revitalized the Pirates. It started a run of 13 wins over the next 16 games en route to the Pirates championship season. Oliver finished the season with a .282 batting average, 64 RBIs, and 14 home runs. The Pirates defeated the

Giants three games to one in the National League Championship Series, and then beat a dominant Baltimore Orioles team boasting four 20-game winners to win the World Series in seven games. Oliver batted .226 with a home run and 7 RBIs in the postseason.

Oliver went on to have an impressive career, and a case can be made for his inclusion in the Hall of Fame. During his playing years, from 1968 through 1985, only Pete Rose and Rob Carew had more hits than Oliver's 2,743. During that period, he was second in doubles (529), third in batting average (.303), and fourth in RBIs (1,326). Over a wider period of time, from 1950 to 1991, Oliver's .303 career BA placed him in the middle of the top 10 in that category for those with a minimum of 9,000 or more at-bats. All members of that list, save for Rose and Oliver, are in the Hall of Fame.[10]

Stargell summarized Oliver as a person this way: "He's a proud man who make no excuses. He possesses as many fine qualities as anybody I ever met."[11]

NOTES

1 Al Oliver and Andrew O'Toole, *Baseball's Best Kept Secret* (Pittsburgh: City of Champions Publishing Company, 1997), 54.

2 John Mehno, "Black and Gold: 1971 Pirates Scrapbook," *Beaver County Times* (Beaver, Pennsylvania), June 20, 2011.

3 Associated Press, "NL Leaders Find Stride," *Columbus* (Ohio) *Dispatch*, August 24, 1971.

4 Bruce Markusen, *The Team That Changed Baseball* (Yardley, Pennsylvania: Westholme Publishing, 2006), 104.

5 Associated Press, "Bucs Sweep, Cubs Win," *Cleveland Plain Dealer*, August 24, 1971.

6 Associated Press, "Aaron Homer Brings Total Bases Record," *Columbus* (Ohio) *Citizen-Journal*, August 25, 1971.

7 "Oliver Makes the Giants Healthier," *San Francisco Examiner*, April 1, 1984.

8 Ibid.

9 Al Oliver, personal interview, March 13, 2017.

10 Oliver and O'Toole, 193.

11 Terence Moore, "Baseball 84," *San Francisco Examiner*, February 24, 1984.

THE FIRST ALL-BLACK LINEUP

SEPTEMBER 1, 1971: PITTSBURGH PIRATES 10, PHILADELPHIA PHILLIES 7, AT THREE RIVERS STADIUM

BY RICHARD PUERZER

THE 1971 PITTSBURGH PIRATES WERE a special team in a multitude of ways. They were probably the most diverse team in the major leagues, featuring 13 players of Latin or African-American descent on their roster, including their best two players, Willie Stargell and Roberto Clemente. That season the Pirates went on to win the World Series, but along the way they also achieved a first in the history of major-league baseball. On September 1, 1971, the Pirates fielded an all-black lineup of African-American and Latino players.

The historic game was played between the Pirates and division rivals the Philadelphia Phillies on a Wednesday night at Three Rivers Stadium in Pittsburgh. The Pirates entered the game with a record of 81-56, and were in first place in the National League East by 4½ games over the St. Louis Cardinals. The Phillies were a lowly 57-77 and in last place in the division. The attendance for the game was 11,278, all of whom got to see history made.

The starting lineup for the Pirates was: batting leadoff and playing second base, Rennie Stennett; batting second and playing center field, Gene Clines; batting third and playing right field, Roberto Clemente; batting cleanup and playing left field, Willie Stargell; batting fifth and catching, Manny Sanguillen; batting sixth and playing third base, Dave Cash; batting seventh and playing first base, Al Oliver; batting eighth and playing shortstop, Jackie Hernandez; and batting ninth and pitching, Dock Ellis.[1]

Aside from the pitcher, the one position and really the only position where a white player was generally more likely to start at this point in the season, was at first base.[2] Bob Robertson generally played first for the Pirates in 1971, especially against left-hand- ed pitching. Despite the fact that the Phillies were starting former-Bucco Woodie Fryman, a lefthander, lefty-swinging Al Oliver got the start at first base for the Bucs.

The occasion of the first all-black lineup came without any warning. Pirates manager Danny Murtaugh posted the lineup, and may not have re- alized himself that he had started the game with all black players. The players themselves did not realize until the game was underway. Al Oliver stated that he had not noticed the lineup until an inning or two into the game when Dave Cash came up to him and said, "Hey Scoop, we've got all brothers out there."[3]

The first inning started out very poorly for Dock Ellis as he walked the first two Phillie batters, Ron Stone and Larry Bowa, to lead off the game. Ellis then righted the ship, getting Tim McCarver to fly out, and striking out Deron Johnson. Ellis was not able to get out of the inning unscathed however, as shortstop Jackie Hernandez was not able to handle a groundball hit by Willie Montanez. The play ended with Stone scoring, Montanez at first, and Bowa at third. Oscar Gamble then singled down the third- base line, allowing Bowa to score. Ellis finally got out of the inning after Terry Harmon, flied out to center. The Pirates roared back in the bottom of the first, with six of the first seven batters reaching base on singles or doubles. By the end of the inning, the Pirates had batted around, knocked out starter Fryman who was replaced byBucky Brandon, and scored five runs.

Ellis was not very sharp in the second inning either, walking leadoff batter John Vukovich and giving up a home run to Ron Stone for his second long-ball of the season. After walking Larry Bowa, Ellis was relieved by Bob Moose. Moose had started the game the previous night, but had gone only two and one-third innings. Two batters later, Moose gave up a two-run home run to Deron Johnson, allowing the Phillies to take the lead, 6-5 on the slugger's 29th blast of the year. Once more, the Pirates came back. After a Gene Clines single, stolen base, and advance to third on an errant throw by McCarver, and a Roberto Clemente walk, Willie Stargell hit a sacrifice fly scoring Clines and Manny Sanguillen hit a home run scoring Clemente. The Pirates finished the inning leading 8-6.

In the third, after Moose gave up a two-out single to Phillies pitcher Brandon putting runners on first and second, Pirates manager Danny Murtaugh chose to replace him with hard-throwingreliever Bob Veale. With Veale's entrance into the game, the Pirates once more fielded an all-black lineup in the field. Veale struck out Phillies batter Ron Stone to get out of the inning. In the bottom of the third, the Pirates manufactured yet another run on a single by Al Oliver, fielder's choice by Jackie Hernandez, sacrifice bunt by Veale, and single by Stennett. The Phillies brought in veteranreliever Dick Selma, who got them out of the inning. The Pirates now led the game by a score of 9-6.

Luke Walker replaced Veale on the mound to start the fourth inning, and the seasoned southpaw promptly loaded the bases with a walk, single, and walk to the first three Phillie batters. Willie Montanez then hit a sacrifice fly allowing Larry Bowa to score. However, Tim McCarver was thrown out attempting to advance to third base on the sacrifice resulting in a double play. Walker got out of the inning, and the Pirates remained ahead of the Phillies by a score of 9-7. The Pirates were held in check in the bottom of the fourth, the first time in the game that they did not score in an inning. Neither team scored in the fifth inning, but the Pirates put together another rally in the sixth, with Gene Clines reaching base on a double, and scoring on a Clemente single, bringing the score to 10-7. Luke Walker then took control of the game, not allowing a Phillie batter to reach base in the seventh, eighth, or ninth innings.

Luke Walker got the win, his seventh of the season, after pitching the final six innings of the game. Bucky Brandon took the loss for the Phillies. Six Pirates batters had two hits apiece, but it was Manny Sanguillen's two-run home run during the second frame, just his sixth of the season, that put the Pirates ahead for good in this rollicking game.

Immediate recognition of the unprecedented event by the press was mixed. There was no newspaper coverage of the event in Pittsburgh as all of the papers were closed due to a strike. The Philadelphia papers did not really recognize the event either. It was not mentioned in the game account in the *Philadelphia Inquirer*,[4] and the only allusion to the unique Pirates lineup in the *Philadelphia Daily News* was reporter Bill Conlin's reference to Danny Murtaugh's "all-soul lineup," with no further explanation.[5] However, a United Press International story that focused upon the all-black lineup that was published in several newspapers around the country. In that article, Danny Murtaugh was quoted as saying, "When it comes to making out the lineup, I'm colorblind, and my athletes know it. They don't know it because I told them. They know it because they're familiar with how I operate. The best men in our organization are the ones who are here. And the ones who are here all play, depending on when the circumstances present themselves."[6] Pirates pitcher Steve Blass commented on Murtaugh's approach to the game, stating, "He treated it with the respect it deserved, but didn't act like it was as big of a deal as they were making—he just put out the nine best Pirates and didn't care if they were white, black, Latino, whatever. It was a tremendous response to that whole thing, which was a big deal."[7]

With the win, the Pirates improved to a record of 82 and 56. They completed the season with a record of 97-65. They went on to defeat the San Francisco Giants in the National League Championship Series three games to one, and then defeated the Baltimore Orioles in the World Series in seven games. Historically, the fielding of an all-black team certainly ranks with that World Series victory.

SOURCES

In addition to the sources cited in the Notes, the author also consulted:

Baseball-Reference.com

Markusen, Bruce. *The Team That Changed Baseball: Roberto Clemente and the 1971 Pittsburgh Pirates* (Yardley, Pennsylvania: Westholme Publishing, 2006).

NOTES

1   On Saturday, June 17, 1967 at Connie Mack Stadium, the Pittsburgh Pirates almost fielded an all-black lineup. Pirates manager Harry Walker's starting lineup was Matty Alou in center field, Maury Wills at third base, Roberto Clemente in right field, Willie Stargell at first base, Manny Mota in left field, Jose Pagan at shortstop, Andre Rodgers at second base, and Jesse Gonder catching. Dennis Ribant was the starting pitcher for that game, but the Pirates also had several black pitchers including Bob Veale, Al McBean , and Juan Pizarrowho all started games that season.

2   Richie Hebner, hospitalized with a viral infection, would have likely been the third baseman since he started 93 games there in 1971, with Jose Pagan (38 games at third base), and Dave Cash (22 games at third base) taking up the slack. Also, Gene Alley (97 games started at shortstop in 1971) was being rested due to a sprained left knee.

3   Al Oliver and Andrew O'Toole, *Baseball's Best Kept Secret: Al Oliver and His Time in Baseball* (Pittsburgh: City of Champions Publishing, 1997), 51.

4   Mark Heisler, "Pirates' Sweep Saddles Phillies With Last Place," *Philadelphia Inquirer*, September 2, 1971: 29-30.

5   Bill Conlin, "Kerplunk! Phils Last," *Philadelphia Daily News*, September 2, 1971: 44.

6   "Pirates Field First All-Black Starting Team," *Tyrone Daily Herald*, September 2, 1971: 5.

7   Colleen Hroncich, *The Whistling Irishman: Danny Murtaugh Remembered* (Philadelphia: Sports Challenge Network, 2010), 178-179.

BLASS, CLEMENTE LEAD PIRATES TO VICTORY IN WORLD SERIES GAME SEVEN

OCTOBER 17, 1971: PITTSBURGH PIRATES 2, BALTIMORE ORIOLES 1, AT MEMORIAL STADIUM, BALTIMORE

BY WAYNE STRUMPFER

IT WAS THE CULMINATION OF THE 1971 baseball season. Game Seven of the World Series pitted the defending world champion Baltimore Orioles vs. the upstart Pittsburgh Pirates. For the Orioles, it was their third consecutive World Series appearance, losing to the New York "Miracle" Mets in 1969 and defeating the Cincinnati Reds in 1970. It was the first World Series appearance for the Pirates since Bill Mazeroski's dramatic walk-off home run against the New York Yankees in 1960.

In 1971, the Orioles were 101-57, winning the American League East Division by 12 games over their nearest rivals, the Detroit Tigers. Baltimore was led by a strong pitching staff that included a record four 20-game winners. Mike Cuellar (20-9), Pat Dobson (20-8), Jim Palmer (20-9), and Dave McNally (21-5) made up the starting rotation for manager Earl Weaver. The Orioles also had a formidable and balanced lineup with five players hitting at least 18 home runs and four players stealing at least 10 bases. Baltimore's defense had a well-built reputation of excellence with Gold Glove winners Mark Belanger at shortstop and Brooks Robinson at third base. Between these two players, they would win 24 Gold Glove awards in their career. The Orioles had swept the Oakland A's in the American League Championship Series, 3-0, to return to the Fall Classic.

The Pittsburgh Pirates won the National League East Division with a 97-65 record, besting second-place St. Louis by seven games. It was the Pirates second consecutive division title. The Pirates were led by veteran manager Danny Murtaugh and 31-year-old slugger Willie Stargell's 48 home runs and 125 runs batted in, and by 36-year-old Roberto Clemente, who batted .341 and recorded 11 outfield assists. Pittsburgh's pitching staff was led by Dock Ellis, who won 19 games, and Steve Blass, who was 15-8 with a 2.85 ERA. Dave Guiusti led a deep bullpen with 30 saves. Pittsburgh beat the San Francisco Giants in the National League Championship Series, three games to one, to gain entrance to the World Series and a matchup against the heavily-favored Orioles.

The first six games of the 1971 World Series were won by the home team. In Baltimore, the Orioles took the first two games, 5-3 and 11-3. When the Series shifted back to Pittsburgh, the Pirates won three in a row, 5-1, 4-3, and 4-0. Back in Baltimore for Game Six, the Orioles staved off elimination with a come-from-behind 10-inning 3-2 victory. Game Seven was played at Baltimore's Memorial Stadium on October 17.

The visiting Pirates sent Steve Blass to the mound. Baltimore countered with Mike Cuellar. It was a rematch of Game Three when Blass pitched a three-hitter to beat Cuellar and the Orioles, 5-1, in Pittsburgh. NBC announcer Curt Gowdy joked before the game, "Poor Earl Weaver, he's down to his last 20-game winner."[1] Cuellar, who was considered by many to be the best screwball pitcher in the majors at the time, was only two years removed from winning the AL Cy Young Award in 1969. Brooks Robinson, in a pre-game interview, commented that he "could really feel it inside" before the game and that a World Series going seven games was "the way it's supposed to be."[2]

The United States Army played the National Anthem and Secretary of State William Rogers, sitting with Baseball Commissioner Bowie Kuhn, threw out the first pitch to Orioles catcher Elrod Hendricks. There was a 15-mile-per-hour wind blowing in from right field and there were high-scattered clouds on the Autumn Maryland day.[3]

Cuellar set the Pirates down in order in the first three innings. Blass started the game shakily by waling leadoff hitter Don Buford. After Blass retired Davey Johnson, Earl Weaver came out of the dugout to complain to the home plate umpire about the Pirates hurler not keeping his foot on the pitching rubber. Curt Gowdy noted he thought the complaint was a "needling tactic" by the Orioles manager. "If he thought of anything to upset Blass or the Pirates, he'll do it," the announcer said.[4] And at first, it seemed to work, as Blass threw three straight balls to slugger Boog Powell. But then Blass regained his composure and retired both Powell and Frank Robinson to end the first inning. Blass later said, "I thank Earl Weaver every time I see him. In the first inning, I was all over the place until Earl came out and it calmed me down with his nonsense."[5]

In the second inning, Blass walked Brooks Robinson and then Pirate first baseman Bob Robertson booted Elrod Hendricks' ground ball to put runners at first and second with one out. But the Pirate hurler induced Mark Belanger to hit into a double play to end the threat. In the third inning, Buford again reached base, this time with a single to right field. However, Blass picked Buford off first base and the Orioles went down quietly.

In the fourth inning, after the first 11 Pirate hitters had been set down by Cuellar, Roberto Clemente hit a home run to left-center field to give Pittsburgh a 1-0 lead. Steve Blass settled down over the next four innings, allowing only one base runner—Elrod Hendricks with a one-out double in the fifth inning—during that stretch. Cuellar matched Blass through seven innings, giving up only a leadoff single to Manny Sanguillen in the fifth inning.

In the top of the eighth, with a 1-0 lead, the Pirates struck again. Willie Stargell led off with a single to left field. Third baseman Jose Pagan then rapped a double off Cuellar scoring Stargell. The Pirates took a 2-0 lead into the bottom of the eighth inning with Blass looking unbeatable. But in the bottom of the eighth, the Orioles bats came to life. Hendricks singled to lead off the inning and he went to second on a single by Belanger. Tom Shopay pinch hit for Cuellar and sacrificed the runners over a base. With runners in scoring position and just one out, Blass was able to get Orioles leadoff hitter Don Buford to ground out to Robertson at first base. Hendricks scored on the play, but Belanger was left stranded at third base when Davey Johnson grounded out to shortstop for the third out.

In the ninth inning, Earl Weaver brought in 20-game winner Pat Dobson to shut down the Pirates. After Dobson retired the first two batters, he gave up consecutive singles to Robertson and Sanguillen. Weaver then brought in another 20-game winner, Dave McNally, from the bullpen to retire Willie Stargell on a groundout to second base.

In the bottom of the ninth, Steve Blass was once again masterful, retiring Boog Powell, Frank Robinson, and Merv Rettenmund in order. Rettenmund hit a bouncer straight up the middle and shortstop Jackie Hernandez fielded it and threw to Robertson at first, and the celebration began. The Pirates were world champions for the fourth time in their franchise history.

Steve Blass, who would be out of baseball by 1974 due to control problems, pitched two complete-game victories in leading Pittsburgh to the championship. Roberto Clemente, playing in his last World Series before his tragic death on December 31, 1972, was named MVP. Clemente, who rarely received national attention due to being overshadowed by the likes of Willie Mays and Henry Aaron, made a statement in the Fall Classic. He collected 12 hits in 29 at-bats and hit two home runs, including the shot in the fourth inning to give the Pirates the lead in Game Seven. Roger Angell wrote that Clemente was "at last the recipient of the kind of national attention he always deserved but was rarely given for his years of brilliant play."[6]

NOTES

1   NBC broadcast, October 17, 1971

2   Ibid.

3   Ibid.

4   Ibid.

5   Bob Hurte, "Steve Blass," SABR Baseball Biography Project, http://sabr.org/bioproj/person/27a6a54d.

6   Ibid.

CLEMENTE COLLECTS NUMBER 3,000 IN LAST AT-BAT

SEPTEMBER 30, 1972: PITTSBURGH PIRATES 5, NEW YORK METS 0, AT THREE RIVERS STADIUM

BY GREGORY H. WOLF

AS THE 1972 SEASON ENTERED ITS last week, Pittsburgh's 38-year-old right fielder, Roberto Clemente, was tired. Coming off an MVP performance the year before in the Pirates' World Series victory over Baltimore, Clemente had labored through arguably the most difficult of his 18 seasons with the Bucs. He had been bothered by a serious intestinal virus for most of the first four months of the season, and suffered from strained tendons on both of his heels. From July 9 to August 22, "Arriba," as longtime Pirates broadcaster Bob Prince liked to call Clemente, started just one game. By August 25 Clemente's averaged had dipped to .301 and he had managed only 82 hits; collecting 36 more in the final five weeks to reach the magical 3,000-hit plateau seemed like a long shot.

Despite the injuries, Clemente had lost none of the drive that made him one of the best players the game had ever seen. "No other player surpasses Clemente in all out strain and effort," wrote Gary Mihoces of the Associated Press. "He runs out every infield grounder as if the World Series were at stake."[1] A four-time NL batting champ en route to his 12th consecutive Gold Glove Award in 1972, Clemente was as easily recognizable for his unique mannerisms, such as rocking his head back and forth trying to get the kinks out while preparing to bat, and his basket catches, as he was for his rocket arm, which earned him the reputation as one the best right fielders in history. But Clemente was more than baseball; he was a proud individual and Puerto Rican. He refused to accept the Americanized name, Bob, that the press had tried for years to heave upon him. And he fought tirelessly on behalf of his fellow Latino ballplayers

and demanded that they be treated with the same respect afforded to Caucasian ones.

As manager Bill Virdon's Pirates cruised to their third consecutive NL East crown by winning 15 of 17 games to move a season-high 15 games ahead of the second-place Cubs on September 14, the focus turned to Clemente's pursuit of 3,000 hits. Just when many counted him out, "The Great One" got hot, pounding out 35 hits in 100 at-bats from August 27 to September 28, leaving him one shy of the milestone. In the first inning against Tom Seaver and the New York Mets at Three Rivers Stadium on September 29, Clemente hit what Al Abrams of the *Pittsburgh Post-Gazette* called a "hard bouncer" to second baseman Ken Boswell, who bobbled the ball.[2] Clemente reached first, but the official scorer, Luke Quay, ruled it an error. "It was a hit all the way," said Clemente bitterly after the game, a 1-0 loss. "This is nothing new. Official scorers have been robbing me of hits for 18 years."[3]

As the Pirates prepared for their second of three games against the Mets on a dreary Saturday afternoon in the Steel City, Clemente seemed disinterested, even unmotivated, according to Bob Smizik of the *Pittsburgh Press*. "What made it so hard for me was that we already clinched the title," said Clemente. "I hate to play exhibition games and these games to me are exhibitions. I can't get up for them."[4] A team-first player, Clemente never looked to pad his statistics and eschewed the spotlight. He seemed worn down psychologically by the attention he had received lately. He was also tired—literally. A noted insomniac, Clemente revealed later that he had been telephoning with friends from Puerto Rico until 4:30 A.M., and then drove his wife, Vera, to the airport.

"When I arrived at the park today," said Clemente, "I had no sleep at all."[5]

A sparse crowd of 13,117 was on hand in Three Rivers Stadium for the 2:15 start time to catch a glimpse of history. On the mound for the Pirates was the 27-year-old enigmatic right-hander Dock Ellis (14-7, 2.80 ERA), hoping that an effective outing might earn him a start in the playoffs. After winning a team-high 19 games the previous season, Ellis had been bothered by tendinitis in his right elbow most of '72 and had not started since tossing 6⅔ scoreless innings against Chicago on September 12. Toeing the rubber for the Mets was rookie southpaw Jon Matlack (14-9, 2.31).

After Ellis tossed a scoreless first, Pirates fans got to their feet when Clemente came to bat with two outs in the first. Standing well off the plate, the noted bad-ball hitter struck out swinging, sending the crowd into a collective sigh.

Clemente came to the plate again to lead off the fourth inning in a scoreless game. Once again the crowd was on its feet, cheering on the former MVP entering the twilight of his illustrious career. "Everyone's standing," said Bob Prince on the KDKA radio broadcast, "and they want Bobby to get that big number 3,000."[6] Clemente looked at Matlack's first pitch. The partisan crowd groaned disapprovingly as home-plate umpire John Kibler called strike one. On the next pitch, Clemente lunged to reach a breaking ball over the outside of the plate and connected. "Bobby hits a drive into the gap in left-center field," said Prince excitedly. "There she is."[7] Clemente scampered to second base standing up while the crowd cheered wildly. "He jumped on the curveball and delivered the type of hit he's produced so many times before," wrote Smizik.[8] Said Clemente after the game, "It was the same pitch he struck me out on in the first inning."[9] Clemente became just the 11th player to reach 3,000 hits. Second-base umpire Doug Harvey briefly stopped the game to give the ball to Clemente, who tossed it over to first-base coach Don Leppert.

It was only fitting that Clemente tallied the game's first and the Pirates' winning run. With the crowd still standing, he scampered to third on a passed

ball, and subsequently scored on Manny Sanguillen's one-out single to left field. Two batters later, Jackie Hernandez tripled, driving in Sanguillen and Richie Zisk (who had walked) to give the Pirates a 3-0 lead.

In between innings, the Mets' Willie Mays, who had become the 10th member of the 3,000-hit club in July 1970, defied custom by leaving the visitors' dugout to congratulate Clemente on the Pirates bench. Afterward Clemente jogged out to right field to start the fifth inning and doffed his cap to a still-standing crowd. Ellis set down the side in order, his fifth consecutive hitless inning.

Clemente was due up with two outs in the bottom of the fifth, but his day was done. Virdon sent in 35-year-old Bill Mazeroski, set to retire at the end of the season, to pinch-hit. A teammate with Clemente and Virdon on the 1960 World Series champion Pirates, Maz popped out to second.

With Clemente out of the game, the remainder of the contest was anticlimactic. Ellis left after the sixth inning, in which he yielded his first and only hit of the game. Willie Stargell and Zisk led off the sixth with walks, and scored when Boswell misplayed Sanguillen's hot chopper to second for a two-base error. Staked to a 5-0 lead, the Pirates' Bob Johnson held the Mets to just one hit in three scoreless innings of relief to preserve the victory for Ellis.

Reporters gathered around Clemente in the Pirates' dressing room after the game. While players congratulated him, there was no champagne or extravagant celebration. An intensively private person, Clemente was quick to deflect attention and give credit to all those who had supported him since he started playing baseball. "I dedicate this hit to the fans of Pittsburgh," he said. "They have been wonderful. And to the people back home in Puerto Rico, but especially to the fellow who pushed me to play baseball. Roberto Marin."[10]

"I'm glad it's over," said Clemente honestly about his chase for 3,000 hits. "Now I can get some sleep."[11] The Pirates announced that he would not play in the club's final three games to rest his aching feet in preparation for their division playoff series with the

Cincinnati Reds, scheduled to open on October 7 in Pittsburgh.

Clemente was honored the next day in a brief ceremony before the finale of the Pirates-Mets series. As the crowd of more than 30,000 gave him a standing ovation, a visibly moved Clemente accepted a trophy. After the game Clemente once again reflected on the support he had received throughout 18 years playing in Pittsburgh. "We are here for the purpose to win for the fans. That is who we work for. Not for (GM) Joe Brown. He does not pay our salary. The fans pay our salary."[12]

Clemente collected his 3,000th hit in his final at-bat of the 1972 season. No one could have expected that it would be his last. On December 31, 1972, the Great One died with four others when his cargo plane crashed off the coast of Puerto Rico en route to delivering relief supplies to Nicaragua following a disastrous earthquake.

NOTES

1. Gary Mihoces (AP), "Roberto Clemente Reaches Baseball Exclusive Ranks," *Danville* (Virginia) *Register*, October 1, 1972: 6D.

2. Al Abrams, "Was Robbed of No. 3000, Roberto Says," *Pittsburgh Post-Gazette*, September 30, 1972: 1.

3. Ibid.

4. Bob Smizik, "Roberto Gets 3,000th. Will Rest Till Playoffs," *Pittsburgh Press*, October 1, 1972: D1.

5. "Clemente Notches 3,000 Officially," *New York Times*, October 1, 1972: 31.

6. KDKA game broadcast from September 29, 1972. Clip available on You Tube at youtube.com/watch?v=XsmqqPxb_xM.

7. Ibid.

8. Smizik.

9. "Clemente Notches 3,000 Officially."

10. Smizik.

11. Ibid.

12. Charley Feeney, "For Clemente After 3,000, Saturday Cheers Linger," *Pittsburgh Post-Gazette*, October 2, 1972: 24.

SOMETHING'S MISSING: NO CLEMENTE IN RIGHT FIELD

APRIL 6, 1973: PITTSBURGH PIRATES 7, ST. LOUIS CARDINALS 5, AT THREE RIVERS STADIUM

BY GREGORY H. WOLF

"YOU KEPT LOOKING IN RIGHT FIELD, and he wasn't there," said Pittsburgh Pirates manager Bill Virdon on Opening Day in 1973. "I kept looking out there."[1]

It was the dawn of a new era for the Pirates. Immensely popular Roberto Clemente had died about three months earlier, on New Year's Eve, when his plane crashed off the coast of San Juan on his home island of Puerto Rico. The 18-year veteran, who had collected his 3,000th hit in his last official at-bat of the 1972 season, had been involved in a humanitarian mission to Nicaragua to assist victims of a massive earthquake.

The Pirates clubhouse was subdued on April 6 as players prepared to take on their divisional rival St. Louis Cardinals to kick off the season. Lacking was the typical raucous party atmosphere as reminders of Clemente's absence were everywhere. The "Great One's" two lockers stood empty. Affable Manny Sanguillen, a two-time All-Star catcher, had the unenviable task of replacing Clemente in right field. "Last night I dreamed about him," said Sanguillen about his close friend, whom he had seen the day he died. "I thought about when we were in the ocean hunting for him. I don't want to talk too much about it."[2] GM Joe L. Brown, fully aware of the pressure-laden task, offered words of reassurance. "Sanguillen is a good ballplayer, he'll handle the job well," he declared.[3] Other Pirates echoed Sangy's comments; their reluctance to talk about Clemente was not a desire to forget the player; rather, they were eager to erase the bitter memories of their decisive Game Five walk-off loss to the Cincnnati Reds in the NLCS and begin their quest for a fourth straight NL East title.

Spring training had produced a few surprises for the Bucs lineup. Sanguillen's move paved the way for highly touted prospect Milt May behind the plate; slugger Willie Stargell with his creaky knees was shifted to left field to make room at first base for Bob Robertson, who had apparently recaptured in spring training the power stroke that had produced 53 home runs in 1970-1971. Rennie Stennett, a flashy 22-year-old Panamanian, started at second instead of Dave Cash, who had taken over taken the same position from another legend, Bill Mazeroski two years earlier.

The pitching matchup featured two of the league's marquee right-handers. Toeing the rubber for the Pirates was 31-year-old Steve Blass. Coming off his best season (19-8, 2.49 ERA), Blass had a 100-67 slate and was making his third Opening Day start. Skipper Red Schoendienst's Cardinals were coming off their second losing season (75-81) in three years, but as usual, Bob Gibson was on the mound—inaugurating a season for the ninth straight time. The 37-year-old was coming off a strong season (19-11, 2.46 ERA), which had pushed his career record to 225-141.

Three Rivers Stadium, was packed with 51,695 spectators for the Friday afternoon game. It was the then-largest crowd in the history of the round, all-purpose stadium, home to both the Pirates and NFL Steelers. No doubt many were on hand for the somber and tear-jerking pregame ceremony honoring Clemente. In attendance were the player's wife, Vera; their three children, Roberto Jr., Luis, and Enrique; and his mother, Luisa Walker Clemente. Situated near home plate, NL President Warren Giles presented Mrs. Clemente with her husband's 12th Gold Glove Award and a lifetime golden pass to attend NL games. The Pirates also announced formally that they were retiring Clemente's number 21. Hanging from the right-field wall, just above where Clemente had patrolled, was another visual reminder of his absence, a homemade banner, "Thank you, Roberto ...We'll never forget the Great One."[4]

Blass labored from the outset. After walking two in the first, he unraveled in the second, issuing another free pass and yielding three singles and a double, and heaving a wild pitch. The Cardinals scored three runs, but it could have been worse. Blass threw out Ken Reitz trying to stretch his single and picked off Lou Brock at first. It was a tough start to the season for the then six-time stolen base champ Brock, who had been thrown out trying to steal an inning earlier. No one could have surmised that Blass's performance was the beginning of his sudden and psychologically distressing exodus from the big leagues. His loss of control seemingly overnight led to what pundits began calling "Steve Blass Disease," an unwelcomed moniker still used four decades later. In the third, Blass loaded the bases with a single, walk, and hit batter. Groundouts by Ted Simmons and Reitz brought home two more runs and the Cardinals led, 5-0.

Blass's struggles contrasted sharply with Gibson's early dominance. He yielded his first hit, a triple by Al Oliver, with two outs in the fourth.

Through five innings the Cardinals maintained their 5-0 lead. After southpaw swingman Luke Walker, in relief of Blass, tossed his first of two scoreless frames, the Pirates finally got on board in the sixth when Stennett drew a leadoff walk, scampered to third on a passed ball and Sanguillen's single, and then scored on Oliver's sacrifice fly. The Bucs tacked on another run in the seventh on Richie Hebner's solo shot, which bounced off the top of the right-field wall. Ironically, Hebner had been given, but missed, the "take" sign from third-base coach Mazeroski.

The Pirates had an explosive offense, even without Clemente. In 1972 the team had led the majors in batting average (.274) and slugging (.397), and finished third in runs scored (691), just 17 fewer than the league-leader Houston Astros. A five-run deficit

didn't concern Blass, in the Pirates clubhouse. "A pitcher can get behind on this team," he said. "[Y]ou never know when this team is going to get a ton of runs."[5]

After an offseason acquisition, left-hander Jim Rooker, held the Redbirds scoreless in the eighth, the Pirates erupted in the bottom of the frame. Consecutive one-out singles by Sanguillen and Oliver and a walk to Stargell sent Gibson to the showers. He was replaced by Diego Segui, a crafty right-hander from Cuba who had led the AL with a 2.56 ERA as a swingman for the Oakland A's in 1970. Segui fanned Robertson, then Hebner knocked in two runs with a bloop to pull the Bucs to within one run. "I was lucky," said Hebner, whom sportswriters affectionately called "The Gravedigger" because of his offseason job. "It was a good pitch. I broke my bat."[6] Pinch-hitting for Rooker, Gene Clines smashed a hard liner into the left-center-field gap. With his dazzling speed, Brock ran down the ball, but it hit off the tip of his glove and rolled away (no error was charged). Clines raced to third, while Stargell and Hebner scored, giving the Pirates a 6-5 lead. Clines, whom most sportswriters expected to be the everyday left fielder and was coming off a superb campaign, batting .334, was upset about his role as a bench player and expressed his desire to be traded. After May was walked intentionally to place Pirates on the corners, Cash, who had pinch-hit for Walker the previous inning and took over at the keystone bag, hit a grounder which shortstop Ray Busse misplayed for his second error of the game, enabling Clines to score.

Pirates left-handed reliever Ramon Hernandez worked around a leadoff walk in the ninth, retiring the next three hitters on outfield flies to preserve the Pirates' come-from-behind victory in 2 hours and 2 minutes.

Rooker earned his first NL victory, after 21 wins (and 44 losses) for the Kansas City Royals, and Hernandez picked up the save. The loss went to Segui. The Pirates were led by Hebner, who collected three of the team's eight hits, scored twice, and knocked in three runs. Stargell, who had assumed Clemente's mantle as clubhouse and team leader, recognized the importance of the game. "Man, it's a big win," he said. "It means a lot to a team winning this way, coming from behind like we did. It means a lot more when we do it against a pitcher like Gibson."[7]

The game underscored the Pirates' resiliency on an emotionally charged afternoon. The trauma of Clemente's tragic death at the age of 38 was still on everyone's mind whether the players talked about it or not. "I don't really want to be there (in right field)," said Sanguillen after the game, "but I have to go on because God, you know, take the Great One away from us. So I have to do my best because that's the only way."[8]

It was difficult for the Pirates to acclimate to life without Clemente in 1973. The Sanguillen experiment in right field failed miserably and he was moved back to catcher beginning June 15. In early July, Richie Zisk, in his first full season, took over right field. The Pirates finished with their first losing season (80-82) since 1968.

SOURCES

In addition to the sources cited in the Notes, the author also accessed Retrosheet.org, Baseball-Reference.com, SABR.org, and *The Sporting News* archive via Paper of Record.

NOTES

1   Phil Musick, "Now Playing Right Field …," *Pittsburgh Press*, April 7, 1973: 6.

2   Ibid.

3   Charley Feeney, "Robby, 1B, Stargell, LF, Take Up Slack," *Pittsburgh Post-Gazette*, April 6, 1973: 10.

4   Musick.

5   Bob Smizik, "Pirates Teach Rooker a Lesson in Winning," *Pittsburgh Press*, April 7, 1973: 7.

6   Ibid.

7   Pat Livingston, "Well, Maybe the First Is the Toughest," *Pittsburgh Press*, April 8, 1973: D3.

8   Ibid.

STEVE BLASS LOSES CONTROL

JUNE 13, 1973, ATLANTA BRAVES 18, PITTSBURGH PIRATES 3, AT ATLANTA STADIUM

BY RICHARD PUERZER

STEVE BLASS WAS ARGUABLY THE best pitcher on the Pittsburgh Pirates during the 1970, 1971, and 1972 seasons, when the Pirates won the National League East each year. In 1971, Blass helped the Pirates to their World Series victory over the Baltimore Orioles by pitching complete-game victories in Games Three and Seven, allowing only 11 baserunners and two earned runs in the 18 innings he pitched. In 1972, Blass pitched in the All-Star Game, won a career-high 19 games with an ERA of 2.49, and finished second in the voting for the Cy Young Award to the Phillies' Steve Carlton. It looked as if 1973 would be another great year for the Pirates, and that Blass would continue to be the ace of the Pirates staff. But instead, 1973 was a bad year in many ways for the Pirates. First, they lost Roberto Clemente, their leader on and off the field, to a plane crash on New Year's Eve 1972. And although they still had a good team, they finished with a record of 80-82, their first season under .500 since 1968. But as bad as the season was for the Pirates as a team, it was a nightmare for 31-year-old right-handed hurler Steve Blass. Blass's performance on June 13, 1973, encapsulated all that went wrong for him that season, and which led to the end of his playing career.

Blass started the Opening Day game for the Pirates against the St. Louis Cardinals on April 6 at Three Rivers Stadium, and clearly was not sharp. He gave up five earned runs in five innings on five hits, four walks, and a hit batsman. What was most uncharacteristic for Blass was his wildness. In his previous seven seasons, he had averaged just under 3.0 walks per nine innings. It was his wildness against St. Louis that foretold Blass's fate in the 1973 season.

Blass's second outing of the season, on April 17 against the Cardinals again, was respectable. In the game at Busch Stadium, he pitched eight innings and gave up three earned runs, but again his walk total—five—was uncharacteristically high. This turned out to be the last game Blass started until August in which he gave up fewer than four earned runs. Clearly Pirates manager Bill Virdon continued to hope that Blass would return to the form he exhibited the season before. He did not have any arm issues or injuries in 1973, or in his entire career, and so the Pirates just hoped that Blass would work things out.[1]

Blass stayed in the starting rotation through June 11, when he gave up five earned runs in 3⅓ innings against the Atlanta Braves. After this outing, Blass's ERA stood at 8.50 for the season, and he was walking 6.6 batters per nine innings. Blass agreed to go to the bullpen and try to work out of his troubles. He received his first call from the bullpen on June 13, in what ended up as one of the worst games in Pirates history.

The starters in the June 13 game at Atlanta Stadium were a pair of seasoned right-handers, Dock Ellis for the Pirates and Ron Reed for the Braves. Entering the game, the Pirates were struggling with a disappointing record of 24-29, while the Braves were a shade worse, at 25-34. The Pirates were nine games behind the National League East division-leading Chicago Cubs, while the Braves were 12 games behind the San Francisco Giants in the NL West.

The game started with the Pirates going down in order in the top of the first. The Braves scored two runs in the bottom of the inning on a wild pitch by Ellis and a run-scoring single by Dusty Baker. In the third the Pirates made a little noise, with leadoff singles by Richie Hebner and Milt May, but both were stranded as Reed worked his way out of the inning. The Braves also had two baserunners in the third, but failed to score.

The fourth inning featured a lot of offense, starting with Richie Hebner smacking a three-run home run, his sixth of the year, scoring Al Oliver and Bob Robertson and giving the Pirates a 3-2 lead. The Braves came back strong in the bottom of the inning with consecutive singles by Ralph Garr, Davey Johnson, Marty Perez, and pitcher Reed, which scored two runs. Reed and Perez moved up on a groundout, and Dick Dietz was intentionally walked to load the bases. Ramon Hernandez relieved Dock Ellis, and the veteran left-hander gave up a grand slam to lefty Darrell Evans, the slugging third baseman's 14th homer of the season. At the end of the fourth, the Braves led 8-3.

The Pirates went down quietly in the top of the fifth inning, and Steve Blass came in to pitch the bottom of the inning. Since he had no physical concerns that would account for his poor performance all season, the Braves thought he was over-anxious and otherwise thinking too much when on the mound. The idea behind bringing him into the game in this situation was to give him an outing with little pressure, as the Pirates were already well behind in the game.[2] Unfortunately for Blass, this outing proved to be perhaps the worst in his life.

Blass began by walking Ralph Garr, allowing him to steal second, uncorking a wild pitch allowing him to advance to third, walking Davey Johnson, and allowing a run-scoring single to Marty Perez to make the score 9-3. Blass managed to get out of the inning on a flyball and two grounders, but he suffered a meltdown in the sixth. He began the inning by walking Darrell Evans and then throwing a wild pitch. He walked Mike Lum and allowed a run-scoring single to Dusty Baker. After getting Ralph Garr to ground out to first base, he gave up a run-scoring infield single to Davey Johnson, walked Marty Perez, gave up a two-run single to opposing pitcher Reed, uncorked another wild pitch, walked Johnny Oates, and gave up a two-run single to Frank Tepedino,

Steve Blass

which swelled the rout to 15-3. Having gotten only one out, Blass was replaced by Bob Johnson, who got the Pirates out of the inning on a 4-6-3 double play. In his disastrous appearance of 1⅓ innings, Blass allowed seven earned runs on five hits (all singles), six walks, and three wild pitches. Blass called it "the worst experience of my baseball life."[3] Johnson went on to finish the game, giving up three more runs in the eighth inning. The final score was 18-3. Despite the many baserunners, the game was played in a relatively quick 2 hours and 37 minutes. The 18 runs were the most runs allowed by the Pirates in a game since 1955.

Blass stayed with the Pirates for the remainder of the season, starting six more games and pitching in relief in three others, but he never returned to his old form. He pitched in one game for the Pirates in 1974, his final game in the majors. He pitched in the minor leagues for the remainder of the 1974 season in a futile attempt to get back to the majors. He retired from baseball in 1975. A profile of Blass by Roger Angell in *The New Yorker* in 1975 and Blass's 2012 autobiography, *A Pirate for Life*, provide extensive details and possible explanations for what Blass went through, and what has become known as Steve Blass disease, in which a pitcher suddenly loses control of his pitches, and never gains it back.[4]

SOURCES

The author relied on Baseball-Reference.com for game details.

NOTES

1   Steve Blass with Erik Sherman, *A Pirate for Life* (Chicago: Triumph Books, 2012), 11.

2   Bob Smizik, "Pirates Pulverized, 18-3," *Pittsburgh Press*, June 14, 1973: 42-43.

3   Roger Angell, "The Sporting Scene: Down the Drain," *The New Yorker*, June 23, 1975: 42-59.

4   Paul Dickson, *The Dickson Baseball Dictionary, Third Edition* (New York: W.W. Norton and Company, 2009), 826.

STENNETT LEADS PIRATE ROUT WITH SEVEN HITS IN NINE INNINGS

SEPTEMBER 16, 1975: PITTSBURGH PIRATES 22, CHICAGO CUBS 0, AT WRIGLEY FIELD

BY DOUG FELDMANN

WHILE PULLING ON HIS GRAY Pittsburgh road uniform in the visitors' locker room at Wrigley Field on the morning on September 16, 1975, Pirates second baseman Rennie Stennett grimaced in pain. Unsure if he would be able to play, Stennett gazed down at a heavily-taped sprained ankle "which he said has been hurting him for about a week," Richard Dozer reported in the *Chicago Tribune*.[1] The previous afternoon, Stennett had started both games of a doubleheader at Wrigley against the Chicago Cubs, but had to be relieved by rookie Willie Randolph in the seventh inning of the nightcap. The twin-bill split had left the Pirates with an 85-64 record and a six-game lead over the Philadelphia Phillies in the National League East with two weeks to play, while the Cubs sat in fifth place with a 72-79 mark.

Meanwhile, there was turbulence within the Cubs' infield lineup as well. In a strange sight, All-Star shortstop Don Kessinger—a fixture at the position since 1964—had, in the past week, been shifted to third base by manager Jim Marshall. The move marked Kessinger's first non-shortstop appearances in his career; he was filling in for the injured Bill Madlock (the National League batting leader at .362, who was sitting out with a fractured thumb). Getting a try at shortstop in Kessinger's place was Dave Rosello, who had scored 100 runs during the summer as the shortstop for the Cubs' Triple-A team at Wichita.

Unbeknownst to all at the time was that Kessinger was performing in his final days in a Cubs uniform –he was traded to the St. Louis Cardinals a month later.

With autumn approaching and the thoughts of Chicago sports fans drifting toward football, only 4,932 showed up at Addison and Clark to witness a historic performance. Among those in attendance was Chicago White Sox pitcher Jim Kaat, who had just returned to the city from a White Sox road trip. Kaat, however, was among the many spectators who would opt to leave the ballpark early. "The Pittsburgh Pirates, who traditionally regard the Cubs as only a minor distraction, pulverized them in an unbelievable, record-filled shutout in Wrigley Field Tuesday," Dozer wrote mournfully.[2]

Taking the mound for Chicago was Rick Reuschel, who despite a respectable 3.49 ERA entered the contest without a victory since August 21. Dueling with him was Pirates rookie John Candelaria, owner of a 7-5 record and a 2.98 ERA since earning a spot on Danny Murtaugh's staff just before the All-Star break.

Reuschel's work on the mound was short-lived, as Stennett willed himself back into the lineup and started the game with a screaming double down the right-field line. A parade of Bucs followed him to the plate (and around the bases); the lone batter Reuschel retired was Dave Parker—on a sacrifice fly.

By the time Stennett batted a second time in the first inning, he faced relief pitcher Tom Dettore, and singled for his second hit, scoring Frank Taveras and sending Candelaria to third. After Dettore threw a wild pitch to Richie Hebner and Candelaria scooted across the plate, Willie Stargell singled home Stennett for the Pirates' ninth run. Parker mercifully ended things in making his second out of the inning, grounding out to first as loud "boos" cascaded from Wrigley's upper deck.

Dettore temporarily quelled the Pirates' bats in the second, but the onslaught continued in the third as Stennett knocked his third hit, a single, before heading home on a long home run onto Sheffield Avenue by Hebner for an 11-0 Pittsburgh lead.

After a lone Pirate run crossed in the fourth, the Steel City attack went into high gear once again in the fifth. As the between-inning music stopped and Stennett took his place in the batter's box, also needing relief (in addition to Marshall) was Wrigley Field organist Frank Pellico—who was replaced by Nancy Faust, normally on duty at Comiskey Park on the South Side.

Stennett drove another double into the gap, and was soon singled home by Al Oliver as Parker finally joined the fun in homering on the first pitch served up by Dettore's replacement, Oscar Zamora.

Rennie Stennett

While standing on second, Stennett was informed by umpire Dutch Rennert that he had an opportunity to set the single-game hits record; and when he returned to the plate for a second time in the fifth, Stennett added a single—matching his two-hit accomplishment from the first inning—to drive in Manny Sanguillen as the Pittsburgh domination moved out to an 18-0 count with half of the game yet to be played. In netting two hits in an inning twice in the same game, Stennett had already tied a record shared by Max Carey, Sherm Lollar, and Johnny Hodapp.

With the Wrigley Field scoreboard resembling the one at the Bears' lakefront home of Soldier Field, bobbles by the Cubs' defense added two more in the sixth—bringing the mind-boggling total to 20-0 as Candelaria cruised easily through the Chicago bats. A single by Stennett in the seventh inning—his sixth hit of the game—contributed to two more Pittsburgh runs, running the count to 22-0.

When Pittsburgh came to bat in the eighth, Marshall emptied the bench and inserted Champ Summers in right field with Paul Reuschel now taking the mound—seeking to quickly end the nightmarish contest his brother had started long ago. He succeeded in retiring the first two Pirates, but the third batter was the white-hot Stennett.

Stennett drove another ball to right and Summers misplayed it into a triple—making Stennett the first major leaguer since 1892 (Wilbert Robinson) to get seven hits in a nine-inning game (and more impressively, in only eight innings of play). It eclipsed the previous high for the season set by Madlock, who had gone 6-for-6 against the New York Mets at Wrigley Field on July 26 and who, in a couple of weeks, would claim his first batting title.

Removed in favor of Randolph as a pinch-runner, Stennett was given a standing ovation by the few fans remaining at Wrigley as he trotted across the field from third base to the Pirates' dugout. "I wanted to rest him," Murtaugh said of his desire to get Stennett and his sore ankle out of the game, "but he kept getting hits."[3] Randolph was left stranded on third, as the second Reuschel mercifully kept the Pirates off the board in the ninth as well.

The final tally stood at 22-0, with every Pittsburgh starter in the lineup—including Candelaria—hitting safely, scoring at least once, and driving in at least one run.

In addition to Stennett's feats, other records had been smashed that day. It was the largest-ever margin of victory by shutout, topping the 21-0 score that the 1901 Tigers and the 1939 Yankees had authored. The 24 hits by the Pirates tied the National League high in 1975, matching the figure notched by the Cincinnati Reds on June 13—which also took place against the Cubs at Wrigley. (Earlier in 1975, the Reds and Pirates had also banged out 18 hits on separate occasions against the beleaguered Chicago pitching staff—which had stood as the previous NL high for the season.)

The domination by the Pirates had been complete. "Lost in the hoopla over Stennett's miraculous achievement," Dozer noted, "was a dandy three-hit pitching job by the rookie Candelaria, who was withdrawn after seven innings."[4] Candelaria had re-aggravated a lingering back injury, necessitating his removal. "I've had a bad back before," the pitcher said. "I had it before I pitched today."[5]

In their pursuit of the NL East title, the Pirates' romp at Wrigley concluded their 1975 season series with the Cubs; they had taken 12 of 18 games from Chicago and dropped their magic number for clinching the title to 7.

What did Stennett plan for an encore, as the Pirates prepared to travel to Philadelphia for a crucial series where they were 0-7 for the year at Veterans Stadium?

"I just want to forget about today and get back to playing my kind of baseball," he told Bob Smizik of the *Pittsburgh Press*—perhaps lamenting the fact that "batting holidays" against the 1975 Cubs had to come to an end *sometime*.[6]

SOURCES

In addition to the sources listed below, the author also consulted Baseball-Reference.com, Retrosheet.org, and SABR.org

NOTES

1   Richard Dozer, "Yes, Cubs Lose: 22-0," *Chicago Tribune*, September 17, 1975.

2   Ibid.

3   Ibid.

4   Ibid.

5   Charley Feeney, "Stennett Seven-Hits Cubs," *Pittsburgh Post-Gazette*, September 17, 1975.

6   Bob Smizik, "Blazing Bucs Enter Inferno," *Pittsburgh Press*, September 17, 1975.

THE TRAGIC DEATH OF BOB MOOSE: HIS LAST APPEARANCE IN THE MAJORS

SEPTEMBER 25, 1976: ST. LOUIS CARDINALS 3, PITTSBURGH PIRATES 0, AT BUSCH STADIUM, ST. LOUIS

BY ROBERT E. BIONAZ

A SPATE OF PREMATURE DEATHS BE- tween 1970 and 1979 brought baseball fans face-to-face with the fragility of human life. In those 10 years, no fewer than 14 active or recently active professional baseball players lost their lives to accidents, disease, murder, and suicide. Most prominent among the deceased players were Hall of Famer Roberto Clemente of the Pirates, who died in a plane crash on December 31, 1972; pitcher Don Wilson of the Houston Astros, winner of 104 major-league games and author of two no-hitters, who died accidentally on January 5, 1975; outfielder Lyman Bostock of the California Angels, a lifetime .311 hitter, murdered in Gary, Indiana, on September 24, 1978; and All-Star catcher Thurman Munson of the New York Yankees, who died in an airplane accident on August 2, 1979. Other notable major leaguers dying in that time period include utilityman Chico Ruiz, pitcher Jim McGlothlin, infielders Danny Thompson and Mike Miley, and pitchers Danny Frisella and Bob Moose, a dependable and versatile Pirate right-hander.[1]

Moose debuted for the Pirates at the end of the 1967 season, making two starts against the Houston Astros. In his second start, on September 29, he won his first major-league game. He made the 1968 team and for the next six years worked effectively in both starting and relief roles. He won at least 11 games each season from 1969 through 1973, and in 1969 had a 14-3 mark for a major-league-leading .824 winning percentage and a 2.91 earned-run average, and pitched a no-hitter in the thick of the National League East Division race against the eventual World Series champion New York Mets. Two years later, Moose played an important role in the 1971 Pirates' drive to the World Series, winning 11 games for the team.

Moose also pitched two scoreless innings against the San Francisco Giants in the National League Championship Series and made three World Series appearances without a decision against the Baltimore Orioles in the Series.

Along with his successes, Moose also suffered the bitter disappointment of ending the 1972 NLCS by throwing a wild pitch that sent the Cincinnati Reds into the World Series. The then best-of-five 1972 NLCS proved a nightmare for Moose. He failed to retire a batter in his second-game start, on October 8, then in the fifth game he seemed on the verge of getting out of trouble when he threw the two-out, ninth-inning wild pitch with Hal McRae batting, allowing the walkoff run to score from third. Pirates teammate Steve Blass recalled that after the devastating loss, Moose "just dealt with it. He shrugged it off. Bob had a wonderful positive attitude. He was a great guy with the ideal temperament for a ballplayer. He had a great approach to what he did, was a fine guy and an ideal teammate." Moose claimed that "[f]or about 10 minutes after the game, the pitch disturbed me. Then I realized it was just part of the game. I didn't have any trouble living with it."[2]

By that 1972 season, Moose was pitching almost exclusively as a starter. He had appeared only once in relief in 31 appearances during the regular season. In 1973, as the Pirates, demoralized by the death on New Year's Eve of Roberto Clemente, staggered through a desultory season, Moose made 29 starts and four relief appearances. With a mediocre 12-13 record, nevertheless he tied for second in wins on a pitching staff in disarray. Already stricken by the loss of Clemente, the Pirates saw their pitching ace, Steve Blass, drop from a 19-8 record with a 2.48 earned-run

149

average in 1972 to 3-9 with an unbelievable ERA of 9.85. Blass simply could not throw strikes. In 1972, he had walked 84 batters in 249⅔ innings; in 1973, he walked the same number of batters in only 88⅔ innings. The Pirates never found anyone to fill the hole created by Blass's ineffectiveness and finished the season 80-82, 2½ games behind the division-winning New York Mets.

The Pirates moved Moose into the second spot in the rotation for the 1974 season. However, after several poor outings, he was obviously not all right physically. By May 23, Moose owned a 1-5 record and a 7.57 ERA. His season ended when doctors discovered a blood clot in his right shoulder near his collarbone.[3] Moose had two surgeries to correct the problem. He recovered sufficiently to make the Pirates' Opening Day roster in 1975, but he struggled on the mound. Again pitching as both a starter and reliever, by the end of June, Moose had an 0-2 record with a 5.88 ERA. The Pirates sent him to Triple-A Charleston, and recalled him at the beginning of September. When he returned to the Pirates, Moose was a new man. In his last six appearances, covering 26⅓ innings, Moose allowed only one earned run. In his final appearance of the season, he beat the Philadelphia Phillies 3-1 in the final complete game of his major-league career. His brilliant September pitching squared his won-lost record at 2-2 and lowered his ERA to 3.72.

Moose ostensibly began the 1976 season as a long reliever. On April 17, Pittsburgh beat writer Charley Feeney wrote of the Pirates in *The Sporting News* that "their middle-inning relievers Bob Moose and Larry Demery should be able to pick up the starters until they are ready to go nine innings."[4] However, when injuries and ineffectiveness hampered Pirates relief ace Dave Giusti, Moose began to pitch regularly as the closer. By July 7, he had notched 10 saves and sported an ERA of 2.16. Moose won his final major-league game, 4-2, in relief on June 12, 1976, when the Pirates scored two runs in the top of the 11th against the Atlanta Braves. His pitching declined the rest of the season. He failed to garner another save,

Bob Moose

and he lost all five of his decisions. His ERA wound up at 3.70.

Moose made his final major-league appearance in a 3-0 loss to the St. Louis Cardinals at Busch Stadium on Saturday, September 25, 1976. The Pirates, who would be eliminated in the division race the next day by the Phillies, were still mathematically alive for the title. Moose entered the game in the bottom of the sixth with the Cardinals leading 3-0. He pitched two scoreless innings, allowing two walks and a single to Jerry Mumphrey. When Ed Kirkpatrick pinch-hit for Moose in the top of the eighth, he was out of the game, and unbeknownst to anyone, at the end of his career.

Two weeks later, on the evening of October 9, 1976, Bob Moose's 29th birthday, an automobile accident on a rain-slicked road near Martins Ferry, Ohio, snuffed out his life. Remembrances of Moose's life and career included Pete Rose calling him "my kind of player. He would fight you to the bitter end."[5] Pirates teammate Al Oliver remembered Moose's poise and strength after the 1972 NLCS loss: "Moose didn't go into hiding after that pitch. He walked off the field with his head high. Later in the clubhouse, he didn't hide from reporters. He answered every question and he didn't alibi. He was a pro." Oliver also remembered Moose as a great teammate. "When I was down, maybe for not hitting," Oliver recalled, "Moose would find a way to talk to me. I appreciated that."[6] Perhaps the most poignant reflection came from Moose's recently retired manager, Danny Murtaugh, who would himself die less than two months later. An obviously pained Murtaugh said, "I can't tell you how depressing this is. Here's a young man in the prime of his life, alive and healthy one minute and not with us anymore the next."[7]

As Murtaugh lamented, Bob Moose died far too young. Putting Moose's tragic death in perspective, Steve Blass juxtaposed the unexpected end of a baseball game with the unexpected end of a human life. "A wild pitch can be abrupt, but nothing like real life."[8]

NOTES

[1] Information on the deaths of active major leaguers comes from: Baseball Almanac, baseball-almanac.com/players/baseball_deaths.php, accessed August 21, 2017; and Baseball Reference, baseball-reference.com/bullpen/List_of_major_league_players_who_died_while_still_playing, accessed August 21, 2017. Game and player career information comes from Retrosheet, retrosheet.org/, accessed August 20, 2017. Don Wilson's death by carbon monoxide poisoning in his garage, was ruled accidental by the medical examiner. See, Matthew Clifford, "Don Wilson," SABR Biography Project, sabr.org/bioproj/person/1643c2b4, accessed August 22, 2017.

[2] Earl Lawson, "Wild Pitch Sets Off Reds' N.L. Pennant Party," *The Sporting News*, October 28, 1972: 9. Quoted in Fran Zimniuch, *Shortened Seasons: The Untimely Deaths of Baseball's Stars and Journeymen* (Lanham, Maryland: Taylor Trade Publishing, 2007), 45. Quoted in Bruce Markusen, "Card Corner: Remembering Bob Moose," National Baseball Hall of Fame: baseballhall.org/discover/card-corner/remembering-bob-moose, accessed August 21, 2017. See also *The Sporting News*, October 23, 1976: 70.

[3] Markusen, "Remembering Bob Moose." See also Floyd Johnson, "Bob Moose," SABR Biography Project, sabr.org/bioproj/person/cc344cf0, accessed August 19, 2017.

[4] Charley Feeney, "Buccos Thankful for Depth on Hill," *The Sporting News*, April 17, 1976: 6.

[5] Markusen, "Remembering Bob Moose."

[6] Charley Feeney, "Pirate Scholarship to Keep Moose Memory Green," *The Sporting News*, January 8, 1977: 36.

[7] *The Sporting News*, October 23, 1976: 70.

[8] Zimniuch, *Shortened Seasons*, 45.

DANNY MURTAUGH'S FINAL GAMES AS PIRATES MANAGER

OCTOBER 3, 1976: PITTSBURGH PIRATES 1, ST. LOUIS CARDINALS 0 (FIRST GAME)

PITTSBURGH PIRATES 1, ST. LOUIS CARDINALS 0 (SECOND GAME), AT THREE RIVERS STADIUM, PITTSBURGH

BY ROBERT E. BIONAZ

THE PIRATES' 1976 SEASON AND Danny Murtaugh's managerial career concluded with a doubleheader against the St. Louis Cardinals on October 3, 1976. Both teams disappointed that year, the Cardinals dropping from 82-80 in 1975 to 72-88 beginning the season's final Sunday. For Pittsburgh, although it had won only two fewer games than in its Eastern Division-winning season of 1975, as the season's final day dawned, the Pirates' 90-70 record put them 9½ games behind the division winners, the Philadelphia Phillies.[1]

Since 1970, the Pirates had dominated the National League Eastern Division, winning five division titles and one World Series in six seasons. As 1976 began, they were well positioned to win another division championship. *Sports Illustrated* predicted another title for the Pirates, opining, "Despite perennial doubts about Pittsburgh's overall quality, almost every year the Pirates win."[2]

However, the 1976 Pirates failed to live up to expectations. They won their first five games, and on April 25 stood in first place. A 7-1 loss to the Los Angeles Dodgers on April 26 dropped them to third place. They never occupied the top spot in the division again. At the end of April, the Pirates were three games behind the first-place New York Mets. By the end of May, they trailed the red-hot Philadelphia Phillies by 6½ games. Although the Pirates had a 16-10 record in June, they fell further behind the Phillies, trailing them by 9 games on June

30. By July 31, the Pirates' deficit had grown to 11½ games. After the completion of play on August 24, the Pirates trailed the Phillies by 15½ games. Then the Pirates got hot. They won 15 of 17, including a three-game sweep of the Phillies September 6-8. On the morning of September 13, the Pirates stood only four games behind. A two-game sweep of the Phillies on September 15 and 16, then a 4-1 win over the Mets on September 17 pulled them within three games. They got no closer. Over the next five days, the Pirates lost five of six to the Mets and Chicago Cubs, dropping them six games back on the morning of September 23. They were eliminated on September 26.

On October 3, the last day of the regular season, Murtaugh concluded his managerial career by guiding the Pirates to two 1-0 victories over the Cardinals. He had announced his retirement two days before, and on the campaign's last day, the Pirates and Cardinals treated 24,228 spectators to two games reminiscent of baseball in the Deadball Era. They combined for two runs and 22 hits, only three for extra bases. All four starters pitched complete games. The teams played the first game in 1:47, the second in 1:48, about the length of an average game in 1920.[3]

In the first game, Jim Rooker won his 15th of the season with a seven-hit shutout. The Cardinals mounted just one threat, when Keith Hernandez and Mike Tyson singled with none out in the fourth inning. Rooker then got Sam Mejias to ground into a double play and retired Charlie Chant on a grounder to shortstop. The Pirates scored the lone run of the game in the sixth on a double by Omar Moreno and an error by first baseman Hernandez. Rooker allowed only two harmless singles after the sixth inning. The win was Pittsburgh's 91st of the season, the fifth time in 12 years that Murtaugh-led teams had won more than 90 games.

The Pirates gave Murtaugh a proper sendoff by winning his final game as manager by the same score. Pittsburgh starter Jerry Reuss pitched even better than Rooker had in the first contest, allowing only five hits and one walk while striking out six. Only two Cardinals baserunners reached third, but the Pirates were stymied by Cardinals left-hander Pete Falcone. In the bottom of the ninth the game remained scoreless. Falcone, who often struggled with control, walked Richie Zisk to lead off the inning. Rookie Miguel Dilone ran for Zisk and stole second. Falcone then retired Bill Robinson and Bob Robertson, bringing rookie Tony Armas to the plate. Armas, making his first start in the majors, promptly got his first major-league RBI with a single to left, scoring Dilone and winning the final game of the 1976 season for the Pirates and Danny Murtaugh.

The day marked the end of an era in Pittsburgh baseball. An unlikely managerial choice when hired in 1957, Murtaugh must be the only major-league manager who got his job because of an orange drink. On the evening of July 31, 1957, the seventh-place Pirates were playing the Milwaukee Braves at County Stadium. After a disputed call at second base, umpire Stan Landes ejected Pirates manager Bobby Bragan. Bragan later described what followed: "I went back to the dugout and told Danny Murtaugh—he was one of my coaches—to get me a hot dog and a cold drink. All they could rustle up was an orange drink with a straw in it, and I took that and went back out there." Bragan offered Landes a sip which resulted in another invitation to leave the field. The next day, Pirates general manager Joe Brown met the team in Chicago and fired Bragan. The now former skipper mused, "Did the orange juice have anything to do with it? The pot had been boiling, and that made it boil over. A cup of cold orange juice."[4]

Clyde Sukeforth, reportedly Brown's first choice to take over, "declined and recommended Murtaugh," who had three-plus years of managerial experience with New Orleans and Charleston. Although Brown named Murtaugh an "interim," he would eventually serve four different stints between 1957 and 1976 as the Pittsburgh skipper. During Murtaugh's managerial career the team won more games than for any other Pittsburgh manager before him except Fred Clarke, and won four division titles, two pennants, and two World Series championships.[5]

Murtaugh did not enjoy his first day as Pirates manager. His team lost both games of that day's doubleheader with the Chicago Cubs and fell into last place. The losses were Pittsburgh's seventh and eighth in a row. The team broke the losing streak two days later and went 25-23 the rest of the season, finishing in a tie for seventh and giving Murtaugh a 26-25 record in his first season as the Pirates manager.

By the end of 1957, Murtaugh was no longer an "interim" and managed the club through 1964, when a heart problem diagnosed in 1962 caused him to retire at age 46. He returned in the middle of the 1967 season, again for 1970 and 1971, and for a final stint from September 7, 1973, through the end of the 1976 season. His teams won the World Series in 1960 and 1971 and division championships in 1970, 1971, 1974, and 1975. Murtaugh's teams won 1,115 games and lost 950, a .540 winning percentage. They proved particularly adept at winning after major-league expansion in 1969. In his five full seasons of managing between 1970 and 1976, his clubs finished first four times and second in his final year. Although clearly a better team than the team he inherited in 1957, Murtaugh's 1976 squad, like the 1957 version, which featured key performers from the 1960 champions, included a number of players who would make key contributions to the 1979 championship team. In 1957, the Pirates featured Roberto Clemente, Dick Groat, Bob Skinner, Bill Mazeroski, Bill Virdon, Roy Face, Bob Friend, and Vern Law. The 1976 team included Dave Parker, Willie Stargell, Ed Ott, Omar Moreno, Bill Robinson, John Candelaria, Jim Rooker, Kent Tekulve, and Bruce Kison. As he headed into retirement, Murtaugh could look back with pride at his managerial career.

Murtaugh's last retirement proved brief. The offseason of 1976-77 proved to be a nightmare for baseball fans in general and Pirates fans and the organization in particular. On October 9, right-hander Bob Moose, a valuable and versatile pitcher and the author of a 1969 no-hitter against the New York Mets, died on his 29th birthday in an automobile accident. Less than two months later, on December 2, Danny Murtaugh suffered a stroke and died. Longtime Pittsburgh sportswriter Les Biederman wrote after Murtaugh's death: "You were someone special, on and off the field. You were kind, considerate, firm, loyal and above all, fair. And you were always modest. Your baseball cap always fit your Irish head." Successful on the field, respected off the field, Murtaugh left an indelible mark on the city and its baseball franchise. To think, it all started with an orange drink.[6]

NOTES

1 All references to game scores, standings, etc., come from retro-sheet.org.

2 *Sports Illustrated*, April 12, 1976: 68.

3 For a discussion of average playing times, seereference.com/sports-active-lifestyle/average-length-baseball-game-cf7787f-6118cdfcd (accessed March 18, 2017). On Murtaugh's retirement,

see Charley Feeney, "Brown, Murtaugh Break Up Their Pirate Act," *The Sporting News*, October 16, 1976: 13.

4 Donald Honig, *The Man in the Dugout: Fifteen Big League Managers Speak Their Minds* (Lincoln: University of Nebraska Press, 1995), 24. Another account of the orange-drink argument can be found here: retrosheet.org/boxesetc/1957/B07310MLN1957.htm (accessed March 18, 2017).

5 Andy Sturgill, "Danny Murtaugh," sabr.org/bioproj/person/d9cd13bd (accessed March 8, 2017). See also Harold Rosenthal, *Baseball's Best Managers* (New York: Thomas Nelson and Sons, 1961), 103, cited in Sturgill, "Danny Murtaugh." For a description of Murtaugh's four terms as Pirates manager, see Robert Dvorchak, "The Next Manager Is … Danny Murtaugh, *Pittsburgh Post-Gazette*, November 29, 2009. *The Sporting News* had extensive coverage of the Bragan firing and Murtaugh's elevation to manager: Les Biederman, "Bragan Gets His Last Laugh as Buc Boss," *The Sporting News*, August 7, 1957: 3; J.G. Taylor Spink, "Luck of the Irish for Murtaugh," *The Sporting News*, August 14, 1957: 4; Les Biederman, "Murtaugh Learned of Firing in Midnight Call on Brown," *The Sporting News*, August 14, 1957: 4. Les Biederman, "Pilots Get Ulcers, Sukey to Raise Christmas Trees," *The Sporting News*, August 21, 1957: 8.

6 "Pirates Moose Killed in Crash on 29th Birthday," *New York Times*, October 11, 1976; "Danny Murtaugh Is Dead at 59; Won 2 Series as Pirate Manager," *New York Times*, December 3, 1976; Les Biederman, "Dan's Cap Always Fit His Irish Head," *The Sporting* News, December 18, 1976: 53. Mike Miley of the California Angels and Danny Frisella of the Milwaukee Brewers also died in vehicle accidents in January 1977. "Angels' Infielder Miley Dies in Auto Accident," *New York Times*, January 7, 1977; "Danny Frisella Dead in Car Mishap at 30," *New York Times*, January 4, 1977.

"POPS" NAMED MVP AS PIRATES COMPLETE COMEBACK TO WIN WORLD SERIES

OCTOBER 17, 1979:PITTSBURGH 4, BALTIMORE 1, AT MEMORIAL STADIUM

GAME SEVEN OF THE WORLD SERIES

BY FREDERICK C. BUSH

AS THE PIRATES AND ORIOLES PRE-pared to meet in the winner-take-all Game Seven of the 76th World Series, there arose a commotion over a column written by Baltimore sports editor John Steadman. The Pittsburgh media provided the Pirates and their fans with the gist of Steadman's opinion, which was that the Bucs calling their team a family was "a cheap grandstand play, a sickening put-on, a bad pun. The Orioles haven't been gagging themselves to keep from ridiculing 'The Family' reference, but it must be amusing."[1] The Orioles probably wished that Steadman had not given the Bucs such "bulletin-board material" to provide extra motivation, especially after Game Seven when the only gagging the Orioles would be accused of doing was choking away what had seemed to be a certain Series victory after Game Four. Such an outlook, however, would sell "The Family's" efforts short as "(i)n truth, the Pirates won the world championship more than the Orioles lost it, beating Baltimore's best pitchers and holding its hitters to only two runs in the final three games."[2]

The atmosphere was electric as 53,733 fans packed Memorial Stadium one more time on a pleasant 65-degree evening.One of the fans in attendance was incumbent President Jimmy Carter, who threw out the ceremonial first pitch to Orioles catcher Rick Dempsey. Carter was the first president to attend a World Series game since Dwight Eisenhower visited Brooklyn's Ebbets Field during the 1956 World Series between the Dodgers and New York Yankees.[3]

Once the game was under way, it appeared as though Baltimore's Scott McGregor and Pittsburgh's

Jim Bibby were going to duplicate the previous game's pitching duel. Neither team mounted any threat in the first two innings, but second baseman Rich Dauer hit a line-drive home run to left field to lead off the bottom of the third that put the Orioles up 1-0. It was the only run Bibby and the Bucs relievers who followed him—Don Robinson, Grant Jackson, and Kent Tekulve—would allow in Game Seven.

The Pirates began to take over the game in the sixth inning. Bill Robinson hit a one-out, bad-hop grounder that was just out of shortstop Kiko Garcia's reach for a single. Willie Stargell batted next and delivered a two-run home run to right-center, giving the Pirates a lead they never relinquished. Stargell's ball was also just out of reach, this time of Orioles right fielder Ken Singleton, who briefly hung on the outfield wall as he watched the ball land in the Pirates' bullpen. In a twist of fate, exactly eight years to the day after he had scored the winning run in Game Seven of the 1971 World Series against the Orioles, Stargell scored the winning run in Game Seven of the 1979 Series against the same team.[4]

The Pirates were in danger of surrendering their 2-1 lead in the bottom of the eighth inning when Jackson gave up one-out walks to pinch-hitter Lee May and Al Bumbry. After the second walk, Tekulve entered the game and retired pinch-hitter Terry Crowley on a groundball to second base that allowed both runners to move up. Singleton was intentionally walked to load the bases, after which Eddie Murray hit a fly ball to deep right field. Dave Parker stumbled but made an over-the-shoulder catch of Murray's ball to end the inning, a play about which Tekulve later said, "I thought, 'I hope his legs don't fail him now,' but he's made those plays all year and somehow I knew he'd get it."[5]

After Phil Garner doubled to lead off the ninth inning, Orioles manager Earl Weaver "paraded a record five pitchers to the mound in a futile bid to stem the inevitable."[6] Mike Flanagan replaced Tim Stoddard with one out and gave up a single to Omar Moreno that scored Garner. Weaver then brought in Don Stanhouse, who surrendered a base hit to left-center by Tim Foli that advanced Moreno to third. Tippy Martinez took the mound next and loaded the bases by hitting Parker with a pitch. Finally, Dennis Martinez, the fifth Orioles pitcher of the inning, hit Bill Robinson with a pitch that brought Moreno home with the Pirates' final run of the game. It did not take an astute spectator to sense the desperation behind Weaver's procession of relievers, all of whom were ineffective and—as a group—gave up the last two runs that resulted in the final 4-1 score.

In the bottom of the ninth, Tekulve struck out Gary Roenicke and Doug DeCinces before getting pinch-hitter Pat Kelly to fly to Moreno in center field for the final out. For their efforts, Jackson got the win, Tekulve got his third save of the Series, and the Pirates got their fifth world championship. As Tekulve said, "(I)t's ours and nobody can take it away."[7]

The Pirates had pounded out 81 hits against the Orioles over the course of the seven-game Series and had compiled a team batting average of .323, which was a record for a winning team in the World Series and second only to the 1960 New York Yankees' .338.; The 81 hits were also second only to the same 1960 Yankees squad's 91 hits.[8]

Five Pirates accumulated double-digit hit totals: Willie Stargell (.400) and Phil Garner (.500) led the way with 12 each, Omar Moreno (.333) tallied 11, and Dave Parker (.345) and Tim Foli (.333) had 10 apiece. Foli also set a record for the most at-bats (30) without a strikeout.[9] Bill Madlock batted .375 while rapping out nine hits and drawing five walks and, in Game Five, became one of three Pirates bat-

Willie Stargell

ters—along with Parker (Game One) and Stargell (Game Seven)—to tie the Series record of four hits in one game. The Orioles' inability to stop the Pirates in the top of the ninth inning of Game Seven was simply a microcosm of the entire World Series, especially those games in which the Pirates bunched their hits together to score more runs.

Stargell's performance stood out above all, and he was the unanimous choice of the nine-man committee as the Most Valuable Player of the World Series.[10] In addition to batting .400 with 7 RBIs, Stargell set a World Series record with seven extra-base hits—four doubles and three home runs (the Pirates' only home runs in the seven games)—and tied Reggie Jackson's 1977 record of 25 total bases.[11] The award made Stargell the first player player to win the regular-season, League Championship Series, and World Series MVPs in the same season. For that matter, the Pirates made a clean sweep of all MVP awards in 1979 as Parker had been voted MVP of the All-Star Game that summer.

President Carter visited the jubilant Pirates' locker room after the game to offer his congratulations and watched the team accept the championship trophy. Manager Chuck Tanner could not remember what Carter said to him because he was so excited, while a jovial Stargell joked, "I wanted to ask him if he had any peanuts on him. But there were too many Secret Service men around, and I was afraid to ask."[12]

Stargell turned serious for a moment when he was asked about Steadman's column that had denigrated the Pirates' use of the word "family" to describe their team. "Pops" Stargell, the Bucs' inspirational father figure, said, "I thought that was unfair. That man didn't live with us all year. He didn't understand that we depend on closeness, that we are a family. No words can express what we've done. We've overcome. We've worked hard. We've scratched and clawed. We took that song 'We Are Family' and identified with it. We weren't trying to be sassy or fancy. We're just a ballclub that is a family in our clubhouse. And that's why we won the World Series, that's why we came from behind."[13] Stargell's response was a fitting summary of the 1979 Pittsburgh Pirates.

NOTES

1   Pat Livingston, "Stand-Up Pirates Set Down Birds," *Pittsburgh Press*, October 18, 1979.

2   Ron Fimrite, "Rising From the Ashes," *Sports Illustrated*, October 29, 1979: 61-64.

3   Murray Chass, "Pirates Capture World Series With 4-1 Triumph," *New York Times*, October 18, 1979.

4   Lowell Reidenbaugh, "Stargell's Bat? Just Plain Poison!," *The Sporting News*, November 3, 1979: 43-44.

5   Dan Donovan, "Whew, It's Over! Bucs Are Champs," *Pittsburgh Press*, October 18, 1979.

6   Reidenbaugh, "Stargell's Bat? Just Plain Poison!"

7   Donovan, "Whew, It's Over! Bucs Are Champs."

8   "World Series Notes: Garner Won the Hard Fight," *Pittsburgh Press*, October 18, 1979.

9   Lowell Reidenbaugh, "Room at Top Just for Bucs," *The Sporting News*, November 3, 1979:40.

10 Reidenbaugh, "Stargell's Bat? Just Plain Poison!"

11 "World Series Notes: Garner Won the Hard Fight."

12 Ibid.

13 Dave Anderson, "Pops Hit One for 'The Family,'" *New York Times*, October 18, 1979.

JIM BIBBY'S NEAR NO-HITTER

MAY 19, 1981: PITTSBURGH PIRATES 5, ATLANTA BRAVES 0, AT THREE RIVERS STADIUM

BY ELIZA RICHARDSON

ON THE EVENING OF TUESDAY, MAY 19, 1981, a scant crowd of 5,514 fans at Three Rivers Stadium saw Jim Bibby throw a near-perfect game against the Atlanta Braves while helping his own cause by hitting two doubles, scoring one run, and collecting an RBI in the process. Bibby later said it was the best game of his career, even better than the no-hitter he threw against the Oakland A's in 1973 when he played for the Texas Rangers.[1] Just two seasons removed from their 1979 World Series championship season, the banged-up Pirates entered the game owning a 12-16 record. Dave Parker, John Candelaria, Tony Peña, Willie Stargell, Rod Scurry, Ernie Camacho, Bill Robinson, and Don Robinson were all sitting out with injuries.[2] Another issue certainly on the minds of players and fans was the players strike deadline looming on the horizon just 10 days away. The main issue on the table was free-agent compensation, and in fact the players would end up striking on June 12, beginning the first midseason strike in major-league history.[3] For a couple of hours on May 19, though, the five thousand in attendance got a glimpse of greatness.

Terry Harper led off the top of the first with a bloop single to right field on the second pitch he saw from Bibby, a fastball away. It was the only base-runner the Braves would have for the game as Bibby settled in and set down the next 27 batters in order, using only 93 pitches and striking out three.

Claudell Washington batted second for the Braves. Bibby popped him up to Tim Foli at shortstop. Next up in the first inning was Biff Pocoroba, the Atlanta third baseman. He grounded out to first base, moving Harper to second, where he was stranded by 1971's American League Rookie of the Year Chris Chambliss, who grounded out to end the inning. It

was the last time all night a Braves baserunner would be standing on a base.

In the bottom of the first inning, 42-year-old future Hall of Famer Phil Niekro took the mound for the Braves. Just a week earlier he had pitched a complete-game two-hit shutout against the Pirates in Atlanta and he picked up right where he left off as Lee Lacy, Tim Foli, and Bill Madlock were set down in order.[4] Lacy and Madlock both struck out.

Center fielder and future NL MVP (1982 and 1983) Dale Murphy led off the second inning followed by Glenn Hubbard and Bruce Benedict. Bibby induced a groundball to short, a lineout to third, and a flyout to center field to take care of all three.

The Pirates opened up the scoring in the bottom of the second inning when Omar Moreno drove in Mike Easler with a single to left field. Easler had reached on a fielder's choice after Jason Thompson's leadoff hit to right field. Phil Garner singled Easler to third before getting caught stealing second base by Benedict.

Big Jim Bibby, whose hands were so large he could reportedly palm eight baseballs facedown, climbed back onto the mound owning the one-run lead that would prove to be all he'd need (but not all he'd get) for the top of the third inning to face the bottom of the Braves order.[5] He struck out Rafael Ramirez looking, made short work of Phil Niekro, who grounded out to third, then got Terry Harper on a fly to left field to end the inning.

Bibby himself led off in the bottom of the third. He had been an All-Star in 1980 and finished third in the National League Cy Young Award voting that year.[6] He would end up missing all of 1982 due to injury, then come back to win five games (losing 12) in 1983 for the Pirates. His 1984 season with the Texas

Jim Bibby

Rangers would be the last season of his major-league career.[7] Bibby grounded out to the shortstop, after which Lee Lacy was out on a foul ball to the first baseman and Foli flied out to left.

The Braves' batters were dispatched quickly and efficiently in the fourth and fifth innings. All remained quiet until the bottom of the fifth inning when Bibby hit the first of his two doubles, a two-out hit up the middle. He came around to score when Lee Lacy, the next batter, hit a double to left field.

Atlanta again offered no resistance to Bibby's dominating pitching performance in the sixth with Ramirez, Niekro, and Harper going down in order.

The Pirates chased Niekro in the bottom of the sixth as Thompson led off with a single to right, followed by another single off the bat of Mike Easler. Niekro got two outs as Garner grounded into a fielder's choice, erasing Thomson at third base, and Moreno flied out to center. But catcher Steve Nicosia, filling in for injured rookie Tony Peña, doubled to center, scoring Easler and Garner, thus ending Niekro's night. Bibby promptly greeted Atlanta reliever Rick Mahler with an RBI double to left, bringing the score to what would be the final: Pirates 5, Braves 0.

In a wonderful final moment of poetic justice, Bibby faced Terry Harper with two outs in the bottom of the ninth and induced Harper to make the last out on — of all things — a fly ball to right field. The entire game took only 1:57 to play.

SOURCES

In addition to the sources cited in the Notes, the author consulted Baseball-Reference.com.

NOTES

1   Charley Feeney, "Harper's Leadoff Single Ruins Bid at Perfect Game," *Pittsburgh Post-Gazette*, May 20, 1981: 17.

2   Phil Musick, "Pirates Turn Into an All-Star Farm," *Pittsburgh Post-Gazette*, May 20, 1981: 17.

3   "Strike 3! Baseball Season Called," *Pittsburgh Post-Gazette*, June 13, 1981: 9.

4   Feeney.

5   Rick Telander, "He's Not Hot Stuff, He's My Brother," *Sports Illustrated*, March 2, 1981. "For the Record," *Sports Illustrated*, March 1, 2010.

6   Rory Costello, "Jim Bibby," in Bill Nowlin and Gregory H. Wolf, eds., *When Pops Lead the Family: The 1979 Pittsburgh Pirates* (Phoenix: SABR, 2016).

7   Ibid.

RICK REUSCHEL INSPIRES STRUGGLING BUCS WITH STRONG FINISH

SEPTEMBER 25, 1985: PITTSBURGH PIRATES 8, MONTREAL EXPOS 2, AT THREE RIVERS STADIUM

BY GORDON J. GATTIE

IN LATE FEBRUARY 1985, PITTSBURGH Pirates general manager Pete Peterson signed veteran right-handed pitcher Rick Reuschel to a one-year deal with the Hawaii Islanders, Pittsburgh's Triple-A affiliate in the Pacific Coast League. The contract provided Reuschel an opportunity to compete for a spot with the Pirates in spring training. In June 1982 he had been diagnosed with a partial rotator cuff tear.[1] Reuschel missed the rest of 1982, pitched only 20⅔ innings in 1983, and then endured his worst professional season in 1984, compiling a 5-5 record and 5.17 ERA in 92⅓ innings with the Chicago Cubs. Upon Reuschel's signing, Peterson commented, "We've made Rick no promises, but I would think that he could be a long-relief man." Pittsburgh skipper Chuck Tanner offered more confidence: "We'll give Rick a look. I know one thing. He knows how to pitch."[2]

Spring training didn't inspire hope among Pirates fans; the team finished with a league-worst 6-18 record. Tanner maintained his optimism throughout the exhibition season, commenting, "We all start out zero-zero. I think our overall pitching will keep us competitive, and there isn't a team in our division capable of running away with it."[3] Sportswriters didn't have high expectations for Tanner's team; *The Sporting News* predicted a last-place finish: "What a shame—a disaster waiting for the vans to pull up to Three Rivers Stadium."[4] The *Pittsburgh Press* forecast a fifth-place finish, writing, "Last year, in August, with his team 20½ games out of first place, Chuck Tanner was plotting ways to win the pennant. It didn't and it won't this year, either."[5]

Heading into their September 25 matchup against the Montreal Expos, the '85 Pirates were suffering through their worst season since 1954, when they compiled a 53-101 record. They occupied the NL East basement with a 51-98 record, 43 games behind the division-leading St. Louis Cardinals and 18½ games behind the fifth-place Chicago Cubs. Their struggles were more offensive than pitching; they scored fewer runs than any other major-league team, while their pitching was below average but not the majors' worst.

The Expos had experienced some midseason success during mid-June when they briefly led the NL East, but they had been mired in third place since July 12 after an extra-inning loss to the Cincinnati Reds. The Expos struggled throughout September, starting the month with a five-game losing streak, then losing six straight from September 17 through 22. The latter streak included two extra-inning losses to Pittsburgh. By late September, the Expos had fallen from contention.

Rick Reuschel was one of the few bright stars in Pittsburgh as the season wound down. Although he had won 139 games through 1984 and passed through the November 1984 re-entry draft with no takers, Reuschel was willing to prove himself in the minor leagues for another job in the majors.[6] Reuschel succeeded, winning six of eight decisions while spending the first six weeks of the season with the Triple-A Islanders. On May 21, GM Peterson called him up. That evening Reuschel pitched his first game in a Pirates uniform and defeated Houston, 3-2. In his major-league return, he allowed only one run on three hits over 7⅔ innings, retiring 15 of the first 16 batters he faced. Tanner commented, "Reuschel pitched like the old pro that he is."[7] In the two months from his season debut through July 20, the Pirates won only 18 games, and Reuschel won eight of them. He regained his expertise with the sinkerball; more than two-thirds of his outs were groundouts.[8] Reuschel carried a 13-7 record with a 2.25 ERA over 175⅔ innings into that evening's matchup against Montreal.

Conversely, Expos right-hander Bill Laskey was struggling to keep a major-league job. After he started at least 25 games in each of his past three seasons with the San Francisco Giants, the team traded him along with Scot Thompson to Montreal in exchange for Dan Driessen on August 1.[9] Laskey hadn't received much run support from the Giants all season; they scored only 14 runs in his 11 losses that season.[10] He lost his first three decisions after joining Montreal, then was moved to the bullpen. However, Laskey had pitched well against Pittsburgh in his most recent outing, allowing two runs in six innings seven days earlier against the Bucs.

Pittsburgh's smallest crowd at Three Rivers Stadium that season—2,648[11]—watched as Montreal leadoff hitter Tim Raines started the game with a fly out to left field and Mitch Webster followed with a fly out to right field. Andre Dawson singled for the game's first base hit, but Hubie Brooks grounded

Rick Reuschel

out to short and ended the inning. In the bottom of the inning, Pittsburgh leadoff hitter Joe Orsulak singled. R.J. Reynolds flied out. With Johnny Ray hitting, Orsulak stole second. Ray walked. Sid Bream singled Orsulak home with the game's first run and moved Ray to third base. Mike Brown walked to load the bases, but the Pirates missed an opportunity to score more runs when Tony Peña fouled out and Jim Morrison flied out to end the threat. Reuschel set down the Expos in order in the second inning on a popout, fly out, and groundout. The Pirates threatened again in the bottom of the inning with runners on first and third with two outs, but Ray flied out to center field for the third out. Reuschel delivered another three-up, three-down inning with two groundouts and a strikeout.

Bream started the third inning by grounding out to second base. Brown doubled, then Peña, Morrison, and Sam Khalifa followed with successive singles; both Brown and Peña crossed the plate during that stretch. Reuschel hit into a fielder's choice, as Morrison was thrown out at home. With Khalifa on second and Reuschel on first, Orsulak plated Khalifa with a single. Reynolds followed with another single, scoring Reuschel and chasing Laskey. Southpaw Gary Lucas ended the inning, but the Pirates used six hits to score four runs and increase their lead to 5-0.

In the fourth inning, both pitchers set down their opponents in order, and each team left one runner on base in the fifth inning as both Reuschel and Lucas established their rhythm. In the sixth inning, Reuschel allowed a leadoff single to pinch-hitter Herm Winningham, who was forced out at second on a fielder's choice as the Expos still couldn't place two runners on base in the same inning after six frames. Montreal right-handed reliever Bert Roberge walked Reynolds, the first batter he faced, who stole second and third base. Reynolds scored on a mishandled sacrifice bunt; Peña doubled home Bream and Brown on the next plate appearance to increase Pittsburgh's lead to eight runs.

The Expos finally scored in the seventh inning when Terry Francona singled and Tim Wallach walloped his 21st homer of the season. Reuschel did not allow another Montreal baserunner for the remainder of the game. Pittsburgh managed a lone walk in the seventh and eighth innings, but scored no more runs. Pittsburgh soundly defeated Montreal, 8-2, with Reuschel allowing five hits while striking out seven batters and walking none. His five-hitter was his eighth complete game over his past nine starts. Tanner complimented Reuschel's tenacity: "The way Reuschel is pitching should be contagious to our young pitchers. They see him go out there and throw strikes and get the job done."[12]

The Pirates ended the 1985 season with a 57-104 record, the worst winning percentage in the majors. Reuschel was a bright spot during a tough year; even though he pitched in Hawaii for the season's first six weeks, he led the Pirates with 14 wins and finished second in games started (26), innings pitched (194), and strikeouts (138), while allowing only seven homers. After his difficult 1984 season, Reuschel was named *The Sporting News'* Comeback Player of the Year for his 14-8 record and 2.27 ERA.[13] He finished fourth in NL ERA, third with 6.2 Wins Above Replacement for NL pitchers, and second lowest with 0.325 home runs allowed per nine innings pitched. Reuschel's comeback story was a breath of fresh air during the 1985 season, when many stories focused on relocation threats[14] and drug-abuse accusations. Writing about Reuschel's 14th victory, Pittsburgh sportswriter Bob Hertzel noted, "But there is something more esoteric about the accomplishment; a message that success can grow out of failure. It is what fans have latched onto, fans tired of reading about drugs and tests and in need of a hero."[15]

SOURCES

Besides the sources cited in the Notes, the author consulted Baseball-Almanac.com, Baseball-Reference.com, Retrosheet.org, and the following:

O'Brien, Jim. *We Had 'Em All the Way: Bob Prince and His Pittsburgh Pirates* (Pittsburgh: Jim O'Brien Publishing, 1998).

NOTES

1   Tribune Wire Services, "Rotator Cuff Torn: Reuschel," *Chicago Tribune,* June 26, 1982: 59.

2   Charley Feeney, "Reuschel Trying for Pirate Job," *Pittsburgh Post-Gazette,* February 28, 1985: 24.

3   Charley Feeney, "Pirates End Exhibition Season With Another Loss," *Pittsburgh Post-Gazette,* April 8, 1985: 31.

4   Bill Conlin, "Cubs Will Avenge Loss in Rematch," *The Sporting News,* April 8, 1985: 18.

5   Bob Hertzel, "Cubs Ready to Defy Critics and Repeat in 1985 …," *Pittsburgh Press,* April 7, 1985: 65.

6   Charley Feeney, "Retread Reuschel 'Never Lost Faith,'" *The Sporting News,* July 1, 1985: 23.

7   Charley Feeney, "Reuschel, Bucs Top Astros," *Pittsburgh Post-Gazette,* May 22, 1985: 13.

8   Charley Feeney, "Odyssey Continues for Rick Reuschel," *The Sporting News,* August 5, 1985: 31.

9   Associated Press, "Laskey Traded to Expos for Driessen," *Santa Cruz* (California) *Sentinel,* August 1, 1985: 10.

10 Bob Padecky, "Giants' Reliever Cracks Down on Hated Dodgers," *Santa Cruz Sentinel,* August 1, 1985: 10.

11 Charley Feeney, "Reuschel Stymies Montreal," *Pittsburgh Post-Gazette,* September 26, 1985: 13.

12 Ibid.

13 "1985 TSN All-Star Squads," *The Sporting News,* October 28, 1985: 18.

14 Phil Musick, "Mayor's Late-Inning Rally Heads Off Pirates at Pass," *Pittsburgh Press,* June 30, 1985: 17.

15 Bob Hertzel, "Incredible: Reuschel Wins No. 14 in Comeback Story," *Pittsburgh Press,* September 26, 1985: 28.

PIRATES BACK WAKEFIELD WITH OFFENSIVE EXPLOSION, SEND 1992 NLCS TO DECISIVE SEVENTH GAME

OCTOBER 13, 1992: PITTSBURGH PIRATES 13, ATLANTA BRAVES 4, AT ATLANTA-FULTON COUNTY STADIUM

GAME SIX OF THE 1992 NATIONAL LEAGUE CHAMPIONSHIP SERIES

BY FRANK ITTNER

AS THE 1992 NATIONAL LEAGUE Championship Series opened, the Pittsburgh Pirates found themselves facing a familiar foe. In 1991, the Bucs had taken the NL's best record into its NLCS matchup with the upstart Atlanta Braves, but despite a 3-2 lead in games and home field in Games Six and Seven, they ultimately fell short of capturing the series. Pittsburgh's vaunted offense was shut out in the final two games, as the Braves won their first pennant since 1958.

The 1992 rematch again featured the two teams with the NL's best records. However, this time the Braves had the home field advantage after a league-leading 98-64 record.[1] After the Braves jumped out to a 3-games-to-1 lead, Pirates Game Five starter Bob Walk pitched a masterful three-hit complete-game 7-1 victory, staving off elimination and sending the series back to Atlanta with the Braves leading three games to two. To win the pennant, the Pirates needed to do what the Braves had accomplished, that is, win the final two games on the road.

A sellout crowd of 51,975 gathered for Game Six at Fulton County Stadium, hoping to see the Braves clinch their first pennant at home since moving to Georgia in 1966. The Braves' starting pitcher was their stellar 26-year-old left-hander Tom Glavine, the reigning Cy Young Award winner, who had just recorded his second consecutive 20-win season, posting a 2.76 ERA and a league-leading five shut-

outs. Opposing Glavine was 26-year-old rookie knuckleballer Tim Wakefield, who had started the season at Triple-A Buffalo and had only been called up to the parent club in late July. The right-handed Wakefield quickly moved into the starting rotation and responded with an impressive overall record of 8-1 and ERA of 2.15 in just 13 starts. His performance was so remarkable that Pirates GM Ted Simmons stated that his team's rotation for the NLCS would be "Doug Drabek, Danny Jackson, and the Miracle (Wakefield)."[2] Pirates manager Jim Leyland compared the 1991 team to this year's by singling out Wakefield: "He's been our one and only surprise this year. The rest of the team, we pretty much knew about."[3]

Despite the obvious mismatch in major-league experience of the starters, the Pirates' confidence had been bolstered in Game Three of the series, when Wakefield had outdueled Glavine, 3-2, with a complete-game five-hitter (despite giving up two solo homers). In fact, the Braves had been so befuddled by Wakefield's knuckleball that manager Bobby Cox had summoned 53-year-old retired Braves knuckleballer Phil Niekro to pitch batting practice before the game.[4] Atlanta shortstop Jeff Blauser likewise remarked that bats were of little use in returning Tim Wakefield`s knuckleball lobs, the Braves should have used (tennis) rackets.[5]

After a scoreless first inning, the Pirates put on an offensive explosion in the top of the second that

163

blew the game open and drove Glavine to an early exit. Cleanup hitter and NL slugging leader Barry Bonds led off with a long home run to right that gave the Bucs a quick 1-0 lead. Jeff King and Lloyd McClendon followed with singles, and catcher Don Slaught launched a two-run double to right, pushing the lead to 3-0. José Lind grounded to shortstop Blauser, who threw to third in an attempt to cut down the lead runner. However, the throw glanced off Slaught and past third baseman Terry Pendleton, allowing Slaught to score, with Lind winding up at second base.[6] Pitcher Wakefield then put down a bunt (on a 1-and-2 count) that was fielded by Glavine, who threw to third too late, putting runners at first and third. The Braves pitcher's frustrations began to show, as he paused to glare at catcher Damon Berryhill for directing him to throw to third.[7] Leadoff hitter Gary Redus followed by fighting off an inside pitch with a flare to right field that landed just inside the foul line, a double that scored Lind and sent Wakefield to third.[8] The next batter, Jay Bell, blasted a three-run homer to left, pushing the lead to 8-0, with still no outs in the inning. That spelled the end for Glavine, who was pulled in favor of Charlie Leibrandt and left to a chorus of boos from the home crowd.[9] While southpaw Leibrandt managed to keep the score intact, he did give up singles to Bonds and McClendon, with the inning ending only after McClendon rounded first base too far, and Bonds was caught between third and home on a bizarre 9-5-3-6-2-5-3 putout.

In the bottom of the second, Wakefield issued a leadoff walk to Sid Bream, and two outs later, walked number-eight hitter Mark Lemke. Braves manager Bobby Cox elected not to pinch-hit for pitcher Leibrandt, who promptly struck out swinging, leaving the score 8-0 after two frames. The decision not to use a pinch-hitter was second-guessed openly by members of the Atlanta media and seemed to indicate that Cox was already looking ahead to Game Seven.[10]

Neither team scored in the third inning, but the Braves finally dented the scoreboard in the bottom of the fourth. Sid Bream led off the inning with a single to center and Ron Gant walked. Wakefield then retired Berryhill and Lemke, again bringing up the pitcher's spot with two out and two on. This time, Cox decided to replace Leibrandt with pinch-hitter Lonnie Smith, who smacked the first pitch into right field for an RBI single. Wakefield then issued his fourth walk of the game to Otis Nixon to load the bases, but was able to avoid a big inning by getting Jeff Blauser on a popup to shortstop to strand the runners.

In the top of the fifth, the Pirates reignited their offense against the new Braves pitcher, "Starvin'" Marvin Freeman, effectively putting the game out of reach. Freeman began by issuing walks to McClendon and Slaught, and Jose Lind followed with a two-run double to extend the lead to 10-1. After Wakefield sacrificed Lind to third, Redus came through with an RBI single. Jay Bell then grounded to first, with Redus taking second on the play. The next batter was Andy Van Slyke, who pounced on the first pitch for a single to score Redus and give the Bucs a 12-1 lead after only 4½ innings.

With a commanding lead, Pirates manager Leyland now had the luxury of resting his bullpen for the inevitable Game Seven, despite Wakefield not being as sharp as in his prior performance.[11] Wakefield gave up consecutive singles to start the fifth inning, but settled down to retire the next three batters, with the final out coming after a diving stop by third baseman Jeff King on Berryhill's hard groundball.[12] The Pirates stretched their lead to 13-1 on a solo homer by McClendon in the sixth, and rest of the game was reduced to a mere formality. Wakefield was touched for two home runs by David Justice, but they were of little consequence. When Sid Bream grounded to short for the final out of the game, Pittsburgh had evened the NLCS with a resounding 13-4 victory.

Tim Wakefield's final line was hardly the stuff of legend: 141 pitches, nine hits, four earned runs, two home runs, four walks, four strikeouts, and one wild pitch. However, by going the distance for the second time in the series, he ensured that the team would have a rested bullpen for the decisive seventh game. Meanwhile, the Pirates' dominant offensive perfor-

mance had already produced the following NLCS records by one team:[13]
- Most doubles, series: 16.
- Most runs scored, series: 33.
- Most total bases, one inning: 16 (second inning, Game Six).
- Most runs, NLCS game: 13 (Game Six, 1992). *Tied with Atlanta Braves (Game Two, 1992) and Chicago Cubs (Game One, 1984).*

Postscript: The next evening, the Pirates took a 2-0 lead into the bottom of the ninth inning behind right-hander Doug Drabek, but were undone by a three-run Braves uprising, culminating when former Pirate Sid Bream slid home with the winning run on a two-out, two-run pinch single by Braves third-string catcher Francisco Cabrera off Bucs reliever Stan Belinda. That final play, often referred to simply as "The Slide," seemed to be a turning point after which the Pirates would struggle for years to come.[14] In the offseason, both Barry Bonds, the 1992 National League MVP, and Doug Drabek, the Pirates' number-one pitcher, left the team to sign free-agent contracts with the Giants and Astros, respectively. The 1993 Pirates played .500 ball through June 28 but never reached that plateau again for the rest of the season. By the end of July, they had released prior-year starting catcher Mike LaValliere, were forced to accept the resignation of GM Ted Simmons, traded away Stan Belinda, and had even sent Tim Wakefield down to Double A after he started the season with severe bouts of wildness, including one game when he walked 10 batters. The Pirates finished the 1993 season in fifth place in the NL East with a record of 75-87, the first of 20 consecutive losing seasons, a streak unmatched in the history of major-league baseball.

SOURCES

In addition to the sources cited in the Notes, the author consulted Baseball-Reference.com and Retrosheet.orgNote: due to an ongoing Teamsters strike, there was no coverage of the '92 NLCS by Pittsburgh's two major newspapers at the time, the *Press* and the *Post-Gazette*.

NOTES

1 The city where League Championship Series games would commence alternated each year from 1969 through 1993 between the East and West Divisions. Even when both LCS formats switched from a best-of-five series to a best-of-seven series in 1985, the regular season won-loss records did not factor into the playoffs until the League Division Series was added.

2 Bill Nowlin, "Tim Wakefield," (SABR Bio Project), sabr.org, December 15, 2016.

3 Mark Maske, "Pirates Pin Hopes on Wakefield," *Washington Post*, October 13, 1992.

4 Furman Bisher, "A 13-Run Massacre on Tuesday the 13th," *Atlanta Journal Constitution*, October 14, 1992: D1.

5 Gordon Edes, "White Knuckles: It`s Braves' Turn," *SunSentinel*, October 13, 1992.

6 Mark Maske, "Pirates Pound Braves 13-4, Send NLCS to 7th Game," *Washington Post*, October 14, 1992.

7 Ibid.

8 Ibid.

9 Ibid.

10 Prentis Rogers, "Chop Talk: What the Players, Fans, and Media are Saying on the Air," *Atlanta Journal Constitution*, October 14, 1992: D6.

11 Jerome Holtzman, "Leyland Defends Wakefield Going the Distance," *Chicago Tribune*, October 14, 1992.

12 Fred McMane (United Press International), "Pirates 13, Braves 4," October 14, 1992.

13 "National League playoff records set so far by the Pirates and Braves," *Atlanta Journal Constitution*, October 14, 1992: D6.

14 J. Brady McCullough, "The Slide: The Moment That Begat a Legacy of Losing for the Pirates," *Pittsburgh Post-Gazette*, April 2, 2012.

CORDOVA, RINCON, AND SMITH PROVIDE FIREWORKS IN 10-INNING NO-HIT VICTORY OVER ASTROS

JULY 12, 1997: PITTSBURGH PIRATES 3, HOUSTON ASTROS 0, AT THREE RIVERS STADIUM

BY FREDERICK C. BUSH

IT TOOK THE DUAL ATTRACTIONS OF a Jackie Robinson number-retirement ceremony and a postgame fireworks show to lure the Pirates' first non-Opening Day sellout crowd since June 5, 1977, to Three Rivers Stadium on July 12, 1997.[1] The surprising Bucs, who had been dubbed "The Freak Show" by announcer Greg Brown because of their unexpected rise to contention, were in first place in the NL Central Division as they entered their first series of the season's second half, which pitted them against second-place Houston.[2] The Astros had registered consecutive dominant shutouts, 7-0 and 10-0, to overtake the Pirates for the division lead. In light of the two disappointing losses, the crowd of 44,119 had come primarily to watch the pregame and postgame festivities on this day; however, they received an additional thrill as the hometown nine won a no-hitter in dramatic fashion in the bottom of the 10th inning.

Before the game, the Pirates formally retired Jackie Robinson's number 42—which had already been retired by Major League Baseball earlier in the season—as part of what was called Breaking Barriers Night. Six Pittsburgh residents, including the Pirates' Hall of Fame first baseman Willie Stargell, were honored for following "Robinson's path by breaking barriers of their own," and Robinson's daughter, Sharon, threw out the first pitch.[3] While this was happening, Pirates starter Francisco Cordova was having difficulty with his control while warming up, and pitching coach Pete Vuckovich worried that Cordova might not last longer than an inning or two. Looking back on what followed, Vuckovich observed, "It just goes to show you, all you're doing down in the bullpen is getting loose and getting ready to go."[4]

Whatever Cordova's own feelings about his warm-up session may have been, his confidence was likely bolstered by the fact that he already had tossed a two-hit, 6-0 shutout against Houston at the Astrodome on June 23. Astros manager Larry Dierker later said about that game, "It was like we were swinging at butterflies. We didn't get a good swing the whole game," and also believed, "Well, (Cordova) might shut us down [on July 12], but there's no way he can pitch better."[5] Though unaware of Dierker's thoughts, Cordova nevertheless proved them to be wrong.

While the game would turn out to be a historic occasion, a perfect game was quickly out of the question when Cordova walked Jeff Bagwell with two outs in the first inning. The next batter, Luis Gonzalez, hit a line drive straight at first baseman Kevin Young for the third out of the frame. Beginning with Gonzalez's lineout, Cordova bore down and retired 20 consecutive Astros batters before issuing his second walk of the evening, to Gonzalez, with two outs in the top of the seventh. Of those 20 consecutive outs, 10 came by strikeout, including a string of five consecutive punchouts from the second inning through the end of the third .

Amid the growing anticipation that a no-hitter might take place, the fact that Pittsburgh was also being kept off the scoreboard appeared to be lost on the crowd. The Pirates batters, however, were well aware that they were involved in a struggle. Astros starter Chris Holt had surrendered a single to the first batter he had faced, second baseman Tony Womack, but he had immediately stifled any potential scoring threat by inducing a 5-4-3 double-play grounder from Jermaine Allensworth. Holt was not as dominant as Cordova, but he held his own in the pitchers' duel as he retired the Pirates in order in the fourth, fifth, and seventh innings and allowed no more than one base-runner in any inning until the bottom of the eighth.

In that eighth inning, Holt allowed two singles that, with two fielder's-choice grounders, left Lou Collier on second and Cordova on first. Collier was the first runner the Pirates had gotten into scoring position in the game, so Dierker brought in Billy "The Kid" Wagner, his fireballing, left-handed reliever, to quash the threat. Wagner obliged by striking out Womack to keep the game in a scoreless tie.

Cordova allowed his final baserunner of the evening with two outs in the top of the ninth when he hit Chuck Carr with a pitch, but Bagwell lofted a lazy fly ball to right field that kept the no-hitter intact. Wagner continued to throw BB's and struck out the side to send the game to extra innings.

At this point the significance of the 0-0 ballgame no doubt dawned on any longtime Pittsburgh fans in attendance. They surely recalled Pirates pitcher Harvey Haddix throwing 12 perfect innings against the Braves in Milwaukee on May 26, 1959, only to lose the game 1-0 in the 13th inning. If a similar fate were to strike the Pirates on this night, it would not befall Cordova alone as Pirates manager Gene Lamont sent Ricardo Rincon to the mound in the top of the 10th. Lamont reasoned, "(Cordova) had thrown enough, a few too many. If I send him back out there, he ends up throwing 135 or 140 pitches. Remember, the game is riding on every pitch. That puts more stress on the arm."[6] Cordova said after the game, "I wanted to keep on going. But it's not my decision."[7]

Cordova may have found some solace in the fact that his no-hitter now rested in the hands of Rincon. The two pitchers were Mexican compatriots who had become friends as teammates with the Mexico City Diablos Rojos (Red Devils) in 1994 and 1995. Rincon issued the Astros' third free pass of the contest (to Derek Bell) with one out, but Bill Spiers struck out and Brad Ausmus popped out to catcher Jason

Kendall to increase the tension inside Three Rivers Stadium. The suspense would soon come to an end in a manner that delighted the crowd and exorcised some of the demons of Haddix's unfortunate loss 38 years earlier.

Wagner was done for the evening, so John Hudek entered the game for Houston in the bottom of the 10th. Initially, Hudek picked up where Wagner had left off and struck out Dale Sveum. However, he then walked Kendall, retired Jose Guillen, and walked Turner Ward (who was pinch-hitting for Collier). With men on first and second and the pitcher's spot due up, Lamont sent Mark Smith to the plate to hit for Rincon.

Smith had been acquired in a four-player trade with the San Diego Padres on March 29 and had 11 RBIs in 59 at-bats for Pittsburgh.[8] In regard to what happened next, Smith asserted, "I got a great scouting report from [batting coach] Lloyd McClendon. He told me to watch for fastballs, that (Hudek) likes to get ahead on fastballs. He started me off with an inside fastball [for a strike]. I watched for the same thing."[9] Smith saw what he was looking for on the next pitch, and he smacked his third home run of the season to deep left field to give the Pirates a 3-0 victory.

Although the Pirates had emerged victorious, Cordova did not receive credit for the no-hitter; in fact, he did not even receive the win, which went to Rincon. In regard to Cordova's plight, Bagwell remarked, "Pretty weird. But I'm sure he's happy they got the win even if he didn't get the no-hitter."[10] Ausmus compared Cordova's no-hit effort to his earlier two-hitter against the Astros, saying, "In this game he threw more off-speed pitches and moved the ball around a little more. He really kept us off balance. I don't think we hit a ball hard, did we?"[11]

The answer to Ausmus's question was no, which was why Cordova and Rincon entered the record books together with the eighth combined no-hitter in major-league history.[12] Their 10-inning effort also tied the major-league record for the longest no-hitter, which had been accomplished four times previously.[13] It was only the third no-hitter by the Pirates in

Pittsburgh in the 110-year history of the franchise, joining John Candelaria's gem against the Los Angeles Dodgers on August 9, 1976, and Nicholas Maddox's no-hitter against the Brooklyn Superbas on September 20, 1907.

Not to be forgotten in the midst of all the fanfare about the no-hitter was the other hero of the day, Smith, who said of his game-winning blast, "It's funny, but I got all fired up sitting on the bench in the ninth inning, thinking how great it would be to win the game with a homer. I can't describe the feeling. It's the greatest feeling you could ever have."[14]

NOTES

1   Alan Robinson, "Pirates Team for 10-Inning No-Hitter," washingtonpost.com/archive/sports/1997/07/13/pirates-team-for-10-inning-no-hitter/85717df9-2a82-4260-883a-881481ffffe7/?utm_term=.95063a7cd082, accessed September 22, 2017.

2   Paul Meyer, "Pirates' 'Freak Show' Hit Zenith With July No-Hitter, *Pittsburgh Post-Gazette*, July 11, 2007: F-1.

3   Bob Smizik, "Pirates Celebrate Jackie," *Pittsburgh Post-Gazette*, July 13, 1997: D-10.

4   Kevin Stankiewicz, "Twenty Years Later, a Look Back at the Francisco Cordova-Ricardo Rincon No-Hitter," post-gazette.com/sports/pirates/2017/07/12/Pirates-Francisco-Cordova-Ricardo-Rincon-20-years-no-hitter-Gene-Lamont/stories/201707120033, accessed September 22, 2017.

5   Ibid.

6   Bob Smizik, "Cordova and Rincon Combine on No-Hitter," *Pittsburgh Post-Gazette*, July 13, 1997: D-1.

7   "Cordova and Rincon," D-10.

8   Ibid.

9   Ibid.

10 Ron Cook, "A Weird Gem for Cordova," *Pittsburgh Post-Gazette*, July 13, 1997: D-1.

11 "A Weird Gem," D-10.

12 As of September 22, 2017, there have been 11 combined no-hitters in major-league history.

13 Three of the other 10-inning no-hitters also occurred in the National League: the Cincinnati Reds' Jim Maloney, 1-0, against the Chicago Cubs on August 19, 1965; the Cincinnati Reds' Fred Toney, 1-0, also against the Cubs, on May 2, 1917; and the New York Giants' Hooks Wiltse, 1-0, against the Philadelphia Phillies on July 4, 1908. The fourth such no-hitter was hurled by Sam Kimber of the old American Association's Brooklyn Atlantics against the Toledo Blue Stockings in a game that ended in a 0-0 tie on October 4, 1884.

14 Robinson.

PIRATES' UNFORGETTABLE COMEBACK

JULY 28, 2001 (GAME ONE OF DAY-NIGHT DOUBLEHEADER): PITTSBURGH PIRATES 9, HOUSTON ASTROS 8, AT PNC PARK

BY PAUL E. DOUTRICH

AS 32,977 PATRONS FILED INTO PNC Park on Saturday, July 28, some knew that they were going to be part of a notable day for the Pittsburgh Pirates, but no one expected the real reason why the day would be unforgettable.[1] Most knowledgeable fans thought it was because the Pirates were about to play the day game of the first day-night doubleheader in the team's history. Others were excited because it was their first trip to their team's beautiful new ballpark. However, no one imagined that the day's lasting memory would instead come with two outs in the bottom of the ninth inning.

The Astros came into Pittsburgh locked in a battle with the Chicago Cubs for first place in the National League Central Division. During the previous six years, Houston had the best record in the division, winning three of the previous four division championships. On the other hand, the Pirates were trying to stay out of the division's cellar. It had been 10 years since Pittsburgh finished the season with a winning record. They were already 23 games under .500, and there was no doubt that 2001 would be the 11th year.

The game began uneventfully. The Astros went down in order in the first inning as did the home team. On the mound were two young right-handed hurlers. Bronson Arroyo, the Pirates pitcher, had been recalled from Triple-A Nashville the day before. He started the season in Pittsburgh but had been pitching for the Sounds since an ugly loss to the Philadelphia Phillies on June 20. Carrying a hefty 6.24 ERA and a 3-6 won-lost record, Arroyo hoped the game against the Astros would keep him in Pittsburgh. Meanwhile, Roy Oswalt was establishing himself as a potential Rookie of the Year candidate.[2] He began the season in the Astros bullpen but became part of the starting rotation in early June. He brought an impressive 8-2 record and 3.39 ERA into the game.

Vinny Castilla led off the second inning for the Astros by launching his 13th home run of the season. Houston had signed Castilla two months earlier as a free agent, after he was released by the Tampa Bay Devil Rays. A 10-year veteran, the slugger was expected to bring some additional punch to the middle of an already potent Astros lineup. He did not disappoint. Since coming to Houston on May 15, he had hit 10 home runs, driven in 43 runs, and was hitting at a .280 clip.[3]

In the bottom of the inning the Pirates matched the Astros' production. Left fielder Brian Giles led off with a double to center field. Two outs later Kevin Young smacked a single to left field, scoring Giles. Since coming to Pittsburgh from Cleveland two years earlier, Giles had quietly established himself as one of the better hitters in the National League. Along with third baseman Aramis Ramirez and catcher Jason Kendall, he was counted on to drive the Pittsburgh attack in 2001. Carrying a .323 average with 24 home runs and 62 RBIs, Giles was living up to those expectations.[4]

After a scoreless third, Castilla opened the Astros fourth with another towering drive to deep left-center field. Giles raced back to the wall, leaped, gloved the ball, and pulled it back into play, robbing Castilla of his second home run. After the game the left fielder said, "It would have landed in the front row, I think. ... Here you can't give up on the ball. It was hit high. Those are really the only balls you have a chance to bring back."[5] Aided by Giles' spectacular catch, Arroyo labored through the rest of the inning, giving up a single, two walks, and a wild pitch before escaping a bases-loaded threat when Oswalt flied out.

The fifth inning did not turn out as well for the Pirates pitcher. Leadoff hitter Craig Biggio singled and was sacrificed to second by shortstop Julio Lugo. Lance Berkman followed with a single that got Biggio to third. Into the batter's box stepped Castilla for the third time and for the third time he launched a missile to left field. This time it could not be brought back and the Astros took a three-run lead, 4-1.

Both starters were gone by the end of the seventh inning. Oswalt's departure came after the Pirates scored a run and had men on second and third with one out. Nevertheless, he left confident that his ninth win was just two innings away. "I counted it as a win," he said after the game.[6] Southpaw Ron Villone came in and quickly put out the fire. During the Pittsburgh rally, Warren Morris, a left-handed hitter batting .154, pinch-hit for Arroyo. When Pirates manager Lloyd McClendon saw that Oswalt was being lifted in favor of Villone, he pulled Morris and sent to the plate right-handed Craig Wilson, who was batting .300. But Wilson struck out and leadoff hitter Tike Redman flied out to center. Meanwhile, Arroyo's exit ended the next day back in Nashville.[7]

The Pirates reliever, Omar Olivares, did not fare as well as Villone. A journeyman right-handed pitcher who was in his 12th and final major-league season, Olivares came into the game with a 6.80 ERA. He was immediately greeted by Castilla, who hammered his third home run of the day into the left-field stands. Only a perfectly timed leap by a self-described "short, fat guy" separated Castilla from a truly historic day of his own.[8] Houston added its sixth run of the day before its half of the inning ended.

Right-handed relief pitcher Michael Jackson, who picked up for Villone in the bottom of the eighth, quickly dispatched the three Pirates hitters he faced. In the ninth, with Olivares still on the mound, the Astros scored twice more, pushing their lead to six runs, 8-2. The only redeeming moment for Olivares was a swinging strikeout of Castilla.

The Pirates' ninth began the way the eighth had ended. Jackson got third baseman Ramirez to fly out to deep left and Johnny Vander Wal on a fly to center. It was then that lightning struck. Kevin Young, who already had a hit and both of the Pirates' RBIs, lashed a double to left. The eighth hitter in the lineup, second baseman Pat Meares, followed with his fourth home run of the season and the last in his career. Still down 8-4, manager McClendon sent up light-hitting Adam Hyzdu to bat for Olivares. Hyzdu singled. Tyke Redman followed with a walk. Hyzdu then scored the Pirates' fifth run on a single by shortstop Jack Wilson.

With his team's lead slipping away, Astros manager Larry Dierker called in his stopper, Billy Wagner. One of the preeminent relief pitchers in the major leagues, Wagner already had 24 saves. A southpaw with a fastball that periodically clocked in at 100 mph, he could be intimidating. Jason Kendall was the first Pirate to face Wagner. During the winter Kendall had signed a six-year, $60 million contract. The catcher's season had not lived up to his new salary. His batting average had fallen by 68 points and his power numbers further reflected the decline. With the Astros just one out away from the win, Wagner's third pitch drilled Kendall in the leg, loading the bases for Giles.[9]

Giles became the ninth Pirates hitter in the inning. In his only previous appearance against Wagner, Giles had struck out. The lefty-versus-lefty matchup certainly favored the pitcher. Giles went to the plate looking for an inside pitch that he could just put into play. "When a guy is throwing that hard, you don't want to try to do too much," he said after the game.[10] On Wagner's second pitch, Giles got what he wanted. He turned on the pitch and crushed a screaming line drive into the right-field stands. Of the swat Giles explained: "I never give high fives to (first-base coach) Tommy Sandt. But I knew it was gone."[11] Pittsburgh's incredible comeback was complete. Only once before in the National League, on June 29, 1952, when the Cubs defeated the Reds 9-8 in the first game of a Crosley Field doubleheader, had a team with two outs in the bottom of the ninth inning rallied back from being six runs down to win.[12] Giles' grand slam duplicated the feat.

As they left PNC that afternoon with fireworks bursting overhead, the happy Pirates fans probably again admired their team's picturesque new ballpark. They certainly remembered Castilla's three home runs and the catch that robbed him of a fourth; but no doubt their most lasting memory was of Brian Giles' grand slam that transformed a memorable game into an unforgettable comeback.

NOTES

1   retrosheet.org/boxesetc/2001/B07281PIT2001.htm.

2   Oswalt finished second to Albert Pujols in the National League Rookie of the Year voting.

3   baseball-reference.com/players/gl.fcgi?id=castivio2&t=b&year=2001#1066-1128-sum:batting_gamelogs.

4   baseball-reference.com/players/gl.fcgi?id=gilesbro2&t=b&year=2001#597-696-sum:batting_gamelogs

5   Robert Dvorchak, "Pirates Stun Astros With 7-Run Rally," *Pittsburgh Post-Gazette,* July 29, 2001: D-7.

6   Ibid.

7   "Notebook," *Pittsburgh Post-Gazette,* July 29, 2001: D-6.

8   Dvorchak, "Pirates Stun Astros."

9   Kendall was the first batter Wagner hit in 2001.

10   Bob Smizik, "Giles Helps Pirates Grind Out Improbable Victory," *Pittsburgh Post-Gazette,* July 29, 2001: D-7.

11   Robert Dvorchak, "Giles' Grand Slam in Ninth Caps Incredible Comeback in 9–8 Victory Against Astros," *Pittsburgh Post-Gazette,* July 29, 2001: D-1.

12   Smizik, "Giles Helps Pirates."

ROSS OHLENDORF WINS HIS ONLY GAME OF THE SEASON

JULY 2, 2010: PITTSBURGH PIRATES 2, PHILADELPHIA PHILLIES 0, AT PNC PARK

BY JORGE IBER, PHD

WHEN A FRANCHISE ENDURES TWO consecutive decades of sub-.500 seasons there are bound to be some close calls to breaking the cycle over the ignominious years (1997 and 2012, when Pittsburgh finished 79-83), and then there are seasons that are outright catastrophes (like 2001 and 2009, when they finished 62-100 and 62-99). The Pirates' 2009 campaign was their then-record 17th consecutive losing campaign. (The losing campaigns would stretch to 20.) With this season, they "surpassed" the ignominy of cross-state rivals, the Philadelphia Phillies of 1933-1948. Not surprisingly, this Pirates squad was proficient neither at the plate (3.95 runs scored per game and a .252 team batting average) nor on the mound (a 4.59 ERA). Still, there were some glimmers of sanguinity for 2010.

One of these indications was the work of Curtis Ross Ohlendorf, a native of Austin, Texas, whom Pittsburgh acquired in late July 2008 after stints with the Arizona Diamondbacks and the New York Yankees. He was a fourth-round draft pick by Arizona out of Princeton University in 2004 and was then part of the trade that sent future Hall of Famer and left-handed pitcher Randy Johnson back to the desert in January 2007. Ohlendorf's time with New York was brief, however, as he was traded to the Pirates after a disappointing ERA of 6.53 in 25 appearances covering 40 innings. Upon his arrival in the Steel City in July 2008, the Texan started five games and finished 0-3 with a 6.35 ERA. The right-hander would, however, begin to demonstrate some promise during the awful campaign of 2009.

A quick review of three outings from that year demonstrates the reason for the Pirates' optimism. First, on August 18, Ohlendorf pitched seven innings against the Milwaukee Brewers, surrendering one earned run and five hits. Pittsburgh triumphed, 5-2. At this point, his record stood at 11-8 for a team that was 48-70. Two other contests, both no-decisions, would provide further encouragement. On September 5, in a 2-1,10-inning Cardinals victory at PNC Park, Ohlendorf pitched eight innings, allowed four hits, struck out 11, and the only run St. Louis scored while he was on the mound was unearned. In this game, he matched a rare feat, striking out all three batters on nine pitches in the fourth. Finally, in another sterling outing, he went seven innings against San Diego, surrendering only one earned run in a 2-1 Padres victory on September 19 in Pittsburgh. This was Ohlendorf's final start of the year, and dropped his ERA to a team-best 3.92 as he finished with an 11-10 mark. Ohlendorf's ERA was substantially below that of the entire staff (4.59). He pitched 176⅔ innings (third on the team) and had a winning record for a club that finished 37 games under breakeven. Certainly, here was a starter Bucs manager John Russell could count on going into 2010. It was not to be, however, as the wheels came off for both the Pirates and Ohlendorf in 2010. The team finished 57-105 (its worst mark since the days of "Rickey's Dinks" that went 42-112 in 1952) Similarly, the once promising career of Ross Ohlendorf went down the same black hole as he finished 1-11, although with a fairly decent ERA of 4.07.

A quick review of the statistics for the Pirates in 2010 makes one cringe. The overall team batting average dropped to .242, last in the National League. Team ERA ballooned to 5.00, also last in the senior circuit. They were shut out in approximately 10 percent of their games (15 times) and scored a measly

Ross Ohlendorf

587 runs for the year (3.62), while surrendering 5.34 tallies per contest. An effective summation of the year came early in the season, as the Brewers won 20-0 at PNC on April 22. Ohlendorf did not pitch that day but he contributed, though less so than his mound colleagues, to this horrendous season. He had several poor outings, with short stints in games against the Atlanta Braves on May 21, a 7-0 defeat (pitching only 3⅔ innings); another ineffective effort occurred on July 17, when, after being staked to a three-run lead, Ohlendorf gave up four runs while retiring just one batter in the top of the second against the Houston Astros. A further negative took place on July 28 in the first inning against the Colorado Rockies at Coors Field, as Ohlendorf took a line drive off his head from the bat of Troy Tulowitzki. To round out the nightmare, he did not record an out while suffering a shoulder injury in his final game of the year, a 10-2 defeat to St. Louis before a paltry home crowd of 12,393 on August 23. Ohlendorf, however, remained one of the "best" Pirate starters that year, with 21 starts and 108⅓ innings pitched.

Even in a gloomily horrendous season, however, there can be brief moments of sunshine, and for Ross Ohlendorf, that ephemeral moment took place at PNC against the team that would win the NL East in 2010, the Philadelphia Phillies. Coming into 2010, the Phillies had appeared in back-to-back World Series, defeating the Tampa Bay Rays in 2008 and

losing to the Yankees the following year. While the denizens of eastern Pennsylvania enjoyed success, the westerners finished a combined 65 games below .500 over those two seasons. The six-game season series against their hated cross-state rivals proved one of the few bright spots for the 2010 Pirates, as they took four of the six contests.

On Friday, July 2, before a crowd of 30,339, Ohlendorf took the mound to confront left-handed veteran Jamie Moyer. Going into the contest, the Pirates were 28-51 while Philadelphia stood at 41-36. In the top of the first, Ohlendorf made short work of Jimmy Rollins, who popped out to third, and then retired both Raul Ibanez and Jayson Werth on called third strikes. Ohlendorf continued to handcuff the Phillies through the rest of his time on the mound, scattering singles to Dane Sardinha in the third, Ryan Howard in the fourth, and Wilson Valdez in the fifth and seventh. The only extra-base hit for Philadelphia was by Ibanez in the sixth. In the eighth, Pirates right-handed reliever Joel Hanrahan retired Rollins, Ibanez, and Werth in order, and in the ninth, right-handed closer Octavio Dotel recorded save 18 of the season as he induced Ryan Howard, Ben Francisco, and Greg Dobbs to fly out.

Pittsburgh chalked up its two tallies in the fourth off Moyer on a single by Andrew McCutchen, strike-outs by Garrett Jones and Lastings Milledge, a single by Ryan Doumit, a walk to Bobby Crosby, and an infield single by Andy LaRoche and a throwing error by Moyer. After four innings, the score stood at 2-0 Pirates, and that was the last of the scoring.

Ohlendorf pitched for Pittsburgh in 2011, but lasted only two starts before going on the disabled list with a back strain after a short outing on April 8. He did not start again until August 23. He had a total of nine appearances, finished with a 1-3 mark and an ERA of 8.15. He was released by the Pirates on December 7, 2011. He then bounced from the Boston Red Sox (no appearances) to the San Diego Padres to the Washington Nationals to the Texas Rangers, the Kansas City Royals (no appearances), and the Cincinnati Reds between 2012 and 2016, finally landing in Japan during 2017 with the Tokyo

Yakult Swallows. His final record in the majors was a pedestrian 30-41 with an unimpressive 4.82 ERA.

While his stint in baseball was not the greatest, Ohlendorf did earn a degree from Princeton in 2006 and has worked for both the University of Texas's Office of Finance and the US Department of Agriculture. Additionally he also continued to work for his family, which has been ranching in Texas since the 1830s, in running the homestead and marketing their Rocking O Longhorns throughout the world.[1] In in the midst of all the negatives on the diamond, in 2010 *The Sporting News* named Ohlendorf one of the smartest athletes in sports, trailing only left-handed reliever Craig Breslow, a student at Yale where he majored in molecular biophysics and biochemistry, and Florida State University football player (and now Dr.) Myron Rolle.[2]

SOURCES

In addition to the sources cited in the Notes, the author also relied on Retrosheet.org and Baseball-Reference.com.

NOTES

1   Ann Hess, "Ohlendorf: Baseball Pitcher by day, Longhorn Rancher by Night," May 11, 2017. See agdaily.com/lifestyle/ohlendorf-baseball-pitcher-longhorn-rancher/.

2   David Gura, "'Sporting News' Magazine Compiles List of the 20 Smartest Athletes in Pro Sports," September 24, 2010. See: npr.org/sections/thetwo-way/2010/09/24/130101713/-sporting-news-magazine-compiles-list-of-the-20-smartest-athletes-in-sports. As of 2017 Breslow had appeared for seven teams during a 12-year major-league career covering 2005-2006 and 2008-2017.

PIRATES LOSE ON A REALLY, REALLY BAD CALL

JULY 26, 2011: ATLANTA BRAVES 4, PIRATES 3 (19 INNINGS), AT TURNER FIELD, ATLANTA

BY JORGE IBER, PHD

WHEN A TEAM GOES THROUGH A two-decade slide like the one the Pirates endured starting in 1993, the seemingly never-ending string of thrashings can run together as a whirlwind of despair in a fan's mind. Still, in this plethora of defeats, some losses carry a much greater sting than do others. After a miserable 2010 campaign, when the team lost 105 games (their worst record since 1952), the website UnNews, which refers to itself as "the mother ship of amateur comedy writing," actually took note of the excruciating calamity playing out in PNC Park by arguing that rather than suffer through what could only be a miserable 2011, management instead had concluded that it was best if the "Pittsburgh Pirates Forfeit Season."[1] Proving that UnNews should stick to comedic scripting and not baseball prognostication, however, it was good that the season was not canceled, as the Pirates' ship actually seemed to be heading in the right direction in 2011.

Indeed, very positive manifestations occurred that year: For example, the team was over .500 at the All-Star break for the first time since 1992; on June 24, after beating the Boston Red Sox, 3-1, the Pirates were 38-37, the latest they had been above breakeven since 1999; and, further whetting the hopes of long-suffering aficionados, the Pirates actually sat atop the NL Central on July 15, 19 and (unfortunately) one final time, on July 25 (actually, a first-place tie with St. Louis with a record of 53-47, but we'll take what we can get, right?).[2] Then came the second game of a four-game set with the Atlanta Braves (of course, it had to be) at Ted Turner Field on July 26. After what can only be termed one of the most heartbreaking defeats in team history, Pittsburgh was

not the same and staggered through a 19-43 record over the last 62 games of the season to finish 72-90, the Pirates' 19th consecutive losing campaign. Defeat number 82 took place on September 14 (in game 149 of the season), at the hands of the Cardinals, 3-2.

Overall, from an offensive perspective, this team was not vastly improved over the previous edition of the club. While in 2010 the Pirates hit a paltry .242, the following season that mark improved to just .253 (nonpitcher totals, .244 with the pitchers added in); ranking number 12 in the NL. The number of runs scored increased slightly, from 587 to 610 (3.77 per contest—number 14 in the NL), while the 57-win squad had tallied only 3.62 runs per outing (dead last in the circuit). The major difference was in the pitching, which, though not spectacular by any stretch of the imagination, was substantively better. In 2010 team ERA was 5.00 (866 runs allowed), in the following year it dropped to 4.04 (with 712 runs allowed). Three starters actually finished with ERAs below the staff average: Charlie Morton (who finished 10-10 with a 3.83); Paul Maholm (who finished 6-14 with a 3.66); and Jeff Karstens (who finished 9-9 with a 3.38). The star hurler was closer Joel Hanrahan, who compiled a 1-4 mark, but with 40 saves and an ERA of 1.83.

Heading into Atlanta, the Pirates had just finished a home series against St. Louis, winning the final contest in the three-game set, 4-3 in 10 innings before 35,402 hometown fans. The July 25 game against the Braves would be the first of a seven-contest road trip. (The next stop would be Philadelphia.) Things started well, as Pittsburgh was triumphant over the Braves on an ESPN national television feed, 3-1, with James McDonald hurling 5⅓ innings and scattering eight hits without allowing a run, and Joel Hanrahan chalking up his 29th save with a three-up, three-down bottom of the ninth.

The starters for the next game were Jeff Karstens for Pittsburgh and Tommy Hanson for the Braves. The official attendance at the start of what would become a 6-hour 39-minute marathon was 22,036; few were left to witness the climax. Right from the start, the Pirates seemed to be picking up where they had left off on the previous day. The leadoff hitter, left fielder Xavier Paul, singled and stole second. As Garrett Jones grounded out, Paul took third, and then he scored on a triple by Neil Walker. Andrew McCutchen flied out, and Pedro Alvarez singled to drive in Walker. Lyle Overbay then lined out to end the Pittsburgh half of the frame. Karsten, staked to an early 2-0 lead, had some troubles in the bottom of the first, walking former Pirate Nate McLouth, who stole second and made it to third on an error by catcher Michael McKenry. The Pirates starter then shut down the threat, inducing Martin Prado to pop out, striking out Brian McCann, and getting Freddie Freeman on a fly ball to deep center.

The Pirates scored again in the second on a one-out, bases-empty home run by McKenry. This made the score 3-0, and would be the final tally for the Pirates over the next 17 frames. Meanwhile, the Braves tied the score in the bottom of the third as they scored three times after two were out. The rally commenced with singles by McCann, Freeman, and Dan Uggla. This plated McCann and sent Freeman to second. Next, Eric Hinske walked to load the bases. Jason Heyward then singled home Freeman and Uggla to knot the score at 3-3. Julio Lugo grounded out to end the inning.

In games like this, there are always moments when a team looks back at missed opportunities. The Pirates had several in regulation: leaving runners stranded in the fourth, fifth (two in this frame), sixth, and ninth. The Braves did not fare much better, leaving the bases loaded in the sixth. After the sixth inning, both starters were gone, and the contest became a battle of the bullpens. For the Pirates, the combination of Tony Watson, Joe Beimel, Jose Veras, Chris Resop, and

Jason Grilliwent eight innings and surrendered only six hits. Daniel McCutchen entered in the bottom of inning 14 and hurled the final 5⅓ frames. Starting in the first extra inning, both squads squandered myriad chances to claim the victory. The Pirates left runners on in innings 10 (two), 13, 14, 16, 17 (two), and 18 (two). Meanwhile, Atlanta stranded teammates in the following at-bats: 11 (two), 12 (bases loaded), 13 (two), 15, 16, 17, and 18 (two). Neither side could get the clutch hit necessary to score the tiebreaking tally.

In the top of frame 19, the Pirates went down in order. Then, the Braves "scored" in the bottom of the inning to claim victory. Heyward grounded out, Lugo walked and Jordan Schafer singled. Lugo took third and Schafer advanced to second on defensive indifference. Pitcher Scott Proctor then hit into what is officially recorded as a fielder's choice. Lugo headed home from third and the throw to McKendry at the plate arrived in plenty of time to nail the runner. McKendry swept a tag across Lugo, and then … the unimaginable happened. Home-plate umpire Jerry Meals inexplicably called Lugo safe. The replay showed (clearly!) that McKendry tagged Lugo not once, but twice before the Braves shortstop touched home plate.

The following days brought numerous discussions about how Meals had blown the call, and MLB also weighed in to acknowledge that the call was "incorrect." In the "too bad, so sad" moment for the Pirates, MLB's vice president for baseball operations, Joe Torre, noted that "no one feels worse than (Meals)."[3] Well, this was certainly debatable.

The Pirates were five games above .500 and would go on to finish 18 games below breakeven after the horrible call by Meals. Although there were many "let's move on" and "tomorrow is another day" quotes, the season, it seemed, turned on that one miserable call. Manager Clint Hurdle tried to rally his troops, but the damage carried on into 2012. With a motto of "Finish" as their theme, the following year's version of the Bucs were on the verge of breaking "the streak," coasting along with a 63-47 mark as late as August 8. Painfully, that club would, like the 2011 version, collapse and end 79-83 (16-36 over the final 52 games), thereby extending the misery of Pirate fans for a 20th campaign.

SOURCES

In addition to the sources noted in the Notes, the author also used information from SABR.org, Retrosheet.org, and Baseball-Refernce.com.

NOTES

1   "Pittsburgh Pirates Forfeit Season," uncyclopedia.wikia.com/wiki/UnNews:Pittsburgh_Pirates_forfeit_season.

2   DJ Gallo, "The 20 Most Depressing 2012 Pirate Facts," October 8, 2012. See: espn.com/blog/playbook/fandom/post/_/id/12516/the-20-most-depressing-pirates-facts-of-2012.

3   David Brown, "Safe?! Stunning Umpire's Call Give Braves Win in 19 innings," July 27, 2011, sports.yahoo.com/mlb/blog/big_league_stew/post/safe-stunning-umpires-call-gives-braves-win-in-19-innings?urn=mlb,wp13987. See also "MLB Acknowledges Blown Call," July 28, 2011, espn.com/mlb/story/_/id/6808357/mlb-acknowledges-jerry-meals-missed-call-pittsburgh-pirates-file-complaint-19-inning-loss.

PIRATES END THE STREAK

SEPTEMBER 9, 2013: PITTSBURGH PIRATES 1, TEXAS RANGERS 0, AT GLOBE LIFE PARK, ARLINGTON

BY STEPHEN PETERSON

DESPITE THE PROMISE OF THE PREVI-ous two seasons, by 2013 Pirates fans were more jaded than ever. There had always been the hope that the losing-season streak, now 20 years long, inevitably had to end at some point. Now, after back-to-back late-in-the-season collapses, there was a feeling that nothing would end the streak. But just as Pirates fans were finally ready to abandon all hope, it finally happened. The Pirates' next winning season took so long that Doug Drabek and Andy Van Slyke's sons would be playing major-league baseball by the time it finally died. It came in a game that on paper was nothing all that interesting. There were no diving, game-saving catches or ninth-inning, base-clearing home runs, just some really solid pitching. Even the celebrating was all but nonexistent. But to Pirates fans, it was quite possibly the greatest baseball game since Bill Mazeroski's home run won the 1960 World Series. When Sid Bream slid into home plate in Game Seven of the 1992 NLCS, there were tears all over Pittsburgh. Almost 21 years later, there would be tears flowing again but these were tears that finally washed away all those years of frustration, heartbreak, bitterness, and embarrassment.

The 2013 season started dreadfully, five losses in the first six games, and Pirates fans almost felt relieved that they wouldn't have to suffer through the tease of a winning record that the previous two seasons had provided. And despite the stigma that came with losing season number 20, it almost came as a relief. Number 20 was over and what difference would 21 make? However, as painful as they were, those two mirage-like seasons were really setting up the actual winning season that was finally coming. During the 2011 and 2012 seasons (Clint Hurdle's first two as

the Pirates manager), the team began to perfect its "torture-ball" style of winning, grinding out a few runs with a meager offense while frustrating teams with stellar pitching, keeping its opponents to a few runs a game. The Pirates didn't collapse the previous two seasons because of some otherworldly curse. They just needed to sustain their winning for a full season. Besides, these players adored one another and their respect and love was infectious.

The starting pitching staff was dominant in 2013, with veterans A.J. Burnett and Francisco Liriano doing some of their best work in years. By mid-July, Liriano had an ERA of 2.00 and a record of 9-3. He would go on to win the National League Comeback Player of the Year Award. Under the tutelage of Burnett, young lefty Jeff Locke went from barely making the starting rotation out of spring training to a surprising All-Star bid. In June, the Pirates called up a former number-one draft pick, right-hander Gerrit Cole. His first appearance couldn't have been scripted better. The reason for the success of Cole, Locke, and Charlie Morton was due in large part to the pitch calling of catcher Russell Martin, who came even better than advertised. Under his tutelage, the starting rotation went from 13th in the league in ERA to second. Meanwhile, Andrew McCutchen began what would eventually become his MVP season, becoming the first real homegrown national baseball celebrity Pittsburgh had seen since Barry Bonds. McCutchen was in his fifth year and unlike most of the team had been part of that 20 years of losing.

But the real key to the Pirates success in 2013 was the Shark Tank. Closer Jason Grilli, Mark Melancon, Tony Watson, Justin Wilson, Jared Hughes, Bryan Morris, and Vin Mazzaro comprised "the best bullpen in baseball," according to Tigers manager Jim

Leyland.[1] They frustrated and eventually terrified opposing teams like sharks sensing blood in the water, earning their nickname. Under the suggestion of the electric Grilli, management even installed a live, working shark tank in the clubhouse. The Pirates bullpen was so dominant that they had reduced games to six innings. If the Pirates had a lead by the time the game was official, it was usually over. Their record at midseason in such games was 40-2.

The National League Central Division was poised to place three teams in the playoffs. By late August the first-place Pirates were a staggering 24 games over .500. The Cardinals started performing better and the Pirates would soon be playing catch-up, while also fighting off the Cincinnati Reds.[2] Amid the wins, number-one Power Rankings, and *Sports Illustrated* covers, the team was dealing with unparalleled pressures. While they had to play with the normal, everyday anxiety that comes with a playoff stretch run, being a Pirate also meant you were inundated with nonstop locker-room questions about the slide, the 20-year losing streak and now "the collapse" or "the swoon" or whatever you wanted to call what happened in August the last two years.

Closer Grilli might have summed it up best: "We weren't a part of all those 20 years, a lot of us, we have nothing to do with that. But we have everything to do with fixing it."[3]

Fortunately for the Pirates, it was going to take the biggest collapse in baseball history to guarantee a losing season in 2013. By September, the Pirates were still rolling and for the first time in 20 years the words "Pirates" and "playoffs" were spoken in the same sentence. But one number was on the minds of every fan in Pittsburgh, .500. The city was going wild, Jolly Rogers were flying, PNC was rocking, repeatedly selling out. But for long-suffering Pirates fans, until it was mathematically impossible for the team to finish with a losing record, no one was ready to celebrate anything.

The streak finally came to an end on September 9, 2013. The Pirates were playing the first in a three-game series against the Texas Rangers in Arlington. After ensuring at least a .500 finish in Milwaukee

the previous week, they lost their next four games. This small, innocuous losing streak was just enough to rattle the nerves of fans who actually thought the Pirates might drop their remaining 20 contests.

The game saw Rangers ace Yu Darvish take on Cole. Ironically, it was the rookie Cole, who had never been on a losing Pirates team, who finally brought the team that coveted win. It was the kind of game the Pirates had been winning all season, just enough offense to complement nearly perfect pitching. Cole and Darvish went back and forth through six innings trading strikeouts and 1-2-3 innings, slowly driving Pirates fans crazy. In the top of the seventh, the dam finally broke. Marlon Byrd hit a two-out double. Pedro "El Toro" Alvarez followed with a run-scoring double to deep center field, giving the Pirates one of the single most important RBIs in the history of the franchise.

Thanks to Cole and eighth-inning man Watson, the Pirates held their tenuous 1-0 lead going into the bottom of the ninth. Pirates fans held their breath as Melancon, filling in as closer for the injured Grilli, came in. Every pitch was tortuous. And when Adrian Beltre grounded a single to left field with two outs, it seemed as if the streak would literally never end. But with a routine groundout by A.J. Pierzynski, Melancon finally shut the door and just like that it was all over. It was win number 82. And despite celebrations all over Pittsburgh, there was no champagne popped in the clubhouse, no celebrating by the team. Hurdle didn't even address the team after the game. It was as if they hadn't realized what they had done. You couldn't blame the night's winning pitcher for possibly not fathoming the significance of the game, and what he had done that night for the city of Pittsburgh. Cole was two years old when the Pirates lost Game Seven of the 1992 NLCS. But the explanation for the muted celebration was clear. This team had not lost all those years—the franchise had, and the fans had. This was not the team's celebration. This was Pittsburgh's.

Only second baseman Neil Walker, the Pittsburgh kid, knew what the fans knew, that this was one of the most significant games in franchise history: "[A] s a fan, that number has some significance, yes. To the other 24 guys, I don't think it holds that much weight."[4]

You can't blame the team for barely acknowledging the win. But for the fans and for the city, it was a 20-year sigh of relief. It put 20 years of misery to bed. It wasn't just a baseball game. It was the end of one of the most miserable chapters in the history of Pittsburgh sports and the birth of a new one.

SOURCES

In addition to the sources cited in the Notes, the author relied on the box-score and play-by-play account at Baseball-Reference.com.

NOTES

1   Lee Jenkins, "The Bucs Start Here," *Sports Illustrated*, September 9, 2013.

2   Pittsburgh was a season-high four games in front on August 10 before St. Louis started chipping away at the Bucs' lead.

3   Jenkins.

4   Jenkins.

LOSERS NO MORE: THE PITTSBURGH PIRATES WIN 2013 NL WILD CARD GAME

OCTOBER 1, 2013: PITTSBURGH PIRATES 6, CINCINNATI REDS 2, AT PNC PARK

BY ROCK HOFFMAN

THE PLAY IS KNOWN AS "THE SLIDE" and it served two functions. The first was immediate; it allowed the Atlanta Braves to beat the Pittsburgh Pirates 3-2 in Game Seven of the 1992 National League Championship Series and advance to the World Series. The second ushered in an era of futility for the Pirates that is unmatched in major-league history. The Pirates won three straight National League East Division titles from 1990 to 1992 and they did not have another winning season until 2013. Twenty losing seasons in a row is not only a major-league record but also the mark for a North American professional sports team.

"The Slide" itself occurred on October 14, 1992, at Atlanta-Fulton County Stadium when Braves first baseman Sid Bream—bad right knee and all—rumbled home from second base with the game-winning run on a single by Francisco Cabrera. His slide managed to avoid the tag of Pirates catcher Mike LaValliere, who needed to move slightly up the first-base line to take the throw from left fielder Barry Bonds.

In 2013, the Pirates, under manager Clint Hurdle, finally broke the string of losing seasons. At the midpoint of the year, they were 51-30 with that 51st victory coming in the last game of a season-high nine-game winning streak. They faded slightly in the second half; after finishing June and July with the best record in baseball, the Bucs were a combined 29-26 in August and September. Hurdle—who was named the 2013 National League Manager of the Year—had his team in first place in the National League Central Division a total of 56 days. They finished the season in second place, three games behind the St. Louis Cardinals.

On September 9, the Pirates shut out the Texas Rangers, 1-0, to score their 82nd win, assuring Pittsburgh of its first winning baseball team in two decades. Two weeks later, a win over the Chicago Cubs put Pittsburgh in the postseason. Finally, 21 years later, the Pirates played in the postseason again, this time as a wild-card team.

"Of all the things I've reported over the years," wrote Ron Cook in the *Pittsburgh Post-Gazette* on September 24, 2013, "this might have the deepest personal significance: I have lived long enough to see the Pirates get back to the playoffs."

Surely, Cook wasn't the only Pittsburgher to express similar sentiments or those of Pirates closer Jason Grilli.

"I hope that [Roberto] Clemente Bridge is swaying a little bit right now," Grilli said while the Pirates celebrated with the time-honored baseball tradition of the champagne shower. "Those bars and everything downtown, I hope people are raising their glass right now. I'm sure they are."[1]

"It's so exciting to see it finally happen after 20 years," said fan Donna Vaughn in the September 25 edition of the *Pittsburgh Post-Gazette*. "We stuck by them, and it's time to celebrate."

While the Pirates made their fans suffer, the professional teams in the city gave them reasons to cheer. In the 21 NFL seasons since the slide, the Pittsburgh Steelers made the playoffs 14 times. They played in four Super Bowls, winning two of them.

In the same time period, the Pittsburgh Penguins of the NHL played 20 seasons (the 2004-05 season was eventually canceled by a labor dispute) and appeared in the postseason in 16 of them. They won what was then the organization's third Stanley Cup in 2009.

"For an entire generation, the Pirates have been the penance that Pittsburgh has served for having the success of the Steelers and the Penguins," said fan Terry Haines.[2]

The Pirates also exorcised some recent demons with their 2013 playoff appearance. In 2011 and 2012 they had late-season collapses that, at the least, cost them the chance at a winning record.

In 2011, Hurdle's first season at the helm, they were seven games over .500 on July 19 at 51-44 but finished out the month by going 3-8. Then their combined mark in August and September was 18-38 and they finished 72-90.

The 2012 season might have been worse, the Pirates were 63-47 on August 8 but the wheels fell off and they finished with a 79-83 record. Over the final 52 games, they were 16-36 including a 7-21 September.

Against this backdrop, the Pirates would host their first playoff game since October 11, 1992, when they beat the Braves 7-1 at Three Rivers Stadium in Game Five of the NLCS. By sweeping the Reds in Cincinnati in the final three games of the regular season, the Pirates earned the right to host them in the wild-card game, a one-game, loser-goes-home format, that MLB had introduced in 2012.

The Reds were 90-72 and had a power offense that scored the third most runs (698) in the league. The pitching staff that manager Dusty Baker had at his disposal was formidable as well. They allowed 589 runs, fourth lowest in the NL; they were fourth in ERA with a 3.38.

The Pirates, with a 94-68 record, ranked ninth with 634 runs scored, second in runs allowed with 577, and third with a 3.26 ERA.

Francisco Liriano, the NL Comeback Player of the Year in 2013, got the start for the Pirates. The seasoned left-hander was 16-8 with a 3.02 ERA in 26 starts. He had 163 strikeouts and 63 walks in 161 innings and allowed only nine home runs. Liriano faced the Reds four times during the season and was 0-3 with 3.70 ERA.

The Reds countered with Johnny Cueto, who was 5-2 with a 2.82 ERA but was limited to just 11 starts because of injuries.[3] He faced Pittsburgh twice in 2013; he received a no-decision after leaving the game with right triceps pain after 4⅓ innings as the Reds lost 3-1 at Pittsburgh on April 13. The next time Cueto took the mound against the Pirates, he threw a gem, going eight shutout innings. He gave up just one hit and allowed only three baserunners while striking out six in a 6-0 win on May 31 at PNC Park. In 13 career starts at PNC, Cueto posted a 1.90 ERA.

A then-record crowd of 40,487 jammed into PNC Park, which was hosting its first playoff game. The Bucs didn't wait long to give them something to cheer about. In the second, Marlon Byrd, who was 7-for-12 in his career against Cueto, homered to left to lead things off. With one out, Russell Martin homered to left-center and the crowd then took to mocking the Reds hurler, chanting "CUE-TO, CUE-TO."

"I loved it, it was awesome," Martin said of the chant, which is usually used after a goalie allows some pucks to slip past him in a hockey game.[4]

Andrew McCutchen, the 2013 National League MVP, led off the third with an infield single. With one out he went to third when Byrd singled to shortstop Zack Cozart. Pedro Alvarez knocked him in with a sacrifice fly to center.

In the fourth, Shin-Soo Choo became the Reds' first baserunner when he was hit by a pitch. Former Buc Ryan Ludwick got the Reds' first hit and Cincinnati had runners on first and second with no out. But Liriano struck out Joey Votto and induced Brandon Phillips to pop to second base. Jay Bruce singled home Choo with a hit to left, Todd Frazier nearly hit a three-run home run but the ball was just foul. Ultimately, he became a strikeout victim.

Starling Marte doubled with one out in the fourth and that was it for Cueto but relief pitcher Sean Marshall wasn't the answer. The veteran southpaw faced three batters and didn't record an out. Neil Walker doubled home Marte, McCutchen was walked intentionally Justin Morneau loaded the bases when he walked. With right-hander J.J. Hoover now on the hill for the Reds, Byrd hit into a force out and Walker scored to make it 5-1.

Cozart's leadoff walk in the fifth didn't amount to anything when pinch-hitter Chris Heisey grounded into an inning-ending 5-4-3 double play. Liriano pitched around one-out doubles in both the sixth and seventh innings.

Meanwhile, the Pirates had yet to be retired in order and the seventh inning was no different. In that inning, Logan Ondrusek became the Reds' sixth pitcher and Martin greeted him with a leadoff homer. Liriano was done after the seventh, after giving up just one run on four hits, a walk, and a hit batter, and striking out five.

In the eighth, Choo hit a ball that a fan reached over the right-field wall to interfere with. It was ruled a home run and a video review confirmed the call but all that really did was set the final score at 6-2.

The Pirates had a winning season, made the playoffs and won the wild-card game. The season would continue, and they would meet the Cardinals in the NL Division Series.

SOURCES

In addition to the sources cited in the Notes, the author also consulted Retrosheet.org, Baseball-Reference.com, Pro-Football-Reference.com, Hockey-Reference.com, and the *2017 Pittsburgh Pirates Media Guide*

NOTES

1   Bill Brink, "Marte's HR Helps Clinch Playoff Berth," *Pittsburgh Post-Gazette*, September 24, 2013: D1.

2   Kaitlynn Riely, "Baseball? In October? Git aht!" *Pittsburgh Post-Gazette*, September 25, 2013: B8.

3   Bill Brink, "Next Stop: St. Louis, Where the Cardinals Await Game 1 of the NLDS on Thursday" *Pittsburgh Post-Gazette*, October 2, 2013: D3.

4   Ibid.

SCHERZER LOSES PERFECT GAME IN THE NINTH, THROWS NO-HITTER AGAINST THE PIRATES

JUNE 20, 2015: NATIONALS 6, PIRATES 0, AT NATIONALS PARK, WASHINGTON

BY BOB WEBSTER

THE PITTSBURGH PIRATES, WINNERS of 21 of the previous 27 games and considered the hottest team in baseball, went up against an equally hot Max Scherzer of the Washington Nationals on a hot and humid Saturday afternoon at Nationals Park in Washington.

Scherzer had taken a perfect game into the seventh inning against the Milwaukee Brewers in his last start, settling for a one-hit shutout with 16 strikeouts and only one walk.

The game-time temperature was 91.[1] The TV announcers and other sources mentioned that the high humidity that day made for one of the hottest days of the summer in Washington.

The Nationals put a run on the board in the fourth when Bryce Harper hit his 23rd homer of the season off Pirates left-handed starter Francisco Liriano, a solo shot to deep center. Harper had strained his left hamstring on Thursday night and missed Friday's game before returning to action this day, but at less than 100 percent.

The Nationals scored four more runs in the sixth and one in the seventh to make the score 6-0.

The right-handed Scherzer entered the bottom of the ninth with a perfect game going after retiring the first 24 batters he faced. Gregory Polanco led off the inning by fouling out to third baseman Anthony Rendon, who made a nice play near the dugout. Jordy Mercer lined out to center fielder Denard Span. Hitting .313 in a reserve role, right-handed batter Jose Tabata stepped up to the plate, pinch-hitting for relief pitcher Vance Worley. With two strikes on Tabata and Scherzer's 103rd pitch of the game,

Tabata appeared to lower his left elbow protector into the path of the ball and was hit by the pitch. Home-plate umpire Mike Muchlinski didn't see it that way and sent Tabata to first, breaking up the perfect game. Scherzer said it was a slider that he didn't finish and it didn't break much. Josh Harrison flied out to deep left to end the game and give Scherzer the no-hitter. The Nationals TV play-by-play announcer, Bob Carpenter, wrapped it up nicely by saying: "Max Scherzer has a no-hitter. Sunday in Milwaukee he was amazing and today in D.C. he was almost perfect."[2]

Scherzer came within one out of throwing the 24th perfect game in major-league history, but did manage to throw the 289th no-hitter in front of a crowd of 41,104 and took 2:21 to complete.

Building on his one-hitter against the Brewers on June 14, Scherzer had faced only three batters over the minimum, retiring 54 of the last 57 batters he faced, giving up one hit, walking one batter and hitting one (Tabata) with a pitch while striking out 26.

The Pirates had won eight in a row before arriving in Washington but had now scored just one run in 18 innings after a 4-1 loss to the Nationals in the series opener on Friday.

As with almost all no-hitters and perfect games, great defensive plays made a difference and this day was no different. The Pirates' Jordy Mercer sent a long drive to left field with one out in the top of the third but Michael A. Taylor jumped and caught the ball right in front of the pad on top of the wall in left field. With two out in the top of the eighth, the shift was on against left-handed-hitting Pedro Alvarez, who hit a groundball past the diving Ian Desmond. Second baseman Danny Espinosa, who was playing short right field in the shift, had to charge the grounder in order to have a chance at getting the speedy Alvarez at first. Espinoza fielded the ball and made a great throw to retire Alvarez and keep the perfect game intact.

Samantha Loss, a reporter and editor for WTOP radio, summed it up nicely. Since it was Father's Day weekend, her dad wanted to go to the game that Saturday afternoon, so they went. She said, "When you go to a World Series game or a Stanley Cup Finals game, you know you are going to something special. No one knew this mid-June baseball game would be anything special until it became special. It's a different feeling, when a regular, ordinary game suddenly becomes extraordinary." She added, "The game started out like any other. But by the fifth inning the sweat-soaked crowd realized that they were watching Max Scherzer pitching a perfect game. After the Nationals scored four runs in the bottom of the sixth, the feeling in Nats Park was electric. It was almost a playoff-like atmosphere."[3]

When the Nationals were at bat, Scherzer watched from the air-conditioned clubhouse, where he changed his undershirt every inning.[4]

After five seasons with the Detroit Tigers, Scherzer returned to the National League for the 2015 season when he signed a $210 million contract with the Nationals. After the win on June 20, Scherzer was 8-5 with a major-league-leading 1.76 ERA and 123 strikeouts, also tops in baseball.[5]

SOURCES

In addition to the sources cited in the Notes, the author also accessed MLB.com, MLB.TV, and Retrosheet.org.

NOTES

1   The temperature is given in the box score at baseball-reference.com.

2   MLB.TV Archives.

3   Samantha Loss, "Greatest Game: Pittsburgh Pirates vs. Washington Nationals—June 20, 2015," October 8, 2015. Retrieved from wtop.com/washington-nationals/2015/10/greatest-game-pittsburgh-pirates-vs-washington-nationals-june-20-2015/.

4   James Wagner, *Washington Post*, June 20, 2015. Retrieved from washingtonpost.com/sports/nationals/2015/06/20/a83b59fe-1761-11e5-9ddc-e3353542100c_story.html?utm_term=.bc98c6af1858.

5   Eric Stephen, June 20, 2015. Retrieved from: sbnation.com/mlb/2015/6/20/8819025/max-scherzer-no-hitter-nationals-pirates.

PIRATES LOSE TO CUBS IN NATIONAL LEAGUE WILD CARD GAME

OCTOBER 7, 2015: CHICAGO CUBS 4, PITTSBURGH PIRATES 0, AT PNC PARK

BY THOMAS J. BROWN JR.

FANS POURED THROUGH THE GATES at PNC Park in Pittsburgh hoping that the Pirates' third consecutive attempt to advance in the post-season would be successful. The Pirates had finished second behind the St. Louis Cardinals in the National League Central division for the third year in a row. Now they would have to play the Chicago Cubs for the right to play the Cardinals, their division rival. It was the first time since divisional play expansion began in 1994 that three teams from the same division finished the season with best records.[1]

The Pirates were disappointed that the Cardinals had edged them out in the Central division. They were also disappointed that they would have to play the Cubs in the NL wild-card game. Pirates pitcher Charlie Morton probably expressed the frustration best: "You hope that the best teams wind up in the playoffs in a series. … Do you really want to see two of the top three or four teams in all of baseball play a one-game playoff? No. And I'm not just saying that because we're one of those teams, I'm saying that because it just doesn't seem like, it just doesn't seem right."[2]

The Pirates were looking to finally advance past the divisional playoffs. For the past two years they had made quick exits. The team and fans were hungry for more. The Cubs, on the other hand, were just excited about making it to the playoffs. They were a team of youngsters who were "a year ahead of schedule," according to the experts, although the young team finished third in the division, with the third-best record in baseball.[3]

The postseason fate was all going to come down to this one game. "When you go into a wild card, it's the seventh game of the World Series as the first playoff game. That's what it is. So you have to try to make your best guess as you put your right lineup out there," said Cubs manager Joe Maddon.

The Pirates sent Gerrit Cole to the mound. He had finished with a 19-8 record. In four starts, he went 2-1 against the Cubs. He would face Jake Arrieta, who had won his last 11 games. He faced the Pirates five times during the season, winning three. He pitched seven scoreless innings in two of the wins.

The Cubs grabbed the lead in the top of the first. Dexter Fowler singled to center and quickly stole second. When Kyle Schwarber hit a line-drive single to left field, Fowler scored easily. Cole settled down and got the next three batters out but the damage was done. More significantly, the Cubs gave Arrieta a 1-0 lead and in eight of his starts during this season that one run was enough for the Cubs to win.[4]

In the bottom of the first, Andrew McCutchen singled, but the Pirates were not able to capitalize on the hit. The same story would repeat itself in later innings.

After an uneventful second inning with both pitchers getting the side out in order, the Cubs took control of the game in the third. Cole started the inning by striking out Arrieta. Fowler stepped to the plate and singled, the second of his three hits that night. Schwarber stepped to the plate. With a 2-and-1 count, Cole threw Schwarber a slider that didn't have any movement. Schwarber hit a homer that sailed over the right-field seats. Cole gave the ball a cursory glance before turning away in recognition that Gregory Polanco was not going to make the play. "Did they measure that thing?" exclaimed the Cubs' David Ross. "He hit that ball and I couldn't even celebrate because I wanted to see how far it went. That was amazing."[5]

Pirates pitching coach Ray Searage visited the mound to speak to Cole. Whatever he said must have worked since Cole got the next two batters out. Miguel Montero showed that other Cubs could hit when he became "the first Cub not named Dexter Fowler or Kyle Schwarber to get a hit" in the fourth inning [6] He was stranded on first when Cole struck out Addison Russell.

Fowler continued to have a night to remember as he homered over the right-field fence in the fifth inning. Although Cole would retire the next two batters, he would not return for the sixth inning. It was a frustrating night for him as he struggled mightily against the Fowler and Schwarber onslaught while dominating the rest of the Cubs' batting order.

Meanwhile, Arrieta continued to keep the Pirates in check as he refused to let anyone else get on base beyond Francisco Cervelli, who was hit by a pitch in

the fifth inning. It looked as if Cervelli had missed getting hit, but clearly he convinced umpire Jeff Nelson that the ball grazed him after he hit the dirt. Again, the Pirates were not able to capitalize on their opportunity.

The Pirates got another chance in the bottom of the sixth when Travis Snider led off with a single, just the second hit allowed by Arrieta. The next batter, Polanco, watched Arrieta's first pitch for a ball before hitting a line drive to the left side of the infield. Kris Bryant, who had just moved to third base from left field, snared the ball and prevented an extra-base hit.

Arrieta plunked Josh Harrison and McCutchen loaded the bases when Russell couldn't handle a groundball up the middle. Pirates fans were on their feet in hopes that they would finally score. But Arrieta was able to get Starling Marte to ground into a 6-4-3 double play to end the threat. PNC Park suddenly became quiet as the crowd realized that the Pirates' best chance might have just ended. They could only

Pirates and Cubs exchange "pleasantries" during their 2015 Wild Card game.

watch dejectedly as Anthony Rizzo pumped his fist in excitement after the play.

Tony Watson took the mound for the Pirates in the seventh. After getting the first two outs, he hit Arrieta on his first pitch. Arrieta was unhurt, but he took offense and started arguing with catcher Cervelli. The benches cleared.[7] There was lots of shoving and yelling by both teams.

The Pirates' Sean Rodriguez was particularly vocal and had to be restrained by three of his teammates. After conferring, the umpires ejected Rodriguez. When he was told, Rodriguez tossed a Gatorade cooler and returned to the dugout stairs, where he shouted some additional choice phrases at the Cubs players before finally heading into the clubhouse. Jeff Nelson, the home-plate umpire, warned both the dugouts about future retaliation before continuing the game.[8]

Arrieta stole second base, which added a little insult to the Pirates' frustrating evening. It didn't lead to anything as Fowler popped out to end the inning, the only time he made an out all night.

After Cervelli hit Arrieta's third pitch to left field to start the seventh, the Pirates fans got their hopes up again. But Arrieta struck out Neil Walker and got Aramis Ramirez to ground into a double play. Bryant made a second stellar fielding play to snuff out hopes of a Pirates rally.

Arrieta got his 10th and 11th strikeouts in the eighth inning. He continued to dominate the Pirates. Arrieta had thrown 103 pitches and was due up fourth in the top of the ninth. He had thrown that many pitches 20 times that season so everyone expected him to take the mound in the ninth. After the game, Maddon joked with reporters that he had Arrieta on a pitch count: "Infinity."[9]

The Pirates season was now on the line. McCutchen, Marte, and Cervelli were due up. They were the three players Pirates fans wanted to see in this situation. But Arrieta was just too dominant. McCutchen and Marte grounded out and Cervelli lined out to second to end the game and the Pirates' hopes of advancing in the post season.

"I'm exhausted. I haven't felt this way all year. This atmosphere, the energy, it was unbelievable," Arrieta told reporters after the game. The Pirates' Walker said of Arrieta: "He was as advertised. He attacked us from pitch one. We weren't able to put much pressure on him or get his pitch count up."[10]

For the second time in as many years, the Pirates had lost the wild-card game. A dejected McCutchen said, "We just didn't do the job tonight, we didn't get it done."[11] Madison Bumgarner struck out 10 batters when he shut out the Bucs in 2014. Now Arrieta had repeated that feat with an 11-strikeout performance. The disappointment of Pirates players and fans could be felt everywhere as the Cubs celebrated in a Gatorade shower on the field.

SOURCES

In addition to the sources cited in the Notes, the author also used the Baseball-Reference.com, Baseball-Almanac.com, and Retrosheet.org websites for box score, player, team, and season pages, pitching and batting game logs, and other pertinent material.

NOTES

1   Bill Brink, "One Game, One Night: Winner Take All," *Pittsburgh Post-Gazette*, October 7, 2015.

2   Ibid.

3   Bruce Miles, "How a Wild-Card Game Changed History for Cubs and Pirates, Daily Herald.com, October 7, 2015.

4   Benjamin Hoffman, "N.L. Wild Card: Cubs vs. Pirates Recap," *New York Times*, October 7, 2015.

5   Michael Rosenberg, "Jake Arrieta's Brilliant Performance Could Be Start of Magical Run for Cubs," Sports Illustrated.com, October 8, 2015.

6   Hoffman, "N.L. Wild Card."

7   Rosenberg, "Jake Arrieta's Brilliant Performance."

8   Hoffman, "N.L. Wild Card."

9   Rosenberg, "Jake Arrieta's Brilliant Performance."

10 Brink, "One Game, One Night."

11 Ibid.

ANDREW MCCUTCHEN HITS THREE HOME RUNS IN ONE GAME

APRIL 26, 2016: PITTSBURGH PIRATES 9, COLORADO ROCKIES 4. AT COORS FIELD, DENVER

BY THOMAS J. BROWN JR.

IT WAS A CHILLY SPRING EVENING AT Coors Field. The Pirates were hoping to rebound from their 6-1 loss on the previous evening when their team leader, Andrew McCutchen, returned to the lineup. McCutchen had struggled on the Pirates' Western road trip, getting only three hits in 23 at-bats before the team's arrival in Denver. Manager Clint Hurdle gave him the day off when the team arrived in Denver, to give him time to sort things out and get back on track. "[I]t was good to have that day to sit back and relax. Just clear my mind," McCutchen said.[1]

McCutchen was determined to overcome his shaky start to the 2016 season and show why he had earned his MVP award in 2013. He came to the ballpark early to watch film of his previous at-bats against Rockies left-hander Jorge De La Rosa. McCutchen had had success against De La Rosa in the past and wanted to be sure that this success continued. After watching the film, he patiently stood in front of his locker in the visitors clubhouse and took one practice swing after another. He explained his thinking later: "I lock in here. I lock in when nobody is watching. So when the game begins, I just play."[2]

The Rockies hoped that De La Rosa would begin to turn things around with this start and reverse the struggles he had experienced in the first month of the season. In his previous start, on April 19, he lasted only two innings and gave up four runs to the Cincinnati Reds.

In the first inning, De La Rosa got leadoff batter Jordy Mercer to fly out to center field before things fell apart for him. McCutchen, the second batter, hit his fifth pitch over the left-field wall. As he arrived at home plate, he tipped his cap to honor his wife, something he started doing after watching Jackie Robinson do the same thing in the film *42*. "We always need our spouses, [Tipping my cap] is my acknowledgement to Maria, letting her know I'm thinking about her, that she's on my mind constantly."[3]

Before the Pirates could finish celebrating, David Freese hit De La Rosa's first pitch over the right-field wall for another home run. De La Rosa struck out Starling Marte but then walked Francisco Cervelli and hit Jason Rogers with a pitch. Josh Harrison singled and suddenly the Pirates were leading 3-0.

Gerrit Cole started for the Pirates. The young pitcher gave up a single in the bottom of the first but the Rockies could not take advantage of the runner. Cole struck out when he led off the second inning. After Mercer grounded out, McCutchen stepped to the plate for the second time in as many innings. After taking a ball from De La Rosa, he hit his second home run of the night over the center-field fence. Once again, he tipped his cap to his wife as he touched home plate. With just two swings of his bat, McCutchen signaled that he was coming out of his slump.

The Rockies scored in the second inning. Cole gave up a single to leadoff batter Ben Paulsen. Paulsen moved to second on a passed ball and ended up at third on DJ LeMahieu's grounder to second. Paulsen came home on another groundball to second by Brandon Barnes.

But this lone run would not matter as the Pirates continued to hammer De La Rosa. After a shaky third inning , in which he walked one batter and hit another, Rockies manager Walt Weiss took him out when he pulled up short of first base while grounding out in the bottom of the third. He told Weiss he might have a groin injury. De La Rosa had never given up three home runs in a game at Coors Field but this was the second time it had happened in his three starts this season.[4] Christian Bergman took over and pitched two solid innings before McCutchen struck again.

This blast, in the sixth inning, would earn McCutchen three RBIs and give the Pirates a commanding 7-3 lead. Bergman gave up a double to Gregory Polanco and a walk to Mercer before McCutchen stepped up to the plate. With the count 1-and-2, he hit another one over the right-field fence. This was McCutchen's second such three home run game. He also hit three home runs in an 11-6 Pirates victory against Washington on April 1, 2009, his first full year in the majors. With this third home run, McCutchen also joined an elite group of Pirates players. Only 10 Pirates have had three-homer games (19 games in all).[5]

After McCutchen homered, Bergman struck out David Freese before Weiss removed him for Gonzalez Germen. Germen threw two balls to Marte. On the third pitch, Marte hit one out of the park for the second Pirates home run of the inning to put them up 8-3.

The Pirates' Cole continued to pitch well although he did give up one more unearned run in the bottom of the sixth. He had relied on his fastball, throwing it on 73 of his 103 pitches. His manager made note of this after the game: "Old-fashioned baseball, boys, here it is. He moved the fastball around—up and down, in and out. That, in and of itself, was fun to watch."[6] The fact that Cole's curveball was not working in the thin air of Coors Field may also have explained why McCutchen was able to power three home runs out of the ballpark.

The Pittsburgh bullpen shut down the Rockies for the final three innings. Although McCutchen had already won the game for the Pirates with his three

Andrew McCutchen

home runs and five RBIs, his teammates added one more run in the top of the ninth. Cervelli singled, moved to third on a walk to Joyce and a fly ball by Harrison and came home when Polanco hit a single. But this run was lost amid all of the excitement in the Pirates' dugout over the return of McCutchen's hitting.

It was clear that the day off had made a difference for him. McCutchen said afterward: "Having the day off to lay back and ... work on [what I had been trying to change] in the cage, and when the game started (Monday), I could just relax. I was able to go around, talk to other people and watch the game and study the game."[7] Clearly that time in the cage and those conversations paid off.

After the game, Hurdle reflected on McCutchen's achievement and how he had bounced back from his slump. "The elite can do it. I never bounced back like that. Maybe in Little League."[8]

McCutchen not only bounced back but added his name alongside Pirates legends Willie Stargell, Roberto Clemente, and Ralph Kiner, the only other Pirates with multiple three-home-run games.[9] "'It's awesome to hit one homer, but to hit three is really cool," McCutchen told reporters. "'Just to be with those caliber of players is tremendous. It's a good day to remember."[10]

Rockies manager Walt Weiss said he knew McCutchen would eventually break out of his slump. He was just hoping that he would do that after the Pirates had finished their series in Denver. "Unfortunately, he's rolling again," Weiss said after the game. "You knew it was a matter of time. ... He looks like he's swinging pretty good to me."[11]

McCutchen had the final word on his spectacular night: "Confidence is always going to be there. You can't always care about results. It's not like I felt myself getting worse. I felt myself getting better and better and better. I knew it was a matter of time."[12]

SOURCES

In addition to the sources cited in the Notes, the author also used the Baseball-Reference.com, Baseball-Almanac.com, and Retrosheet.org websites for box-score, player, team, and season pages, pitching and batting game logs, and other pertinent material.

NOTES

1   "McCutchen Hits 3 Homers, Pirates Beat Rockies 9-4," Sports Illustrated.com, April 26, 2016.

2   Stephen Nesbitt, "Andrew McCutchen Hits Three Home Runs as Pirates Blast Past Rockies for 9-4 Win," *Pittsburgh Post-Gazette*, April 27, 2016.

3   Burt Wilson, "Pirates Outfielder Andrew Mccutchen Tips His Cap After Each Home Run to Honor His Wife," *Pittsburgh Post-Gazette*, May 6, 2016.

4   Patrick Saunders, "Rockies' Pitching Woes Continue as Pirates Cruise to Victory, *Denver Post*, April 26, 2016.

5   Nesbitt.

6   Ibid.

7   Travis Sawchik, "McCutchen's 3-HR Game Provides Proof That Taking Day Off Can Be Beneficial," TribLive.com, April 27, 2016.

8   Nesbitt.

9   Ibid.

10 "McCutchen Hits 3 Homers, Pirates Beat Rockies 9-4."

11 "Rockies Roughed Up by McCutchen, Pirates in 9-4 loss," *USA Today*, April 27, 2016.

12 Jamal Muhammad, "Andrew McCutchen Hits Three Home-Runs in a Single Game for the Second Time," Imediago.com, April 26, 2016.

CONTRIBUTORS

JEFF BARTO joined SABR just as he left Pittsburgh in 1992 to teach at UNC-Charlotte. He has been teaching a History of Baseball course at the university since 2005. Recently he began teaching a second course on baseball that focuses on critical thinking. He enjoys anything Pittsburgh and has started contributing to research on Pirate projects, including this one.

JOHN BAUER resides with his wife and two children in Parkville, Missouri, just outside of Kansas City. By day, he is an attorney specializing in insurance regulatory law and corporate law. By night, he spends many spring and summer evenings cheering for the San Francisco Giants and many fall and winter evenings reading history. He is a past and ongoing contributor to other SABR projects.

ROBERT E. BIONAZ hails from California and is a lifelong fan of the San Francisco Giants. He spent 22-plus years in law enforcement before returning to school, ultimately earning a Ph.D. at the University of Iowa. He is currently an Associate Professor of History at Chicago State University. His research interests revolve around working-class politics and culture during the U.S. Progressive Era, sport (particularly baseball) and culture in the United States, and the effects of political corruption on higher education in Chicago. He has authored a number of articles on working-class politics, and a variety of baseball-themed topics, He is currently working on a manuscript about political corruption and university governance at Chicago State University.

THOMAS J. BROWN JR. is a lifelong Mets fan who also became a Durham Bulls fan after moving to North Carolina in the early 1980s. He is a retired high school science teacher who volunteers with ELL students at his former high school. He also is a mentor to those students after graduation. Besides traveling as much as possible and spending summers watching the Durham Bulls, he enjoys writing about baseball games and biographies, mostly about the NY Mets.

FREDERICK C. (RICK) BUSH, his wife Michelle, and their three sons Michael, Andrew, and Daniel live in the greater Houston area, and he teaches English at Wharton County Junior College in Sugar Land. An avid Astros fan, he was overjoyed about the team's first World Series championship but nevertheless fears it may be a sign of an impending apocalypse. As a SABR member, he has contributed articles to both the Biography and Games Projects and to numerous books. He was also an associate editor for *Dome Sweet Dome: History and Highlights from 35 Years of the Houston Astrodome* and, together with Bill Nowlin, co-edited *Bittersweet Goodbye: The Black Barons, The Grays, and the 1948 Negro League World Series*.

ALAN COHEN remembers running home from high school to catch the end of the seventh game of the 1960 World Series. He has been a SABR member since 2011, serves as Vice President-Treasurer of the Connecticut Smoky Joe Wood Chapter, and is the datacaster (stringer) for the Hartford Yard Goats. He has written more than 40 biographies for SABR's BioProject. He has expanded his research into the Hearst Sandlot Classic (1946-1965), an annual youth All-Star game which launched the careers of 88 major-league players, including Dick Groat of the Pirates. He has four children and six grandchildren and resides in West Hartford, Connecticut with his wife Frances, one cat (Morty), and two dogs (Sam and Sheba).

PAUL E. DOUTRICH is a professor of American History at York College of Pennsylvania where he teaches a popular course entitled "Baseball History." He has written numerous scholarly articles and books about the revolutionary era in America and has curated several museum exhibits. For the past 15 years his scholarship has focused on baseball history. He has contributed manuscripts to various SABR publications and is the author of *The Cardinals and the Yankees, 1926: A Classical Season and St. Louis in Seven.*

DOUG FELDMANN is a professor of teacher education at Northern Kentucky University. He was once a scout for the Cincinnati Reds and has written nine books on major-league baseball, including 2013's *Gibson's Last Stand: The Rise, Fall, and Near Misses of the St. Louis Cardinals, 1969-1975.* He has also published articles in several education journals and the book *Curriculum and the American Rural School. Dr. Feldmann lives in Villa Hills Kentucky.*

JEFF FINDLEY is a native of Eastern Iowa, where he did the logical thing growing up in the heart of the Cubs/Cardinals rivalry - he embraced the 1969 Baltimore Orioles and became a lifelong fan. An informational security professional for a large insurance company in central Illinois, he compiles a daily sports "Pages Past" column for his local newspaper.

T.S. FLYNN is president of the Halsey Hall Chapter of SABR. A Minneapolis-based educator and writer, he's working on his first book, an excavation of the 63-year baseball career of Tom Sheehan.

GORDON J. GATTIE serves as a human-systems integration engineer for the U.S. Navy. His baseball research interests involve ballparks, historical records, and statistical analysis. A SABR member since 1998, Gordon earned his Ph.D. from SUNY Buffalo, where he used baseball to investigate judgment/decision-making performance in complex dynamic environments. Ever the optimist, he supports the Cleveland Indians and nearby Washington Nationals. Lisa, his lovely bride who also enjoys baseball, challenges him by supporting the Yankees. Gordon has contributed to multiple SABR publications.

TOM HAWTHORN is an author and journalist in Victoria, B.C. His latest book is *The Year Canadians Lost Their Minds and Found Their Country: The Centennial of 1967.* He has contributed to more than a dozen SABR books. He has been a member

of selection committees for two sports halls of fame in Canada.

ROCK HOFFMAN has been a SABR member since 1995, he co-hosts Sports Page, a sports talk radio show Saturday at 10 PM on WRDV-FM (WRDV.org) in suburban Philadelphia. He's active in the Connie Mack Chapter by helping at local meetings and running the chapter Facebook site. He was a member of the local organizing committee for the 2013 SABR National Convention in Philadelphia and volunteers to judge oral and poster presentations at the national conventions. He enjoys disc golf and American Civil War history. His home in Ardsley, Pennsylvania is a Ruthian clout from the final resting place of Hall of Fame pitcher Charles Albert "Chief" Bender. Previously, he contributed to the SABR book *When Pops Led the Family: The 1979 Pittsburgh Pirates.*

PAUL HOFMANN is the Associate Vice President for International Programs at Sacramento State University. He is a native of Detroit, Michigan and lifelong Detroit sports fan. His research interests include 19th century and pre-World War II Japanese baseball. He is also an avid baseball card collector. Paul currently resides in Folsom, California.

MIKE HUBER is a Professor of Mathematics at Muhlenberg College who first joined SABR in 1996. He enjoys researching and writing about rare events in baseball, including games in which players hit for the cycle. He has vivid memories of both the 1971 and 1979 World Series, in which the Pirates bested the Baltimore Orioles.

JORGE IBER was born in Havana, Cuba and raised in the Little Havana neighborhood of Miami, Florida. He taught in the public schools of Miami before pursuing a PhD at the University of Utah. He currently serves as Associate Dean in the Student Division of the College of Arts and Sciences and Professor of History at Texas Tech University. His initial academic focus was on Mexican American history, but over the past 15 years or so has shifted research interests to examine the story of Mexican Americans/Latinos and their participation/role in the history of US sports. He is the author/co-author/editor of 10 books and numerous scholarly and encyclopedic articles. His most recent project is a full-length biography of Mexican American former MLB pitcher, Mike Torrez (he of the pitch to Bucky Dent in the 1978 playoff game between the Boston Red Sox and the New York Yankees). He is currently working on two other projects: an anthology on Latinos/as and sport, and a book on Latino participation in all levels of football.

FRANK ITTNER is a New England native now living in the greater Atlanta, Georgia area. He is a lifelong baseball fan, a contributor to the SABR Games Project, and keenly interested in baseball history, trivia, and visiting major and minor-league stadiums throughout the country. He has attended baseball games in over 50 minor- and major-league stadiums from Florida to Alaska, including both Three Rivers Stadium and PNC Park in Pittsburgh.

MATT KEELEAN is a business analyst for Florida State University in Tallahassee, Florida, but grew up in Grand Rapids, Michigan, as a devoted Tigers fan. He is a founding member of the SABR North Florida/Buck O'Neil Chapter, based in Tallahassee, and currently serves as the Chapter's president. Matt and his wife Diana (a fellow SABR member and lifelong Pirates fan) live in Havana, Florida, and are longtime Florida State baseball season-ticket holders.

RUSS LAKE lives in Champaign, Illinois, and is a retired college professor emeritus. The 1964 St. Louis Cardinals remain his favorite team, and he was distressed to see Sportsman's Park (aka Busch Stadium I) being demolished not long after he had attended the last game there on May 8, 1966. His wife, Carol, deserves an MVP award for watching all of a 13-inning ballgame in Cincinnati with Russ in 1971—during their honeymoon. In 1994, he was an editor for David Halberstam's baseball book, *October 1964*.

BOB LEMOINE lives in New Hampshire, where he works as a high school librarian and adjunct professor. A SABR member since 2013, he has con-

tributed to several SABR projects, including being a co-editor with Bill Nowlin on 2016's *Boston's First Nine: the 1871-75 Boston Red Stockings* and is similarly working another book about the Glorious Beaneaters.

LEN LEVIN is a retired newspaper editor who spends a lot of time as the copyeditor for SABR publications. He is a lifelong Red Sox fan.

MARK MILLER is a retired Recreation Department Director in Springfield, Ohio, where he lives with his wife Connie, A high school baseball coach for 22 years, he was inducted into the Springfield/Clark County Baseball Hall of Fame in 2014. He is currently Chairman of the Dayton SABR Chapter. His research, speaking and writing are related to local baseball topics.

SETH MOLAND-KOVASH lives in suburban Chicago but is a passionate fan of the Minnesota Twins. His early professional training was as a historian, so digging through old newspapers and unearthing long-lost stories has long been a passion. Professionally, Seth has served as a Lutheran pastor for over 15 years throughout the Chicagoland area. He is married and is the father of a 12-year old son who has inherited the baseball bug in a major way.

BILL NOWLIN grew up (and remains) a Red Sox fan. The Yankees just won too often in the 1950s, no matter who they were playing. So it was a moment of wonder for this 15-year-old when Bill Mazeroski hit his home run to win the 1960 World Series. Bill has helped edit a few dozen books in SABR's very active and ongoing series.

A Pittsburgh native and professor emeritus of English at Southern Illinois University, **RICHARD "PETE" PETERSON** is the author of *Growing Up With Clemente, Pops: The Willie Stargell Story*, co-author of *The Slide: Leyland, Bonds, and the Star-Crossed Pittsburgh Pirates*, and editor of *The Pirates Reader*.

STEPHEN PETERSON is the co-author of *The Slide: Leyland, Bonds and the Star-Crossed Pittsburgh Pirates*. He has worked as a teacher and screenwriter for the last 10 years. He resides in Los Angeles, California.

RICHARD J. PUERZER is an associate professor and chairperson of the Department of Engineering at Hofstra University.He has contributed to a number of SABR Books, including *When Pops Led the Family: The 1978 Pittsburgh Pirates (2016)* and *Bittersweet Goodbye: The Black Barons, the Grays, and the 1948 Negro League World Series (2017)*.His writings on baseball have also appeared in: *Nine: A Journal of Baseball History and Culture, Black Ball, The National Pastime, The Cooperstown Symposium on Baseball and American Culture* proceedings, and *Spitball*.

ELIZA RICHARDSON is an associate professor of geophysics at Penn State University. Some of her earliest memories are listening to the Cardinals on KMOX with her dad, who is a lifelong Cardinals fan. The trajectory of her life can be told through minor league baseball. Growing up in southwest Virginia, there was the Salem Avalanche. She earned her undergraduate degree in Geology and Geophysics from Princeton University (Trenton Thunder), then pursued a PhD in Geophysics at MIT (Lowell Spinners, Pawtucket Red Sox). Eliza came to Penn State and has been there as a professor and State College Spikes season ticket holder ever since. When not throwing batting practice to their five children, Eliza and her husband are avid homebrewers.

C. PAUL ROGERS III is co-author of several baseball books including *The Whiz Kids and the 1950 Pennant* with boyhood hero Robin Roberts and *Lucky Me: My 65 Years in Baseball* with Eddie Robinson. In recent years, he co-edited two SABR team books: *The Team That Time Won't Forget — the 1951 New York Giants* and *The 1950 Philadelphia Phillies - The Whiz Kids Take the Pennant*. He is president of the Ernie Banks — Bobby Bragan DFW Chapter of SABR and a frequent contributor to the SABR BioProject, but his real job is as a law professor at Southern Methodist University where he served as dean for nine years. He has also served as SMU's faculty athletic representative for over 30 years.

HARRY SCHOGER is 20 years a retiree who spent his working career in the U.S. primary steelmaking management. As a kid he lived near Indianapolis, where he watched a lot of Indianapolis Indians games. At the time they were a Pittsburgh affiliate (1948-51), as they are now. He has lived in northeast Ohio, where the fan base is largely split between the Indians and Pirates, for the past four decades. He is a history buff who loves the history of baseball.

BLAKE W. SHERRY is a lifelong Pittsburgh Pirates fan who resides in Dublin, Ohio. A retired Chief Operations Officer of a public retirement system, he has been a member of SABR since 1997. He co-leads the Hank Gowdy SABR Chapter in Central Ohio, and currently runs the chapter's quarterly baseball book club.

WAYNE STRUMPFER has collected baseball cards and been a Giants fan for 47 years. Currently an attorney in Sacramento, California, Wayne writes occasionally for SABR's Games Project and BioProject. His favorite subject is baseball in the 1960's and 70's.

JOSEPH WANCHO has been a member of SABR since 2005. He currently serves as the chair for the Minor League Committee. He was editor of *Pitching to the Pennant: 1954 Cleveland Indians* (University of Nebraska Press, 2014),and is lead editor on a forthcoming SABR book on the 1995 Indians.

BOB WEBSTER grew up in NW Indiana and has been a Cubs fan since 1963. He has earned degrees from Linfield College and Marylhurst University. Now living in Portland, Oregon and recently retired, Bob is currently researching and documenting the History of the Northwest League and is a Gameday Stats Stringer for the Hillsboro Hops. He is a member of the Northwest Chapter of SABR, on the Board of Executives of the Old-Timers Baseball Association of Portland, and a manager in the Great American Fantasy League.

STEVEN C. WEINER, a SABR member since 2015, is a retired chemical engineer and a lifelong baseball fan starting with the Brooklyn Dodgers of the 1950s. During his undergraduate years at Rutgers University, Steven authored newspaper articles and helped prepare media guides for the sports information office. On WRSU radio, he enjoyed doing baseball and basketball play-by-play in addition to evening sports news and interviews. Steven obtained his doctoral degree in engineering and applied science from Yale University. He has contributed hydrogen and fuel cell safety knowledge to the *International Conference on Hydrogen Safety* and technical literature to the *International Journal of Hydrogen Energy*. Steven currently contributes essays to the SABR Games Project, volunteers as an in-classroom tutor at a local middle school, and serves as a fundraising volunteer for the Washington Nationals Dream Foundation. You can often find him at Nationals Park for a ballgame.

A lifelong Pirates fan, **GREGORY H. WOLF** was born in Pittsburgh, but now resides in the Chicagoland area with his wife, Margaret, and daughter, Gabriela. A professor of German studies and holder of the Dennis and Jean Bauman Endowed Chair in the Humanities at North Central College in Naperville, Illinois, he has edited seven books for SABR. He is currently working on projects about Crosley Field in Cincinnati, Wrigley Field and Comiskey Park in Chicago, and the 1982 Milwaukee Brewers. Since January 2017, he has served as co-director of SABR's BioProject, which you can follow on Facebook and Twitter.

JACK ZERBY, a retired attorney and trusts/estates administrator, grew up in 90 miles north of Pittsburgh, close enough to follow the Pirates via the inimitable Bob Prince on KDKA radio. He enjoyed regular trips to Forbes Field with his dad and still has a foul ball hit by Hank Foiles in 1958. Jack writes, edits, and does fact checks for the SABR Games Project and the BioProject, which he joined at inception in 2002. He lives in Brevard, North Carolina, with his wife Diana, a professional violinist. While living in southwest Florida, he co-founded the SABR Seymour-Mills regional chapter there. Jack has been a member of SABR since 1994.

SABR BioProject Team Books

In 2002, the Society for American Baseball Research launched an effort to write and publish biographies of every player, manager, and individual who has made a contribution to baseball. Over the past decade, the BioProject Committee has produced over 6,000 biographical articles. Many have been part of efforts to create theme- or team-oriented books, spearheaded by chapters or other committees of SABR.

THE 1986 BOSTON RED SOX:
THERE WAS MORE THAN GAME SIX
One of a two-book series on the rivals that met in the 1986 World Series, the Boston Red Sox and the New York Mets, including biographies of every player, coach, broadcaster, and other important figures in the top organizations in baseball that year. .
Edited by Leslie Heaphy and Bill Nowlin
$19.95 paperback (ISBN 978-1-943816-19-4)
$9.99 ebook (ISBN 978-1-943816-18-7)
8.5"X11", 420 pages, over 200 photos

THE 1986 NEW YORK METS:
THERE WAS MORE THAN GAME SIX
The other book in the "rivalry" set from the 1986 World Series. This book re-tells the story of that year's classic World Series and this is the story of each of the players, coaches, managers, and broadcasters, their lives in baseball and the way the 1986 season fit into their lives.
Edited by Leslie Heaphy and Bill Nowlin
$19.95 paperback (ISBN 978-1-943816-13-2)
$9.99 ebook (ISBN 978-1-943816-12-5)
8.5"X11", 392 pages, over 100 photos

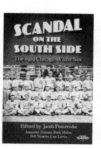

SCANDAL ON THE SOUTH SIDE:
THE 1919 CHICAGO WHITE SOX
The Black Sox Scandal isn't the only story worth telling about the 1919 Chicago White Sox. The team roster included three future Hall of Famers, a 20-year-old spitballer who would win 300 games in the minors, and even a batboy who later became a celebrity with the "Murderers' Row" New York Yankees. All of their stories are included in Scandal on the South Side with a timeline of the 1919 season.
Edited by Jacob Pomrenke
$19.95 paperback (ISBN 978-1-933599-95-3)
$9.99 ebook (ISBN 978-1-933599-94-6)
8.5"x11", 324 pages, 55 historic photos

WINNING ON THE NORTH SIDE
THE 1929 CHICAGO CUBS
Celebrate the 1929 Chicago Cubs, one of the most exciting teams in baseball history. Future Hall of Famers Hack Wilson, '29 NL MVP Rogers Hornsby, and Kiki Cuyler, along with Riggs Stephenson formed one of the most potent quartets in baseball history. The magical season came to an ignominious end in the World Series and helped craft the future "lovable loser" image of the team.
Edited by Gregory H. Wolf
$19.95 paperback (ISBN 978-1-933599-89-2)
$9.99 ebook (ISBN 978-1-933599-88-5)
8.5"x11", 314 pages, 59 photos

DETROIT THE UNCONQUERABLE:
THE 1935 WORLD CHAMPION TIGERS
Biographies of every player, coach, and broadcaster involved with the 1935 World Champion Detroit Tigers baseball team, written by members of the Society for American Baseball Research. Also includes a season in review and other articles about the 1935 team. Hank Greenberg, Mickey Cochrane, Charlie Gehringer, Schoolboy Rowe, and more.
Edited by Scott Ferkovich
$19.95 paperback (ISBN 9978-1-933599-78-6)
$9.99 ebook (ISBN 978-1-933599-79-3)
8.5"X11", 230 pages, 52 photos

THE TEAM THAT TIME WON'T FORGET:
THE 1951 NEW YORK GIANTS
Because of Bobby Thomson's dramatic "Shot Heard 'Round the World" in the bottom of the ninth of the decisive playoff game against the Brooklyn Dodgers, the team will forever be in baseball public's consciousness. Includes a foreword by Giants outfielder Monte Irvin.
Edited by Bill Nowlin and C. Paul Rogers III
$19.95 paperback (ISBN 978-1-933599-99-1)
$9.99 ebook (ISBN 978-1-933599-98-4)
8.5"X11", 282 pages, 47 photos

A PENNANT FOR THE TWIN CITIES:
THE 1965 MINNESOTA TWINS
This volume celebrates the 1965 Minnesota Twins, who captured the American League pennant in just their fifth season in the Twin Cities. Led by an All-Star cast, from Harmon Killebrew, Tony Oliva, Zoilo Versalles, and Mudcat Grant to Bob Allison, Jim Kaat, Earl Battey, and Jim Perry, the Twins won 102 games, but bowed to the Los Angeles Dodgers and Sandy Koufax in Game Seven
Edited by Gregory H. Wolf
$19.95 paperback (ISBN 978-1-943816-09-5)
$9.99 ebook (ISBN 978-1-943816-08-8)
8.5"X11", 405 pages, over 80 photos

MUSTACHES AND MAYHEM: CHARLIE O'S THREE TIME CHAMPIONS:
THE OAKLAND ATHLETICS: 1972-74
The Oakland Athletics captured major league baseball's crown each year from 1972 through 1974. Led by future Hall of Famers Reggie Jackson, Catfish Hunter and Rollie Fingers, the Athletics were a largely homegrown group who came of age together. Biographies of every player, coach, manager, and broadcaster (and mascot) from 1972 through 1974 are included, along with season recaps.
Edited by Chip Greene
$29.95 paperback (ISBN 978-1-943816-07-1)
$9.99 ebook (ISBN 978-1-943816-06-4)
8.5"X11", 600 pages, almost 100 photos

SABR Members can purchase each book at a significant discount (often 50% off) and receive the ebook edtions free as a member benefit. Each book is available in a trade paperback edition as well as ebooks suitable for reading on a home computer or Nook, Kindle, or iPad/tablet.
To learn more about becoming a member of SABR, visit the website: sabr.org/join

THE SABR DIGITAL LIBRARY

The Society for American Baseball Research, the top baseball research organization in the world, disseminates some of the best in baseball history, analysis, and biography through our publishing programs. The SABR Digital Library contains a mix of books old and new, and focuses on a tandem program of paperback and ebook publication, making these materials widely available for both on digital devices and as traditional printed books.

GREATEST GAMES BOOKS

TIGERS BY THE TALE:
GREAT GAMES AT MICHIGAN AND TRUMBULL
For over 100 years, Michigan and Trumbull was the scene of some of the most exciting baseball ever. This book portrays 50 classic games at the corner, spanning the earliest days of Bennett Park until Tiger Stadium's final closing act. From Ty Cobb to Mickey Cochrane, Hank Greenberg to Al Kaline, and Willie Horton to Alan Trammell.
Edited by Scott Ferkovich
$12.95 paperback (ISBN 978-1-943816-21-7)
$6.99 ebook (ISBN 978-1-943816-20-0)
8.5"x11", 160 pages, 22 photos

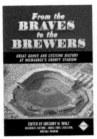

FROM THE BRAVES TO THE BREWERS: GREAT GAMES AND HISTORY AT MILWAUKEE'S COUNTY STADIUM
The National Pastime provides in-depth articles focused on the geographic region where the national SABR convention is taking place annually. The SABR 45 convention took place in Chicago, and here are 45 articles on baseball in and around the bat-and-ball crazed Windy City: 25 that appeared in the souvenir book of the convention plus another 20 articles available in ebook only.
Edited by Gregory H. Wolf
$19.95 paperback (ISBN 978-1-943816-23-1)
$9.99 ebook (ISBN 978-1-943816-22-4)
8.5"X11", 290 pages, 58 photos

BRAVES FIELD:
MEMORABLE MOMENTS AT BOSTON'S LOST DIAMOND
From its opening on August 18, 1915, to the sudden departure of the Boston Braves to Milwaukee before the 1953 baseball season, Braves Field was home to Boston's National League baseball club and also hosted many other events: from NFL football to championship boxing. The most memorable moments to occur in Braves Field history are portrayed here.
Edited by Bill Nowlin and Bob Brady
$19.95 paperback (ISBN 978-1-933599-93-9)
$9.99 ebook (ISBN 978-1-933599-92-2)
8.5"X11", 282 pages, 182 photos

AU JEU/PLAY BALL: THE 50 GREATEST GAMES IN THE HISTORY OF THE MONTREAL EXPOS
The 50 greatest games in Montreal Expos history. The games described here recount the exploits of the many great players who wore Expos uniforms over the years—Bill Stoneman, Gary Carter, Andre Dawson, Steve Rogers, Pedro Martinez, from the earliest days of the franchise, to the glory years of 1979-1981, the what-might-have-been years of the early 1990s, and the sad, final days.and others.
Edited by Norm King
$12.95 paperback (ISBN 978-1-943816-15-6)
$5.99 ebook (ISBN978-1-943816-14-9)
8.5"x11", 162 pages, 50 photos

ORIGINAL SABR RESEARCH

CALLING THE GAME:
BASEBALL BROADCASTING FROM 1920 TO THE PRESENT
An exhaustive, meticulously researched history of bringing the national pastime out of the ballparks and into living rooms via the airwaves. Every play-by-play announcer, color commentator, and ex-ballplayer, every broadcast deal, radio station, and TV network. Plus a foreword by "Voice of the Chicago Cubs" Pat Hughes, and an afterword by Jacques Doucet, the "Voice of the Montreal Expos" 1972-2004.
by Stuart Shea
$24.95 paperback (ISBN 978-1-933599-40-3)
$9.99 ebook (ISBN 978-1-933599-41-0)
7"X10", 712 pages, 40 photos

BIOPROJECT BOOKS

WHO'S ON FIRST:
REPLACEMENT PLAYERS IN WORLD WAR II
During World War II, 533 players made the major league debuts. More than 60% of the players in the 1941 Opening Day lineups departed for the service and were replaced by first-times and oldsters. Hod Lisenbee was 46. POW Bert Shepard had an artificial leg, and Pete Gray had only one arm. The 1944 St. Louis Browns had 13 players classified 4-F. These are their stories.
Edited by Marc Z Aaron and Bill Nowlin
$19.95 paperback (ISBN 978-1-933599-91-5)
$9.99 ebook (ISBN 978-1-933599-90-8)
8.5"X11", 422 pages, 67 photos

VAN LINGLE MUNGO:
THE MAN, THE SONG, THE PLAYERS
40 baseball players with intriguing names have been named in renditions of Dave Frishberg's classic 1969 song, Van Lingle Mungo. This book presents biographies of all 40 players and additional information about one of the greatest baseball novelty songs of all time.
Edited by Bill Nowlin
$19.95 paperback (ISBN 978-1-933599-76-2)
$9.99 ebook (ISBN 978-1-933599-77-9)
8.5"X11", 278 pages, 46 photos

NUCLEAR POWERED BASEBALL
Nuclear Powered Baseball tells the stories of each player—past and present—featured in the classic Simpsons episode "Homer at the Bat." Wade Boggs, Ken Griffey Jr., Ozzie Smith, Nap Lajoie, Don Mattingly, and many more. We've also included a few very entertaining takes on the now-famous episode from prominent baseball writers Jonah Keri, Joe Posnanski, Erik Malinowski, and Bradley Woodrum
Edited by Emily Hawks and Bill Nowlin
$19.95 paperback (ISBN 978-1-943816-11-8)
$9.99 ebook (ISBN 978-1-943816-10-1)
8.5"X11", 250 pages

SABR Members can purchase each book at a significant discount (often 50% off) and receive the ebook editions free as a member benefit. Each book is available in a trade paperback edition as well as ebooks suitable for reading on a home computer or Nook, Kindle, or iPad/tablet.
To learn more about becoming a member of SABR, visit the website: sabr.org/join

SABR BioProject Books

In 2002, the Society for American Baseball Research launched an effort to write and publish biographies of every player, manager, and individual who has made a contribution to baseball. Over the past decade, the BioProject Committee has produced over 2,200 biographical articles. Many have been part of efforts to create theme- or team-oriented books, spearheaded by chapters or other committees of SABR.

THE YEAR OF THE BLUE SNOW:
THE 1964 PHILADELPHIA PHILLIES
Catcher Gus Triandos dubbed the Philadelphia Phillies' 1964 season "the year of the blue snow," a rare thing that happens once in a great while. This book sheds light on lingering questions about the 1964 season—but any book about a team is really about the players. This work offers life stories of all the players and others (managers, coaches, owners, and broadcasters) associated with this star-crossed team, as well as essays of analysis and history.
Edited by Mel Marmer and Bill Nowlin
$19.95 paperback (ISBN 978-1-933599-51-9)
$9.99 ebook (ISBN 978-1-933599-52-6)
8.5"X11", 356 PAGES, over 70 photos

DETROIT TIGERS 1984:
WHAT A START! WHAT A FINISH!
The 1984 Detroit tigers roared out of the gate, winning their first nine games of the season and compiling an eye-popping 35-5 record after the campaign's first 40 games—still the best start ever for any team in major league history. This book brings together biographical profiles of every Tiger from that magical season, plus those of field management, top executives, the broadcasters—even venerable Tiger Stadium and the city itself.
Edited by Mark Pattison and David Raglin
$19.95 paperback (ISBN 978-1-933599-44-1)
$9.99 ebook (ISBN 978-1-933599-45-8)
8.5"x11", 250 pages (Over 230,000 words!)

SWEET '60: THE 1960 PITTSBURGH PIRATES
A portrait of the 1960 team which pulled off one of the biggest upsets of the last 60 years. When Bill Mazeroski's home run left the park to win in Game Seven of the World Series, beating the New York Yankees, David had toppled Goliath. It was a blow that awakened a generation, one that millions of people saw on television, one of TV's first iconic World Series moments.
Edited by Clifton Blue Parker and Bill Nowlin
$19.95 paperback (ISBN 978-1-933599-48-9)
$9.99 ebook (ISBN 978-1-933599-49-6)
8.5"X11", 340 pages, 75 photos

RED SOX BASEBALL IN THE DAYS OF IKE AND ELVIS: THE RED SOX OF THE 1950s
Although the Red Sox spent most of the 1950s far out of contention, the team was filled with fascinating players who captured the heart of their fans. In *Red Sox Baseball*, members of SABR present 46 biographies on players such as Ted Williams and Pumpsie Green as well as season-by-season recaps.
Edited by Mark Armour and Bill Nowlin
$19.95 paperback (ISBN 978-1-933599-24-3)
$9.99 ebook (ISBN 978-1-933599-34-2)
8.5"X11", 372 PAGES, over 100 photos

THE MIRACLE BRAVES OF 1914
BOSTON'S ORIGINAL WORST-TO-FIRST CHAMPIONS
Long before the Red Sox "Impossible Dream" season, Boston's now nearly forgotten "other" team, the 1914 Boston Braves, performed a baseball "miracle" that resounds to this very day. The "Miracle Braves" were Boston's first "worst-to-first" winners of the World Series. Refusing to throw in the towel at the midseason mark, George Stallings engineered a remarkable second-half climb in the standings all the way to first place.
Edited by Bill Nowlin
$19.95 paperback (ISBN 978-1-933599-69-4)
$9.99 ebook (ISBN 978-1-933599-70-0)
8.5"X11", 392 PAGES, over 100 photos

THAR'S JOY IN BRAVELAND!
THE 1957 MILWAUKEE BRAVES
Few teams in baseball history have captured the hearts of their fans like the Milwaukee Braves of the 19505. During the Braves' 13-year tenure in Milwaukee (1953-1965), they had a winning record every season, won two consecutive NL pennants (1957 and 1958), lost two more in the final week of the season (1956 and 1959), and set big-league attendance records along the way.
Edited by Gregory H. Wolf
$19.95 paperback (ISBN 978-1-933599-71-7)
$9.99 ebook (ISBN 978-1-933599-72-4)
8.5"x11", 330 pages, over 60 photos

NEW CENTURY, NEW TEAM:
THE 1901 BOSTON AMERICANS
The team now known as the Boston Red Sox played its first season in 1901. Boston had a well-established National League team, but the American League went head-to-head with the N.L. in Chicago, Philadelphia, and Boston. Chicago won the American League pennant and Boston finished second, only four games behind.
Edited by Bill Nowlin
$19.95 paperback (ISBN 978-1-933599-58-8)
$9.99 ebook (ISBN 978-1-933599-59-5)
8.5"X11", 268 pages, over 125 photos

CAN HE PLAY?
A LOOK AT BASEBALL SCOUTS AND THEIR PROFESSION
They dig through tons of coal to find a single diamond. Here in the world of scouts, we meet the "King of Weeds," a Ph.D. we call "Baseball's Renaissance Man," a husband-and-wife team, pioneering Latin scouts, and a Japanese-American interned during World War II who became a successful scout—and many, many more.
Edited by Jim Sandoval and Bill Nowlin
$19.95 paperback (ISBN 978-1-933599-23-6)
$9.99 ebook (ISBN 978-1-933599-25-0)
8.5"X11", 200 PAGES, over 100 photos

SABR Members can purchase each book at a significant discount (often 50% off) and receive the ebook editions free as a member benefit. Each book is available in a trade paperback edition as well as ebooks suitable for reading on a home computer or Nook, Kindle, or iPad/tablet.
To learn more about becoming a member of SABR, visit the website: sabr.org/join

THE SABR DIGITAL LIBRARY

The Society for American Baseball Research, the top baseball research organization in the world, disseminates some of the best in baseball history, analysis, and biography through our publishing programs. The SABR Digital Library contains a mix of books old and new, and focuses on a tandem program of paperback and ebook publication, making these materials widely available for both on digital devices and as traditional printed books.

CLASSIC REPRINTS

BASE-BALL: HOW TO BECOME A PLAYER
by John Montgomery Ward
John Montgomery Ward (1860-1925) tossed the second perfect game in major league history and later became the game's best shortstop and a great, inventive manager. His classic handbook on baseball skills and strategy was published in 1888. Illustrated with woodcuts, the book is divided into chapters for each position on the field as well as chapters on the origin of the game, theory and strategy, training, base-running, and batting.
$4.99 ebook (ISBN 978-1-933599-47-2)
$9.95 paperback (ISBN 978-0910137539)
156 PAGES, 4.5"X7" replica edition

BATTING by F. C. Lane
First published in 1925, *Batting* collects the wisdom and insights of over 250 hitters and baseball figures. Lane interviewed extensively and compiled tips and advice on everything from batting stances to beanballs. Legendary baseball figures such as Ty Cobb, Casey Stengel, Cy Young, Walter Johnson, Rogers Hornsby, and Babe Ruth reveal the secrets of such integral and interesting parts of the game as how to choose a bat, the ways to beat a slump, and how to outguess the pitcher.
$14.95 paperback (ISBN 978-0-910137-86-7)
$7.99 ebook (ISBN 978-1-933599-46-5)
240 PAGES, 5"X7"

RUN, RABBIT, RUN
by Walter "Rabbit" Maranville
"Rabbit" Maranville was the Joe Garagiola of Grandpa's day, the baseball comedian of the times. In a twenty-four-year career that began in 1912, Rabbit found a lot of funny situations to laugh at, and no wonder: he caused most of them! The book also includes an introduction by the late Harold Seymour and a historical account of Maranville's life and Hall-of-Fame career by Bob Carroll.
$9.95 paperback (ISBN 978-1-933599-26-7)
$5.99 ebook (ISBN 978-1-933599-27-4)
100 PAGES, 5.5"X8.5", 15 rare photos

MEMORIES OF A BALLPLAYER
by Bill Werber and C. Paul Rogers III
Bill Werber's claim to fame is unique: he was the last living person to have a direct connection to the 1927 Yankees, "Murderers' Row," a team hailed by many as the best of all time. Rich in anecdotes and humor, Memories of a Ballplayer is a clear-eyed memoir of the world of big-league baseball in the 1930s. Werber played with or against some of the most productive hitters of all time, including Babe Ruth, Ted Williams, Lou Gehrig, and Joe DiMaggio.
$14.95 paperback (ISNB 978-0-910137-84-3)
$6.99 ebook (ISBN 978-1-933599-47-2)
250 PAGES, 6"X9"

ORIGINAL SABR RESEARCH

INVENTING BASEBALL: THE 100 GREATEST GAMES OF THE NINETEENTH CENTURY
SABR's Nineteenth Century Committee brings to life the greatest games from the game's early years. From the "prisoner of war" game that took place among captive Union soldiers during the Civil War (immortalized in a famous lithograph), to the first intercollegiate game (Amherst versus Williams), to the first professional no-hitter, the games in this volume span 1833–1900 and detail the athletic exploits of such players as Cap Anson, Moses "Fleetwood" Walker, Charlie Comiskey, and Mike "King" Kelly.
Edited by Bill Felber
$19.95 paperback (ISBN 978-1-933599-42-7)
$9.99 ebook (ISBN 978-1-933599-43-4)
302 PAGES, 8"x10", 200 photos

NINETEENTH CENTURY STARS: 2012 EDITION
First published in 1989, *Nineteenth Century Stars* was SABR's initial attempt to capture the stories of baseball players from before 1900. With a collection of 136 fascinating biographies, SABR has re-released *Nineteenth Century Stars* for 2012 with revised statistics and new form. The 2012 version also includes a preface by **John Thorn**.
Edited by Robert L. Tiemann and Mark Rucker
$19.95 paperback (ISBN 978-1-933599-28-1)
$9.99 ebook (ISBN 978-1-933599-29-8)
300 PAGES, 6"X9"

GREAT HITTING PITCHERS
Published in 1979, *Great Hitting Pitchers* was one of SABR's early publications. Edited by SABR founder Bob Davids, the book compiles stories and records about pitchers excelling in the batter's box. Newly updated in 2012 by Mike Cook, *Great Hitting Pitchers* contain tables including data from 1979-2011, corrections to reflect recent records, and a new chapter on recent new members in the club of "great hitting pitchers" like Tom Glavine and Mike Hampton.
Edited by L. Robert Davids
$9.95 paperback (ISBN 978-1-933599-30-4)
$5.99 ebook (ISBN 978-1-933599-31-1)
102 PAGES, 5.5"x8.5"

THE FENWAY PROJECT
Sixty-four SABR members—avid fans, historians, statisticians, and game enthusiasts—recorded their experiences of a single game. Some wrote from inside the Green Monster's manual scoreboard, the Braves clubhouse, or the broadcast booth, while others took in the essence of Fenway from the grandstand or bleachers. The result is a fascinating look at the charms and challenges of Fenway Park, and the allure of being a baseball fan.
Edited by Bill Nowlin and Cecilia Tan
$9.99 ebook (ISBN 978-1-933599-50-2)
175 pages, 100 photos

SABR Members can purchase each book at a significant discount (often 50% off) and receive the ebook editions free as a member benefit. Each book is available in a trade paperback edition as well as ebooks suitable for reading on a home computer or Nook, Kindle, or iPad/tablet.
To learn more about becoming a member of SABR, visit the website: sabr.org/join

Society for American Baseball Research

Cronkite School at ASU
555 N. Central Ave. #416, Phoenix, AZ 85004
602.496.1460 (phone)
SABR.org

Become a SABR member today!

you're interested in baseball — writing about it, reading about it, talking about it — there's a place for you in the Society for American aseball Research. Our members include everyone from academics to professional sportswriters to amateur historians and statisticians to dents and casual fans who enjoy reading about baseball and occasionally gathering with other members to talk baseball. What unites SABR members is an interest in the game and joy in learning more about it.

BR membership is open to any baseball fan; we offer 1-year and 3-year memberships. Here's a list of some of the key benefits you'll ceive as a SABR member:

- Receive two editions (spring and fall) of the *Baseball Research Journal*, our flagship publication
- Receive expanded e-book edition of *The National Pastime*, our annual convention journal
- 8-10 new e-books published by the SABR Digital Library, all FREE to members
- "This Week in SABR" e-newsletter, sent to members every Friday
- Join dozens of research committees, from Statistical Analysis to Women in Baseball.
- Join one of 70 regional chapters in the U.S., Canada, Latin America, and abroad
- Participate in online discussion groups
- Ask and answer baseball research questions on the SABR-L e-mail listserv
- Complete archives of *The Sporting News* dating back to 1886 and other research resources
- Promote your research in "This Week in SABR"
- Diamond Dollars Case Competition
- Yoseloff Scholarships

- Discounts on SABR national conferences, including the SABR National Convention, the SABR Analytics Conference, Jerry Malloy Negro League Conference, Frederick Ivor-Campbell 19th Century Conference, and the Arizona Fall League Experience
- Publish your research in peer-reviewed SABR journals
- Collaborate with SABR researchers and experts
- Contribute to Baseball Biography Project or the SABR Games Project
- List your new book in the SABR Bookshelf
- Lead a SABR research committee or chapter
- Networking opportunities at SABR Analytics Conference
- Meet baseball authors and historians at SABR events and chapter meetings
- 50% discounts on paperback versions of SABR e-books
- Discounts with other partners in the baseball community
- SABR research awards

hope you'll join the most passionate international community of baseball fans at SABR! Check us out online at SABR.org/join.

- -

SABR MEMBERSHIP FORM

	Annual	3-year	Senior	3-yr Sr.	Under 30
tandard:	❑ $65	❑ $175	❑ $45	❑ $129	☐ $45
Canada/Mexico:	❑ $75	❑ $205	❑ $55	❑ $159	❑ $55
)verseas:	❑ $84	❑ $232	❑ $64	❑ $186	❑ $55

(International members wishing to be mailed the Baseball Research Journal should add $10/yr for Canada/Mexico or $19/yr for overseas locations.)

enior = 65 or older before Dec. 31 of the current year

Participate in Our Donor Program!

Support the preservation of baseball research. Designate your gift toward:
❑General Fund ❑Endowment Fund ❑Research Resources ❑_____
❑ I want to maximize the impact of my gift; do not send any donor premiums
❑ I would like this gift to remain anonymous.

Note: Any donation not designated will be placed in the General Fund.
SABR is a 501 (c) (3) not-for-profit organization & donations are tax-deductible to the extent allowed by law.

me _____

nail* _____

dress _____

y _____ ST_____ ZIP_____

ne _____ Birthday _____

ur e-mail address on file ensures you will receive the most recent SABR news.

Dues $_____

Donation $_____

Amount Enclosed $_____

Do you work for a matching grant corporation? Call (602) 496-1460 for details.

If you wish to pay by credit card, please contact the SABR office at (602) 496-1460 or visit the SABR Store online at SABR.org/join. We accept Visa, Mastercard & Discover.

Do you wish to receive the *Baseball Research Journal* electronically? ❑ Yes ❑ No
Our e-books are available in PDF, Kindle, or EPUB (iBooks, iPad, Nook) formats.

Mail to: SABR, Cronkite School at ASU, 555 N. Central Ave. #416, Phoenix, AZ 85004

CPSIA information can be obtained
at www.ICGtesting.com
Printed in the USA
BVHW012216100119
537597BV00006B/103/P